Music Publishing

The Real Road to
Music Business Success

Revised and Expanded Fourth Edition

Foreword by James Stroud

TIM WHITSETT

6400 Hollis Street, Suite 12
Emeryville, CA 94608

Library of Congress Catalog Card Number: 97-71973

Book design, cover, and layout: Linda Gough

Production staff: Mike Lawson: publisher; Lisa Duran: editor; Randy Antin: editorial assistant;
Sally Engelfried: editorial assistance; Teresa Poss: administrative assistant; Georgia George:
production director; Tom Marzella: production assistant

6400 Hollis Street, Suite 12
Emeryville, CA 94608
(510) 653-3307

Also from MixBooks:
The Songwriters Guide to Collaboration
How to Run a Recording Session
Critical Listening and Auditory Perception
Keyfax Omnibus Edition
The AudioPro Home Recording Course
Modular Digital Multitracks: The Power User's Guide
Concert Sound
Sound for Picture
Music Producers
Live Sound Reinforcement

Also from EMBooks:
Making the Ultimate Demo
Tech Terms: A Practical Dictionary for Audio and Music Production
Making Music With Your Computer

Also from CBM Music and Entertainment Group:
Recording Industry Sourcebook
Mix Reference Disc
Mix Master Directory
Digital Piano Buyer's Guide

MixBooks is a division of Cardinal Business Media Inc.

Printed in Auburn Hills, Michigan

ISBN 0-918371-16-3

For my children,

Timothy and Joanna,

in memory of

their mother and my wife,

Janis

Contents

Foreword vii

Preface viii

Chapter One 1

MUSIC PUBLISHING: AN OVERVIEW
A money machine . . .
Music publishing is a growth industry
Solid investment opportunities
Demographic sources of copyright income
Expanding market opportunities
Market genre segments
International scope of the market
Commercial lifespan of a song
Product development remains inexpensive

Chapter Two 6

WHAT IS MUSIC PUBLISHING?
History of music publishing
Flow of song rights
Music publishing vs. other types of publishing
A day in the life of a music publisher
Costs of product
Specific sources of copyright income
How much can a hit song earn?
Different kinds of publishers

Chapter Three 16

STARTING YOUR OWN PUBLISHING COMPANY
Why start a music publishing company?
What it takes to be a publisher
How much money do you need to start?
When to expect a return on investment
Specialization
Choosing a company name

Location
Researching start-up costs
Office facilities
Equipment & furnishings
Insurance
Legal
Licenses and regulations
If you need to raise money . . .
Recruiting personnel
Company formation
Business plans
Meeting competition

Chapter Four 36

ACQUISITIONS
How publishers acquire product
Acquisition philosophy
Financial aspects of acquisitions
Advances
Purchasing copyrights
The buying and selling process

Chapter Five 51

COPYRIGHT
What copyright protection covers—what it doesn't
Duration of copyright protection
"Published" vs. "unpublished" works
International copyright protection
Copyright notice
Common law copyright
Copyright registration
Public domain
Termination of publisher's rights
Infringement
Fair use
Compulsory licensing
Summary

Chapter Six 59

SONGWRITER CONTRACTS

Divisibility of rights
Negotiable contract terms
Analyzing a single-song contract
Analyzing exclusive songwriter agreements
Summary

Chapter Seven 72

CO-PUBLISHING

Writer collaborations
Incentive assignments
Little publisher/big publisher
Division of ownership rights
Administration of co-published works
Analyzing a co-publishing contract

Chapter Eight 77

MECHANICAL-RIGHT LICENSING

Statutory mechanical royalty rate for audio-only
    recordings
Controlled composition clause
Rate discounts, splits, cut-ins
First use
Compulsory mechanical licenses
Negotiated mechanical licenses
What a typical mechanical license contains
Videocassettes
Mechanical-right licensing societies
Mechanical rights in cyberspace

Chapter Nine 85

PERFORMING-RIGHT LICENSING

Various types of performance uses
Performing-right societies
Performing-right societies in the United States
Why U.S. publishers must form two or more
    companies
Collaboration between writers belonging to different
    societies
How performance royalties are divided
    between publishers and writers
Publishers don't collect writer's performance royalties
Administering performing-rights licenses
How performance royalties are calculated
Jukeboxes
Performing-right society membership requirements
SOCAN
Overseas performing-right societies
Performing rights in cyberspace
ASCAP vs. BMI

Chapter Ten 93

SYNCHRONIZATION RIGHT LICENSING

Different types of synchronization licenses
Other licenses needed for audiovisual works
Theatrical synchronization licenses (music in
    movies)
Nontheatrical synchronization licenses
Videogram synchronization licenses
Promotional video clips
Television synchronization licenses
Movies and television shows based on existing songs
Synchronization rights in cyberspace
Synchronization licenses for commercial advertising
Publisher's follow-through after licenses are issued

Chapter Eleven 106

FOREIGN LICENSING

Subpublishing
European Union
Foreign taxes on overseas earnings
Dealing with unpredictable currency exchange rates
Licensing foreign catalogs
Establishing contacts with overseas publishers
Maintaining good working relationships with
    subpublishers
Analyzing subpublishing agreements

Chapter Twelve 119

LICENSING PRINT RIGHTS

Printed music formats
Royalties to copyright owners
Exclusion of public domain works
Reserves
Term of agreement and sell-off period
Catalog agreements vs. single-song agreements
Lyric reprint licenses
Print advertisements
Greeting cards
Games
Album covers and inserts

Chapter Thirteen 124

GRAND RIGHTS AND DRAMATIC RIGHTS

Key characteristics of grand rights
Distinction between grand rights and dramatic rights
Licensing grand rights and dramatic rights
Grand rights and dramatic performance rights and
    copyright owners
Who owns grand rights?
Financial aspects
Music publishers and grand rights

Chapter Fourteen 128

LICENSING SONGS
FOR COMMERCIAL ADVERTISING
Commissioned jingles
Licensing existing songs for commercials
Considerations for licensing commercials
Radio commercials
Print advertising

Chapter Fifteen 133

MISCELLANEOUS LICENSING ISSUES
Special use permits and permissions
General licensing principles
Negotiating tips
Parodies
Medleys
Sampling
New media
Electrical transcription licenses
Consumer products
DART

Chapter Sixteen 144

EXPLOITATION
Market targeting
Market research
Songplugging
Analyzing songplugging tactics
Getting others to market your songs
Record production
Artist/producer development
Video production
Promo videos
Getting songs into television programs and movies
Theme commissioning
Bluebirds, standards, and evergreens
Generic catalog marketing
Boosting performance royalties
Recorded music libraries
Promoting copyrights overseas

Chapter Seventeen 163

MARKETING 101
What is marketing?
Marketing consistency
Marketing plans
Professional consultants
Projecting your message
Sales
The marketing mix
Marketing tools
Trade shows
Advertising
Publicity/public relations

Chapter Eighteen 187

COMPANY MANAGEMENT
The publisher's challenge
Management by objectives (MBO)
Education and information
Management games
Catalog and roster reporting
Creative management control
General personnel management
Hiring managers and key-employees

Appendix 199

Books for further reading
Consumer publications
Mechanical licensing
Online databases
Performing-right societies
Selected overseas licensing agencies
Trade associations and support groups
Trade directories and guides
Trade publications
Trade shows and conventions
U.S. government
Web sites

Index 204

Foreword

As a musician, producer, label head, music publisher, and long-time friend of Tim Whitsett's, I was honored to be asked to write this foreword. The extraordinary amount of knowledge that he shares with you comes from Tim's firsthand experience as an innovative entrepreneur, learning by trial and error, through his tremendous success as a worldwide music publisher.

It is through his all-encompassing music industry experience that you will benefit from this step-by-step, how-to-do-it-right-the-first-time instructional tool. It is thorough and to the point; an absolute necessity for anyone choosing a music publishing career and an essential reference guide for existing publishers.

Music Publishing: The Real Road to Music Business Success, is destined to become part of the standard curriculum in recording industry management programs at colleges and universities worldwide.

Tim, I am fortunate to have worked with and befriended such a sincere, generous, and wise individual. Thank you.

JAMES STROUD

James Stroud, three-time *Billboard* Top Country Producer, founded The Writer's Group, a Grammy-winning powerhouse that helped launch the careers of Thom Schuyler, Fred Knobloch and Paul Overstreet. He currently produces such multiplatinum acts as Clint Black and Tim McGraw and has worked with Melissa Etheridge and the Neville Brothers. He is also the co-owner of Hamstein Cumberland Music Group, winner of 25 BMI and 16 ASCAP awards.

Preface

There have been many changes in the world of music publishing since the original 1989 publication of *Music Publishing: The Real Road to Music Business Riches*. This edition has been totally revised and much of it is completely new material.

Music publishing is one of the least understood but most important segments of the multibillion dollar music industry. This book reveals why music publishing is vital to anyone actively engaged in the music business, and it tells you how to profit from it.

Information in this book empowers you to succeed on whatever level you choose in the business of copyright ownership and music publishing. Whether you aim to start your own publishing company, climb the corporate ladder in your present job, or add profits to your current music business activities, this book is designed to show the way.

This book's holistic approach equips you to operate the kind of company you envision. After reading it, you'll be able to make intelligent assessments of people whom you appoint to handle any aspects of the business you prefer not to personally pursue at this time.

Copyrights, licensing, and contracts are covered in depth. In addition, an array of tactical steps and strategic concepts are provided to enable you to practice publishing successfully. You will learn how to forecast sales, calculate advances, evaluate copyright purchases, negotiate favorable contracts and licenses, market product effectively, manage personnel and company affairs efficiently, and maximize commercial potential.

A music publishing company can't prosper without creative people. However, there must be balance between creativity and sound business practices. The purpose of this book, then, is to show how to reconcile creativity with commercial considerations, impose management disciplines on the creative process, apply business techniques to acquiring and marketing music, and maximize productivity in order to generate the profits necessary for creative forces to flourish.

Although phonograph records are practically obsolete, the term "record" is used in this book as a term of convenience, applicable to recorded product in all formats (compact discs, cassettes, digital audio cassettes, etc.).

All costs, royalty rates, industry averages, and pricing structures used in this book are for illustrative purposes only. You must do your own research to determine what is current and applicable to your situation.

Because copyright issues are always in flux in a changing world with emerging technologies, and because each deal is unique to the parties involved, you should always seek legal and financial counsel about your specific situation before making decisions regarding litigation, contracts, and licensing agreements. Use this book for reference, not as a substitute for expert advice.

CHAPTER 1

Music Publishing: An Overview

▼

*All the glitter and gold of the multibillion
dollar music business revolves around one simple
raw product: songs!
Music publishers operate from the heart of the
business because they control the songs.*

A money machine . . .

You hear music everywhere you go. But unlike the air
we breathe, music isn't free. Wherever music's playing, someone's paying. Music publishers collect royalties and fees every time songs are recorded,
broadcast, printed, used in movies and advertising,
played on juke boxes, or performed live.

Music publishing is one of the few remaining
businesses where a savvy entrepreneur can build an
empire on a shoestring or make a fortune operating
solo. It's a low-risk way to build assets, establish an
extra profit center, and strengthen deal-making
clout. And, like a healthy pension, royalties keep
coming for years.

Copyright values are soaring. Revenues more
than doubled in the past ten years. Rapidly expanding markets for songs in entertainment, education,
and business make *now* the best time ever for music
publishers.

Copyright ownership is a smart step forward for
ambitious record company executives, managers, studio owners, songwriters, producers, musicians, artists,
and *anyone* representing music business clients in *any*
capacity. The search for hit songs is never-ending. You
needn't be a full time publisher to tap this gold mine
and hit the jackpot when someone you know needs a
song.

Music publishing is a growth industry

Revenues from copyrights, especially from music and
films, represent one of the fastest-growing sectors of
the American economy. In recent years, U.S. copyright earnings grew at a real annual rate of more than
twice the overall economy, contributing more to the
GNP than the construction and transportation industries combined. And foreign sales from U.S. copyrights in software, movies, records, tapes, songs,
books, and magazines generate more revenue than
the aerospace industry.

The music publishing segment of the copyright
industry had revenues of well over $5.83 billion
worldwide in 1994, up 16% over 1993 and more than
double the approximately $2.7 billion generated five
years earlier. Of this total, about 21% ($1.24 billion)
was earned within the United States. Another $700
million was earned by American-owned song copyrights in Europe.

Solid investment opportunities

As a vital segment of the copyright industry, music
publishing is fast becoming recognized as a money-
spinning business within financial circles. Shrewd Wall
Street investors know that music publishing overheads
are low and that profit margins can be substantial.

Wall Street analyst Lisbeth Barron told *Hollywood
Reporter*, " . . . Publishing companies are very stable
and have some of the highest margins." In the same
article, investment banker Gordon Quinn noted,
"Publishing companies are among the most liquid of
entertainment industry investment opportunities."

Increasingly, companies and individuals are
acquiring copyrights as a means of entry or expansion
into the leisure industry—as well as for sound investment opportunities. Superstar recording artists,
understanding copyright values, have invested in
music publishing holdings.

Paul McCartney bought the venerable E.H. Mor-
ris Company and the Buddy Holly catalog, but lost out
on a bid to buy ATV Music, which contained the Beatles' hits he wrote with John Lennon. ATV was purchased by Michael Jackson for $40 million in 1985.
Ten years later, Sony Music paid Jackson $110 million
to merge ATV into a new Sony/ATV publishing entity.

Numerous high profile examples illustrate Ric-
cobono's contention. East/Memphis Music Corp.
(publisher of songs by Otis Redding and Isaac Hayes)
was purchased for around $1 million by an investor
who merged it with another company he bought for
$500,000. Without making any significant additions
to the catalog, the investor sold the two companies six
years later for $10 million.

PolyGram sold its Chappell Music Ltd. publishing division in 1984 for a record $100 million. How-
ever, PolyGram execs quickly realized (and publicly
admitted) the sale was a "great mistake." Said Poly-
Gram executive Ted Green, "A day after selling, we
regretted it." PolyGram then launched an intensive
effort to re-enter the music publishing business, purchasing Lawrence Welk's publishing operation for

$25 million, Dick James Music (containing early
Elton John songs) for $20 million, the catalogs of
country music stars Mel Tillis and Webb Pierce for $5
million, and others. Meanwhile, in 1987, Warner
Brothers bought Chappell for $200 million, doubling
the price PolyGram sold it for three years earlier.

CBS sold its publishing arm, CBS Songs, to SBK
Entertainment in 1986 for $125 million to raise cash
after fending off a takeover bid. SBK then sold the
catalog to EMI for $337 million in 1989, a 170%
increase in value in two years time. Meanwhile, CBS
was purchased by Sony and quickly reestablished
itself as a major force in the music publishing industry, fulfilling CBS executive Harvey Shapiro's goal
when he said, "We want to be back in the publishing
business and build another asset base."

RCA cashed in its publishing division a few years
ago, then almost immediately sought to replace it.
The new company, called BMG, rapidly built up a staff
of 124 in 14 countries under CEO Nick Firth who said,
"I'm always an optimist about music publishing."

In 1984, British songwriter Tim Hollier put
together a management team and obtained financing
from a venture capital firm to form a publishing operation called Filmtrax. Within four years, Filmtrax had
become the third largest British publishing company
by virtue of acquiring Columbia Pictures Corp. ($65
million) and Ivan Mogull Music ($5 million). Within
six years of its formation, the company was generating $10 million annually in net receipts (after pay-
ment of royalties to writers). Then, in August 1990,
EMI gobbled up Filmtrax for a reported $115 mil-
lion—about 11.5 times annual net royalty income.

In a report entitled "Inside the Music Publishing
Industry," consultant Paula Dranov concluded,
"Profit margins may be substantial . . . [and] judging
from the annual reports of the parent companies of
music publishers, these divisions are consistently
profitable." And, in the case of investors who acquire
good copyrights but don't even attempt to promote
or exploit the product, she says, "They . . . can't lose,
for their investment will always pay itself back."

LOW RISKS, HIGH RETURNS

Dranov also noted that "music publishing is not
regarded as a risky business." And she points out that
although the music publishing industry's revenues

represent only about 16% of the $35-plus billion generated by the recording industry globally, the ratio of success to failure is much more favorable for music publishers. After all, publishers don't have to risk thousands of dollars on recording, artwork, manufacturing, and marketing a record that may never sell; nor do publishers have to deal with invoicing, shipping, returns, or warehousing.

NEW TECHNOLOGIES GENERATE MORE EARNINGS

There's an exciting explosion of income opportunities for publishers. VCRs, CDs, portable cassette players, DAT, CD-ROMs, MIDI, and karaoke are innovations that didn't exist 20 years ago. The rapid pace of technological change since the early 1980s has had a big, beneficial impact on the music industry.

Music sales have been enhanced by new formats like compact discs, as well as new marketing opportunities, such as dedicated music channels on cable TV. And there are still more exciting developments to come: fiber-optic delivery of pay-per-play, 500-channel digital television, cable radio, etc. Moreover, expanding global computer networks and advanced technology will likely revolutionize how music is distributed to consumers.

PolyGram's Ted Green told *Billboard*, "It's a good time to be in music publishing. The usage of songs is on the increase. Look at such new technologies as home video, compact discs, pay-per-view, and DAT. Pop music is the mainstream of society." Nick Firth agreed: "History shows that as long as music publishers have controlled the rights in all technologies, such rights are very valuable." And Everest Music's Mike Stewart confirmed this to *Hollywood Reporter*: "New technology always requires copyrights. It's the software syndrome. VCRs, CDs, cable are all new revenue sources for the same songs."

Indeed, with each new technological breakthrough, old songs are reissued in new formats, fueling further consumer sales of prerecorded music and bringing new profits to publishers. Technological innovation always augurs well for music sales, multiplying new uses for music in entertainment, education, and business, through interactive media such as CD-ROMs, DVDs, karaoke, and smaller, more portable hardware, like Walkmans.

NEW MARKETS, NEW MONEY OPPORTUNITIES

But that's not the only reason publishing values have skyrocketed. Music is increasingly important in television, film production, and commercials. Radio stations specializing in specific formats (country, R&B, rock, oldies, etc.) provide programming opportunities for all types of copyrights. All-music TV programming (such as MTV and CMT) provides further profits while promoting publishers' copyrights at the same time. And since the revision of the Copyright Act in 1976, publishing royalties on records, compact discs, and tapes have more than tripled for each unit sold in the United States.

Other new markets are fast opening up: cable and satellite delivery are reaching all corners of the globe as governmental regulations are relaxing and state broadcasting monopolies are breaking up. The iron curtain's melt-down presents future opportunities in the former no-man's land of Eastern Europe, where once it was only possible to barter copyright earnings for things like tractor parts—if at all. Worldwide, reciprocal treaties for copyright-law harmonization are being forged to make meaningful markets for music out of hitherto black holes in Latin America, Africa, and Asia.

As a result of these trends and developments, a good catalog now tends to increase in value from 10% to 20% each year without any significant promotional activity on the part of its owner. Jim Fifield, CEO of EMI Music Worldwide, told *Billboard*, "I personally think that the publishing business has more growth [capacity] than [the rest of] the music business." And Windswept Pacific's CEO Chuck Kaye predicted in *Billboard*: "Music publishing will soar in the '90s. A creatively managed and aggressively administered music publishing company can expect a growth pattern unlike that of any other decade." By 1997 this prediction seems almost an understatement.

Demographic sources of copyright income

Music consumers are distributed fairly equally between the sexes, and music is an integral part of life in virtually all countries, among all races, cultures, and classes. Though different types of music appeal to different types of peoples at different times, the fact remains that music is a universal commodity, and copyright ownership presents an inexhaustible range of financial opportunities.

The largest segment of music consumers is aged 25 and older; the 20-24 age group is second; and the 10-19 group third. It is forecast that the 25+ grouping (the fastest growing segment) will continue music buying habits they established in their younger years, more so than did their preceding generation.

While baby boomers have been eager music purchasers, Generation X seems even more extreme in their music consumption. This is probably because they grew up with contemporary music ingrained as an essential element of their culture via exposure to VH1, MTV, CMT, BET, etc., and they had more opportunities to indulge in listening to music while engaged in other activities.

Expanding market opportunities

The market for song copyrights is vast and expanding. Music becomes more and more accessible as hardware becomes more compact and portable. Walkman-type audio and video cassette players, for instance, allow consumers to take music jogging, boating, or camping. New hardware technologies provide new income opportunities for new music—as well as for rereleased existing music—to be issued in new software formats (CDs, CD-ROMs, DAT, DVDs, etc.). Worldwide proliferation of cable, satellite, pay-per-view, and interactive media heavily increases demand for new programming, and, subsequently, the need for more music.

Continuing population growth expands the market universe for music of all types. Rising disposable income and the expansion of leisure time available to all segments of the population creates wider demands for all forms of entertainment. All of these trends are of beneficial, long-range importance to the music publishing industry.

Market genre segments

Popular music today is segmented into markets for several genres, usually designated as follows:

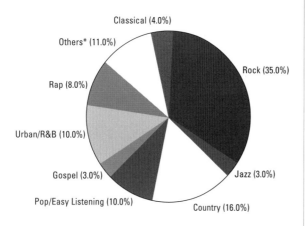

Classical (4.0%)
Others* (11.0%)
Rock (35.0%)
Rap (8.0%)
Urban/R&B (10.0%)
Gospel (3.0%)
Jazz (3.0%)
Pop/Easy Listening (10.0%)
Country (16.0%)

Others: Soundtracks, New Age, Ethnic, World, etc.

These percentages fluctuate from year to year as fashions change. But it's often difficult to categorize the market scope of individual copyrights since many hit songs enjoy *crossover* success within two or more genre segments. The success of a song in one particular market demonstrates an inherent commercial appeal, which a competent publisher can exploit to other markets as well. And if a song achieves popularity with a particular style of music that doesn't appeal to other markets, the onus is on the publisher to have the song rearranged for viable promotion to other targeted market segments.

International scope of the market

The music business is increasingly international. Overseas earnings can augment a publisher's domestic revenues by as much as 25 percent to 40 percent.

Although there are certain cultural and language barriers, a song's success in one country often leads to success abroad. U.S. repertoires, particularly, cross borders frequently. English has become the modern *lingua franca*, and popular entertainment tastes worldwide are heavily influenced by the dominance of the U.S. film, television, and music industries.

Analysis of Top 100 charts in Europe, Australia, and Japan reveal a great many copyrights originating in the U.S., just as U.S. Top 100 charts contain many foreign-originated copyrights. Proven popular acceptance of a work domestically should stimulate the publisher to exploit the song overseas. Any publisher with good international representation and the right kind of repertoire will reap profits from overseas catalog activity.

Commercial lifespan of a song

Hit songs are often thought of as disposable entertainment, achieving a brief flame of popularity, and then fading until forgotten. But hit songs can be successfully exploited to generate money throughout the life of copyright. A song that achieves popularity during one generation is often resurrected in succeeding generations. And a generation in pop music terms is about ten years or less.

Renewed popularity may be spontaneous, but publishers often initiate updated arrangements and creatively exploit older songs by resurrecting them for contemporary recording artists and producers of television shows, films, and advertising commercials.

Songs that are revived and rerecorded by other artists over the years are called *standards*, or *evergreens*. For example, "Alexander's Ragtime Band" has been recorded and performed innumerable times since it was written by Irving Berlin in 1911. Berlin died in 1989 at age 101, outliving the copyright to the song in the USA (where, even with renewals, copyrights lasted only 56 years under the Copyright Act of 1909, which was in effect when the song was written). But in Europe, where copyright protection lasted 50 years after the death of the writer (as American copyright law provides now) "Alexander's Ragtime Band" remains in copyright until 2039.

Another example is "All in the Game," which

has been a hit for many artists since it was co-written by Charles G. Dawes, vice president of the United States under Calvin Coolidge (1925-1929) and recipient of the 1925 Nobel Peace Prize. Standards such as these form the backbone of all valuable catalogs.

For instance, in the '80s, four Top 10 records in the UK included "Lipstick, Powder and Paint" (performed by Shaking Stevens), "Dancing in the Streets" (performed by David Bowie and Mick Jagger), and "Knock on Wood" and "Light My Fire" (both performed by Amii Stewart). Each of these copyrights is over 25 years old; all were hits by other artists prior to these more recent successes, and all are now standards. (Coincidentally, all of these songs originated in the U.S. as R&B hits and subsequently gained international pop and rock hit status.)

Not all of today's standards achieved commercial acceptance when first exploited. There are numerous examples of songs that were greeted with great yawns from the public on first release, and then became chart toppers later because their publishers remained convinced of their viability and kept promoting them. There are also countless examples of songs that were first unsuccessful in one market or country, and then achieved hit status after later reexploitation in another market or country.

Product development remains inexpensive

With all the financial benefits that publishers receive from continuing technological advances and expanding market opportunities, one very interesting fact stands out: *Publishers don't have to invest a cent to reap the rewards of progress.*

The essential elements of the publisher's product are always the same: music and lyrics. It's a product that's conceived and constructed in someone's head. Songs never need capital outlays for R&D, engineering, or manufacture. No matter what happens, creating new copyrights remains as inexpensive as it was 100 years ago. Through every fashion shift and technological change, music publishing generates steady revenues and solid profits.

▼

A market without constraints
The market for song copyrights is not confined to the time, market segment, or locality in which they are initially exploited or in which they first enjoy hit status. Copyrights can be recycled again and again. The market is of international proportions; it has demonstrated considerable growth and shows every sign of continued expansion.

☞ Billboard *magazine stated editorially a few years ago: "With all the changes that have occurred [recently] . . . all that's certain is that publishing will continue to be one of the most lucrative, steady revenue generators in the music industry."*

CHAPTER 2

What is Music Publishing?

Although music publishing can be an exceptionally lucrative business, it is also often misunderstood. Many laymen think music publishing primarily involves printing and selling sheet music. Very few publishers print sheet music these days, however. In fact, most music publishers today don't manufacture product in any physical form, nor do they sell product directly to consumers. Instead, music publishers *license* other companies *the rights* to use, perform, copy, and sell songs in various types of media.

The public misconception of music publishing no doubt originates with the general history of publishing and from the more common definitions of the word *publishing* found in most dictionaries.

Publishing is defined as:
1. preparing and issuing material for distribution or sale to the public
2. making known
3. bringing to the attention of the public
4. spreading information via public advertisement or announcement
5. publicizing, broadcasting
6. issuing a publication

History of music publishing

Publishing evolved with the invention of printing technology in the 15th century. Until that time, creative works had to be meticulously reproduced by hand, which limited the availability of intellectual output to an elite few. Printing created a commercial market for intellectual works and brought about the establishment of publishing houses (printers of books and manuscripts) as distinct from booksellers (retailers). Thus, the term *publishing* became popularly associated with printed material.

Over time, publishing houses tended to concentrate on certain types of product (e.g., literature, maps, or music), and by the 19th century, music publishing became a separate business. Indeed, some of today's major music publishing companies can trace their roots back to this time. Warner-Chappell, for instance, was founded as Chappell Music in London in 1811.

Just as the printing press led to the establishment of the publishing business, newer technologies expanded methods of publishing beyond that of printing. The development of sound recording, for example, enabled music to be reproduced (published) on records.

It might have been a logical step for music publishers to issue music on records, but, as things unfolded, *record companies* emerged to "publish" recorded performances by musicians and singers. That meant that record companies had to obtain permission from the music publishers who owned the songs performed by the recording artists. The upshot was that, instead of selling product per se, music publishers began dealing in rights.

▼

*Copyright literally means
"the right to copy."*

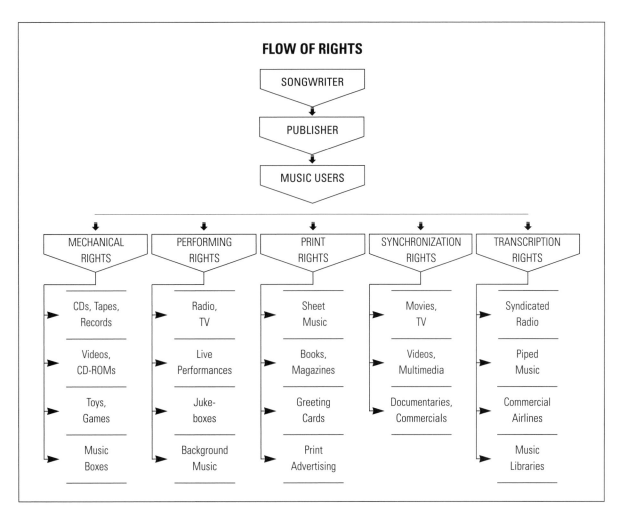

FLOW OF RIGHTS

SONGWRITER

↓

PUBLISHER

↓

MUSIC USERS

MECHANICAL RIGHTS	PERFORMING RIGHTS	PRINT RIGHTS	SYNCHRONIZATION RIGHTS	TRANSCRIPTION RIGHTS
CDs, Tapes, Records	Radio, TV	Sheet Music	Movies, TV	Syndicated Radio
Videos, CD-ROMs	Live Performances	Books, Magazines	Videos, Multimedia	Piped Music
Toys, Games	Juke-boxes	Greeting Cards	Documentaries, Commercials	Commercial Airlines
Music Boxes	Background Music	Print Advertising		Music Libraries

Flow of song rights

A song's creator is endowed by law with total control over how it can be used. This control exists in the legal term *copyright*. Only the copyright owner can legally perform the song, reproduce copies of it for sale and distribution, or authorize others to do so. Songwriters usually assign copyright ownership or management control to music publishers, who then become the guardian of all rights to the songs.

RIGHTS LICENSED BY MUSIC PUBLISHERS

Anyone who wants to record, print, copy, or publicly perform a song must obtain a *license* from its music publisher. In return for issuing a license to use the song, the copyright holder receives either a fee or a royalty for each performance or copy sold.

▼

The exclusive right to print, perform, broadcast, reproduce, manufacture, distribute, and sell a song, in whatever form, belongs to the person or company that controls the song's copyright.

COPYRIGHT PROTECTION ISN'T FOREVER

A copyright is a perishable asset. There is a statutory limit to a copyright's life, after which legal protection ends. At that time, the song enters the *public domain* and can be used by anyone without need of a license or payment of royalties. However, copyright life is long enough to be considered a long-term asset.

Copyright is in effect from the time a song is *fixed* in permanent form (recorded or written down) until 50 years after the songwriter's death. In the case of a song written by two or more writers, copyright remains in effect until 50 years after the death of the last surviving collaborator. (As of 1996, legislation was being considered to extend copyright protection to 70 years after the songwriter's death.)

Music publishing vs. other types of publishing

What sets modern music publishers apart from other types of publishers is the fact that most music publishers don't deal in the physical product that delivers the song to the consumer. Publishers of books, magazines, newspapers, records, films, and software resemble music publishers in that they own the rights to the material they publish, but they also own the physical copies made from the material (records, tapes, discs, books, etc.). Thus, until the copies are sold to consumers, other types of publishers own *tangible assets* (physical copies of the product) as well as *intangible assets* (copyrights to the material contained on the physical copies).

Since most music publishers, then, have no physical product, copyrights constitute their sole stock in trade. Copyrights are intangible assets (i.e., they don't have physical properties you can see or touch). Music publishers "rent" the rights to intangible properties (songs) to *users*, such as record companies, artists, record producers, broadcasters, film producers, advertising agencies, and software developers, etc. The users make physical copies of the songs (records, sheet music, etc.) and sell them to consumers.

HOW THE PRODUCT REACHES CONSUMERS

This illustrates another difference that sets music publishing apart from other types of publishers. Book publishers and record labels market product directly to consumers. Music publishers rarely promote or market songs directly to people who buy discs, tapes, or sheet music. Music publishers focus most of their marketing energy behind the scenes.

The publisher's mission is to market songs to users. The users, in turn, produce physical copies of the songs to sell directly to consumers. Though many music publishers ultimately participate in marketing finished product to consumers, this exercise is, for the most part, the responsibility of the users.

And, rather than "selling" product to users, publishers, in effect, *rent* product. That is, publishers retain copyright ownership and issue licenses that grant *limited rights* to use the songs, which may be revoked if the licensing terms aren't kept. These limited rights are usually *nonexclusive*; the publisher may, in most cases, allow others to also use the same song in similar fashion at the same time. (There are, of course, exceptions where songs are licensed exclusively.)

It is the user's task to make songs available to consumers via discs, tapes, films, print, jingles, live and broadcast performances, etc. It is also the user's task to render the songs in a manner that results in commercial acceptance by the public. Publishers collect royalties and fees from users and pay a percentage of this income to the songwriters who created the copyrights.

Music publishing is difficult for the general public to grasp because:
• the product is intangible
• music publishers tend to operate out of the spotlight
• publishers don't usually deal directly with consumers
• publishing was historically associated with printing

A day in the life of a music publisher

In the course of a day, publishers may deal with songwriters, recording artists, record producers, recording engineers, arrangers, musicians, record salesmen, marketing executives, promotion men, disc jockeys, booking agents, the press, PR consultants, artists' managers, record company management, lawyers, accountants, video producers and directors, overseas licensees, print licensees, and more.

Also in the course of the day, publishers may assume interchangeable roles of recruiting agents, drill sergeants, mother hens, psychoanalysts, confessors, cheerleaders, super-salesmen, brokers, and wheeler-dealers. Indeed, publishers wear as many hats as necessary to discover and nurture songwriting talent and launch songs successfully into the marketplace.

WHAT DO PUBLISHERS DO?

In a sense, music publishers are much like agents, or brokers. They are middlemen between the product's creator (songwriter) and its end-users (record companies, film producers, broadcasters, etc.). Music publishers are the connection, the linchpin between the originator of a song and the vehicle by which it is ultimately brought to the public's attention.

As an agent, the publisher represents the writer by licensing rights to use the song. The better job the publisher does of representation and negotiating deals, the more both he and the writer can earn. But the publisher usually has more of a stake in a song than that of a mere agent. Most often, the publisher also owns either the copyright to the song or has some degree of management control over the copyright. Therefore, the more the publisher increases the income of songs he controls, the more he increases the value of his catalog as an asset, and, by extension, the value of his company.

As any business school student knows, the first duty of a company director is to increase the value of the company's stock to its owners. In music publishing, the company is essentially the song copyrights it controls. From a holistic standpoint, therefore, the publisher's role and goal is always to protect the integrity of his copyrights and to increase the income generated by them.

The business of music publishing involves:
- acquiring songs
- marketing songs
- managing songs
- business management

These four functions include negotiating contracts and licenses, copyright administration, creative direction and guidance of writers, collections, royalty accounting, and the management of finances, taxes, investments, personnel, and facilities.

Since the publisher's product is songs, it goes without saying that acquiring quality songs with commercial potential is the first order of business. A company without quality product is doomed. Equally, no matter how good its product, a company can't succeed without the ability to market that product.

But, quality product and savvy marketing aren't enough to ensure lasting success. Management skills are essential in music publishing, just as in any other business. Music publishing is a glamorous business, chock-full of rags to riches stories. Unfortunately, there are also many riches to rags stories, because some practitioners forget that the music business is a business.

▼

Never forget: Music publishing is a business.

Costs of product

Unlike other segments of the copyright industry (software manufacturers, record companies, film producers, book publishers, etc.), music publishers don't mass produce product in physical form to reach consumers. For this reason, music publishing overhead can be low and profits high. Operating costs are relatively modest, since music publishers don't need to stock inventory, invest in a manufacturing plant and equipment, or employ an army of personnel. It doesn't take a lot of money to start a music publishing company, and fortunes can be made operating solo on a shoestring.

But music publishing is like every other business. It involves *risk*. Publishers risk time and money, two precious resources, acquiring and promoting copyrights. Normally, the biggest financial risk is investment for product acquisition, though product development can also become risky if pursued aggressively via expensive demo or master production, marketing, or promotion.

Capital investment and working capital are needed for:
- **Product acquisition** (signing writers, buying copyrights)
- **Product development** (producing demos and masters)
- **Marketing** (shopping songs to users, augmenting user's promotion efforts)
- **Copyright administration** (copyright registrations and collection fees)
- **Operating overhead** (office facilities, supplies, salaries, etc.)

Sources of product acquisition

The product is created by songwriters. Publishers then acquire the finished songs through copyright assignment from either the songwriters or their original publishers. The assignment may either be temporary or permanent, by doing one of the following:
- **Purchasing** existing catalogs or individual song copyrights
- **Licensing** overseas catalogs (or individual songs) for domestic representation
- **Contracting** songwriters to write exclusively
- **Assigning copyrights** to individual songs from nonexclusive writers
- **Co-publishing** arrangements with other publishers

Except where acquisition is made by purchase, publishers usually pay *advances* (recoupable against royalties) to songwriters or original publishers in order to acquire copyrights. (Methods of assessing the purchase price of an existing song or copyright catalog and of calculating how much monetary advance a song or catalog is worth, are discussed in the chapter on *Acquisitions*.)

Specific sources of copyright income

The two prime sources of copyright income for most publishers are: *mechanical royalties* (from sales of discs and tapes) and *performance royalties* (broadcast, background, live performances).

MECHANICAL INCOME

In the early 1980s, mechanical income faced growth constraints from declining record sales and counterfeiting of legitimately-licensed recorded product. Home taping was another problem (and still defies easy solution).

However, record sales rebounded in the late '80s and continued to grow considerably through the '90s. Worldwide sales of prerecorded music in 1988 leaped 19%, to $20.3 billion, and approached $35.5 billion by 1994. 1989 saw total U.S. sales of $6.63 billion on 806 million shipments of CDs, records, and cassettes. And even in the midst of the 1990 recession, shipments further rose to 866 million units, and revenues were at an all-time high of $7.5 billion (up 14.6% over 1989). The trend upwards continued strongly, with U.S. sales totaling $12.1 billion in 1994 (up 20% over 1993).

"Despite the economy's woes, recorded music sales have held up well," RIAA president Jay Berman commented. "It proves, once again, that music is still a bargain and the best buy for the entertainment dollar."

Meanwhile, purveyors of unlicensed and counterfeit product are being caught and prosecuted successfully in several countries. At the same time, increased mechanical-royalty rates in America and unit-price rises overseas have combined to raise publishers' mechanical income. The Harry Fox Agency (which collects mechanical royalties for most U.S. publishers) more than quadrupled annual collections between 1984 and 1994 (from $80 million to nearly $358 million). And Harry Fox's collections jumped again in 1995, to over $392 million.

PERFORMANCE INCOME

Meanwhile, U.S. performance income more than doubled between 1976 and 1984, (from $157 million to $328 million) then doubled again over the next decade. This impressive growth should continue even more dramatically with the rise of new technologies and the spread of more broadcasting outlets. There are over 9,000 radio and television stations in America alone, and still more broadcasting outlets are coming online (each home will soon have access to some 500 television channels).

Performance income has also soared in Europe. For instance, the British performing rights society, PRS, collected some £60 million in 1982, but its 1995 collections approached £150 million (approximately $225 million).

OTHER INCOME

Income from *synchronization* licenses (music used in films) has grown substantially (to as much as 20% of some publishers' total gross) and will continue to do so as producers require more music to meet increased demands for visual programming.

Besides performance, mechanical, and synchronization licensing, other sources of publishing income include print rights, commercials, jingles, transcriptions, and grand rights. Revenues from all of these income sources continue to grow impressively.

Breakdown of global music publishing revenues

WORLDWIDE MUSIC PUBLISHING REVENUES—1993

Performing rights	$2,190,000,000	43%
Mechanical rights	$1,890,000,000	38%
Print rights	$577,350,000	11%
Synchronization & other	$243,310,000	5%
Interest & investments	$126,360,000	3%
Total	$5,027,020,000	100%

(Source - NMPA)

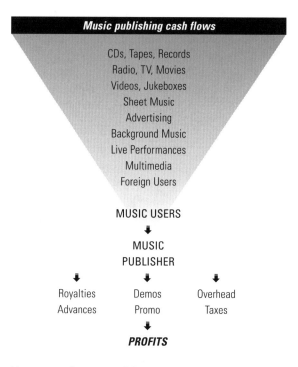

Music publishing cash flows

CDs, Tapes, Records
Radio, TV, Movies
Videos, Jukeboxes
Sheet Music
Advertising
Background Music
Live Performances
Multimedia
Foreign Users

MUSIC USERS
⬇
MUSIC PUBLISHER

Royalties	Demos	Overhead
Advances	Promo	Taxes

⬇
PROFITS

How much can a hit song earn?

Although songs are published in virtually all media, most consumers purchase them in recorded form. So a "hit" is normally determined by record sales. But how many record sales make a hit? There is no magic number.

Beauty is in the eye of the beholder, and it could be said that a hit is defined by who's counting. Some musical genres have larger market potential than others, and some markets are larger than others. Sales of any one song must be measured against sales of similar types of songs released in similar circumstances. The comparison must be between apples and apples, not apples and oranges.

Bluegrass music, for instance, appeals to a rather small niche market. Therefore, 50,000 sales of a bluegrass album is a notable achievement. And 50,000 sales of a new artist's debut release on a small indie label might be a cause for rejoicing. But, 50,000 sales of a heavily promoted pop album by a big-name act on a major label may make all concerned want to hang black crepe. Yet you can pop the cork on a bottle of champagne if you sell 50,000 albums in a small market like Norway, where it only takes 25,000 sales to earn a gold record.

POTENTIAL PUBLISHER EARNINGS FROM A MILLION-SELLER

Any discussion of how much money a publisher might earn from a hit must begin with establishing an exact number of records sold. For the purpose of examining potential earnings, therefore, we'll use a platinum single (one million unit sales) as an example, since a million-seller is a hit by every definition.

Historically, one million sales of a single earned a gold record award in the U.S. In recent years, however, sales of singles have declined in favor of album purchases, so a single now needs only 500,000 sales to be certified gold. (1 million sales now earns a platinum designation, versus 2 million units required previously.)

The starting point for our projections is the *mechanical royalty*, which is what the record company pays the publisher for each disc or tape sold. The gross amount of mechanical royalties earned directly from a million sales in the U.S. is $69,500, assuming that the publisher is paid the full statutory mechanical royalty rate currently in effect (1996-97). But a million-seller also generates income from sources other than record sales.

It is impossible to precisely predict how much a song will earn in addition to record sales. There are many variables affecting the amounts of *performance royalties* (from broadcasting, jukeboxes, etc.), *print income* (sheet music sales, lyric reprints, etc.), *foreign earnings*, and income from a myriad of potential *miscellaneous usages*.

For instance, country songs tend to earn more performance royalties than R&B. Rock songs may generate more foreign sales than country. Melodic ballads sell more sheet music than rock. Rap is unlikely to be covered by other artists or sell any sheet music at all. But pop hits are likely to be covered by other artists, used for background music and commercials, and included in TV-marketed "best of" albums. Moreover, a megahit may well crossover to sell in several markets, generating more performance income from a greater range of broadcasting outlets and more print income from a wider variety of formats.

In view of these variables, income from several types of songs was averaged below in order to arrive at realistic projections of possible earnings from a hypothetical million-selling single.

Potential gross from a million-selling record

Income Sources	Low Estimate	High Estimate
Mechanical (CDs/Tapes)	$69,500	$69,500
Performances (Radio/TV)	$50,000	$250,000
Print	$15,000	$35,000
Foreign (All Sources)	$75,000	$250,000
Miscellaneous	$15,000	$75,000
Total	$224,500	$679,500

ASSUMPTIONS USED IN TABLE

Mechanicals. This is the only nonvariable, since mechanical royalties are paid on reported sales, and one million sales = one million sales. The above projected mechanical income assumes that the royalty paid is the full statutory rate in effect as of 1996-1997, which is 6.95¢ per song (for under five minutes in playing time), and that there is no *negotiated rate reduction* or *controlled composition clause*. (See the chapter on *Mechanical-Rights Licensing*.)

The amount shown above is the *gross* paid by the record company to the publisher. The publisher must share this with the songwriter(s) and any co-publishers. If there is just one publisher, and the songwriter(s) receive(s) the standard 50% royalty, the publisher nets $34,750 ($69,500 ÷ 2).

Performances. Performance royalties are collected by *performing-rights societies* from broadcasters, jukebox operators, and venues that use live and background music. The societies (BMI, ASCAP, and SESAC in the U.S.) then pay *net* royalties to the songwriters and publishers respectively. This means that the performance income shown above isn't shared with the songwriter(s).

Performance royalties on a hit vary widely. A song that reaches Number One on the U.S. pop charts generally earns between $70,000 and $100,000 in performance royalties from radio play alone. But a Number One song will certainly be performed in other media as well. Further, a Number One pop hit tends to crossover to other market genres, thereby increasing radio airplay and other types of performances. So the total shown above includes performances logged from TV, jukeboxes, clubs, concert arenas, etc., as well as airplay on radio stations geared to formats other than pop.

Print. As will be seen in the chapter on *Licensing Print Rights*, there are numerous printed formats in which music is published, and a million-seller will most likely be issued in several. Also, this category includes fees for lyric reprints in magazines and books, etc. Assuming the publisher in this scenario licenses all print rights (i.e., doesn't print his own sheet music), the amount shown above is *gross* and must be shared with the songwriter(s) and any co-publishers. Usually, publishers share licensed print income with songwriters on the same percentage basis as all other nonperformance income, which is 50% in this case.

Foreign. This category includes income from all overseas sources (mechanicals, performances, print, and miscellaneous). Typically, the publisher licenses foreign rights to overseas publishers (*subpublishers*). The amount shown above represents *gross* income received from the subpublisher, after the subpublisher's fee and any other contractually allowed costs are deducted. The publisher splits these receipts with the songwriter(s) and any co-publishers, usually on the same percentage basis as with other nonperformance licenses.

Miscellaneous. This category includes income from a range of possible sources, such as synchronizations (fees and royalties from the song's use in films and other visual media), computer software (CD-ROMs, MIDI files, etc.), karaoke, commercials, and so on. Again, the above sum represents the gross amount received by the publisher, who must then share the income with the songwriter(s) and any co-publishers.

Assuming, then, that the song in this projection has one publisher, and the songwriter receives the standard 50% royalty on nonperformance income, the chart below illustrates the potential earnings *net* to the publisher.

Potential net from a million-selling record		
Income Sources	Low Estimate	High Estimate
Mechanical (CDs/Tapes)	$34,750	$34,750
Performances (Radio/TV)	$50,000	$250,000
Print	$7,500	$17,500
Foreign (All Sources)	$37,500	$125,000
Miscellaneous	$7,500	$37,500
Total	$137,250	$464,750

NOTE: The above figures apply to the 'A' side of a million-selling single only. 'B' sides would essentially earn income only from record sales, since there wouldn't be significant radio airplay or sheet music sales.

Ultimately, however, achieving a million record sales is usually just the start of a copyright's earning potential over many years. The above figures reflect only the most immediate income to be expected in the first 12-18 months. In time, additional income may be generated from:

- Album sales by the artist capitalizing on the single's success
- Cover versions by other artists
- "Greatest hits" compilations and TV-marketed albums
- Videocassettes
- Continuing print licenses ("best of" and "personality" folios, etc.)
- Continuing performance income for live and broadcast performances
- Background music uses
- Record club sales
- Commercial advertisements
- Synchronization in motion pictures, etc.
- New media (karaoke, sampling, MIDI Files, CD-ROMs, etc.)

Different kinds of publishers

There are approximately 70,000 music publishing companies registered with the three U.S. performing-right societies, ranging from one-man operations based in back bedrooms to multinational giants with hundreds of employees and richly-appointed offices. However, a great many of these companies share common ownership, so the actual number of separately owned publishing entities is probably in the range of 10,000-20,000. But many of these companies are largely inactive. In fact, only a few hundred publishers have songs on the U.S. charts each year.

Lack of chart activity, though, doesn't necessarily mean inactivity, and inactivity doesn't necessarily mean lack of profitability. Obviously, many music publishing companies fold each year for one reason or another, and many more are founded with high hopes by individuals of both genders and all races, ages, tastes, talents, and abilities. It's very difficult, therefore, to say exactly how many active music publishing companies are in existence, except to say that there is a vast number of all types and sizes.

People start publishing companies for a variety of reasons, and there are a variety of ways publishing companies operate. Even companies of similar size targeting the same markets develop different operating styles, or corporate cultures, because each company reflects the individual personality of its founder or the collective personality of its management team. There is no cookie-cutter formula that must be adhered to in order to succeed.

But though no two publishing companies are exactly alike, there are some broadly defined categories that classify to one degree or another any particular company's type of operation. Essentially, these categories are as follows.

DESK DRAWER PUBLISHERS

Also called *vest pocket* publishers, the term refers to publishers who keep their copyrights in a desk drawer, figuratively speaking, rather than dusting them off for active marketing. This type of publisher is entirely passive, or reactive, meaning that he licenses copyrights when requested by users but makes no effort to sign new writers or promote new uses of the songs.

This situation arises when a small publishing company's owner retires without selling his catalog but still receives royalty earnings from previous activity. It also happens when a publisher dies and his catalog is looked after by an *administrator* who fulfills licensing requests and collects royalties. (The administrator may be a surviving family member, lawyer, accountant, trustee, or hired manager.) Another example is an investor who acquires a copyright catalog and is content that the continuing income stream from the previous owner's activities is sufficient to pay back the investment and return a profit.

COPYRIGHT-HOLDING COMPANIES

This type of operation can be classed somewhere between active and passive. They actively spark the creation of music but aren't necessarily fully-fledged publishing companies, because they don't develop songwriting talent or market songs outside their own area of business. Examples include television, film, jingle, and record-production companies who commission works specifically for in-house productions. They can also include recording artists and producers who acquire copyright interests in songs they record but don't actively exploit the works to other users.

LONE RANGERS

These are active, one-man operators who single-handedly acquire material and hustle it into the marketplace. They include writer-publishers, artist-publishers, producer-publishers, and entrepreneurs. Most concentrate on a particular genre (e.g., country, R&B, pop, rock) that the owner has some expertise in. Many do their own copyright administration, licensing, and collections, while others enter into joint-ventures or arrangements with larger publishers or service organizations to handle specific functions.

ADMINISTRATIVE PUBLISHERS

These operations service desk drawer publishers, lone rangers, and other copyright owners who, for whatever reason, choose not to or cannot handle necessary catalog management duties. These duties entail royalty collections and accounting, registrations, licensing, and contracts. Administrators usually retain around 10%-15% of all income they collect. Administrative publishers don't promote or exploit songs, and they normally don't offer advances.

BANKER PUBLISHERS

These are usually well-heeled organizations that don't get much involved on the creative side of publishing but do pursue strategic alliances with creative people in order to develop publishing catalogs. Their modus operandi essentially involves acquiring ownership interest in copyrights by financing writers who have recording commitments as artists or producers and by bankrolling co-publishers to market and exploit the catalogs they bring to the table.

Banker-publishers are usually more concerned with profit opportunities than with any certain musical genre. They therefore tend to control catalogs that are more diversified than those of lone rangers and small, creatively oriented publishers.

FULL-SERVICE PUBLISHERS

These are fully staffed operations involved in all areas of publishing. They may act as banker-publishers or administrative publishers in some cases, but they also sign and nurture songwriting talent; develop artists; finance demos, videos, and recording sessions; purchase catalogs; pay advances for new works from well-known writers; sublicense catalogs from overseas publishers; market material to recording artists; and promote songs in all media. While larger operations of this type do their own collections, administration, and licensing, smaller ones may make arrangements with service firms to handle specific functions.

Among full-service publishers are a range of company sizes, corporate cultures, musical styles, and marketing orientation. Smaller, independently owned companies, for instance, tend to focus on the musical genres that their founders are enamored of. As companies grow and prosper, they may begin to diversify.

The most successful independents are usually those that align themselves with other segments of the industry, such as record labels, production companies, and management. And the most successful independents also become highly desired targets for acquisition or merger.

Indeed, there has been quite a lot of consolidation over the past few years as copyright-rich indies have been absorbed by larger companies. As a result, there are today only a handful of truly giant publishing operations, most of which are very profitable divisions of still larger corporations that are also significant players in film, television, records, and other segments of the entertainment business. Though the trend towards consolidation means that the media giants have formidable locks on market share, there is always opportunity for aggressive, intelligent new blood to enter the business and make a mark.

SERIOUS MUSIC PUBLISHERS

While the types of publishers discussed above focus on more mainstream areas of publishing (i.e., popular music of all genres), there are other kinds of publishers who profit very well from strong markets in the *serious* field of music publishing, which includes educational, classical, concert, children's music, religious, and theater. Most of the megapublishers are also involved in these areas, but there are many more smaller companies that concentrate solely on one or two of these niche markets.

The table below illustrates the departmental breakdown and functions of a major, full-service publisher. Managerial and departmental titles vary from company to company.

Departmental functions of a full-service publishing company	
DEPARTMENT	FUNCTIONS
Business Affairs	Legal, Contracts, Licensing, Negotiations, Corporate Matters, Insurance, Leases, etc.
Administration	Copyright Registrations, Contract Filings, Routine Licenses & Permissions, Registration (Performing- & Mechanical-Right Societies)
Financial	Accounting, Bookkeeping, Royalties, Taxes, Investments, Equity & Debt Management, Payables, Billings, Collections, Payroll
Creative	Acquisitions, Auditions, Songplugging, Writer & Catalog Exploitation & Development, Demo & Record Production, Artist Development
Marketing	Promotion, Advertising, Press & Media, Public Relations, Sales, Artwork, Design
Operations	Personnel, Facilities, Purchasing, Equipment, Maintenance, Shipping, Communications, Printing, Copying, Manufacturing, Inventory, Computer & Information Systems, Library
Print	Arrangements, Design, Artwork, Printing, Shipping, Distribution, Sales, Inventory, Billings, Collections, Licensing
International	Foreign Acquisitions, & Licensing, Exploitation, Liaison With Overseas Branches & Licensees
Recorded Music Library	Acquisitions, Production, Marketing
Film & Television	Synchronizations, Theme Commissioning
Jingles	Production, Marketing, Synchronizations
Concert	Arrangements, Licensing, Permissions
Theater	Grand & Dramatic Rights Licensing

Employees of smaller publishers usually wear several hats with overlapping responsibilities. Indeed, many smaller indie publishers do not pursue every area of publishing opportunity (recorded music libraries, or concert and theater licensing, for instance). And many publishing functions routinely handled by larger firms may be contracted out by smaller publishers. The table below illustrates how a small to mid-size indie publisher may divide publishing tasks between in-house staff and outside contractors.

Departmental functions of a small, independent publishing company	
IN-HOUSE OPERATIONS	SUBCONTRACTED OPERATIONS
Acquisitions	Legal Affairs
Songplugging	Copyright Administration
Promotion	Licensing
Demo Production	Contracts
Record Production	Press/P.R.
Nonroutine Licensing	Print Sales
Creative Direction	Foreign
Contract Negotiations	Accounting
Artist Development	Bookkeeping
Personnel Management	Royalties

CHAPTER 3

Starting Your Own Publishing Company

Why start a music publishing company?

A music publishing career can provide personal fulfillment and great financial rewards. It has obvious attractions for anyone seeking a good business to start or to be in. But you don't have to pursue music publishing as a full time occupation to benefit from much of what it has to offer. If you're involved with the music business in any way, there are always opportunities to profit from copyright ownership.

Remember, the music business revolves around songs. The search for the right song is never-ending. If you're active in performing or recording, someone you know needs a song. This also holds true if you represent artists, producers, or songwriters in a legal, financial, booking, public relations, or management capacity. If you happen to have the right song at the right time, you may well reap a fortune.

▼

Being in the right place at the right time with the right song = $$$.

Music publishing is a low-risk method of building assets and establishing an additional profit center, no matter what area of the music business you've chosen to focus on. Indeed, setting up a music publishing company should be a natural move for anyone engaged in, or connected with, the music industry. This is especially true considering music publishing companies don't necessarily need staff, offices, or expensive equipment. The annualized costs of starting and maintaining a publishing enterprise can amount to just a few dollars a day.

BENEFITS OF OWNING A MUSIC PUBLISHING COMPANY

The benefits of owning a music publishing company should be particularly obvious to those in the following fields of activity.

Established songwriters

A songwriter who has established a track record of hits is in the enviable position of being beseeched for new material by artists, producers, and other users. Though a major publisher may have been instrumental in the songwriter's initial success, there comes a time when the writer may want more control over his or her own creative works and career. The publisher's services must be reevaluated in relation to the percentage it retains from the writer's income.

Moreover, the writer may now begin to look ahead to when he or she will no longer be actively writing. Copyright ownership can provide income-generating assets for future financial security. If an established writer wants to retain a relationship with a major publisher, a co-publishing venture can be structured whereby the writer retains a portion of ownership in the copyrights he or she creates.

In addition, established songwriters inevitably attract younger writers seeking mentors to help them break into the business. It is not at all unethical for an established writer to sign upcoming writers to his or her own company. Indeed, it makes good business sense. Younger writers have much to gain from the knowledge, experience, and contacts established writers have earned over the years, and established writers deserve to be compensated for their time and guidance.

New songwriters

It is usually very frustrating for new writers to try to get publishers to accept their work. It's also difficult for unpublished writers to gain access to record labels and producers. In fact, most major labels won't accept unsolicited material unless it comes from a publisher. Some fledgling writers short-circuit the process by setting up their own publishing company. They can then submit material directly to record labels, producers, and artists in the guise of a publishing company rather than that of an unpublished writer (no one has to *know* they're self-published).

Record producers

The pivotal role producers have between artists, labels, publishers, and songwriters places them in an ideal position to get songs recorded. They have numerous opportunities to sign unpublished songs or make co-publishing deals with indie publishers and self-published writers in return for including songs on the recording projects they produce.

Recording artists

Like producers, artists can record material submitted to them in return for an interest in publishing rights that may be available. Artists may feel justified in receiving some of the future copyright earnings from songs they help popularize. It makes even more sense for *self-contained artists* (i.e., those who primarily record self-penned songs) to retain publishing rights to their own material. After all, one of the main reasons for signing with a publisher is to get material recorded, and the self-contained artist takes care of that himself.

Artists' managers, music business attorneys, accountants

Anyone representing artists, songwriters, or producers will do well to offer publishing services to their clients. The clients may not have the time, inclination, or capacity to manage music publishing interests, but they will certainly benefit from copyright ownership. It should therefore be the duty of their representative to point this out and help them structure a copyright holding company. The manager, attorney, or accountant also benefits, either by increasing the client's income (which increases the representative's fees or percentage) or through shared ownership in the copyrights accumulated by the client, or both.

Record labels

Every record company should set up a separate entity to publish songs they release that aren't already signed to other publishers. Often co-publishing material by self-contained artists is a condition laid down by the record company in the artist's contract. Also, it frequently happens that publishing income makes the difference between profits and losses on an artist's release. Moreover, publishing interests add an additional profit center and asset base to the record company operations.

Film, video, and television producers

Movie and television production companies are in a similar situation to that of a record label. That is, they can reduce cash outlay and increase asset value by taking ownership interests in music copyrights used in their productions. And, by commissioning songwriters to write material specifically for their projects as *employees for hire*, the production company owns the copyright to the works created.

Studio operators

Recording studio owners are often approached to rent facilities on "spec" during times that the studios are otherwise unbooked. If the would-be clients have publishing available as collateral for later payment or to sweeten the deal, studio operators might be more inclined to speculate on the project, in consideration of the windfall profits that might accrue from copyright ownership. It certainly takes no heavy lifting for the studio operator to set up a music publishing company in order to benefit from opportunities that arise.

Entrepreneurs and investors

The music business is one where fast profits can be made. Though there are risks, any entrepreneur smitten by the allure of the music business should be aware that music publishing requires less investment relative to risk than almost any other segment of the industry. But even when an entrepreneur chooses to pursue one of the more high profile segments (like a record label, studio, or artist management company), music publishing ought to form part of the overall plan, for the reasons discussed above. Certainly, music publishing is an attractive proposition worth serious consideration by anyone seeking a potentially high return on investment.

Though the benefits of owning a music publishing operation are clear, there are shortcomings to self-publishing if one isn't well grounded in the business or isn't capable of proper copyright administration, licensing, and marketing. A full time publisher can greatly enhance the value and income of your copyrights. So if you're unable or unwilling to devote the necessary time and energy to managing your copyrights, consider making an administrative or co-publishing deal with a larger publisher. While the full time publisher takes care of all the details and minutiae, you can build cash-generating assets for the future without being sidetracked from your current goals.

ANCILLARY BENEFITS OF COPYRIGHT OWNERSHIP

In addition to the direct benefits of starting or owning a music publishing entity, there are numerous indirect or ancillary benefits.

Copyright ownership gives you leverage when negotiating deals with major publishers and labels; you have something of value to trade for more front money, more points, etc.

The more diverse you are, the more secure you are when one area of your career or business goes south. The old saying about not putting all one's eggs in the same basket is still as much a word to the wise as it ever was. Whatever your main interests, if you're involved in the music industry, establishing a music publishing company as a separate entity should be a no-brainer insurance policy—a lifeboat in case your flagship runs into stormy seas.

What you might not be interested in doing today, you might well want to do tomorrow. If you're concentrating now on a performing career, for instance, the time may come when you're too decrepit to tour but are still enamored of the business, and music publishing revenue can fund other activities.

Assuming you're still years away from even thinking about life in a rocking chair, you should nevertheless make retirement plans. If you start building copyright ownership now, you'll have assets in place later to provide cash flow for your sunset years, to sell or borrow against in case of emergency, or to fund a life on the golf course.

What it takes to be a publisher

You don't need a license per se to become a publisher (but check locally for general business-license requirements in your city and state). You will, however, need to become a member of a *performing-right society*—not because membership is required, but because the societies collect a major portion of publishers' income. There are no stringent requirements for membership in a performing-right society. (See the chapter on *Performing-Right Licensing.*)

As for the personal qualities you'll need: it would help if you love music, if you're a fan and can bring a missionary zeal to promoting your catalog. But it's not entirely necessary. You may, instead, possess the typical entrepreneurial flair for conceiving, starting, and operating a business. That means, if you aren't endowed with all the attributes needed for suc-

cess in a particular business, you recruit associates who're strong where you're weak. You, or the team you put together, should have a basic business sense and an instinct for what is musically commercial.

The ideal publisher combines the following attributes:
- the ability to recognize hit songs
- the ability to match the right song with the right artist
- negotiating skills
- attention to administrative detail
- understanding contracts and licenses
- financial integrity

Publishers have a fiduciary responsibility to their songwriters. Music publishers collect royalties and fees due from usages of songs, and must properly account to songwriters for their share of the income. Failure to make accurate and timely accountings can result in the loss of copyrights and the imposition of damages and legal fees.

How much money do you need to start?

You can start a publishing company on a shoestring, keeping your files in a shoe box. As long as you go about it intelligently and have an ear tuned to the market, you have as good a chance to make it big as someone starting off with a hundred grand and plush offices. Many multimillion dollar publishing companies were founded on less than $1,000.

To be more specific, however, the amount of start-up money *you* need depends entirely on how you intend to operate in the early stages. So, to calculate your start-up costs, ask yourself these questions:

Do you need an office at this stage, or can you operate from home? Do you need to hire personnel, or are you confident of your abilities to recognize and market hit songs and to administer copyright catalogs properly? (You certainly would not be wise to sink a lot of money into office space and personnel until your needs and publishing income warrant such expenditures.)

Do you have access to good songs and songwriters that don't require payment of advances? If your talent sources at this stage do require funding, how much? Do your songwriters provide finished demos, or will you need to finance the recordings?

Do you own, or have access to, playback and tape-duplicating equipment, a word processor, a fax machine, an answering machine, etc.—or will you need to buy or lease some or all of this essential equipment?

Can you type your own letters, labels, contracts, etc., or will you need to budget for secretarial services?

Do you live near a major recording center, or will you have to dredge up expenses for postage, packaging, long-distance telephone, faxes, and travel, in order to plug your songs into the marketplace?

Do you have a source of income for personal needs until the business takes off and can afford to support you? It can take a long time to build cash flow, even if you're successful right away. How much can you set aside for contingencies? Remember the old adage: Whatever can go wrong will. The whole point of contingency planning is to be prepared for unforeseen delays and setbacks in every area. If you calculate you'll have a royalty check for $50,000 in 90 days, what happens if it actually doesn't arrive for 120 days? And supposed it's only for $40,000 due to deductions, withholdings, reserves, or whatever, that you hadn't counted on?

When to expect a return on investment

Most songs earn money only after being released in recorded format. Recorded songs generate mechanical royalties (record sales) and performance royalties (airplay), which provide the bulk of all publishing earnings. Even sheet music sales and miscellaneous licenses, including those that pay upfront fees or advances, are usually spin-off results of a song's popularity in recorded format.

Chapter 2 examined how *much* a hit song can earn, but you should understand how *long* it takes to actually receive royalties from a hit record. Unfortunately, music publishing isn't as simple as retail merchandising, where customers exchange cash on the spot for product.

Before publishers see significant money from a hit record, they must wait for it to pass through a chain of other hands. Ironically, this chain is inversely arranged so that the product's originators are paid last. This is because the record business has traditionally operated on a consignment, or sell-or-return basis.

Normally, the only time money changes hands *before* goods or services are rendered is when consumers buy the finished product from retailers. The retailers then pay the distributor, or wholesaler, from whom they obtained the product. The distributor subsequently pays the manufacturer, or record company. The record company, in turn, pays the music publisher (as well as the artist and producer). Last in the chain is the creator of the raw material that started the whole process—the songwriter—who is paid by the music publisher.

All in all, from the time you acquire a song and start marketing it, you should never expect to see any earnings until a year has elapsed—and that's the most optimistic timeline imaginable. More often, it takes much longer to get a new song cut, manufactured, released, marketed, and paid for.

BEST CASE SCENARIO
First three months
Assume you acquire a song today and demo it next week. Your next task is to get it recorded and released. You begin shopping the work to various producers you think may be interested in this type of song.

This process can take a very long time indeed, ranging from days to years. But let's say you're particularly lucky: The song is recognized as a hit by the first producer you play it to, and he wants to record it for his next project.

The recording session takes place a month or two later. Following our rosy scenario, then, your song is recorded within three months from the time you acquire it.

Second three months
The record company chooses the song as the artist's next single and schedules it for "rush" release three months later. Thus, six months after you've acquired the song, it hits the streets in record form.

Third three months
It takes a month or so for the record company's promotion and marketing team to get the record into the charts, and the record has about two months of peak sales activity thereafter. Now you're nine months from the date you first acquired the song.

Fourth three months
The record company's mechanical-license agreement with you provides a quarterly accounting. So expect three more months before you receive any royalties. Royalties from radio airplay (paid to you by the performing-right society) will begin to flow about the same time or shortly thereafter. Bear in mind, these first royalty accountings are for the initial sales period only. A further three months or more will lapse before you begin to see earnings from the peak sales period.

To sum up, under the most optimistic timeline, it should take approximately 12 months or more for you to get a song recorded, released, charted, and then for the money to trickle back from consumers to retailers to distributors to the record company to you, the music publisher. Income from performance royalties, sheet music, and other spin-off usages arrives about the same time or a little later, but rarely sooner.

IMPORTANCE OF CASH FLOW MANAGEMENT

This waiting period can play havoc with a new music publisher's cash flow. Established publishers have catalogs of income-producing songs accumulated over the years. These catalogs generate a steady flow of royalties, so established publishers aren't dependent on current hits to sustain operations. Current hits provide the foundation for later income to finance future operations. The challenge for start-up publishers is to survive during the time it takes to build a catalog of income-producing songs.

However, once a song shows signs of commercial success, the publisher may be able to raise cash on the strength of its demonstrated potential. Particularly, the publisher might get royalty advances from sheet music distributors, lyric-reprint magazines, and overseas publishers. It is also possible to get loans using projected royalties as collateral.

Knowing the pay-off timeline is important so that you can project cash flow and prioritize expenditures. Cash flow is as essential to success as profits. You can operate at a loss for years, as long as you can meet ongoing expenses. But an otherwise profitable company can go out of business if there is no cash to sustain operations until accounts receivable are converted to money in the bank. The point is, you must be in a position to sustain your business in the early months, because there'll be no cash flow until you've built up a catalog of income-producing songs.

The timeline is also important when calculating how much to advance a songwriter or pay for a copyright. The longer it takes to recoup an investment, the more iffy that investment is, and the less you should risk upfront.

Specialization

It is difficult to devise one promotional strategy to use for each and every songwriter, artist, song, or record release. The product is not uniform. You are not marketing thousands of identical widgets. Each product is unique and was created emotionally as well as intellectually. There is always a degree of unpredictability.

Each song and record release must be approached with this question: What is the optimum strategy for launching (or furthering) the career of the songwriter/artist with this particular song/release? Different songwriters and different artists require different strategies and tactics at different stages in their careers. For some, certain barriers have already been overcome; others are at the starting line.

Companies concentrating on a single product, like shampoo, can hone a grand marketing plan that's applicable for years. They have opportunities to test and reject dozens of advertising themes and ideas. Music publishers don't have that luxury, because each song is a unique product. And for record releases, the window of marketing opportunity is open only for a few months (or weeks).

A shampoo manufacturer's million-dollar campaign saturates the market with one message about one product. A music publisher's marketing budget must be allocated between dozens of songs, each requiring different strategies and tactics. You don't have time and money to develop a brilliantly sophisticated campaign for each release, but somehow you've still got to peak interest, convey excitement, and motivate people to buy.

Newer publishers might, therefore, do better specializing in one particular genre, at least during the formative years. By fiercely concentrating on a single genre, you accumulate expertise in product development, marketing, promotion, and sales in that arena. In time, you acquire certain instincts and a basic game plan evolves that you can modify with ease to match each new songwriter or release.

When you've acquired a feel for a certain market, your projections are more realistic. You know just where to start working a new product, the best advertising vehicles, the key radio stations and press you must get, the venues where the artist needs to appear. You know the personalities, the players, the stores, all the things needed to leverage your way upwards to success. You've learned what works where and what doesn't. You can maximize your marketing dollars, because you've been there repeatedly.

But delving into an unfamiliar market genre is like starting over. There are competitors already established who have a leg up on you. You have to inform yourself about different market forces, make new contacts, build credibility all over again.

This isn't necessarily bad; new challenges bring new opportunities and prevent stagnation. And since musical tastes are cyclical, having a product line and marketing expertise in several genres provides insurance against peaks and valleys of consumer interest (and sales) in one genre or another. But your safest path, when starting out, is to master one area before trying to diversify.

Choosing a company name

Choosing a company name and logo are among the most important and difficult decisions faced when launching a new venture. Your trade name should be unique and project the image that you want to convey about your company. (See further discussion about company names and logos in the chapter entitled *Marketing 101*.)

Before you settle on a name for your company, you must first decide whether to affiliate with ASCAP, BMI, or SESAC. When you apply for affiliation with a performing-right society, you must submit your name for approval. You cannot, of course, use a name already in use. The performing-right society you apply to will check the thousands of companies already registered and cross-reference those listed with the other societies. You will be asked to submit two alternate name choices in case your first (and/or second) choice is already taken. Consider yourself one of the lucky few if even your third choice is available. It will seem that every clever name has already been co-opted.

Location

Some companies thrive in localities far removed from centers of music business activity. But there are decided advantages to being located "where the action is." Early this century, that meant New York for American publishers. Later, of course, Los Angeles and Nashville joined the Big Apple as a formidable triumvirate driving the U.S. music industry.

An energizing effect is gained from being surrounded by one's peers, especially in creative fields such as publishing, songwriting, and record production. There is also access to contacts who provide essential marketing ideas and deal-making opportunities in the cities that have an active music scene.

Contacts are a publisher's second most valuable asset (after catalog), and must be cultivated assiduously—something that is harder to do from a remote location. And it's often easier to find, develop, and market music successfully in a city where talent congregates and support facilities flourish on a wide scale.

Veteran record and publishing executives have commented that the quality, commerciality, and professionalism of some types of musical product often suffer when created in isolation, away from the mainstream. The contention is that the further away you get from major recording centers, the further off-center the product gets.

Using radio alone to gauge what's happening in the market is misguided. By the time a song is written, pitched, cut, and released, a year passes before it is heard on the radio. Thus, someone in the hinterlands relying on radio is working on last year's model. Chances for mainstream success are better when you're involved in a setting where you can actively learn from successful peers.

Having said this, however, it is certainly possible to succeed virtually anywhere if your product is good and you work to overcome the disadvantages of distance by diligent pursuit of contacts via phone, mail, e-mail, fax, and travel. The communications revolution has made it possible to stay in relatively close touch with the market and important contacts the world over, no matter where you're based.

Indeed, being away from a music center can actually work to your advantage. There may be a lot of native talent in your area but no solid music companies on the ground to tap into what is available. If that's true, you won't have to compete for talent with more established companies down the street. Also, operating expenses are usually lower away from the music business capitols.

Instead of trying to emulate fashions prevalent in major music centers, you can capitalize on the uniqueness of your own area, marketing your *sound* as definitive, new and exciting. And, if you're successful, your company may take on a somewhat exotic air.

There was always something special about the Memphis Sound of Stax and Sun Records, the early Motown Hit Factory operating from Detroit, and the Mersey Beat scene in Liverpool that brought forth the Beatles and other British Invasion groups. Because they were away from the mainstream, these companies and their product seemed to stand out from the pack.

Other successful, regional examples include Prince's Paisley Park Records (Minneapolis), SubPop (Seattle), Mammoth (North Carolina), TK Records (Miami), Fantasy Records (San Francisco), Chess and Vee-Jay Records (Chicago), Ichiban Records and Lowery Music (Atlanta), and Gamble-Huff Productions (Philadelphia). And, there is an endless list of classic hits that emanated from indie labels, publishers, producers, and studios operating from Muscle Shoals, New Orleans, Jackson, Austin, and other locations too numerous to mention.

Researching start-up costs

Among a new company's start-up costs are incorporation fees, business licenses, and deposits for utilities, telephone, insurance, leases, etc. There may also be costs of financing when you're raising investments or loans for your operation.

Quick calls to your city hall, secretary of state, or county clerk should reveal the types of licenses you need and their costs. Your phone and power companies will tell you about deposits. Your attorney will tell you the costs of incorporation fees, investor's agreements, and other legal work.

Other start-up costs include supplies, furnishings, and equipment. The list may get surprisingly long before you're through. You'll not only need the obvious things: playback equipment, fax machine, answering machine, word processor, desks, chairs, etc., you'll also need all sorts of minutiae: blank cassettes, stationery, rubber bands, paper clips, staples, and so forth.

Catalogs are the best way to figure the costs of supplies, equipment, and furnishings, and to make sure you're covering everything you need. Collect catalogs from office supply houses, computer stores, and sound equipment emporiums where you intend to acquire most of your needs. Go through them page by page, checking the items you must have.

For example, from stores like Office Depot or Office Max, you'll get comprehensive catalogs of goods at relatively low prices. Based on the number of your staff and their respective functions, determine how many staplers you'll need, how many pairs of scissors, how many rulers, desk trays, lamps, waste baskets, and so on. Write these items down with prices next to them. Do the same thing for computer equipment, telephone system, sound system(s), furniture, shelving, decor (pictures, potted plants, whatever). Soon you'll have a complete list of everything you need to open your doors, and you'll know the total cost.

Office facilities

Many start-up music publishers operate initially from back bedrooms or kitchen tables. But any company seeking growth and serious success requires office facilities as soon as possible. Once a management team is in place, the first priority is acquiring a base where business and planning can be conducted without domestic interruptions, a place that is conducive to meeting with writers and producers. With proper office facilities, a new company becomes more concrete, less abstract. Efficiency and productivity begin to mushroom.

New companies selecting first-time premises go through a balancing act to obtain suitable space without sinking money into bricks and mortar that would be better spent acquiring and marketing product. It makes sense, therefore, to rent or lease, rather than to build or buy. And, unless the nature of your business absolutely requires a prestigious address, it's not wise to invest your company's future in lavish furnishings or a pricey location.

Don't scrimp unwisely, however. Saving on rental expenses is not a good reason to make a long-term commitment to a seedy building or a space that restricts growth. Nor do you want to move too soon or too often, because moves are disrupting and expensive.

If you plan to seek investors, the balancing act also extends to how you want potential funding sources to view your company and its prospects. You don't want to appear unrealistic about money by taking on unnecessarily large or expensive offices. But you also don't want to give the impression of a poverty-stricken, fly-by-night operation that smells of failure.

Ideally, you'll find adequately respectable facilities available on a long-term lease with room for expansion. In fact, a long-term lease at reasonable rates in a desirable building is a plus factor from an investor's point of view, since short-term leases can subject you to unforeseen rent hikes or moves. And, if remodeling or construction must be done, you should negotiate to have it done as a condition of taking the lease or arrange for reduced rent while work is being done.

When leasing office space, keep in mind that your product is music. You must have well-insulated facilities to play your sound-system without generating complaints; nor do you want to be disturbed by other tenants or activities nearby. You'll want 24-hour access and the assurance of security. Also, check out parking and ease of access, as well as costs of utilities, janitorial services, and maintenance.

Before you commit to a lease, weigh the advantages and disadvantages of the premises as follows:
- location
- usage (office, studio, etc.)
- type of building
- square footage
- access to parking/shipping/public transportation
- storage capacity
- length of time expected at this site
- if you foresee a move within the next three years, when (approximately), and to what type of facility?
- length of lease, monthly payment, restrictions, concessions, and other terms
- if it's a short-term lease, what allowances do you make for increased expenses should you face a rent hike upon renewal or have to relocate?
- what improvements are needed to the facility, and who makes them (e.g., the landlord or yourself)?
- who pays for the improvements, and how does this reflect on the terms of your lease?
- what are the average monthly costs of utilities, maintenance, janitorial service, and insurance?

A small, established publishing company could operate efficiently with approximately 1,200 square feet, partitioned to provide space for:
- reception/secretarial/filing area
- supplies/library/copying room
- executive office
- songpluggers' office
- demo studio
- board room (and work area for part-time help)

Equipment & furnishings

Most of the following items are essential to a music publishing operation:

- sound playback system(s)
- cassette duplicator
- computer system with laser printer
- software to handle functions of: financial planning, accounting, bookkeeping, database management, word processing, mail merge
- TV/VCR
- answering machine
- fax machine
- electric typewriter
- photocopier
- postage meter
- filing cabinet(s)
- executive desk(s)/chair(s)
- secretarial desk(s)/chair(s)
- miscellaneous chairs for visitors
- work table(s) for packaging, shipping, labeling, editing, etc.
- credenza(s)
- sofa(s)
- cassette/CD racks and library shelving
- miscellaneous accessories (lamps, ashtrays, wastebaskets, etc.)
- miscellaneous decor (pictures, plants, etc.)

LEASE, BUY, OR RENT?

Rather than purchasing the items needed to set up an office, you might find better leverage leasing everything as a package. While you'll want to present a good image, elaborate or ostentatious furnishings aren't necessary. Prudent expenditure on furnishings leaves more capital available for vital marketing and acquisitions.

It's always a good idea to review your plans with an accountant. Whether you lease, rent, or buy affects your tax position (depreciation), overhead (ongoing costs versus one-off expenditures), and balance sheet (assets versus liabilities).

There are other financial implications as well. Large capital investment in equipment may leave you stuck with something difficult to offload in favor of newer technologies. A long-term lease may provide for upgrades and maintenance, or there may be penalties for early termination.

When making the choice of whether to lease, buy, or rent equipment, furnishings, and company vehicles, there are five points to consider:

Cash flow may be the determining factor for a young start-up venture that needs to husband financial resources. Outright purchases, of course, significantly reduce the company's available cash that may be needed for product acquisition, development, and marketing. Even installment purchases requiring large down payments can have an adverse effect on cash resources. Lease or rental payments, on the other hand, free cash resources for more productive use in the early stages.

Commitment is the second consideration. When you buy something, you're usually going to incur almost immediate depreciation, making it difficult to offload the item quickly at a price that affords suitable replacement without additional cash outlays.

Leasing, on the other hand, may also keep you locked in over a period of time during which the item becomes obsolete or otherwise no longer suited to its purpose. Many lease contracts, however, do provide for early termination (with financial penalties) or for upgrades. Renting is the most flexible in terms of commitment, but it's also the most expensive over the long haul.

Cost as a factor has to be judged by (a) the amount of initial outlay, if cash flow is paramount, and (b) the long-term, depending upon the nature of the item and the commitment to it. Buying usually provides the best long-term value for money over leasing. Renting, the most expensive option, should be reserved for items needed rarely or very occasionally (a few days or weeks).

Taxes can be lowered through depreciating the cost of a purchase or lease of large-ticket items. Thus, if you buy an item outright, the cost is depreciated over a number of years, rather than in the year in which the money was spent. The downside is that you may spend $15,000 for an item but will only be allowed to deduct, say, $3,000 in that year. The upside is that you can continue to deduct depreciation in succeeding years even though no additional outlays are necessary. Rental expenses, however, are current expenses and may be deducted in full as they occur.

Obsolescence (except for rentals, which can be terminated quickly), is a factor that must be considered along with commitment. If you commit to an item via long-term lease or purchase, you want to be sure it isn't obsolete before your commitment is ended. This must especially be addressed with high-tech items like computers and recording equipment.

Insurance

Insurance is a significant issue for some types of businesses. If you have a studio, for instance, your insurance will be much more expensive and essential than if you're a small music publishing operation. But to some degree or another, you will need adequate insurance to cover losses of equipment, furnishings, data, inventory, vehicles, etc. You may also need liability insurance, and you may want to provide health and life insurance benefits for yourself and/or employees.

Key-man insurance might be required by investors or lenders. After all, they're banking on you to make your proposal work. If anything happens to you or one of the other founders, the entire venture may be jeopardized. You should consider key-man insurance for yourself and other indispensable members of your team for the same reason, even if isn't required by funding sources. Often, the loss of just one key member reduces an organization's effectiveness to that of a one-legged stool.

Along the same lines, if you're making a large advance to a songwriter, you may want to consider insurance to cover the unthinkable. But think about it. If, after you pay the advance, the songwriter meets with disaster before writing or submitting commercially viable material, you'll have no hope of recouping your investment.

A wide range of insurance options are available for every situation, so you'll want to consider a variety of plans from several different companies before making your choice. But cost shouldn't be the single most important factor. The insurance company's reputation, rating, service, exemptions, deductions, and package of coverages must all be considered along with the premium payments.

Legal

Investors and lenders want assurance that you're represented by good legal counsel. After all, your stock in trade revolves around contracts, licenses, and copyrights. These must be negotiated and drafted with expertise. Even then, at some point, there will be problems, especially, as you grow and prosper. As the old saying goes, you know you've got a hit when you get a writ.

While you want to establish a working relationship with an attorney who is experienced in music business matters, you may find that you'll need different legal specialists to handle different problems or opportunities. For instance, you need an attorney versed in securities matters if you plan to offer stock or limited partnerships.

Licenses and regulations

All businesses must comply with a host of regulations and obligations imposed by a host of governments—city, county, state, and federal. Although you can wade through various bureaucracies to find out what burdens you face, you would do well to seek competent advice from a lawyer and accountant to insure

that everything pertaining to your specific operation is nailed down. Depending upon the size and nature of your business, some of the following licenses, permits, and compliances may be required:

- Articles of incorporation filed with the state
- Annual corporate reports filed with the state
- Registration as a foreign corporation if your company is based in a state other than the one in which it's incorporated
- Securities and Exchange Commission (SEC) regulations and registration (if you're seeking equity investors or selling limited partnerships; there are also varying laws among states dealing with sales of stock and partnerships)
- State sales permit (if you sell retail, you'll have to collect sales tax on behalf of the state; this might also apply to your city)
- State resale tax exemption certificate (so you won't have to collect sales tax if you sell to distributors, wholesalers, or retailers)
- Property tax assessment filing (usually with your county)
- Local business license (usually with your city)
- Fictitious name registration (usually with your state)
- Trademark registration (usually with your state, but also federal)
- Workers' compensation (usually with your state)
- Employer identification number (IRS form SS-4)
- Employee withholding allowance certificate (IRS form W-4)
- Employee withholding exemption certificate (IRS form W-4E)
- Withholdings of income and social security taxes from employees must be deposited with the IRS either semi-monthly, monthly, or quarterly (obtain form 501 from the IRS)
- Quarterly filing of IRS form 941 detailing employee withholdings
- IRS form W2 supplied to each employee by January 31 stating amount of wages paid and taxes withheld during the preceding calendar year
- City and state withholding forms (similar to W2) supplied to employees if applicable
- State and federal unemployment taxes and disability insurance be required as withholdings
- IRS form 1099 detailing payments to independent contractors (must be filed with the IRS by February 28 for work done during the preceding calendar year)
- Various state and federal laws concerning hours and conditions of work, minimum wage, health and safety standards, discriminatory hiring practices, etc.

NOTE: Licenses, permits, and obligations vary in form or name in different jurisdictions.

TIP: Some tax assessments require payments or deposits in advance based upon your projected sales or earnings. You're naturally confident the venture you're launching will meet its projections, and you'll be inclined to tell all and sundry how well you expect to do. But don't volunteer your optimism to a tax assessing authority. Rather, you should adopt an attitude of, "Gee, we just hope we can keep our doors open long enough to pull in some business." You want to pay the least amount possible where advance payments are required. Why tie up working capital to pay taxes on income you've not yet earned?

REGULATORY RED TAPE

As long as your situation is routine, there will not likely be any issues that hold up permits or licenses for your operation. However, if your circumstances are subject to some agency or governmental ruling that could delay or alter your plans, you should be prepared to deal with the situation in order to overcome any obstacles.

Examples of possible roadblocks:
- **Zoning**. Will your type of business be allowed to operate in the neighborhood you've chosen? Are there restrictions on access, noise, signs, or business hours?
- **Building codes**. Does your business meet all health, safety and environmental regulations? What about sound insulation, etc.?
- **Conversion**. Permission is required to convert buildings of historical or architectural importance.
- **Environmental impact**.
- **Workplace health and safety**.

If you need to raise money . . .

Sophisticated money sources know that it takes *people* to make companies work. They will therefore attach more weight to your management team than anything else about your proposal. In fact, decisions whether to invest or lend may be based 80% on the quality of the founders and management team and 20% on the business concept or market potential.

▼

Superior management can flourish with mediocre product, and mediocre management can fail with superior product.

Hands-on experience is a major criteria for success. Funding sources are reluctant to let someone go to school at their expense. So, when recruiting, get the most experienced people you can find for each position. Brains, fancy degrees, good looks, and shining personalities are all wonderful attributes but fail to impress investors and lenders if not backed by proven experience.

It will benefit you to have a full team on board to help craft your business plan, and it'll make raising capital that much easier. However, in your company's early stages, it may not be feasible to have every slot filled. Aside from the outlay for salaries, contributions, and benefits, there may not be enough activity to justify a full body count. Under-utilized people can become demoralized and unmotivated; it's also demoralizing to those who do have a full plate when others around them seem to be doing little or nothing. The interim answer, then, is for full-time staffers to wear more than one hat, while using part-timers, consultants, and/or subcontractors as needed.

One often overlooked ingredient for success is the number of employees (including the founders) a start-up company has at the outset. A frequently quoted statistic is that 90 per cent of new businesses fail, most within the first year. But that's because most new businesses are one- or two-man operations. When you take these out of the mix, you find that the first-year survival rate for companies with 5-10 employees is over 75%. Companies with 11-20 employees have a better than 85% first-year survival rate; the rate rises to 95% for companies with over 20 employees.

Why is this? If you combined the Marx Brothers and the Three Stooges, you'd have the minimum threshold number to give you excellent chances for survival, but obviously it is not just quantity that matters. What drives the survival rate is the fact that entrepreneurs who can recruit experienced, talented people do so because the company they're founding is an attractive proposition, and, by extension, they're then able to raise the capital necessary to make it viable.

That's not to say solo operators can't succeed. But it's tough being the Lone Ranger, especially if Tonto isn't at your side. No one can be an expert at everything, nor can one person physically do all that's needed in the time required. Typically, a successful one- or two-man operation provides a decent living for the owners. The opportunity for real wealth arises with a full-scale operation.

Money talks—but don't let it talk too much. What if a prospective co-founder is in a position, and is willing, to invest a substantial sum in the new company? Respectfully decline. Never let any founder invest a cent more than any other founder. The reason is entirely psychological. Someone who puts $50,000 into the venture will have 50 times the influence of someone who can only contribute $1,000. But the larger investor may not have 50 times the brains or talent, and his inflated influence may tilt the company in the wrong direction.

Allowing a team member to dominate because he can outspend the others is analogous to allowing a bad singer to front your band because he has a great sound system you can use. The initial, material advantage is lost with the damage done to your long-term prospects. Limit investments by founders to the maximum amount all the others are able or willing to invest.

Of course, nonmanagement investors are a different matter. When you're ready to raise capital, those who make substantial investments may want and deserve a seat on the board of directors. But no single investor should gain undue influence if you structure stock distribution so that sweat equity is proportionate to monetary contribution.

☞ *The synergistic value of a well-rounded, like-minded team driving towards a goal is immense. It's much easier to recognize and seize opportunities, surmount obstacles, and stay the course when you have a reservoir of experience, talent, and moral support to draw from.*

Recruiting personnel

The most far-reaching decisions you'll make when forming your company are the people you choose to join your founding team. It cannot be emphasized enough that the quality of this team not only determines your ability to get funding, it also determines your likelihood of success.

After you analyze the functional roles required to run your company, it's time to enlist the right people to fill the key positions. Your recruiting drive must be intelligently planned, candidates rigorously tested, and trap-door mechanisms devised so that team members who don't pan out can be replaced with as little damage to the company as possible.

A prime entrepreneurial motivator is the desire to own a piece of the action and be in control. Entrepreneurs are naturally confident they can turn dreams into reality. But the entrepreneurial ego has to be channeled to recognize where additional talents and skills are required to round out those that the entrepreneur himself lacks. And the entrepreneur's ego must be sufficiently strong to give him the confidence to join forces with those who might indeed have more talent than he does himself.

An entrepreneur who wants true success would rather be vice president of a strong, flourishing company in which he has a significant stake, than be chairman and majority stock-holder of a weak, struggling entity. Or, to use a football analogy, is it more satisfying to be the only outstanding player on a team that finishes the season 0-16 or to be one of many stars on the team that wins the Superbowl?

▼

First-class people strive to recruit first-class people, while second-raters usually recruit third-raters for fear of being overshadowed.

A strong leader sees the benefits of being surrounded with other strong leaders, resulting in a championship team. There will inevitably be clashes where strong wills are involved, but if candidates are screened and selected on the basis of trust, respect, and compatibility, these clashes will be healthy rather than destructive. If all team members share a goal with a clear strategic vision of how to get there, then the tactical choices of how that strategy should be carried out may be better made when there's a lively devil's advocate debate during the decision-making process.

▼

Avoid the danger of building a team that looks and sounds too much alike.

Birds of a feather tend to flock together, but in business that may lead to disaster. Don't automatically discount candidates whose looks, ages, and personalities don't mirror yours. Superficial filters can cost you valuable team members.

If all your founders share the same personality traits, are about the same age, and have similar life and career experiences, you may get along famously on your way to ruin. Balance optimists with pessimists, and vice versa. The optimist might take off without filing a flight plan or checking the weather. A pessimist may never get off the ground at all.

Creative types may conjure up all sorts of projects, but there should be sound financial checks on what they want to do. On the other hand, a team overloaded with financial bean-counters may find reasons to never try anything. When one side is forced to build a case to prove an idea's validity, it's more likely the idea will be better planned and thus have a better chance of success.

The ideal team balances youth with maturity, optimists with pessimists, risk-takers with bean-counters, high-fliers with mission-controllers, designers with mechanics, creators with implementers, thinkers with doers, enthusiasts with realists, a good offense with a good defense. Above all, don't allow factions to evolve or petty jealousies to fester. Fill all positions with strong, qualified people who are self-confident enough to rise above internecine warfare and who will dedicate themselves to the cause.

Choose team members with complementary disciplines and who understand what all the other departmental managers have to face to bring the company's goals to reality. While each team member has to focus on his own departmental goals, he also has to aim at the same bulls-eye as every other member.

If your sales manager is concentrating on numbers of units sold rather than profits per unit, he'll clash with the finance manager. If the finance manager is too intent on risk avoidance, there'll be a clash with the creative department whose productions and acquisitions are constrained. And, if the creative department feels paperwork and management information systems are unimportant, something to attend to "later on," there'll be clashes with administration or business affairs.

The point is, every team member has to have a feel for what's important to other team members and why. Everyone has to see the forest as well as the trees. That's why, from the beginning, team members have to be involved in structuring the company, seeing how the various components come together to make a smoothly functioning whole with one overriding purpose: success, as defined by your company's objectives and goals. Any team member who feels above it all and that he or she doesn't have to play by the rules is not a team player and doesn't deserve to be on the team.

Company formation

As soon as the nucleus of your management team is assembled, you must, together, address a range of issues. Among the most crucial are the following:

- Legal entity: proprietorship, partnership, limited partnership, corporation, etc.
- A timeline for the company's goals and objectives during its first three years, including the amounts of capital needed at each stage of development
- Sources and plans for raising capital
- Methods of raising and leveraging capital and details required for pro forma budgeting
- Responsibilities for writing specific sections of the company's business plan
- Additional profit-center opportunities
- Requirements for office and storage space, furnishings and equipment, etc.
- Purchasing guidelines and facilities procurement parameters (e.g., lease, rent, buy, and budgetary limitations)
- Management information systems for financial reporting

- Sales and cashflow forecasting procedures
- Pro forma budgets
- Accounts payable, billing, and collection policies
- Personnel policies and financial security controls
- Decision trees for market testing of new product, image development, and media thrusts
- Promotion, distribution, and sales policies, including how these functions should be structured and/or pursued (i.e., to what degree should independents and subcontractors be utilized vis-à-vis in-house personnel)
- Departmental organization charts, reporting relationships, and management control techniques
- Departmental budgetary controls
- Incentive systems for founders, management, key-employees, and nonkey-employees
- By-laws, corporate formation, and corporate goals for the next three years and beyond, including possible exit strategies for investors
- Timeline for product acquisition and releases, with decision-tree scenarios to determine numbers of acquisitions and releases in years two and three
- Parameters of authority for negotiating deals
- Milestone budget allocations for acquisition and product development during first three years

CHOOSING A LEGAL ENTITY

There are three basic types of company organization: *sole proprietorship, partnership,* and *corporation.* Each has its own legal and financial characteristics. Your choice may be influenced by how it affects your personal tax situation, or the tax exposure of your partners, co-founders, or investors.

Consultation with knowledgeable tax attorneys or accountants should precede your choice of company formation. Ultimately, your choice depends upon factors unique to your personal goals and circumstances.

Sole Proprietorship. The most basic company form is sole proprietorship. The owner is 100% responsible for all management decisions, retains 100% of all net profits, and is also personally liable for all company debts.

Advantages of sole proprietorship:
- Simplest and least expensive form of company to start
- Fewer regulatory burdens and less required paperwork than other forms of business
- Owner answers only to himself
- Owner maintains 100% control over company's direction
- Owner keeps 100% of profits
- Owner can offset other taxable income with business deductions and losses

Disadvantages of sole proprietorship:
- Unlimited liability—owner's personal property may be at risk if the company's debts or obligations exceed its assets.
- Owner is taxed as an individual on all company net income.
- As a self-employed person, the owner must file estimated state and federal income tax returns quarterly and make tax payments in advance on money not yet earned.
- Company has an "unstable life"; owner's death or illness could cause a cessation of business.
- Because of company's instability, it is harder to raise capital.

Partnerships. A partnership exists when two or more people operate an ongoing business in which they share ownership and profits. Partners can be individuals, corporations, other partnerships, or various combinations thereof. Three common types of partnerships are *general partnerships*, *limited partnerships*, and *joint ventures*.

General Partnerships. All partners share profits, assets, liabilities, and responsibilities. Assets belong to partners collectively. Each general partner has authority to enter into contracts on behalf of the partnership. Each partner is accountable for actions by any other partner and is equally responsible for the partnership's debts and losses.

The partnership itself pays no taxes. Partners must individually account for their shares of profits or losses on their personal returns.

When a general partnership is disbanded, assets are liquidated and proceeds are used to (1) pay creditors, (2) repay loans to the partnership by any of the partners, and (3) compensate partners who have contributed funds or assets. Money left over is distributed between partners in proportion to their shares in the business.

Limited Partnerships. At least one partner acts as *general partner*, assuming total responsibility for managing the venture. The remaining, "limited" partner(s) must not have any say or role in managing the venture.

Whereas general partnerships are formed by like-minded individuals who collectively contribute assets, capital, expertise and/or time to the company, limited partnerships usually arise when one party seeks to raise money to pursue a specific venture. The function of the limited partners is to provide operating capital.

Limited partners are repaid a percentage of the venture's profits. Normally a limited partnership has a finite life. Limited partnerships may be formed to finance specific projects (e.g., an album production, a series of productions, the purchase of a copyright catalog, or the launch of a record company). But the limited partners are not in it forever.

Once limited partners receive a preagreed return on investment, or a certain period of time lapses (or both), the limited partnership is dissolved. Usually, the assets then become the property of the general partner, and the limited partners have no further association with the venture.

Should the venture fail, limited partners lose only their investment; they are not liable for losses or damages beyond what they put into the venture. However, if a limited partner makes management decisions, he ceases to be a "limited" partner, and exposes himself to the full liability of a general partner.

Limited partnerships are popular vehicles for raising capital with certain types of investors. But limited partnership agreements must comply with government regulations and can be very complex and expensive to structure. You may be in violation of securities laws simply by advertising for investors unless certain precautionary steps are taken. Therefore, limited partnerships should only be undertaken with counsel of an attorney versed in securities laws.

Joint Ventures. The difference between a joint venture and a general partnership is that a joint venture is formed to achieve a specific goal, as opposed to being an ongoing business. When this specific goal is fulfilled, the joint venture comes to an end. All other similarities with general partnerships apply, however, with regards to responsibilities, shares of assets, profits, losses, and liabilities. Therefore, it's essential to detail levels of responsibility, accountability, and disposal of assets when the venture is dissolved.

Joint ventures are useful when two companies pool resources to further a project that benefits them both. For example, a record company and publishing company might finance a film production company to produce a movie featuring music owned by the publisher and performed by the record company's artists. The joint venture benefits (1) the film production company, which gets financing to produce the film; (2) the publishing company, which earns a share of the film's profits while exploiting its copyrights; and (3) the record company, which gets rights to the soundtrack album, gains exposure for its artists, and shares in the film's profits.

Advantages of partnerships:
- Lower start-up costs required than corporations for filing fees and franchise taxes
- Less regulatory requirements than corporations

- More management expertise available than with sole proprietorships, and more flexible management organization than corporations
- Possible tax advantages: owners can offset other taxable income with business deductions and losses
- Capital may be raised by recruiting additional partners
- Stability of the business can be defined, either by fixing a limited life for the company or by amending the partnership agreement to allow indefinite continuity in the event any partner leaves or dies

Disadvantages of partnerships:
- Unlimited liability for all general partners (personal property is risked when company debts or obligations exceed assets)
- Possible instability. Unless the partnership agreement provides otherwise, the addition or departure of any partner causes the partnership to automatically terminate
- Difficulty in raising long-term financing or large sums of capital without substantial personal guarantees by the partners
- Just one partner or employee (whether authorized or not) can bind the other partners, leaving them personally liable
- Individual partnership interests are not easily transferable or sold; partnership shares are difficult to liquidate
- Tax-supported fringe benefits allowed to corporations, such as pensions and profit-sharing, are unavailable
- Partners are taxed as individuals on all company net income, which may, in some cases, be disadvantageous

Corporations. While sole proprietors and general partners risk personal assets if business goes bad, owners of failed corporations risk only what they invest in the company. All business losses are borne by the corporation—and by its creditors, when losses exceed the value of liquidated assets.

Corporations are legal entities separate and apart from their owners. They have a life of their own, may enter into agreements, purchase property, make investments, raise money, sue and be sued, all in the name of the corporation. Even a corporation owned 100% by one person continues to exist after the owner dies—the deceased's shares pass to his estate. The corporation exists so long as it remains solvent, or until it is voluntarily dissolved by its owners. And as long as it exists, no matter how often it changes hands, it remains bound by any contracts, debts, and obligations entered into by previous owners.

Corporations are regulated by the state in which they operate. Some types of corporations must also comply with federal regulations. As in the case of partnerships, a corporation may be owned by individuals, partnerships, other corporations, or any combination thereof.

The extent of ownership or equity a person has in a corporation is represented by shares of stock. Each shareholder has a "security" interest, or a claim, on the assets of the company equal to the value or percentage of shares owned. If a corporation is wound up or sold, liquidated assets pay (1) accrued taxes, (2) creditors in order of security, and (3) accrued salaries. Any remaining balance is distributed to shareholders in proportion to the amount of stock owned.

To maintain corporate status as a separate legal entity, personal affairs of shareholders and directors must not spill over into corporate activities. Otherwise, the IRS may declare the corporation as an "alter ego" of the owner(s) and nullify the corporate status for tax purposes. Mixing personal and business records may also pierce the corporate veil of limited liability for shareholders, exposing personal assets to claims from creditors and winners of lawsuits.

Corporations are separately taxable entities. After-tax income is reinvested in the company as operating capital and distributed as dividends to shareholders.

Corporate income is thus taxed twice: first, the corporation is taxed on net earnings; secondly, shareholders are taxed personally on dividends received from the corporation's after-tax earnings. Except in the case of "S" corporations, shareholders cannot offset personal income with deductions for corporate expenses or losses. An "S" corporation provides owners with tax benefits of a partnership—losses and deductions can be claimed on personal returns—while extending corporate benefits of protecting personal assets from losses or damages incurred by the company.

One-man corporations. Shareholders of small or infant corporations frequently double as directors and officers. In fact, one person can own all the shares, carry out the legal functions of the board, act as CEO as well as secretary-treasurer, and also be a salaried employee of the corporation.

A one-man corporation is, in essence, a sole proprietorship that has been incorporated. The proprietor owns 100% of the stock and is accountable only to himself for company management and distribution of profits. Though the business is owned and operated by one person, the company is treated as an entity separate from the person of the owner, and it has the same advantages, attributes, obligations, and restrictions as any other corporate form of organization.

"S" Corporations (aka Small Business Corporation or Subchapter S Corporation). A small corporation, meeting certain requirements, can elect to have its profits and losses allocated to individual shareholders for tax purposes rather than being taxed on a corporate basis. Depending upon the shareholders' personal circumstances, this can provide tax savings, since business profits to individuals may often be taxed at a lower rate than corporations, and individuals may be able to use business deductions and losses to offset taxable income from other sources. At the same time, individual "S" Corporation shareholders enjoy limited liability protection and all other advantages of doing business as a corporation.

Close Corporations. In a close corporation, all outstanding stock is owned by the individuals who control and manage the affairs of the business. There are no other classes of stock and no publicly held shares. Close corporations are organized to extend limited liability to the owner-managers, which is not available in partnerships. The trade-off for limited liability, is of course, accepting the obligations, requirements, and restrictions inherent in any corporate structure, including incorporation and filing fees, franchise taxes, board and shareholder meetings, and other corporate burdens. Neglecting any of the corporate requirements may subject the company to reclassification for tax purposes and expose the owners to penalties and unlimited personal liability

Holding Companies. A holding company exists to own stock in other corporations. Usually, the holding company controls the voting shares. ABC Entertainment Corp., for instance, may function as a holding company by having controlling interest in DEF Records, Inc.; GHI Music Publishing Corp.; JKL Studios Ltd.; and MNO Management, Inc.

Publicly Owned Corporations. After a company passes successfully through certain stages of growth it may "go public" by selling stock on the open market. Going public can raise substantial capital, which in turn positions the company to maximize its potential. At the same time, founders and original investors can personally reap immediate financial rewards for their efforts in building the company. Indeed, for many investors, taking the company public is the ultimate and most desirable exit strategy.

There are possible pitfalls and disadvantages in going public, but the benefits can far outweigh the negatives. However, the resulting corporate structure must be designed to minimize any possible conflicts and tensions developing between new shareholders and management.

Perceived disadvantages of going public usually center on the founders' fear of losing control of the business. Management can be ousted by shareholders in the event of slow growth, no growth, or a series of losses. But only a majority vote can oust directors and management, and going public doesn't mean you have to give up a majority of the stock.

However, if the founders' poor performance leads to a shareholders' revolt, it may well be best for the founders themselves if management passes to more capable hands. After all, the founders still retain stock, which should improve in value with better management. Why insist on retaining control to the point where the company goes under, the stock becomes utterly worthless, and the founders wind up with nothing? The founders would be better off seeking other opportunities (or jobs); they could still become wealthy by virtue of owning stock in a growing, well-managed company.

Going public requires an enormous amount of preparation, a considerable amount of money, compliance with oversight from regulatory agencies, and it will make you accountable to new shareholders. But these drawbacks pale in comparison with the real benefits gained from a properly designed public offering.

Advantages of incorporation:

- Owners' liability is limited only to the amount they invest in the company; they are not personally liable for debts, losses, or other obligations incurred by the corporation.
- Owners' personal assets are protected from company creditors.
- Stability: The business continues despite disability, death, or departure of individual shareholders.
- As a distinct legal entity, the corporation can borrow, lend, sue, enter into contracts, own, buy and sell property.
- Ability to bring together a wide range of investors; flexibility in raising money through various types of loans, securities, common stock, preferred stock, bonds, debentures.
- Shares in the company are easier to transfer or sell, though the sale price depends upon the stock's market value.
- Shares in the company can be offered in lieu of cash for services rendered and as inducements to recruit valued employees, artists, songwriters, producers, etc.
- Corporations can more easily obtain discounts and favored-customer treatment from suppliers, travel agencies, hotel chains, rental car firms, etc.
- Tax-supported benefits are more readily available to corporations, such as pension and retirement plans, profit sharing, stock options, etc.

Disadvantages of incorporation:

- Government regulations and paperwork requirements are more burdensome.
- Corporations are expensive to organize, though limited partnerships may be equally so.
- Except in the case of an "S" corporation, there is double taxation; first, on corporate profits before dividends, and second, shareholders are personally taxed on dividends.
- Required accounting and audit procedures are more expensive.
- Changing the corporate structure or winding up the company can be expensive and complex.
- Because shareholders enjoy limited liability, the corporation's credit is limited to its own net worth without regard to the status of individual shareholders.
- Free transferability of stock opens the door to uninvited shareholders whose goals and aims may be incompatible with original founding owners.
- Minority shareholders must bow to the wishes of majority shareholders, subject only to protection against fraud and breach of trust by the majority.
- In large corporations with widespread ownership of stock, shareholder control over strategic decisions may be diluted, resulting in inertia on the part of many owners and manipulation by a few.
- Daily management and control of the corporation is separated from those owners who are not also directors or officers.

Business plans

Attempting to raise serious money requires a business plan. There are numerous business books available to help you craft a solid, appealing plan; there are also many excellent software programs that hold your hand through the process. The following points don't constitute all you need to know about putting together a plan, but they are worth remembering when you get down to work.

EXECUTIVE SUMMARY

A good song grabs you from the start. You're not forced to wallow through two minutes of avant-garde self-indulgence before finally finding the melody and storyline.

When you pitch a song or master, it might take just seconds for an A&R man to reject material that took weeks or months to create. Investors and lenders review your proposal with the same cold dispatch. They need less than five minutes to decide whether your plan warrants further reading.

Investors ask essentially the same questions as A&R people:

- Does it have a good hook?
- Is it a potential hit?
- Does it fit? (Country labels don't want rap; music publishing start-ups won't excite investors specializing in genetic engineering.)

The Executive Summary is the first section of the plan. It summarizes, or highlights, all that follows. So, you've got to get to the nub, peak their interest, and entice them to read on. Investors and loan officers quickly scan your Executive Summary to see:

- Who you are, as a company
- What your goals are
- How much money you're seeking
- How this money will empower you to achieve your goals
- How investors/lenders will be compensated

If the Executive Summary passes muster, the money source may skip to the *Financial* section and study your projections. Then he may turn back to the *Management* section to see if there's sufficient experience to achieve the intended results. Then your *Exit Strategy* will be reviewed to see how the investor or lender gets out of the deal with satisfactory profit.

Executive summaries quickly tell investors

- What the business is about
- Whether the targeted market can support the business concept
- If the management team can do the job
- Whether financial projections are realistic
- If funding requested is within reason
- If funding requested is within the investor's range
- Whether return on investment is worth the risk

Quick rejection can come if any of these factors fails to meet the investor's criteria. But, if all seems good on the surface, the investor will take time to study your plan in depth.

HOW LONG SHOULD YOUR PLAN BE?

The more money you seek, and the more complex your venture, the more information you'll need to substantiate your proposal. But even the simplest proposal should contain a minimum of ten pages, not including the Financial section and Appendices. Anything less may leave the impression that not enough research and thought went into considering all the variables.

Most plans range from 15-25 pages, not including Financials and Appendices. A plan more than 30 pages runs the risk of being tedious. Financials and

Appendices should certainly not be longer than the plan itself.

Save nuts-and-bolts details for the Appendices. The plan itself should make for easy, flowing, punchy reading. If, after reading the plan, an investor wants to know the manufacturing cost of jewel boxes or the printing costs of J-cards, he can refer to the Appendices. Otherwise, such minutiae interrupt the flow of the plan.

Even so, you can't include *everything* in the Appendices. If an investor is the type that wants to know the function and history of every little thing under the hood, he'll ask for specifics.

Investors and lenders are not unlike busy A&R personnel. Faced with 20 cassettes to audition, the inclination is to listen first to those containing one song each. The A&R person feels more has been accomplished after listening to ten tapes of one song each than if just one tape containing ten songs had been reviewed. If an investor has a stack of plans to read, the thickest ones will probably be the last to get attention.

HOW FAR INTO THE FUTURE SHOULD YOUR PLAN GO?

Financial projections should extend through the time investors or lenders are expected to exit the deal with their promised payoff. This usually means three to five years.

For the first year, at least, show projections of income and expenses broken down month by month. For years two and three, make financial projections on a quarterly basis. You can summarize projections on an annual basis for years four and five, because it's more difficult to accurately predict results the further out you get.

Take the same approach when detailing your proposed operations. Give a timetable for reaching specific milestones in the first two years; subsequent years can be more generalized.

If your company is already operating, include financial history and accomplishments to date. Financial data should go back at least three years, if you've been in business that long.

WRITE TO THE POINT

How your plan is written and presented reveals much about your chances for success. Pay great attention to spelling, grammar, and math. Inattention to seemingly small matters points to big mistakes on things that really count. Proofread, proofread, proofread—and then get someone else to proofread.

Don't load your text with technical language, but don't be pedantic or talk down to readers either. If you must use terms that might confuse a layman

(like *mechanicals*, *synchronizations*, etc.), consider adding a glossary.

Avoid attempts at cuteness, humor, and sarcasm. Don't use slang, don't use down home or streetwise language. You're not writing a chatty newsletter or a puff piece. You're writing to inform and convince, not entertain.

Keep your tone upbeat and professional. Write with authority, conviction, and professionalism. Write short, sharp sentences that suggest action. Eliminate unessential words. Edit out tangled syntax, confusing, or redundant phrases. Convert passive phrases ("we will have been") to active ("we will"). Edit with an ear to simple, clear language. Keep text punchy, flowing logically, and, above all, interesting.

Back claims with facts, numbers, and sources: "The market for this music is growing rapidly. According to *Billboard*, sales jumped 28% over the last two years." Don't rely on your Financials and Appendices to impress readers with numbers and statistics. They may never get that far if you don't convince them earlier that you're on to a good thing. Use numbers in your text wherever possible to illustrate points you're trying to make. Instead of, "There is a vast number of radio stations now programming our type of music," say: "There are now 1,225 FM stations programming this music, as opposed to just 700 stations three years ago."

Don't make subjective claims, such as, "John Jones is the greatest songwriter that ever lived." Who says so? But, you might say, "Paul McCartney said, 'John Jones is the greatest songwriter that ever lived'" (if, in fact, McCartney did say that). Or you can quote press reviews and articles: "*Tunesmith Magazine* editorialized, 'John Jones writes better songs than any living songwriter.'" You can also cite lesser lights to polish the shine on your writer: "John Jones was voted 'Best New Writer of 1997' by the Paducah Amateur Songwriters Association."

Avoid superlatives like: greatest, best, incomparable, etc. Again, who says so? You can convey a sense of convincing quality without resorting to hollow adjectives if you substantiate claims with facts. For instance, instead of: "Our management team has a fantastic track record in all aspects of music publishing," you can say: "Our management team has a combined total of 35 years experience in copyright administration, licensing, catalog acquisition, writer development, songplugging, marketing, and record production."

You can use superlatives in stating your company goal or mission, if you give credence to them by explaining how you will back up your claims. You can state your goal, "We will become the most effective music publishing company in this genre," if you follow up by declaring *how* you will become "the most effective." This can be done by adding: "Existing music publishers in this field tend to sign new, unproven talent within small demographic confines. We concentrate on a few, select signings who have demonstrated market appeal. Financial resources from this funding, together with our experienced marketing team, position us to aggressively market product to new, wider audiences, which existing publishers have so far neglected."

VISUAL PRESENTATION

Submitting an audition tape with fireworks, dancing girls, and ice cream won't get you a deal if the music's not in the groove. It's the same when you present your plan to money sources. Leather-binding, gold trim, multi-colored graphs, and pop-ups impress, but the only thing that gets you the money is a well-formulated and documented concept that convinces investors they will profit from dealing with you.

But presentation is not irrelevant. It raises—or lowers—expectations. A sloppy presentation does not inspire faith that your company will be well run. Use a word processor with a daisy wheel printer, or, preferably, a laser printer. If you don't have facilities to do this yourself, most copy shops provide such services at a reasonable cost.

If you use a computer, choose typefaces and type-sizes with a judicious eye for business-like appearance and ease of reading. You can use *italics*, **bold**, and CAPS for emphasis.

Use 1¼ spacing between lines of text and double-space between paragraphs. Leave at least an inch of margin on each side of the page, and roughly two inches at the top and bottom. Investors and lenders like room to make notes. In fact, lots of white space draws attention to the text. Filling a page to capacity makes it visually foreboding. And never use both sides of a page; print on one side only. For paper, use good quality, standard white bond. Never use off-colors or paper that's heavier or lighter than normal typing paper.

Use block paragraphs, not indents. Keep paragraphs short. Where possible, break paragraphs containing pertinent facts and numbers into statements highlighted with bullet-points for emphasis.

For example, instead of saying: There are 1,225 FM stations programming this type of music. These stations reach an estimated 26 million listeners, who spend $260,000,000 on recorded music per year, according to *Billboard*.

Format the paragraph this way:
According to *Billboard*:
- 1,225 FM stations program this type of music.
- 26 million people listen to these stations regularly.
- $260,000,000 is spent per year on recorded music by these listeners.

In the second example, these statistics leap out, emphasizing key facts about your market. The first example hides this information in the text and may be missed by someone quickly scanning the page.

Graphs and charts offer another way to emphasize information. Use them within the body of the plan; don't relegate them to the Appendices. Visual aids draw attention and are absorbed faster than text. They also break up the monotony of blocks of text. But use only charts generated by computer. Hand-drawn charts distract and imply amateurism.

Four types of charts and graphs:
- **Pie Charts** for market shares, CD/cassette sales-ratios, etc.
- **Line Graphs** for sales trends, market growths, comparisons
- **Flow Charts** for organizational structure, distribution channels
- **Bar Charts** for sales trends, market growths, comparisons

Photos and illustrations also enhance business plans—if professionally done. Don't use hand-drawn illustrations or Polaroids. Photos and illustrations generally belong in the Appendices and might include logos, album covers, artists, and studio or office facilities. But don't include photos of the management team. Best-seller charts listing your product, as well as favorable reviews and press coverage, also support your product's alleged potential for success.

Binding
Though you don't need genuine leather, gold-edged binders, endeavor to use something that denotes quality. A ten-cent school report-cover does not make a good impression. Best bet: Have the plan professionally bound at a copy center. Don't use spiral binding, which tends to come unraveled. Use a binder that allows the plan to lay flat when opened to a page.

Print your company name, logo, and address on the cover. Choose a dark, professional color, such as royal blue, deep burgundy, charcoal gray, or black. Avoid pastels and, especially, white or lighter colors, which show fingerprints and smudges.

Meeting competition

Competition within the music industry differs somewhat from more conventional businesses. Car salesmen can tout their models' advantages over competitors by claiming more safety features, better mileage, lower maintenance, or higher resale value. They can, perhaps, clinch sales by throwing in extras at no additional cost: air conditioning, cassette decks, sun roofs. Customers can then rationalize purchase decisions.

But music is an emotional purchase, an intangible commodity. The product's quality and desirability are very subjective features; consumers either react favorably, or they don't. You can't convince someone to like a particular record or song with hard sell or other standard sales tactics.

Assuming two songs are well-crafted, professionally performed, and in the same genre, how do you explain, exactly, why you like one better than the other? And how does it sometime happen that your brother, sister, or spouse, whose tastes generally mirror your own, reacts just the opposite?

Since competition is not so straightforward or objectively defined in music as in other businesses, you might think that competition is not much of a factor, and that all you have to do is produce good music. Should you make such a statement, however, any sophisticated investor or lender will immediately tag you as naive and unprepared. There *is* competition.

If you truly had no competition, the conclusion could be made that not many people are interested in your type of product. Strong competition is an indicator of consumer interest in a particular genre. Thus, existing competition makes it more likely your type of product already has marketplace acceptance, and this fact could make your proposal more interesting to money sources.

But a musical product doesn't quite compete head-to-head, like detergents, tires, or toothpaste. So, what is the nature of your competition? In the broadest sense, music is a luxury, a leisure activity. Music has to compete for the dollars, time, and attention that people can afford to allocate for entertainment.

There's competition from television, movies, sports, video games, travel, books, etc. And in the music field itself, there are many genres other than your own; within your genre, there are other companies promoting their own product.

Competing companies can crowd you in more ways than you might imagine. Not only can they outposition you for product visibility by dominating in-store play, display space, or airplay, they can also snatch away artists, writers, catalogs, or songs you wanted to acquire. They might also raid your staff, enticing away valued employees.

While you should respect strong competition, don't be intimidated by it. And never discount new kids on the block or be dismissive of competitors you perceive as weak. Paths cross and recross, upwards and downwards, in the music business.

BUSINESS CYCLES

Every industry goes through at least three, and, more often, four cycles. If you're seeking investors or lenders, you may be asked to describe the cycle you think the music publishing business is in and how that affects your chances. The four business cycles are as follows:

New. This is a time of opportunity for the first companies on the block, and the growth rate is high. It's also a time of great risk, since a permanent, definable market hasn't been established. The challenges to companies in a new industry are to gain exposure, establish credibility, and secure a market base.

Expansion. Comes on the heels of fast growth in a new industry, bringing new competition, and, thus, a shake out among companies trying to carve market shares. Market leaders begin to emerge, standards are set, and growth continues apace.

Stabilization. The rate of growth levels off, market leadership is settled, competition is firmly rooted, and the challenge is to maintain market share, or grow by nibbling away at the competition. It's hard for newer companies to break into the mainstream unless they resort to guerrilla tactics or devise some sort of edge. Successful new entries sometime thrive, although on a smaller scale than entrenched, established companies, by concentrating on niche markets.

Decline. Now there is low, no, or negative growth; competition is weakening as some companies leave the field. The challenge is survival.

So, where does the music industry fit into all this? Certainly, it is not a new industry, and it is not in decline. The answer lies somewhere between expansion and stabilization. Some segments are expanding, thanks to new technologies and fashion shifts. These two elements, always dynamic, keep throwing out new challenges and opportunities, thus making it possible for start-up companies to find a niche and succeed.

The music industry has been around long enough to allow entrenchment; much of the mainstream power of distribution, marketing, control, and influence now rests with a handful of multi-national giants. It's next to impossible for an upstart to pry a significant market share from the clutches of these behemoths. In that sense, the business has stabilized.

On the other hand, because of the dynamics of changing fashions and technologies, there are always underlying characteristics of the expansion cycle and a sense of renewal. There are always genuine opportunities for successful entrepreneurial forays into the fray. Significant money can be made, even if the major players horde most of the market share. And when an entrepreneurial upstart really succeeds, there are always lucrative opportunities, if desired, for partnership with, or a sell out to, one of the multinationals.

CHAPTER 4

Acquisitions

▼

*Acquiring marketable copyrights is a
prerequisite for successful publishing.*

How publishers acquire product

Music publishers find new product in a variety of
ways. Once a publisher hangs out his shingle, so to
speak, an increasing flow of unsolicited material
arrives "over the transom." Most of these submissions
are decidedly amateurish, but everything must be listened to, because occasionally something worth pursuing does come through.

Aggressive music publishers actively scout new
songwriters. They check out bands and solo performers at gigs and showcases. They are on the alert for
news of established songwriters whose current publishing deals are coming to an end. They court new
record companies signings who write their own songs
and foreign publishers who have material available
for subpublishing.

A strong network of music business contacts is
often the best source for locating talented, unsigned
writers. Publishers get referrals from A&R personnel,
artist managers, promotion people, booking agents,
deejays, lawyers, etc. And publishers in the market to
purchase copyrights make their needs known to
prominent music business attorneys, accountants,
and managers who frequently have clients wishing to
sell catalogs.

Publishers build catalog through the following methods:
- *individual song agreements*–signing one song at a
time
- *exclusive agreements*–signing songwriters to write for
the company
- *administration agreements*–acquiring temporary
management of copyrights
- *co-publishing agreements*–acquiring part-ownership
of songs
- *subpublishing*–acquiring temporary rights to
foreign catalogs or songs
- *purchase*–buying existing copyrights

Acquisition philosophy

▼

*The first principle of acquisition is
selectivity—quality over quantity.*

Obviously, not every song is a hit. Nor does every new
writer live up to expectations. A catalog containing
hundreds of substandard songs nobody wants to
license is more than useless. It is a drain on a company, because of the fruitless time and money spent
acquiring the songs, negotiating contracts, filing registrations, producing demos, feeding administrative
details into the system, and spinning promotional
wheels that go nowhere.

Before an acquisition is made, therefore, everyone within the company who has to deal with songs at
the marketing level should be given a vote in the decision process. This ensures a highly selective acquisition
policy and an enthusiastic professional commitment
from all marketing staff to work the product. While
selectivity doesn't guarantee hits, those songs that are

acquired have a much better shot at commercial success, because the entire company is committed to making them happen.

▼

Selectivity includes knowing what to do with the product once you have it.

There should be no acquisition without a clear plan for exploitation. Acquisitions should always be made on market-oriented principles. The company's marketing staff must be able to apply the classic marketing techniques of defining the product, identifying its target audience, then presenting the product in a manner that meets the market's needs and demands.

Financial aspects of acquisitions

Acquisition of quality copyrights nearly always requires a capital investment. Sometimes, publishers pick up a song on condition they will get it cut or used in some other specified manner, such as a movie soundtrack. But, more commonly, the writer or original copyright owner also requires monetary motivation to assign away potentially valuable rights.

Copyright acquisition normally requires one of two types of financial transactions: an advance or a purchase. Each of these transactions has its own accounting and tax implications, but our focus here is how to approach the problem of arriving at a fair price in either case.

Of course, each copyright is unique and no one's crystal ball is infallible when it comes to forecasting how well or how badly an investment will fare. A lot depends on instinctive knowledge of how a fickle marketplace will receive a subjectively judged product. But there are also time-tested techniques for minimizing risks of investment.

Advances

In the pursuit of acquiring potentially commercial songs, publishers frequently offer *advances* to songwriters as inducements to assign their copyrights. An advance is a form of loan. But conventional loans obligate borrowers to repay certain sums by certain dates. They are also usually made on terms that include interest and some type of collateral that is forfeited if the loan isn't repaid as agreed.

Advances are *interest-free* loans with no fixed repayment schedule. They are *recoupable* against royalty income that may or may not materialize. Advances are recouped piecemeal as royalties are earned by writers over rather indefinite periods of time. Furthermore, advances are usually *nonreturnable* —there is no recourse if not enough royalties are earned, because recipients aren't obligated to repay unrecouped advances.

If you advance a songwriter $1,000 as an inducement to assign a copyright to you, you're entitled to withhold (recoup) the first $1,000 from the songwriter's royalties. The songwriter receives royalties only after the advance is repaid but doesn't have to pay you back at all if the song never earns a dime.

Key features of a typical advance vs. a typical conventional loan		
Features	Advance	Conventional loan
Collateral	No	Yes
Interest	No	Yes
Fixed payments	No	Yes
Fixed term	No	Yes
Nonreturnable	Yes	No
Recourse if unpaid	No	Yes

GENERAL PRINCIPLES FOR NEGOTIATING ADVANCES

When negotiations start with a figure suggested by the other party (or a competitor's figure you feel compelled to match or top), you must calculate how many record sales are required to recoup the advance. Then determine (1) if your sales projections match the level required to recoup, and (2) whether the timeline for recoupment justifies the risk compared with other investment opportunities, including safe, marketable securities.

If negotiations are to start with a figure suggested by you, you must project how many records you reasonably expect to sell during the given time frame. You can then arrive at a figure by multiplying the number of projected units by the dollar amount of the royalty rate. Allow yourself a margin of error in case actual sales ultimately fall short of your projections.

Competition with other publishers to sign a particularly desirable song, songwriter, or catalog may complicate the decision-making process. There may also be negotiating conflicts when your idea of a reasonable advance is less exalted than the other party's. Just because you have $10,000 to pay for an advance doesn't mean you can *afford* it if the deal is only worth $2,000.

Each case is unique, and the size of an advance ultimately comes down to a judgment on the commercial merits of the product under consideration. You must resist pressures that come into play during negotiations, and focus on how much money you can afford to tie up between the time the advance is paid and the time it takes to recoup at a profit.

CASH FLOW CONSIDERATIONS

As in war, the first rule in business is survival. You can suffer numerous defeats and still win the war as long as you live to fight another day. Cash is the key to survival in business; without it, you can't keep the doors open.

▼

The essence of cash flow management is to ensure that income matches or exceeds payments for trade credit, royalties, loans, dividends, daily transactions, etc.

Cash flow must not be equated with profits. The level of profits (or losses) is a measure of company performance, which can be affected and even manipulated on paper by various, legitimate accounting techniques. But what counts in the real world is whether enough cash is available for daily operating requirements.

Cash flow isn't so much a measure of performance as it is a measure of solvency. A company with healthy cash flow can survive a succession of losses, but when it runs out of cash it is insolvent. Insolvency can lead to bankruptcy, even though there may be profits on paper.

Money is a limited resource. There is a time value to money, and there are innumerable ways and means to invest money at a profit. If you don't think a deal will repay your investment faster than interest on funds deposited, you're smarter to keep your money safely earning interest. It's better to stay funded and ready for the right kind of business than to plunge into an ill-conceived venture that depletes your financial resources, limits your future opportunities, and, perhaps, risks your company's viability.

Sure, you're in the publishing business, and your object is to acquire copyrights. But there is always another deal around the corner, though there is not always enough money. Don't risk capital on a deal you reckon will earn, at best, 10% a year (and possibly nothing at all), when you can safely place the money in risk-free certificates of deposit while waiting for a deal with more lucrative potential.

This may be easier said than done in the heat of negotiations. If several companies are bidding in an auction atmosphere, the psychology favors the songwriter or catalog owner that is being courted. Since your peers are heavily courting the same songwriter or product, you might be blinded to the reality of whether or not the object of all this interest is actually viable.

That's what makes the herd atmosphere dangerous. It's easier to lose sight of reality and fail to trust your own judgment, when competitors are rushing after the same object. You may begin to think the object is to win the race, rather than to acquire a winning deal. The result may be short-lived triumph at beating out your competitors and long-term chagrin for grossly overpaying to make the deal. Balance enthusiasm with realism. Let someone else grab the brass ring if a deal seems too expensive for the risk involved.

▼

*The deal is not the object.
The object is to acquire potentially lucrative copyrights at a reasonable price.*

☞ *Methods discussed here for forecasting sales and calculating affordable advances also apply to other financial decisions, such as demo and record production, artist development, hiring personnel, committing resources to facilities, and equipment, and major marketing campaigns. In all these areas, you must have clear expectations of the pay-off. You must have a fix on how much income can be generated in relation to the investment required, and whether or not potential profits are worth the risks.*

☞ *Also, keep in mind that techniques for calculating how much you should pay to acquire copyrights and catalogs are the same you should use when seeking advances for your catalog (or songs) from overseas publishers, sheet music distributors, etc. Your calculations can demonstrate in black and white how much revenue your copyrights should realistically generate under a proposed deal, how much you should net, what your copyrights are worth in terms of an advance, and why you're justified in asking for that amount.*

CALCULATING ADVANCES

Record sales are the usual method by which copyrights become sufficiently popular to produce meaningful income. Therefore, in order to determine whether the size of an advance is reasonable, you must determine:

1. How many records must be sold before the advance is recouped;
2. Whether that many sales can be realistically achieved;
3. If sales projections are large enough to return a reasonable profit;
4. If the needed sales can be achieved within an acceptable time frame;
5. If you can afford to tie up working capital for the period it takes to recoup; and
6. Whether the potential return on investment within the time frame for recoupment justifies the risk compared with other investment opportunities.

PAYING AN ADVANCE TO ACQUIRE ONE SONG

For purposes of illustration, let's examine a deal proposal to publish one song based on the following conditions:

- The deal is for one song.
- Advance asked is $1,000.
- Writer assigns 100% copyright ownership, life of copyright.
- Songwriter's royalties are 50% of all income received by the publisher.
- The song is being released as the 'A' side of a single.
- The record company pays the full statutory mechanical royalty rate.

Advances are always based on the writers' share. Do not include your share as part of the royalty income from which you will recoup.

If you advance $1,000 to acquire one song, and the writer's royalty is the standard 50%, the song must gross $2,000 before you recoup the advance. (The song must gross $4,000 to recoup if your share is 25%.)

Since the song in this case will be released as the 'A' side of a single, there will hopefully be some measure of performance income resulting from radio airplay. But don't base your calculations on too much hope. Reckon that at least 75% of gross income will come from record sales. Performance royalties and other income will account for the other 25%. That means the writer must earn a minimum of $750 from mechanical royalties (record sales), and an additional $250 through performance royalties and other income before the advance is recouped.

The current gross statutory mechanical royalty rate (through 1997) paid by U.S. record companies to publishers for record sales is 6.95¢ per unit sold. The writer's 50% share is therefore 3.475¢. Divide $750 by 3.475¢, and you find that the record has to sell 21,583 units to recoup ($750 ÷ 3.475¢ = 21,583).

If the song is an album cut or 'B' side, you must totally discount potential performance income and base the advance solely on anticipated record sales. Divide $1,000 by 3.475¢, and you see the record must sell 28,777 units to recoup.

If the release does in fact sell 21,583 units, and 25% of the total earnings do in fact come from performance and other income, the publisher will make a profit of 50%, as follows:

$1,500 - gross mechanical royalties (21,583 units x 6.95¢)
+ 500 - gross performance and other income
= $2,000 - gross income

$2,000 - gross income
- $1,000 - songwriter's share
= $1,000 - publisher's share

$1,000 - publisher's share
+ $1,000 - songwriter's share recouped against advance
= $2,000 - retained by publisher

$2,000 - retained by publisher
- $1,000 - publisher's initial investment
= $1,000 - publisher's profit = 50% ($1,000 ÷ $2,000 = .50)

When an advance is based on the expectations of one record release, you must be certain of the following:

- the song will, in fact, be released;
- it will be an 'A' side—otherwise, base the advance on 100% of sales; and
- airplay and other activity (foreign, print, etc.) must generate sufficient income to bridge the gap between projected mechanical royalties and other earnings—otherwise, base the advance on 100% of sales.

You must also be certain that the required sales level for recoupment can be realistically achieved. Be sure the following statements are true:

- the artist's target market is broad enough to achieve the required sales level;
- the artist's most recent release sold enough units to have recouped this advance;
- the artist's record company can *and will* effectively market the product; and
- the artist's record company can be counted on to pay royalties.

If you're considering an advance to a co-publisher, foreign publisher, or songwriter who is to receive more than the standard 50% royalty, you must obviously alter the basis of your calculations to reflect the different percentages. Example: if your share is 25%, and you're making a $1,000 advance to a songwriter/co-publisher whose take totals 75% (writer's share = 50% and co-publisher's share = 25%), then you must gross $4,000 ($3,000 = 75% of $4,000) in order to recoup.

PAYING AN ADVANCE FOR A CATALOG OF SONGS

Many of the same considerations come into play when negotiating exclusive songwriter agreements covering a writer's back catalog and/or output during the term of the agreement. An exclusive writer commanding a $10,000 advance, at a royalty of 50%, must sell an aggregate 287,770 units ($10,000 ÷ 3.475¢) to recoup, discounting performance royalties and other income.

It is chancy to gamble on a new writer's works selling nearly 300,000 records, unless there are extenuating circumstances. One such circumstance might be that the writer's works are being recorded by an established artist, or a hot new act is guaranteed significant promotional support by a major label. More established writers have track records from which past sales can be extrapolated into meaningful forecasts of future earnings potential.

Blended royalty rate

When calculating how many record sales are needed to recoup an advance for a catalog of songs, one must remember to factor in the prospect that many, if not most, of the copyrights in question will likely earn less than the full statutory mechanical royalty rate. Some songs may be subject to *controlled composition clauses* (see the chapter on *Mechanical-Right Licensing*), others may have been licensed at *reduced rates* for other reasons, and many may be split (co-written) with one or more other songwriters. Indeed, the mix of splits and licenses issued at reduced royalty rates may be so complex that realistic projections can only be made after a statistical model has been formulated.

One would need to comb through the catalog, extract the income-producing copyrights, then make note of the songwriter's net share earned from each current income-producing license. For instance, a catalog of 500 songs might contain 100 songs that actively generate earnings. An examination of those 100 songs might reveal the following data:

Number of songs	Licensed rate	Gross royalty	Writer's share	Writer's net
11	100%	6.95 x 11	50%	38.23
19	100%	6.95 x 19	25%	33.01
23	75%	5.2125 x 23	50%	59.94
24	75%	5.2125 x 24	25%	31.28
16	100%	6.95 x 16	33.33%	37.07
7	75%	5.2125 x 7	33.33%	12.16
Total: 100				211.69

The songwriter's per unit net royalty for these 100 songs totals 211.69¢ ($2.1169). The songwriter's *blended* net royalty per unit is therefore 211.69 ÷ 100 = 2.1169, or approximately 2.12¢ per record sold.

Although this statistical analysis of current licenses issued for the writer's works in no way guarantees that future earnings will reflect a similar blended royalty rate, it is as good an indication as any as to how this songwriter's future net royalties will break down. It reveals that the writer's copyrights are frequently split with other songwriters, and that many of the songs are licensed at less than the statutory mechanical royalty rate.

So, with a blended royalty due the writer of 2.12¢ per unit, and an advance of $10,000, the writer's works must sell 471,698 units in order to recoup ($10,000 ÷ .0212). But that's recouping on record sales alone. Since the analysis was made on the writer's current income-producing songs, there is a history of performance royalties and other types of income, which can also be blended.

For purposes of illustration, assume the writer's mechanical income amounted to 45% of his royalty earnings, while performance income and other royalties totaled 55%. If these statistics hold up, the writer's works must generate only $4,500 in record sales to recoup, which means sales of just 212,264 units (471,698 x 45%). The balance of the advance ($5,500) could reasonably be expected to be recouped from performance royalties and other types of income.

FORECASTING SALES

Of course, knowing how many sales are required to recoup an advance is one thing. The bigger question is whether or not the songwriter's works are likely to sell that many records in order to recoup the advance.

You must know, before making an advance, whether you can generate enough sales not only to recoup (break even), but to achieve profitability within the time frame you've set. Forecasts are the key to assessing the risks of failure against the potential rewards of success.

It is important to base sales forecasts on solid research and hard reality—not wishful thinking. Even so, it isn't easy to get it right. No matter how carefully done, forecasts rarely turn out to be 100% accurate. But if you're conservative, honest, and realistic, you can reach valid assumptions and come up with a workable estimate of potential sales.

Some marketing experts in other industries claim the ability to build complex statistical models that can predict sales volume within plus or minus 5 percent. However, it is unlikely record sales can be forecast with such accuracy, due to the highly subjective nature of the product.

Music is not a basic need. People like a song or they don't, and not everyone likes every song. It is therefore difficult to build a statistical model factoring in all the esoteric minutiae characteristic of industries centered on less subjective product. So we're left with less exotic tools to work with in forecasting record sales.

Historical-based forecasting

If you're contemplating an advance to an established songwriter (or catalog owner) with a verifiable sales history, you can extrapolate past sales into forecasts based on what has already been achieved and then add in how much better you expect to do with the copyrights, given your marketing capabilities. Likewise, if you're working out a new advance to renew an agreement with one of your existing songwriters, there is an established or historical financial pattern to work from. You can forecast sales based on past performance, factoring in pipeline royalties from previous releases as well as the increased volume you expect to achieve with new copyrights contributed during the renewed contract period.

But if you're considering an advance to a new songwriter with no earnings history, you have to dig deeper to come up with meaningful forecasts. You can't just pull a number out of a hat or base your projections on hope.

Executive judgment

If you, your partners, or associates have a collective track record of success in the music business, your instincts and experience are valuable forecasting tools. Your forecasting team cannot, however, be too far removed from grassroots or street-level marketplace sensitivities. The more time spent in executive-suite isolation, the more the feel for the market's pulse diminishes.

Jury of experts

You can use a jury of experts. Veteran record salesmen are excellent candidates for jury duty. They can draw on past experience with similar product to estimate sales. Input from retailers and distributors is also useful for the same reason. Such a jury would probably use *comparative analysis* to arrive at their estimates.

Comparative analysis

You can compare like with like to arrive at sensible forecasts: Your product is like so and so, which sells such and such. Ergo, given the same marketing capability as so and so, and given that your product has similar commercial appeal, you have a reasonable chance of also selling such and such.

However, your analysis must truly be comparative. You can't say that because your song is recorded by Joe Newartist, who is much like Mike Megastar, Joe should therefore sell as many units as Mike. Joe Newartist, wonderful though he may be, has not yet established the loyal fan base and market penetration Mike Megastar enjoys. The playing field isn't level. The comparison is only realistic when you use Mike Megastar's debut results as a benchmark, and then consider such factors as market conditions now versus then, as well as the marketing methods planned for Joe versus the methods used to break Mike's debut release.

A source for comparative data is *Billboard* magazine's Soundscan system, which collects computer-generated sales results from retail outlets by scanning barcodes of recorded product. Accessing Soundscan thus provides insight into how many sales it takes before an album registers number 50 on the pop charts, or number 75 on the country charts, or whatever.

Concentrating on your own market niche (pop, country, rap, rock), you'll learn the scales of success up and down the charts. And comparing product in the same genre as your own, by artists of similar caliber to your own, you can form an educated guess as to how many sales your own product can achieve, assuming your marketing ability is on a par with the product compared. (See the chapter on *Exploitation* for details of Soundscan.)

The Delphi Method

This method of analysis actually blends two other methods: *Group Discussion* and *Democratic Pool*. In the Group Discussion method, members of a group or committee submit forecast figures for discussion. A consensus is then reached whereby all members of the group decide upon a number that the group as a whole is happy with.

In the Democratic Pool, each member of the group submits a forecast estimate, which is accepted without question. These estimates are then averaged, and the average number becomes the accepted forecast.

The Delphi Method takes the numbers submitted by members of the Democratic Pool and then opens them to Group Discussion. The resulting give-and-take may lead to individual members revising their original estimates. The final numbers are then averaged to arrive at the forecast. Thus, the Delphi Method uses the strengths of both Group Discussion and the Democratic Pool.

Market surveys

This method requires going into the marketplace and testing product with prospective customers, either one-on-one or through focus groups. This might be fine if you're marketing a single product, like detergent or perfume, or if you're testing the market viability of one particular artist. But it is rather prohibitively expensive and time consuming from the point of view of a catalog with many different songs, each one of which has different attributes. Also, test results can be misleading unless the survey is conducted with respondents who are scientifically selected as representative of the market, and the right questions are asked in the right way.

FORECASTING A MULTIPRODUCT LINE

One of the difficulties in forecasting sales for a song catalog is that you're not dealing with a single product. It is one thing to arrive at a forecast for a particular artist in a particular genre, but you need to project how many sales you can reasonably expect for a variety of songs released by a variety of artists over a finite period. Some of these artists aren't yet on your radar screen, and each release by each artist will have a different sales potential depending upon numerous factors, including the level of market acceptance an artist has achieved (or lost) at the time of release.

You're therefore working with many unknowns. What you have to do, then, is project the average number of sales you expect per release. For example, say you're working out an advance to a songwriter-producer who is slated to produce four different artists during the contract's first year.

Two of these artists (A & B) have had albums out already, which sold approximately 100,000 units each. By virtue of the groundwork already laid and the increased marketing strength you will bring to the deal, you expect sales to increase for each of these artists by 25%, at least. The other two artists (C & D) are releasing debut albums, but you feel confident they'll each sell at least 25,000 units, because they each have a growing fan base, and their labels have committed substantial marketing muscle and tour support.

However, being cautiously realistic, you hedge your bets by forecasting that sales will increase by 25% on just one of the two established artists (A & B); the other's sales will increase by only 15%. And you count on just one of the two new artists to sell 25,000 units; the other's debut will do only half that. So your forecast looks like this:

Artist	Sales
A	125,000
B	115,000
C	25,000
D	12,500
Total:	277,500

Combined sales projections for these four artists total 277,500 units. Each artist therefore averages sales of 69,375 units (277,500 ÷ 4).

But, each album will contain a minimum of 3 songs written by your prospective songwriter-producer. That gives you 12 songs (4 albums x 3 songs each). Since each album averages 69,375 units, the total sales of *songs* yielding mechanical royalties is 832,500 (12 x 69,375). At the full, statutory mechanical rate, the 12 songs would gross $57,858.75 (6.95¢ x 832,500). Thus, if each song was written 100% by your songwriter-producer, and the record companies paid the full royalty on each one, the writer's royalties from record sales would be $28,929.38 ($57,858.75 x 50%).

However, let's assume the songwriter-producer co-writes each of the 12 songs with another songwriter, and your guy's royalty share is 50% (25% of gross). Let's further assume the record labels involved are paying mechanical royalties based on a 75% controlled composition rate. This reduces your writer's royalty share per song as follows:

.0695¢	- statutory mechanical royalty rate
x 75%	- controlled composition rate
= .052125¢	- gross royalty per song

.052125¢	- gross royalty per song
÷ 2	- divided 50/50 between publisher and songwriters
= .0260625¢	- writers' share

.0260625¢	- writers' share
÷ 2	- divided 50/50 between two songwriters
= .01303125¢	- your writer's net share

.01303125¢	- your writer's net share
x 832,500	- total sales
$10,848.52	- total net mechanical royalties to your songwriter

Trend analysis

Once you've made a forecast for the coming year, you need to forecast forward into all the other years covered by the contract under consideration. It's not likely each year will be the same. The question is, will sales increase or decrease in each of these years?

The answer depends upon whether you expect your writer's prospects as a producer to steadily improve, thereby creating more opportunities for getting his songs cut; whether you can establish market acceptance of his works with other users (for cover records, jingles, print, soundtracks, etc.); and, finally, whether you expect the target market for the writer's genre to expand or shrink.

In this hypothetical case, you believe the writer's

star as a producer is on the rise. It's safe to assume, then, that he'll continue to produce at least four artists per year whose albums will each contain at least three of his works.

Your writer is also fairly prolific. You have a high regard for the commercial quality of his work, and you confidently expect he'll create several songs per year that you can exploit, in addition to those he produces himself. You think you can get at least two songs cut by third-party users in years two and three of the contract.

As to the market for the writer's type of material, you need to do some research to discover any shifts in the demographic makeup of the target market, as well as sales patterns of product in this genre, over the past few years. From your research, you make a *Trend Analysis*, which enables you to make reasonable assumptions about the level of growth (or shrinkage, or stagnation) expected for the next three to five years (assuming economic conditions remain otherwise constant).

The key to projecting rates of growth (or decline) is not the average rate over a period, but the *trend*. The pattern below shows growth at an average of 4.2% over a five-year period.

Year	Growth
1 - 1992	7%
2 - 1993	5%
3 - 1994	4%
4 - 1995	3%
5 - 1996	2%
Total:	21%

The total growth over 5 years is 21%. The average growth per year is therefore:

21 ÷ 5 years = 4.2%.

However, the growth trend is downwards! So, despite the five-year average annual increase of 4.2%, the rate of growth is steadily diminishing, down to just 2% in the most recent year. Therefore, you'd be advised to predict very low or no growth during the near future.

On the other hand, the average five-year growth can still be 4.2% per year when the growth trend is upwards.

Year	Growth
1 - 1992	2%
2 - 1993	3%
3 - 1994	4%
4 - 1995	5%
5 - 1996	7%
Total:	21%
21 ÷ 5 years =	4.2%

In this case, you might be justified in predicting continued growth of at least 4.2% because the trend is upwards. But you should limit your projections to three years, at maximum. After the third year, taper any projected rate of growth, since Years 4 and 5 are a long way out for safe predictions. Lots can happen, and probably will.

☞ *Always be conservative when forecasting. Err on the side of caution. It's great when things turn out better than expected, but rotten when things turn out worse.*

So, let's assume your trend analysis of the market for your writer's works shows 4.2% average growth per year with a healthily improving rise over the last five years (the growth was 7% in the most recent year). It may, then, be safe to predict a 5% average growth rate over the next three years, the term of the contract under consideration.

Putting all this together, we expect 12 songs released in the first year, with average sales each of 69,375 units. We expect at least 14 songs released in each of Years 2 and 3, with average sales growing at 5% per year. Our projections, then, for this writer's mechanical royalty income during the proposed three-year-deal are as follows:

Year	Average unit sales	No. of songs released	Total projected sales	Writer's royalty	Writer's earnings
1	69,375	12	832,500	0.01303125	$10,848
2	72,844	14	1,019,813	0.01303125	$13,289
3	76,486	14	1,070,807	0.01303125	$13,954
Totals:		40	2,923,120	0.01303125	$38,091

Forecasting the sales blend

When forecasting a song catalog's financial performance, you also need to consider all sources of income. In addition to mechanicals, there will likely be income from performance royalties, print royalties, foreign royalties, and, perhaps, royalties and fees from such miscellaneous usages as jingles, soundtracks, sampling, etc. Even if you accurately predict the number of record sales and amount of mechanical royalties received, the actual blending of other types of income can dramatically alter the dollar amount grossed.

For example, say your songwriter actually does sell 2,923,120 units, netting him $38,091 in mechanical royalties during the contract's three-year-term, as forecast above. If you projected *blended* income of 60% mechanicals, 20% performances, 15% foreign, 3% print, and 2% miscellaneous, you'd forecast total songwriter earnings of $63,486.

Source of income	% of gross	Amount
Mechanical royalties	60	$38,091
Performance royalties	20	$12,697
Foreign royalties	15	$9,523
Print royalties	3	$1,905
Miscellaneous	2	$1,270
Total:	100	$63,486

But suppose mechanicals only amount to 35% of total earnings, and the percentages of performance and foreign royalties are significantly higher, because the writer's songs are released as 'A' side singles from the albums and do very well overseas. Your projections may then look like this:

Source of income	% of gross	Amount
Mechanical royalties	35	$38,091
Performance royalties	40	$43,533
Foreign royalties	20	$21,766
Print royalties	3	$3,265
Miscellaneous	2	$2,177
Total:	100	$108,832

The resulting songwriter's net earnings would be $108,832. This is $45,346 more than if mechanical royalties totaled 60% of all income, even though the number of records sold and the amount of mechanical royalties earned are still exactly the same.

Now, suppose, instead, none of the writer's works are used as 'A' sides. And it then turns out that mechanical royalties account for 85% of all earnings, because there is very little performance income from airplay, none of the songs are issued in print, foreign earnings aren't so great, and no "miscellaneous" usages materialize. The resulting total income for the songwriter may then look like this:

Source of income	% of gross	Amount
Mechanical royalties	85	$38,091
Performance royalties	7	$3,137
Foreign royalties	8	$3,585
Print royalties	0	$0
Miscellaneous	0	$0
Total:	100	$44,813

The songwriter's earnings of $44,813 are $18,673 less than the first projection (based on mechanical royalties of 60%), and a whopping $64,019 less than they would have been if mechanical royalties were 35%, even though the number of records sold and the amount of mechanical royalties earned are exactly the same in all three scenarios.

Needless to say, faulty projections of the sales blend can cause a publisher to miscalculate the size of an advance with disastrous results. Let's examine the publisher's profits in each of these three cases.

1. If the publisher forecasts mechanicals will total 60% of all income, he might pay an advance of $65,000, based on projected total songwriter earnings of $63,486 over a three-year-period. Suppose, however, the mechanical projections were correct as to the number of units sold and royalties earned, but the *percentage* of mechanicals was 85% of total songwriter earnings. The songwriter would still owe $20,187 at the end of the term, but the publisher would nevertheless profit, as follows:

Mechanicals=85%	Gross Income=$89,626
Advance	$65,000
Publisher's Share (50%)	$44,813
Less Publisher's investment (advance)	($65,000)
Balance	($20,187)
Plus recoupment from songwriter's share	$44,813
Publisher's net	$24,626

The publisher's profit is thus 38% ($24,626 ÷ $65,000 = 0.37886), or a return of about 12.66% a year. While this isn't terrible, it is by no means the happiest of outcomes, considering the risk involved and the safer, alternative investment opportunities available.

2. True disaster would occur had the advance been $100,000 based on projections that mechanical royalties would have accounted for 35% of the total earnings, but mechanical royalties turned out instead to be 85% of the total. The result would be:

Mechanicals=85%	Gross Income=$89,626
Advance	$100,000
Publisher's Share (50%)	$44,813
Less Publisher's investment (advance)	($100,000)
Balance	($55,187)
Plus recoupment from songwriter's share	$44,813
Publisher's net	($10,374)

3. On the other hand, if everything works out exactly as projected, where mechanicals are 60% of all earnings, and the advance is $65,000, the results are as follows:

Mechanicals=60%	Gross Income=$126,972
Advance	$65,000
Publisher's Share (50%)	$63,486
Less Publisher's investment (advance)	($65,000)
Balance	($1,514)
Plus recoupment from songwriter's share	$63,486
Publisher's net	$61,972

Although the contract term ends with the songwriter still in the red by $1,514, there will certainly be enough earnings in the pipeline to recoup the balance in a reasonably short time. Moreover, the publisher's net of $61,972 over and above the advance that was paid represents a profit of 95% ($61,972 ÷ $65,000 = 0.95341), or a return of approximately 32% a year.

BEST CASE/WORST CASE SCENARIOS

A prudent publisher makes projections based on what he thinks will occur, then accounts for *what if.* Can he still profit if his projections are off by 10%? By 20%? The publisher will make his projections carefully, with thorough research and sales forecasting techniques, then do *what ifs* based on *best* case, *most likely* case, and *worse* case scenarios.

If you're reasonably confident the deal is worth a $65,000 advance, you might exercise caution and treat earnings of $65,000 as the *best case* scenario. Then, lop off 10% ($6,500) and figure total songwriter earnings of $59,500 as the *most likely* scenario. Then take off 20% and figure $52,000 as the *worst case* scenario. Then, if the worst case materializes, your profit would be:

Worst Case Scenario=60%	Gross Income=$104,000
Advance	$65,000
Publisher's Share (50%)	$52,000
Less Publisher's investment (advance)	($65,000)
Balance	($13,000)
Plus recoupment from songwriter's share	$52,000
Publisher's net	$39,000

The profit under the worst case scenario would then be 60%, or 20% a year. That could be a workable deal, if it's the worst that can happen. Otherwise, your projections were so far off as to be embarrassing. Remember, carefully work out what you think will happen, then use that as your *best* case bottom line. And then, if after knocking off at least 20%, you think you can still afford the deal under the worst case scenario, and there are no safer alternatives, consider it a go.

Again, the best forecasting tools for blended sales, trend analyses, and best case/worst case scenarios are the techniques discussed above for sales forecasting. Do your research with care, consult experts, and consider what ifs. Although publishing involves risk-taking (no forecast is fail-safe, as meteorologists will tell you), you can reduce the chances of disaster from a reckless gamble to a carefully calculated risk, thereby greatly increasing the odds of success in your favor.

STRUCTURING ADVANCES

Advances might be made for one song, a catalog of songs, or for all songs written during the period of an exclusive contract. It is always prudent to pay advances in installments, rather than in one lump sum. After the initial cash advance paid as a signing inducement, future payments should be conditional upon either *milestone achievements* or your exercise of *options* to renew the contract beyond the original term.

Milestone achievements might include:

- delivery of a specified number of commercially acceptable songs
- a minimum number of record releases
- a minimum level of sales
- recoupment of earlier advances
- chart activity

Options

Contracts are typically entered into for an initial period of one year (or one album release or *X* number of songs). The publisher usually has contractual options to extend the agreement each year for additional periods of one year (or for an additional *X* number of songs or album releases containing *X* number original songs). Options generally must be exercised before each anniversary date of the contract.

Song delivery

The agreement may call for delivery of *X* number of *commercially acceptable songs* with options to pick up an additional specified number of songs. Whether or not a song is "commercially acceptable" is up to the publisher. If a writer splits a song 50/50 with a co-writer, that song counts as half a song toward the delivery commitment.

Record releases

Advances can be paid on the basis of record releases. For instance, self-contained bands or singer-songwriters with recording deals may receive an advance upon the release of one (or more) album(s) containing at least X number original songs. The publisher has options to pick up an additional specified number of albums, each of which contains at least X number original songs, upon payment of further, specified advances.

Incremental advances

It is also common to increase the amount of advance payments with the exercise of each option. For instance, instead of shelling out $50,000 for a three-album deal, the agreement may call for payments of $10,000 for the first album, $15,000 for the second album, and $25,000 for a third album.

This might also be structured as a three-year deal with payments of $10,000 for the first year, $15,000 for the second year, and $25,000 for a third year. The company reserves options to pick up the second and third albums (or years) and is not committed to paying out the remaining portions of the advance if the deal doesn't seem to work as originally envisioned.

Songwriter advances may be doled out in even smaller installments. Rather than annual lump sums, they can be divided into quarterly, monthly, biweekly, or weekly payments. For instance, a $5,000 annual advance may be paid in 26 biweekly installments of $192 each.

By making advances conditional, and by staging payments in increasing increments, you can better control working capital so funds aren't tied up in nonproductive investments. The structure of advance payments is, of course, a matter of negotiation, but you must be able to cut your losses if a deal isn't working out.

Chart activity

Bonus amounts might be offered for each song that makes the *Billboard* Top 100. For instance, $X is paid for each song breaking the top 50; $Y for each song breaking the top 10; and $Z for each song that reaches number one.

Minimum/maximum advance formula

This is another method of computing advances on milestone achievements. In this case, the amounts of future advances payable during each option period are calculated on a percentage of income generated during the previous period up to a pre-agreed maximum amount. There may also be a guaranteed minimum amount payable, no matter what the previous period's earnings were.

For instance, the first advance might be, say, $25,000 with an option after one year to renew the agreement upon payment of either a minimum amount of $30,000, or 75% of earnings up to a maximum of $50,000, whichever is higher.

Thus, if the first year's earnings are $25,000, the publisher would pay $30,000 to renew. If the first period's earnings were $50,000, the publisher would pay $37,500 ($50,000 x 75%). But, if the earnings were $75,000, 75% of that would be $56,250, so the publisher could renew the agreement upon payment of the maximum amount of $50,000.

RECOUPING EXPENSES

Many publishers charge songwriters' advance accounts for certain promotional, administrative, and developmental costs. These expenses are deducted from gross writers' royalties before the split is made and before cash advances are recouped.

For example, assume a songwriter receives an advance of $1,000 for one song, and there are additional expenses totaling $500 for demo production, promotion, copyright fees, and administrative and collection costs. And further assume the song grosses $5,000. The money breaks down as follows:

$5,000 - gross royalty earnings
- 2,500 - net publisher's 50% share
= $2,500 - **gross writer's 50% share**

$2,500 - gross writer's share
- 500 - recoupable expenses
= $2,000 - **net writer's share**

$2,000 - net writer's share
- 1,000 - applied to advance account
= $1,000 - **net royalties due writer**

In this example, the publisher retains $4,000 from $5,000 gross ($2,500 net publisher share + $500 expense recoupment + $1,000 advance recoupment = $4,000). Put another way, the publisher's cash investment was $1,500 ($1,000 advance to acquire the product + $500 for demo and copyright expenses). The publisher's profit is thus $2,500, or 62.5%.

Whether or not you add certain expenses to a writer's advance account is a policy decision. Some publishers absorb these expenses as a cost of doing business; others may absorb them as a result of a writer's negotiating strength. But any category of expenses charged to a writer must be specified in the contract.

CROSS-COLLATERALIZATION

Another matter of negotiation is whether the publisher is allowed to *cross-collateralize* advances. The term simply means that you can recoup advances for earlier works from earnings generated by later works. Thus, if you exercise the option for a second album release of original songs when the first album hasn't been recouped, you can apply the balance of the first advance against royalties earned by the second release.

Cross-collateralization may also extend to artist or producer royalties when the writer records or produces tracks for the publisher's affiliated record company. The writer may justifiably argue that separate artistic endeavors (e.g., songwriter, artist, producer) should be compartmentalized. But where writer royalties are concerned, the publisher is on stronger ground. Any resistance to cross-collateralization of songwriter royalties can be met with the argument that you'd naturally be reluctant to exercise options without an opportunity to recoup outstanding balances.

Purchasing copyrights

When copyright assets are bought and sold, *or used as collateral for loans*, an appraisal must be made of their fair market value. Be wary of buying copyrights at prices based on nothing more than hunches about their potential. You cannot safely use potential as a basis for calculating market value. You must be reasonably assured that the level of income generated over the next three to five years will return a suitable profit on your investment. In order to make reasonable assumptions of future income, you must first examine the recent earnings history.

The examination of earnings should preferably cover the preceding five years, at least. Obviously, if the catalog is under five years old, appraisal must be made on however many years of historical financial information are available. But, the more years an appraiser has to work with, the better he can project future catalog earnings. And it is the projected earnings that determine what the catalog is worth, because there must be sufficient income to profitably repay any investment by a purchaser or lender.

FINANCIAL EVALUATION OF COPYRIGHTS

Valuing intangible properties, like copyrights, presents challenges. Certain concrete attributes, such as recent earnings, are used to form an initial assessment, which must then be used to project the assets' commercial future. Since no one can predict to the penny what a copyright will earn over the next few years, this judgment must be subjective. Each copyright catalog has unique qualities, as well as drawbacks, from the perspective of assessing future earnings, which are the basis of its present value.

The appraisal of copyrights leaves aside other assets that the copyright owner might have, such as real estate, furnishings, or equipment. The formula used to appraise a copyright catalog's value is as follows:

1. *add* the preceding three to five years *gross receipts*
2. *subtract* all royalty payments to songwriters and co-publishers
3. *divide* the result by the number of years totaled to find *the average annual net income*
4. *multiply* the average annual net income by a *multiple*

THE MULTIPLE

A catalog's appraisal hinges on the *multiple* of its average annual net earnings. The multiple used for valuation is commonly between four and ten times the average annual net receipts. Different appraisers might use different multiples to value the same catalog, just as one appraiser might value two catalogs with identical average annual earnings differently.

There can be no argument about the average annual net income, since this is derived from simple, indisputable math. But there may be a natural tug of war between negotiating parties over which multiple produces a fair market value.

Buyers and lenders tend toward caution. Since they don't want to risk loss of profit, they use a conservative multiple to value the copyrights. Sellers and borrowers, on the other hand, want to raise the maximum amount of money possible, so they argue for a higher multiple. Ego may also come into play when copyright owners seek to demonstrate their catalog is worth a higher sum.

The multiple selected depends upon the following:
1. *Duration of rights* to key copyrights owned by the publisher
2. Contractual *commitments to pay advances* to writers
3. *Advances owed to publisher* by writers
4. *Advances owed to licensees* by publisher
5. Contractual *commitments by licensees to pay additional advances*
6. *Income trend* over previous three to five years (rising or falling?)
7. The appraiser's opinion of the catalog's *future commercial potential*

Example One: valuing the catalog of Smith Music
Suppose Smith Music is just three years old. Its net income was $75,000 in the first year, $90,000 the second year, and $125,000 the third year, for a total of $290,000. The average annual net earnings are then

$96,667 ($290,000 ÷ 3).

In this example, income increased each year. Also, Smith Music owes no advances to licensees and retains the catalog for life of copyright. A multiple of *seven* might therefore seem reasonable for appraisal. If an appraiser uses a multiple of *seven*, Smith Music's catalog is worth $676,669 ($96,667 x 7).

Smith Music	
Year	Net income
1	$ 75,000
2	90,000
3	125,000
Total	$290,000
	÷ 3 years
	$ 96,667 (average annual net income)
	x 7 (multiple)
Market value:	$676,669

Example Two: valuing the catalog of Jones Music

By contrast, consider Jones Music, also three years old. Average annual net income is exactly the same ($96,667), but the income trend is reversed ($125,000 the first year and $75,000 the third year), indicating a loss of momentum. Further, Jones owes $50,000 to foreign licensees and has rights to certain key income-producing copyrights for only another 20 years. Obviously, Jones Music must be appraised lower than Smith Music, perhaps using a multiple of *five* and subtracting the $50,000 owed to foreign licensees:

Jones Music	
Year	Net income
1	$125,000
2	90,000
3	75,000
Total	$290,000
	÷ 3 years
	96,667 (average annual net income)
	x 5 (multiple)
Market value:	$483,335
	- 50,000 (advances owed)
Adjusted market value:	$433,335

Though both companies average $96,667 net income annually over three years, Smith Music is worth $243,334 more than Jones Music, in this appraiser's opinion.

The industry trend has been to nudge upwards the multiples used to value publishing catalogs. Multiples as high as 12-15 have been used recently where there were well-known songs in the catalogs, and the purchasers recognized that expanding market opportunities offer increased copyright earnings potential.

For example, EMI purchased Filmtrax at a reported multiple of 11.5, and it was rumored a few years ago that Jobete Music (then netting $10 million per year) drew serious interest at a potential price of between $150 million and $200 million (a 15- to 20-year multiple). Although such a multiple was unprecedented, and was based primarily on the unique quality of Jobete's catalog, *Billboard* magazine editorialized:

> [The] . . . real-world price for Jobete [would be] in the $85 million to $95 million range [a multiple of 8.5 to 9.5] . . . [but] in this age of seemingly anything-goes music publishing prices, one is tempted to say, why not?

COMPANY NAME

The appraisals in the above examples are based on copyright assets only, and don't include other assets (real estate, equipment, stock, etc.). However, the company name is also often part of the deal, even though the purchaser plans to merge the copyrights into another catalog entity. A company name may be considered as an asset with goodwill value. The price of the name, in addition to the copyrights, is subject to negotiations.

CASH VS. ACCRUAL VALUATIONS

Also, these appraisal examples were made on a *cash basis*. The purchase price multiple of net income may be calculated either of two ways: *cash* or *accrual*.

Cash is a real-time method of valuation, in that income and royalty payments are accounted for only if actually received and paid during the valuation period. It is the simplest method of pricing, but doesn't necessarily take into account the true value of the assets since accounts receivable and payable are not factored.

Suppose, for example, that using the cash basis analysis, $1 million was received during the past year and $250,000 paid in royalties, leaving a net of $750,000. *But*, though not due to be paid for another three months, an additional $250,000 is owed in royalties. The true net is then actually $500,000, which would be evident if the accrual basis were used to calculate the value.

The buying and selling process

THE PROSPECTUS

Whether a copyright owner is attempting to sell a catalog or raise money using the copyrights as collateral, a *prospectus* must be prepared describing the assets. The prospectus summarizes income generated in each of the previous three to five years. Summaries for each year are broken down into the following categories:

Income source	Gross income	Royalties paid	Royalties owed	Net income
Domestic:				
Mechanicals:				
Performances:				
Synchronizations:				
Print:				
Miscellaneous:				
Foreign:				
Mechanicals:				
Performances:				
Synchronizations:				
Print:				
Miscellaneous:				
Totals:				

In addition, summaries of all existing contracts and major licenses are detailed with the following information:

- type of agreement (songwriter, co-publishing, administration)
- expiration dates (options, retention rights, etc.)
- percentages (writers/co-publishers, etc.)
- subpublishers (percentages, territories, retention rights, options, etc.)
- advances owed *to* third parties
- advances owed *by* third parties
- commitments *by* third parties (product guarantees, financial obligations, etc.)
- commitments *to* third parties (product guarantees, financial obligations, etc.)
- print licenses, synchronization licenses, special permissions, other pertinent facts

Since this information is proprietary, the seller usually insists that a letter of confidentiality be signed by interested buyers in order to protect the integrity of the business.

DUE DILIGENCE

After terms of a copyright or catalog purchase have been agreed in principle, a process called *due diligence* must be undertaken by the buyer. Any sale agreement should be subject to the findings of due diligence. The results of due diligence can affect the price the purchaser is willing to pay, or even whether or not the purchaser goes through with the deal.

Discrepancies turned up during due diligence audits either result in the purchase price being adjusted or the deal being aborted. In essence, the

due diligence process determines whether the claims of the seller are accurate with regard to two major aspects of the catalog: financials and legalities.

Financials

The seller's books and records are examined and compared with actual royalty statements received during the period to insure reported income is accurate. Statements examined include those from performing- and mechanical-right societies, subpublishers, print licensees, and other major users, such as ad agencies and film producers.

There is also an examination of statements issued to songwriters, co-publishers, and other third parties. The seller's relevant bank records are also examined to substantiate claims of royalties paid by the seller.

A third area of examination tests the validity of the seller's claims regarding advances it is owed by songwriters and third parties, as well as balances on advances still owed by the seller to subpublishers and other licensees. All pipeline monies owed *by* and owed *to* the seller must be substantiated.

Due diligence audits are designed to isolate anomalies in income that may skewer the financial picture presented by the seller and alter the appraisal. Anomalies can include such things as the receipt of judgment awards for infringements, or receipts of payments owed by third parties for usages that occurred before the accounting period began but were not received until after the period began.

Another type of anomaly might be the receipt of a large advance received during the examination period from a third party, such as a subpublisher, and which is still mostly unrecouped. Unrecouped advances might significantly reduce future earnings as licensees retain all income until the advances are repaid.

Legalities

While accountants pour over the financials, lawyers pursue due diligence on the legal aspects of a potential copyright purchase. This phase of the process examines the files and records of the seller. Particular interest is paid to such things as copyright registrations, contracts, and licenses to determine validity, enforceability, and obligations, financial or otherwise.

Copyright registrations must be examined to ensure claims are valid, remaining terms of copyright are properly disclosed, ownership percentages are accurate, and renewals are perfected, etc. This usually involves a copyright search in the Library of Congress.

Actual contracts and major licenses are checked out to ensure rights claimed in the prospectus are accurate and have not in any way been diminished by failure on the part of the seller. All contracts and licenses must be signed. Chains of title are checked to ensure the validity of rights claimed and that there are no undisclosed restrictions or prohibitions on rights claimed. Specifically, there must be no restrictions or prohibitions on transferring or selling any of the copyrights and no reversions of copyright to assignors in the event of such a sale.

Court records are also searched to reveal any problems, such as undisclosed loans, mortgages, or liens existing on any of the copyrights, and to ensure that no litigation is threatened, pending, or underway. Any of these things could impose unwanted liabilities on the buyer and affect the legality of any sale.

CHAPTER 5

Copyright

Copyright literally means *the right to copy*. Copyright owners have the exclusive right to perform or make copies of their songs (or authorize others to do so). No one may use or make copies of a copyrighted song in any manner without the owner's permission. This permission takes the form of a *license*, which lays out precise conditions and limitations under which the song may be used, including what fees or royalties must be paid to the copyright owner.

The U.S. Copyright Act of 1976 (effective January 1, 1978) replaced the Copyright Act of 1909. Revision became necessary because of technological advances not dreamed of by the framers of the old law—tape recorders, photocopiers, television, radio, long-playing records, piped music, synchronization of music onto film, etc. (And since 1976, of course, there have been further technological advances not dreamed of by the revisers of the 1909 law—CDs, DAT, MIDI, CD-ROMS, etc.) Copyright laws in other countries have undergone revisions and amendments for the same reason.

What copyright protection covers—what it doesn't

Any original work is automatically copyrighted once it has been "fixed in any tangible medium of expression." A "tangible medium" is any format "now known or later developed" from which the song "can be perceived, reproduced, or otherwise communicated, either directly or with the aid of a machine or device."

Translation: A song is "fixed" sufficiently for copyright protection the moment the writer jots down the lyrics on paper with musical notations or records a rough demo on a cassette recorder.

EXPRESSION VS. IDEAS

Copyright protects the way a song is expressed, not the idea behind the work. For instance, if the song is about lost love, the lyrics and music are copyrightable, but not the subject matter. The theme of lost love has been, and will be, applied to thousands of songs.

FIRST SALE

Copyright doesn't protect the physical property which contains the song. When you purchase a CD, you own the disc. You can play it, sit on it, sail it like a Frisbee. But you do not own the songs, nor the artist's performance of the songs, on the disc. You may not, therefore, make copies of the CD or even play it publicly for profit without authorization from the copyright owners.

The copyright owner is paid on the *first sale* of the product embodying the copyright (e.g., a CD). The purchaser then is the owner of the physical product, though not the copyright. But, as owner of the physical product, the purchaser can resell the product without additional payment to the copyright owner. Which means you can sell your CD collection without having to compensate the music publishers or recording artists.

The concept of *first sale* is the legal basis that video stores use to buy videos that they in turn rent out and ultimately resell as used videos. Many record stores also buy and sell used CDs on the same legal grounds.

COPYRIGHT DOESN'T PROTECT TITLES

A lot of thought often goes into choosing a song title. But though a title is very important and sometimes unique, you cannot copyright a song title. (Titles of motion pictures can be protected by registration, however.) Dozens of copyrighted songs share the same title. You can therefore register a song called "I Don't Care" without fretting that there already exists several dozen copyrighted works with the same title.

However, certain songs have become so famous that the Library of Congress may refuse to register a new song with a title that would be easily confused with an established song. For example, the *Doctrine of Unfair Competition* might apply if you were to try and register a new song called "Rudolph the Red-Nosed Reindeer."

Duration of copyright protection

Copyright protection is in effect from the time a song is *fixed* in physical form (recorded or written down) until 50 years after the songwriter's death. Thus, a song written in the year 2000 by a 20-year-old songwriter who dies in 2060 at age 80 would remain under copyright protection until the year 2110, or 110 years. If there are two or more writers, copyright remains in effect until 50 years after the death of the last surviving collaborator.

However, a work created by an *employee for hire* as a *work for hire* is the property of the employer. A work for hire's copyright is in effect for 75 years from the date of publication or 100 years from the date of creation, whichever comes first.

Congress is currently considering extending the term of copyright to the life of the songwriter plus 70 years. The term of protection was recently increased to life of the songwriter plus 70 years in Great Britain, to conform with most other European nations.

SONGS WRITTEN BEFORE JANUARY 1, 1978

Under the old Copyright Act of 1909, copyright protection was given for an initial term of 28 years with the right to renew copyright protection for a further 28 years. This offered a maximum copyright life of 56 years. Thus, a song created and published in 1960 had protection until 1988, with renewal rights available for an additional 28 years, until 2016.

However, the 1976 Copyright Act (effective January 1, 1978) extended the copyright life of pre-1978 copyrights. Any song created prior to January 1, 1978 was given copyright protection for 75 years from the date of publication. So, a song first published in 1960 now remains in copyright until 2035 (75 years from the original publication date).

Prior to the 1976 Act, many songwriters and publishers lost copyright protection through errors and oversights when it was time to file a renewal claim. So, if you're considering the purchase of songs written prior to 1978, you would be wise to call in a competent copyright attorney to examine the copyrights closely. You must make sure required renewals were complied with, because once a copyright is lost it cannot be restored. And, if renewals were filed, you need to determine how many years of protection remain, so you will know how many more years you can earn royalties from them.

"Published" vs. "unpublished" works

The 1976 Copyright Act provides copyright protection to both *published* and *unpublished* works. For a work to be considered published, it must be fixed (recorded or printed) and distributed in tangible form (discs, tapes, sheet music, etc.) to the public by sale, lease, rental, or lending. Unpublished works may be fixed (written down or recorded as a demo), but not publicly distributed in manufactured form. Live performances are not considered publication.

International copyright protection

There is no "international copyright" that automatically protects a work throughout the world. Copyright protection in each country depends upon that country's own operative copyright laws. But most countries have laws to protect foreign works under certain conditions. Moreover, international treaties have greatly simplified copyright protection so that, for all practical purposes, protection is extended to every significant country.

The two major copyright treaties are the *Berne Convention* and the *Universal Copyright Convention* (UCC), both of which the United States signed. Copyright claims by citizens of any country belonging to either treaty are recognized in every other signatory country. The United States is also a signatory to the *Buenos Aires Convention*, which includes all North and South American countries. (For a list of countries maintaining copyright relations with the U.S., write the Copyright Office and ask for Circular 38a.)

Until recently, U.S. copyright owners could protect works in all UCC member nations by affixing the copyright symbol © or the word "copyright," followed by the name of the copyright owner and date of copyright. Protection in the member nations of the Buenos Aires Convention was assured by adding the words "All Rights Reserved" to the copyright notice.

On March 1, 1989, however, the United States signed the Berne Convention, an international treaty that required certain changes in U.S. copyright law.

These changes are not retroactive and are effective only with regard to works created on and after March 1, 1989. One of the more notable changes deals with requirements for a *copyright notice* on published materials in order to affect copyright protection.

For detailed information about the amendments to U.S. copyright law under the Berne Convention agreement, request circulars 93, "Highlights of U.S. Adherence to the Berne Convention," and 93a, "The United States Joins the Berne Union" from the Copyright Office.

ISWC (INTERNATIONAL STANDARD WORK CODE)

A new method for identifying music copyrights has been developed in order to ensure that copyright owners receive fast, accurate, and efficient distribution of royalties earned by their songs throughout the world. Upon registering a work with a performing-right society, the society issues an ISWC number that is unique to the song.

The ISWC is a nine-digit number preceded by the letter *T* and tagged with a one-digit check number. The society with which the work is first registered links the number to the international "WorksNet" database in New York. Any rights agency anywhere in the world can then identify a work by plugging its ISWC number into the database, thereby locating the proper copyright owner. (See the chapter on *Performing-Right Licensing* for further details.)

Copyright notice

The 1976 Act continued the 1909 Act's requirement that a *notice of copyright* be placed on all published copies of a song. This extended to printed copies (sheet music, lyric reprints, film/TV/video credits); however, copyright notices were not required on label copies or album covers of discs and tapes for the songs contained therein.

In other words, a song published in sheet music form, or lyrics published in a magazine or book, had to be accompanied by the appropriate copyright notice. If the notice was not included, a song could be considered "dedicated to the public." As such, it would fall into *public domain*. Once a song (or any other copyrightable work) becomes public domain, copyright can not be restored, and the owner forever loses claim to copyright!

The law put the burden on the copyright owner to notify the public of a claim to copyright. Innocent errors or omissions of copyright notice from a relatively few copies could be corrected to prevent permanent loss of copyright. However, if someone used a work thinking it was public domain because of the lack of notice, and proved innocence of criminal

intent to infringe the copyright, the owner might not be able to recoup payment for copies sold prior to the time the error was corrected and the user notified of the claim.

The copyright notice had to be in an obvious place on the published copy of the work, generally the title page or first page of the music. Notice included the copyright symbol © (the letter *C* enclosed in a circle), or the word "copyright," or the abbreviation "copr.," followed by the year of publication and the name of the copyright claimant.

Example:
© 1999 by Smith Music
or
Copyright 1999 by Smith Music

Sound recordings are copyrighted by the record manufacturer using a different copyright symbol (a letter P enclosed by a circle), which represents the manufacturer's claim to copyright in the recorded performance of the song—not the song itself.

However, since signing the Berne Convention, copyright notice is not required by the U.S. for works created on or after March 1, 1989. Failure to place a copyright notice on works created since March 1, 1989, no longer results in loss of copyright.

Nevertheless, placing a notice of copyright on published works is still strongly recommended. First, you want potential users to be able to identify you as the owner, so that you could be contacted for future licensing. Secondly, with a notice, an infringer can not claim that he or she "innocently infringed" a work, thinking it was in public domain. (In such cases, there might be a reduction in damages for infringement that the copyright owner would otherwise receive.)

The Berne Convention Act is not retroactive. Thus, all works first published and distributed in the United States before March 1, 1989, must still be published with the appropriate copyright notice. If a work was first published without the required notice before 1978, copyright was lost immediately (with the possible exception of works seeking "ad interim" protection). Once copyright is lost, it can never be restored in the United States, except by special legislation.

Common law copyright

The 1976 Copyright Act provides owners protection for songs "fixed" in tangible form. But there is also protection under *common law* for songs that have not yet been recorded or written down.

No formal copyright registration is required under common law. Copyright protection begins the moment a work is created and continues until the work is fixed in tangible form. The work can be performed live if the performance is not recorded so that someone may later have access to the recording. No one may use a song protected by common law copyright for commercial purposes without the owner's authorization. As long as a song is not fixed, common law copyright protection can continue virtually forever. Once fixed, a song's protection is subject to the Copyright Act of 1976.

Copyright registration

The 1976 Copyright Act lays down the formalities of registering a claim to copyright with the Library of Congress. However, it isn't necessary to register a claim to copyright with the Library of Congress to validate ownership, although it is most advisable. What registration does is make a public record of your claim to copyright from the date you registered the work. Registration itself does not preclude someone contesting your claim.

Though the mandatory requirement for copyright notice has been abolished, U.S. copyright owners must still *deposit* two complete copies or phonorecords in the Copyright Office. Copies deposited must represent the *best edition*. Deposit is required of any work publicly distributed in the United States, whether or not the work contains a copyright notice.

The Copyright Act requires a published work to be *deposited* with the Copyright Office at the Library of Congress within three months of publication, although you won't lose your copyright protection if you fail to do this. You can register the work at any time during the lifetime of the copyright (from the date the song was fixed until 50 years after the death of the last surviving writer).

But it is highly prudent to register your claim as quickly as possible. Here's why: If someone uses your work without authorization, and/or without payment, you may not be able to take legal action until you first register your claim with the Library of Congress. And even then, you may not be able to receive statutory damages and royalties arising from unauthorized usage that occurred before you belatedly filed your registration. Thus, you can lose a substantial sum of money because you neglected to register your claim in a timely manner.

☞ *If you have registered your claim and can prove someone has willfully infringed your copyright, you may be entitled to statutory damages ranging from $500 to $20,000 (even up to $100,000 in some blatant cases), plus any profits the infringer made from your work.*

REGISTRATION PROCEDURES

Registration is a simple process. Forms for filing copyright registration are available free from the Copyright Office. The quickest and simplest method of obtaining registration forms is to phone:

The Forms and Publications Hotline, 202-707-9100

Alternatively, you can write:
The Register of Copyrights
Publications Section, LM-455
Library of Congress
Washington, DC 20559

Ask that the forms you need, as described below, be sent to you. The forms contain simple instructions, and you should have no trouble supplying the necessary information to register your claim.

When you've filled out the form, return it to the Copyright Office as per the instructions, along with two copies of the *best edition* of the song (if the work is published), and a check for $20, which is the filing fee. Within a few weeks, you'll receive the form back from the Register of Copyrights, validated with a copyright number, which verifies you've laid claim to copyright in the particular work.

Best edition means a copy of the song in its published form at the time of registration, e.g., printed sheet music as opposed to a handwritten lead sheet. (Lead sheets—sometimes called top lines—consist of the melody line and the lyrics, with chord changes usually indicated by letter symbol rather than being fully scored.) A compact disc would be considered the best edition if the song was published simultaneously on cassette.

If your work is published, send two copies of the sheet music, or two copies of the recording (including sleeve or jacket), along with the completed form and filing fee. However, if the work is one of several in a *collection*, such as a book of songs, or recorded album, you need only send one copy of the best edition.

As noted, the 1976 Copyright Act requires copies of the best edition of a published work to be deposited with the Library of Congress within three months of publication date, although failure to do so will not invalidate copyright protection. However, the Copyright Office can at any time demand that you make a deposit, and failure to comply with such demand may result in fines of up to $2,500.

If you're registering an *unpublished* work, send the completed form, the $20 filing fee, and one copy of the song (either a lead sheet or demo recording, whichever best represents the work). If the song is later published, it's a good idea to reregister it as published.

FORMS YOU NEED:

- **Form PA** for registering both published and unpublished songs.
- **Form SR** for published and unpublished sound recordings. (If you're registering a recorded performance *and* the songs rendered on the recording, you may register both claims with this one form, rather than separately filing an SR for the recording and a PA for the song.)
- **Form TX** for non-dramatic literary works. Use this form if you register a book of lyrics.
- **Form CA** for filing corrections or additional information about works previously registered.
- **Form VA** for registering visual arts (photos, models, prints, posters, album covers, designs, advertisements, etc.).

If you need to speak with a Copyright Office information specialist or request further information, you can telephone *202-707-3000* or write:

Copyright Office
Information Section, LM-401
Library of Congress
Washington, DC 20559

POOR MAN'S COPYRIGHT

Some songwriters and fledgling publishers attempt to save money by not registering copyright claims with the Library of Congress. Instead, they document their claim to copyright by putting a copy of the song in a sealed envelope and sending it to themselves by certified mail. They then leave the envelope sealed, believing the postmark will validate their copyright claim when the envelope is opened in a court of law.

The idea is to be able to prove that a copyright claim was made on a certain date, and that the work in question, therefore, could not have been cobbled together later in order to make a spurious claim against someone else's work. This method of copyright is sometimes acceptable by courts attempting to settle rival claims, but it is an iffy way to establish copyright ownership. It is always preferable to register your work with the Library of Congress, following the procedures laid down by the 1976 Act, because you could lose legal status to claim damages and royalties earned from unauthorized usages prior to the date of formal registration.

SHOULD YOU REGISTER A CLAIM FOR EVERY SONG?

Copyright fees add up at $20 a pop. Should you rush to file copyright claims on every new song you acquire, or should you wait until they're published? Remember, registering is not "copyrighting" a work. The work is already copyrighted upon creation. Your object is to establish it as a fact that you claim copyright to the work as of a certain date.

It's a bit paranoid to think that any legitimate producer or record company will rip off a song you send on demo, but you never know who might hear a tape once it leaves your hands. As long as the song is unreleased or otherwise unpublished, you could take a chance on using the poor-man method of sending copies to yourself by certified mail.

But a better bet is to compile a demo reel of numerous songs and register them all as one collection with the Library of Congress. Then, if and when one particular song is recorded or published in any form, you can file an individual copyright claim.

REJECTIONS OF COPYRIGHT CLAIMS

The Library of Congress is fairly liberal about what it will accept for registration. As noted above, mere registration does not imply the validity of a claim—just that a claim was made on a certain date to a work rendered on a copy deposited with the Library of Congress.

So, when you receive a certificate and copyright number for a song from the Register of Copyrights, you have not been given definitive judgment that your claim is impeccably valid; rather, you've been given certification that you have made claim to the work in question. If you register a song that is identical with another song, the work that is registered first obviously enjoys the advantage when a dispute arises over ownership.

Obvious rip-offs that the registrars at the Library of Congress can detect will be rejected. But just because they issue a certificate and copyright number does not mean that a work is not a rip-off, or that the copyright claim may not be invalidated by judicial procedures that establish infringement.

Public domain

Copyright protection is not forever. Under the 1909 Copyright Act, U.S. copyright owners could protect songs under copyright for an initial 28-year term with the opportunity to renew protection for a further 28 years. The 1976 Copyright Act brings the U.S. copyright law into line with most other countries (i.e., copyright protection can be claimed from time of publication until 50 years after the death of the writer).

Any work that outlives copyright protection is said to be in the *public domain*, or *PD*. Anyone can use a PD song in any manner, without permission or payment.

You cannot take a work from the public domain, such as "Yankee Doodle," and copyright it. But you can devise an arrangement of a public domain song and copyright the arrangement.

Thus, you can record a snatch of melody from a Mozart aria and release it without having to pay mechanical royalties. But you can also do this: You can rearrange the Mozart aria musically, set new lyrics to it, and then copyright the new arrangement. Then, if anyone wants to record your arrangement of Mozart's work, they have to obtain a license from you and pay you royalties.

Some publishers have managed to maintain a degree of copyright protection for works that were due to enter public domain by copyrighting new arrangements. For example, European copyright of Gilbert and Sullivan operettas expired in the 1970s. The publisher, Chappell Music, Ltd. (now Warner-Chappell), commissioned and copyrighted new arrangements of the works. Thus, Chappell still licenses Gilbert and Sullivan for theatrical productions, albeit the newly copyrighted versions.

The performing-right societies accept registration for new arrangements of public domain works, but they usually will not pay the full royalty rate. They evaluate the amount of new material in the arrangement and pay royalties based on the extent of the new work. For instance, they might judge that the amount of original material added to the PD work warrants payment of 25% of the normal royalty rate . . . or 50%, or whatever.

When filing a copyright claim for a new arrangement of a public domain work with the Library of Congress, the claimant must clearly designate the new matter added that justifies the claim.

Termination of publisher's rights

Songwriters can reclaim songs from publishers at any time during a five-year period after the 35th year of publication, or after the 40th year of assignment to the publisher, whichever comes first. The songwriter must notify the publisher that he intends to reclaim the copyright not less than two years (nor more than ten years) before the date of availability.

Under the old Copyright Act of 1909, as discussed, the initial term of copyright protection ended after 28 years, with a renewal provision for a further 28 years. Many songwriters were able to negotiate contracts that stipulated all rights would revert to themselves after the initial 28 years so they could make new publishing deals for the duration of the renewal period.

Under the 1976 Copyright Act, there is no renewal period, but songwriters can now reclaim songs from publishers at any time during a five-year period after the 35th year of publication (in sheet music, or record release, for instance), or after the 40th year of assignment to the publisher, whichever comes first.

For example, songwriter Jones assigns his song to Smith Music on January 1, 1979. A record is released of the song one year later, on January 1, 1980. If Jones wants to, he can take the publishing rights back from Smith Music any time between the years 2016 and 2021 (35 years after the first publication).

If, however, Jones made the assignment to Smith Music on January 1, 1979, and the song wasn't published until 1989, Jones can't exercise his right to reclaim the song until the year 2019 (40 years after the assignment was made to Smith, but still five years sooner than the 35th anniversary of the publication date).

The publication date, therefore, can be very important in determining the length of time a publisher controls a song. So it is essential that you, the publisher, carefully document actual publication dates for each song in your catalog.

In order for a songwriter to reclaim his song from a publisher under the Copyright Act's termination clause, he has to notify the publisher in writing that he intends to do so. Notification has to be given to the publisher not less than two years (nor more than ten years) before the date within the five-year period of availability that the songwriter wants to reclaim the right.

For instance, say writer Jones will be eligible to reclaim his song between the years 2015 and 2020. He decides he wants the song back at the first opportunity, the year 2015. He must, therefore, serve notice of reclaim to Smith Music sometime between the years 2005 and 2013.

If Jones forgets that he can do this and suddenly wakes up to the fact in the year 2017, for instance, he can notify Smith Music that he intends to reclaim the song in 2019. But if he neglects to reclaim the song within the five-year window of availability, he cannot do it thereafter.

If the songwriter is dead when the termination period looms, his heirs can terminate the publisher's right to the song. If there was more than one writer, the majority of them (or their heirs) must agree to the termination. Otherwise, the publisher may be able to maintain control of the work.

PUBLISHER'S RIGHTS AFTER TERMINATION
After termination, the publisher can no longer license or authorize further usages of the song, or collect monies arising from new usages. However, the publisher can continue to collect monies arising from *derivative* works (i.e., records, sheet music, synchronizations, etc.), which were duly authorized before

the termination took place—subject, of course, to the publisher continuing to account to the writer for all royalties as per their original agreement.

In other words, if Smith Music licenses a song to be released as a record in the year 2010, and writer Jones terminates Smith's right to the song as of 2015, Smith can continue to collect royalties from the record released in the year 2010 as long as it continues to sell.

EXCEPTION FOR "WORKS FOR HIRE"

Termination rights do not apply to songs created as *works for hire*. This applies to cases where songwriters are signed to exclusive agreements as *employees for hire*, as well as when composers are *commissioned* to write specific material for employers, such as movie themes. On works for hire, copyright claims are registered listing the employer (publisher) as "author" and the songwriter/composer as "employee for hire."

Since the songwriter waives copyright ownership *before* the work is created, copyright inherent upon creation belongs to the employer. Thus, the songwriter cannot *re*-claim a work for hire, since the writer never owned the copyright in the first place. The owner of a work for hire enjoys copyright protection for a period of either 75 years after date of publication, or 100 years after date of creation, whichever comes first.

Infringement

Copyright infringement occurs when someone makes an unauthorized copy of a copyrighted song. It also occurs when someone uses enough elements of a copyrighted song to be considered "substantial similarity." In other words, infringement is not limited to cases where copies are made note-for-note or word-for-word.

Infringement is a violation of copyright law, and is usually handled through civil lawsuits brought by the aggrieved party in federal court. In order to sue for copyright infringement, you must have first registered your copyright with the Library of Congress. If a case is proved, the court can issue an injunction against the defendant to cease and desist any further infringement. Criminal penalties can be imposed if the injunction is ignored.

The court can also order all copies of the infringing work to be destroyed and the defendant to reimburse the plaintiff for all financial loss incurred by the infringement. This can include an amount equal to all profits the infringer has made from the usage.

If someone uses your copyright as a movie theme or TV jingle, you can have expert witnesses testify as to what the fair market value of a synchronization license would be in similar usages to establish how much you should be awarded. In addition, the copyright owner may be awarded statutory damages for each work infringed (usually between $250 and $10,000), plus all court costs and reasonable attorney's fees.

Infringement doesn't necessarily have to be intentional. Indeed, cases abound where the guilty party wasn't consciously aware of copying an existing work. The situation is different, however, when someone, such as an organized counterfeiting organization, knowingly infringes a copyright for profit. Although infringement is normally treated as a civil matter, cases of blatant infringement might constitute criminal activity. In such cases, the copyright owner can bring criminal charges, and, if proven, the court can levy criminal penalties of imprisonment and fines of as much as $50,000 for each work infringed.

Fair use

One defense against a charge of infringement is the principle of *fair use*. This concept is incorporated into copyright law, and permits the reproduction of small amounts of copyrighted material for the purposes of critical review, parody, scholarship, news reporting, etc. The amount of copying must have no practical effect on the market for, or on the value of the original work, and must be used only for purposes of teaching, illustration, comment, criticism, quotation, or summary.

Compulsory licensing

In addition to the principle of "fair use," the Copyright Act makes certain exceptions to the monopoly of rights a copyright owner has with regard to licensing works. In particular, four special provisions are included which permit *compulsory licensing*. The term *compulsory license* means that the copyright owner *must* issue a license to a qualified user under certain conditions and upon payment by the user of statutory fees or royalties.

COMPULSORY LICENSING APPLIES TO:

Noncommercial transmissions by public broadcasters
This applies notably to Public Broadcasting System (PBS) and National Public Radio (NPR). Because they are partially taxpayer-funded, nonprofit operations, legislation was passed allowing public television and radio to use copyrighted material upon payment of preset fees, as opposed to the more market-oriented rates negotiated between the performing-right societies and commercial broadcasters.

Secondary transmission of works on cable

Because cable was the only means by which some households could receive television broadcasts, this provision of the Copyright Act allows cable companies the right to rebroadcast, transmit, or distribute programming by local television stations and networks. Cable companies can acquire compulsory licenses to rebroadcast copyrighted programs upon payment of specified fees.

Recording of musical compositions

(This subject is discussed in detail in the chapter on *Mechanical Licenses.*) The compulsory licensing provision of the Copyright Act applies only in cases where a song has been previously released. Until then, the copyright owner can withhold a license under the principle of *first use.*

First use means that until a song is released in phonorecord format, the copyright owner can (1) refuse to license anyone to record or release it or (2) charge any mechanical royalty rate without regard to the statutory rate established by the compulsory licensing provision of the copyright law.

The idea behind compulsory mechanical licenses is to prevent copyright owners from denying use of copyrighted material in phonorecords, as long as the user agrees to pay the statutory royalty monthly, the use is confined to non-dramatic performances of musical works in phonorecords only, and the work has been previously distributed to the public in phonorecord format.

Jukeboxes

The 1976 Copyright Act provided for a compulsory license to publicly perform nondramatic musical works by means of coin-operated phonorecord players (jukeboxes). However, the Berne Convention Implementation Act amended the law to provide for *negotiated licenses* between jukebox operators and copyright owners. This led to the establishment of the *JLO* (*Jukebox Licensing Office*), which is discussed in the chapter *Mechanical-Right Licensing.* Negotiated licenses now take precedence over compulsory licenses.

Summary

The subject of copyright is complex and frequently open to dispute and interpretation. Thick tomes are written about copyright; heated arguments arise in and out of court over the meaning of this or that clause, sentence, word, or punctuation mark. Also, copyright law in this and most major countries is in flux. There are amendments, adjustments, and precedent-making adjudications continuously.

You should keep abreast of changes and challenges to the law as it exists. Read more about it, attend seminars, and, as the last resort, hire a good copyright lawyer. Remember, *copyright law is the guardian of your product* as a publisher. That is why it is vital to understand and appreciate what it entails, and why it is vital to remain vigilant against any attempts from any quarter to dilute the protection the concept and law provides.

See the Appendix for a list of suggested books for further information about copyright law, and request a copy of the 1976 Copyright Act (as amended) from the Library of Congress, which is free for the asking.

CHAPTER 6

Songwriter Contracts

When a song is written, the songwriter is automatically vested with copyright ownership. Publishers then acquire copyrights from songwriters in one of two ways: on a song-by-song basis or under terms of an exclusive songwriter contract.

Under terms of a *single* or *individual song contract*, a songwriter assigns either *permanent* copyright ownership or *temporary* exclusive rights to the copyright of *one* song. Under terms of an *exclusive songwriter contract*, the songwriter assigns either *permanent* copyright ownership or *temporary* exclusive rights to the copyrights of *all* songs written during the term covered by the agreement.

In either type of assignment, the writer technically *sells* the copyright(s) to the publisher. Unless otherwise stated in the agreement, the sale is unconditional. This means there is no recourse for the writer to recapture the copyright if the publisher fails to initiate some form of commercial use of the song.

Divisibility of rights

When a writer assigns a song to a publisher, the publisher normally becomes the beneficial owner of all rights to the copyright for the duration of the term of assignment provided for in the agreement. But copyrights are *divisible*, meaning writers can theoretically assign (1) mechanical rights to one publisher, (2) print rights to another publisher, (3) performance rights to a third publisher, and (4) synchronization rights to yet a fourth publisher.

In practice, publishers strongly resist divisibility, since it severely limits potential benefits they might earn from a song's long-term success. They argue that their time and investment earns them the right to profit from any success the song has in every area. And

it stands to reason that a publisher won't put forth much effort to fully exploit a work in order for someone else to reap much of the rewards. Nor can publishers justify investing the same amount of effort in a copyright to which they have only partial rights as they would in one they fully control. Therefore, publishers expect and demand an assignment of all rights (the *bundle of rights*).

BUNDLE OF RIGHTS

The *bundle of rights* refers to those rights inherent in copyright ownership. A songwriter owns this bundle of rights by virtue of, and immediately upon, writing a song. Only the copyright owner may make and sell copies of the song—or authorize others to do so—in any format existing now or hereafter. Only the copyright owner may use or perform—or authorize others to use or perform—the song live, on film, radio, television or by any other method existing now or in the future.

When a songwriter assigns the bundle of rights by contract, the publisher in effect acquires every conceivable right in the territory covered by the agreement to use, license, and authorize the use of the song, or any part of the song (including title, lyrics, melody, chorus, storyline, etc.), for every conceivable purpose in any conceivable media or technology whether existing now or in the future.

The Bundle of Rights:
- to *reproduce* copies of the work (i.e., sheet music, phonorecords, etc.)
- to *distribute* copies of the work to the public by sale, rental, lease, or lending
- to *prepare* derivative works (adaptations, arrangements, dramatizations, etc.)
- to *perform* the work publicly
- to *display* the work publicly

So, despite divisibility allowed under current copyright law, it is rarely an issue, because writers normally assign publishers *an undivided interest* in all rights without quibble. After all, the songwriter doesn't really benefit from divisibility, and it is administratively messy for all concerned.

WHAT UNDIVIDED INTEREST MEANS

The term *undivided interest* might be confusing. There is always just *one* copyright in a work. Ownership of a copyright might be shared any number of ways, but there is still just one copyright. So, if three songwriters equally contribute to the creation of a song, each owns an undivided one-third interest in the copyright. The *ownership is divided* three ways, but the *copyright itself always remains undivided.*

Each of the three songwriters might assign or sell their respective ownership shares to a music publisher, and each music publisher can further assign the shares they acquire. In other words, various rights to the copyright can be divided and transferred or shared, but each divided portion of the copyright remains a portion of the whole, and all portions, when added together, total 100 per cent of one undivided copyright. Thus, if ownership of a copyright is "divided" into ten equal parts, each owner is deemed to own an undivided 10% interest in the copyright.

Negotiable contract terms

Some writers can demand better terms than others. This is especially true for writers with numerous hits to their credit, or when there is competition between publishers to acquire a song.

Songwriter contracts include these negotiable terms:
- Exclusions
- Duration
- Territory
- Advances
- Timing of advance payments
- Cross-collateralization
- Recoupment of expenses
- Royalties
- At source calculation of royalties

- Accounting period
- Performance clauses
- Options

EXCLUSIONS

Exclusions contractually prohibit a publisher from making certain uses of a copyright or authorizing others to do so. Depending upon the songwriter's negotiating clout, some exclusions may be absolute; others may merely require the publisher to first consult with and obtain permission from the writer before specific usages are made or authorized. Examples include the following.

First use mechanical licensing

The concept of *first use* is that a copyright owner can prevent anyone from releasing a recorded version of a song that has not yet been recorded and released. Once a recording has been authorized for release, however, the copyright owner can no longer prevent anyone from making similar use of the song as long as a mechanical license is obtained under the compulsory mechanical licensing provision of the Copyright Act.

Since the copyright owner controls the first use of a new song, a writer who is also a recording artist may fairly and understandably want to maintain the right of approval over who the publisher chooses to grant a mechanical license to for first use. The writer/artist may intend the song to be released first by himself/herself. If the writer is an established artist, this may pose no problem for the publisher who expects the song's value will be enhanced by the writer/artist releasing it.

But such consideration should not be indefinite. It would be unfair to the publisher for a writer to sit on a song throughout the term of agreement. Further, if the writer is not an established artist, withholding first use permission could impact on the song's value if the publisher is prevented from licensing a release by a really major act.

Compromise may take the form of the publisher agreeing to not issue a first use license until *X* months have elapsed from the time the writer first notified the publisher in writing that the song should be held. Or, a limit might be placed on the number of songs a writer can withhold from first use, either (a) during the term of the agreement or (b) at any one time.

Reduced royalty rates

The writer may successfully negotiate to prohibit the publisher from issuing mechanical licenses at rates less than the current statutory mechanical rate to any company affiliated or financially connected with the publisher. Prohibition of lower royalty rates and licensing fees may also apply to other users connected in any way with the publisher (e.g., jingles, films, television productions, foreign licensing, print, merchandising, etc.). In other words, any usage authorized by the publisher to a parent, subsidiary, or affiliated company must be made *at arm's length*, so as not to favor the publisher, parent company, affiliates, or subsidiaries at the writer's expense.

Altering, changing, editing, adapting

Publishers usually insist on the right to change, adapt, arrange, translate, or otherwise alter all works assigned by a writer. However, more established writers may negotiate the right to be consulted first, to approve or disapprove any changes, and to not have any royalty share diminished by the addition of other songwriters who make such changes. A songwriter may also insist on the right to be allowed to first make any changes proposed by the publisher, allowing third parties to attempt the changes only in the event the writer declines to do so, or in the event the writer's efforts fail to meet the publisher's objectives.

Specific types of licenses

Some songwriters, particularly more established ones, may insist on right of approval before the publisher can license the works in commercials, films, or other usages. Many writers get particularly hung up about "trivializing" their output through uses in commercials, parodies, sampling, etc. Others may be offended by the use of their material in X-rated movies, political campaigns, or for the promotion of certain products, such as tobacco or alcohol.

DURATION

Duration deals with the length of time the publisher has the rights to the song. The duration of the assignment can range from a few years to *life of copyright*. But, even though a contract might say "life of copyright," the writer can reclaim copyright within 35 to 40 years, unless the agreement states that the song is a *work for hire*, either because it was *commissioned* by the publisher, or was written by the songwriter as an *employee for hire*.

Publishers naturally strive to secure rights to songs for as long as possible, preferably for the life of copyright. Writers may try to negotiate contracts allowing them to recapture copyright after a much shorter period of time, say five or ten years.

Publishers argue that their expertise, time, and investment in a song earns them the right to benefit from any success the song has over the long term. But a writer with a track record of hits may successfully insist on getting the copyright back much sooner as a condition of assignment.

Also, publishers vying with competitors to sign established writers may acquiesce to writers' demands to return the copyright after a limited period of time. Thus, duration of copyright assignment is ultimately determined by the songwriter's negotiating power.

In any event, agreements between songwriters and publishers normally result in long relationships. Even after a publisher's rights terminate, when a songwriter recaptures the copyright, the publisher generally continues collecting royalties earned from licenses issued prior to the date of termination. So agreements should be carefully understood by both parties at the time of signing, because publishers and songwriters will be in business together for years to come, as far as the works involved are concerned.

TERRITORY

Territory deals with the particular country or countries in which the copyright assignment is operative. Standard songwriter contracts assign the publisher rights to the song for the *world*. But, again, a songwriter's negotiating power may enable him to limit the territory to one country or group of countries (the United States, or the United States and Canada, for instance).

A songwriter might resist worldwide assignment to an indie publisher who doesn't have foreign offices, and therefore licenses rights to subpublishers. The songwriter might argue that sublicensing would reduce his foreign royalties and could want to negotiate contracts directly with overseas publishers himself.

The publisher could counter that if he makes the song a hit, thereby increasing the copyright's worldwide value, he should rightfully benefit from his efforts. Also, he might add, it is unrealistic for a songwriter who isn't somewhat established, with solid overseas contacts, to expect to be able to obtain competent foreign representation in every territory. A standoff might be avoided if the publisher agrees to calculate the writer's foreign royalties *at source* (see below).

ADVANCES

Advances represent a commitment by the publisher that his efforts to promote the song will earn at least a certain sum of money for the writer in the near term. Where the publisher is acting in a banker capacity, the advance is a form of loan against earnings the publisher and the songwriter mutually believe will materialize near term. In addition to the size of the advance, related issues include the *timing* of payment or payments, whether certain publishing *expenses* may be added to the advance account and recouped from royalties, and whether *cross-collateralization* is allowed.

Not every songwriter contract calls for an advance. Some writers are satisfied with certain commitments by the publisher to achieve certain goals within a specified period of time (see *performance clauses,* late in this chapter). Advances are usually *nonreturnable*, meaning writers do not have to repay them if the song fails to *recoup* (earn sufficient income for the publisher to get his investment back).

See the chapter on *Acquisitions* for detailed discussion of advances, including methods used to calculate the size of an advance, forecasting income, structuring payments, cross-collateralization, and recoupment of expenses.

TIMING OF ADVANCE PAYMENTS

The *timing of advance payments* determines whether or not the publisher must part with the agreed advance in one fell swoop or parcel it out in installments over time, perhaps triggered by milestone events. With individual song contracts, advances are usually paid in one lump sum, upon signing. For exclusive songwriter contracts, incremental or installment payments are more common.

CROSS-COLLATERALIZATION

Cross-collateralization is a method publishers use to reduce the risks of not being able to recoup advances. It allows royalties earned by one song to be applied against the unrecouped advances still owed for other songs.

For example, if Smith Music advances songwriter Jones $100 for each of two songs published under separate, cross-collateralized agreements, then Jones owes Smith Music $200 against any royalties earned by either work. If Song A earns Jones $500 in royalties, but song B never earns a penny, Smith Music can deduct the full $200 advanced for both songs from the earnings of Song A, paying Jones a net $300.

If Jones successfully demanded there be no cross-collateralization, Smith Music could only deduct the $100 specifically advanced for song A from its $500 earnings. Smith would have to write off the $100 advance for song B.

RECOUPMENT OF EXPENSES

Recoupment of expenses is a rather controversial policy from the writer's viewpoint. Under this provision, the publisher adds ordinary publishing expenses, such as copyright registration fees, lead sheets, demos, copying, etc., to the writer's advance account. The publisher then reimburses its expenses from the writer's royalties.

Songwriters generally feel these expenses should be absorbed by the publisher as a cost of doing business. They question the justification of recouping the cost of publishing from their earnings. The publisher's likely answer would be that he is bankrolling the writer, that he is bearing the financial risk, and that he is the one who stands to lose if the song doesn't earn any money. This may or may not satisfy the writer. But even

where a publisher normally charges writers' accounts for such expenses, exceptions may be made for writers with sufficient negotiating clout.

ROYALTIES

Publishers normally pay newer writers 50% of all income received from licensees. More established writers and some self-contained acts with recording deals may warrant higher percentages (60% - 75%), or even the right to retain a percentage of the publishing ownership (i.e., 50% writer's royalty, plus 50% of publishing = 75% of income). Self-contained acts might argue for the higher royalty rate because, from their point of view, a significant part of the publisher's role (getting the songs commercially released) has been eliminated by their own status or initiative.

In cases where publishers print their own sheet music, songwriters' royalties are specified in dollars and cents or a percentage of the selling price of the printed music. Otherwise, the writer usually receives the same percentage of the publisher's print royalty receipts as with other types of income (i.e., mechanicals, performances, synchronizations, foreign, etc.).

AT SOURCE ROYALTY CALCULATIONS

At source is a term describing a method of calculating royalties. It usually applies to subpublishing songs with overseas companies, but can also pertain to any situation where the publisher sublicenses a copyright. Essentially, a contract provision requiring the publisher to pay the writer based on income earned *at source* means that the publisher cannot calculate royalties on net receipts, or income received after the licensee has deducted its percentage.

Typically, songwriters without sufficient clout to negotiate at source royalty calculations are paid a percentage of what their publishers receive from subpublishers or other licensees. For example, if a writer's contract calls for 50% of all net receipts, and the publisher's German subpublisher retains 25% of earnings in that country, then the writer would receive 50% of 75% of any income earned in Germany.

But, if the writer is paid based on earnings at source, and the German publisher retains 25%, the publisher must factor the subpublisher's share back into net receipts and pay the writer 50%. The effect is that of all earnings in Germany, the writer receives 50%, the subpublisher retains 25%, and the publisher is left with 25%, instead of 37.5% (50% of 75%).

	Writer's share based on net receipts	Writer's share based on at source earnings
Total Earnings	$100.00	$100.00
Subpublisher share (25%)	$25.00	$25.00
Net receipts	$75.00	$75.00
Writer share (50%)	$37.50	$50.00
Publisher net	$37.50	$25.00

If a writer and publisher cannot agree on whether at source royalty calculations will be made on foreign earnings, a compromise might be reached whereby a subpublisher's retention fees are limited to a maximum percentage of gross at source income. For instance, if the writer successfully negotiated to be paid based on allowing subpublishers a maximum retention fee of 20%, then the writer would be paid 50% of 80% (40%) of all earnings at source. And if, in that case, the subpublisher's retention fee was actually 25%, the earnings would be distributed as follows:

Writer's share based on maximum of 20% allowed for subpublisher retention fee	
Gross receipts	$100.00
Maximum allowed subpublisher share (20%)	$20.00
Net royalty calculation base (80%)	$80.00
Writer share (50%)	$40.00
Actual subpublisher share (25%)	$25.00
Publisher net (35%)	$35.00

As you can see, if the publisher allows the writer a ceiling on net receipts royalty calculations, and makes a subpublishing deal that gives the subpublisher a retention fee above that ceiling, then the publisher must absorb the difference. (In the above example, the writer gets 40% and the publisher ends up with 35%.) In any case, the writer's share of performance income is collected and paid directly by the performing-right societies, and is not subject to dilution by any subpublishing fees.

ACCOUNTING PERIOD

Publishers normally provide royalty statements twice yearly, within 30, 45, 60, or 90 days of 30 June and 31 December, along with payment for any monies due less any advances outstanding. Writers naturally want payment quickly, and so might argue for statements within 30 days of the accounting period's end, and more sought-after, established writers may be able to negotiate quarterly rather than semi-annual accountings.

In a few extreme cases of songwriter negotiating clout, the publisher may even agree to pay the writer's share of all income within 15-30 days of receipt, which means the publisher would be issuing payments frequently during the year. Few songwriters see any reason why publishers should hold on to their money longer than it takes to write out a check, especially since publishers may have received much of the royalties several months before the required time to account.

Publishers prefer to hold the money in an interest-bearing account for as long as possible. The optimum period from the publisher's standpoint, then, is semi-annual accountings within 90 days of the period's end. Publishers with large catalogs can accumulate significant extra income from interest on writers' money.

The one thing every publisher should try to avoid is contractual obligations to pay different writers at different times. Royalty accounting should be a uniform procedure, and statements for all writers should be issued at the same time every period.

PERFORMANCE CLAUSES

As a condition of copyright assignment, some writers demand the publisher accomplish (perform) certain milestone achievements within a specific period of time. This occurs frequently when there is no, or a relatively low, advance paid, in order to put some onus on the publisher to justify the songwriter's parting with the copyright. (An advance usually carries with it the implication that the publisher will work the song in order to recover the investment.) Performance clauses may impose one or more of the following obligations on the publisher:

- Obtain a record release within one year (or six months) of the agreement's date.
- Publish the song in sheet music form.
- Get the song used in a feature film, television production, or advertising jingle.
- Pay an additional advance (sometimes a nominal sum of $50-$100) as a condition of retaining rights to the song if the performance obligation has not been met within the allotted time.

OPTIONS

Options usually permit the publisher to extend the length of the copyright assignment upon giving notice to the writer. An option may also be used to extend the length of time a writer's exclusive services are committed to the publisher. Typically, publishers must either meet certain conditions, such as payment of an additional advance or getting a record released, in order to pick up an option, but not always. Sometimes, an option may be exercised if the writer fails to meet some obligation, such as turning in a certain number of commercially acceptable songs.

Analyzing a single-song contract

A *single-song agreement* between a publisher and writer of a specific song typically contains the following recitals and provisions:
- Date of agreement
- Name and address of publisher
- Name and address of songwriter(s)

In the event the song has more than one writer, the agreement specifies the share of royalties due each writer. For example: Smith and Jones write a song together. Jones writes all the music (50%) and half the lyrics (25%), for a total share of 75%; Smith's share is thus 25% (0% for music and 25% for lyrics).

There follows a boilerplate declaration worded something like:

WITNESSETH: In consideration of the following agreement and of the sum of one ($1.00) dollar and other good and valuable consideration in hand paid by the publisher to the writer, receipt of which is hereby acknowledged, the parties agree as follows:

The writer hereby sells, assigns, transfers, and delivers to the publisher, its successors or assigns, the original musical composition entitled [*title of song*] as written and composed by the above-named writer, including all rights, claims and demands of every nature to the title, words, and music, and all copyrights thereto, including but not limited to the copyright registration number [*copyright registration number*] of the composition, including but not limited to the grand rights and exclusive copyrights relating thereto *throughout the world*, and to have and to hold the said copyrights and all rights of whatsoever nature now or hereafter existing under any agreements relative thereto, *for and during the full term of all said copyrights*.

WARRANT OF EXCLUSIVITY

Next, there follows a *warrant of exclusivity* wherein the writer declares that the lyrics and music of the song were written solely and exclusively by himself/herself, that the work is wholly original and does not infringe upon any other copyrighted material, that no other claims exist to the song (from other writers or publishers, etc.), and that the writer therefore is fully empowered to make the agreement.

CONSIDERATION OF AGREEMENT

Then comes a further *consideration of agreement* (in addition to the token $1.00 cited in the first paragraph) wherein the publisher promises various compensations to the writer, namely advances and royalties.

Advance

The first compensation specified is the amount of any advance against potential royalties the publisher will pay the writer. The usual contractual wording would be something like this:

Publisher hereby agrees to pay the writer the sum of $__ as a non-returnable advance against royalties payable to writer hereunder. *Said advance, and any further advance that may be paid, shall be deducted from any payments due the writer hereunder or due to the writer heretofore or hereafter under terms and conditions of any other agreement now existing or later entered into between the parties hereto.**

*NOTE: This allows the publisher to cross-collateralize advances.

Royalties

Then follows an itemization of royalties and fees the publisher agrees to pay on earnings of the song. Sometimes the itemization is dealt with in an attached *Exhibit* to the agreement, rather than being spelled out within the body of the agreement.

The usual royalty schedule is as follows:

Piano copies:
____¢ per copy for each piano copy sold and paid for in the U.S. and Canada.

8¢-10¢ is the normal rate; *piano copy* is the terminology for printed sheet music of a single song. This rate applies only to piano copies printed by the publisher.

All other printed editions:
___% of the net wholesale price of each copy *printed by the publisher* of all other printed editions (folios or other collected works), *prorated by the number of songs* contained in the edition, sold and paid for in the U.S. and Canada.

10%-12% of net wholesale price per copy sold is a normal rate. If the writer's song is contained in folios and collections with other works, the royalty rate as stated above shall be *prorated* in ratio to the number of all works contained in the edition licensed by the publisher. In other words, a folio of ten songs, selling for $15 with a 10% royalty rate, would pay the writer a royalty of 15¢ for one song ($15 x 10% = $1.50 ÷ 10 = 15¢).

Printed editions licensed:
____% of all net sums received by the publisher for all piano copies, folios, or other collected works *licensed by, but not issued by the publisher*, sold and paid for in the U.S. and Canada. (*50% is the normal rate.*)

For works issued in folios and collections with other works, the royalty rate as stated above shall be prorated in ratio to the number of all works contained in the edition licensed by the publisher. In other words, if the publisher receives $100 for a folio of ten songs, for which the combined writers' share is 50%, then $50 is divided by ten, and the writer of the song in this agreement receives $5.

Mechanical and synchronization royalties:
____% of all net sums received by the publisher from mechanical and synchronization licenses (records, discs, tapes, usages of the song in theatrical and television films, etc.).

50% is the normal rate, though writers with significant bargaining power have negotiated as much as 75%.

Note the terminology of all net sums received by the publisher. Many publishers issue mechanical and synchronization licenses through a mechanical-right licensing agency, most notably the Harry Fox Agency in New York.

For mechanical licenses, the Harry Fox Agency retains 4.5% for its services. Thus, the publisher receives 95.5% of the total monies collected for record sales, and pays the writer 50% of that, or 47.75% of total monies earned.

For synchronization licenses, Fox charges publishers 5% of the fee or $2,200, whichever is less.

Foreign royalties:
____% of all net sums received by the publisher from sales and all other usages in countries outside of the U.S. and Canada.

50% is the normal rate, although, again, writers with strong bargaining power have negotiated as much as 75%.

There is a usual disclaimer here that the publisher may sublicense or otherwise assign some or all of the foreign rights to various overseas publishers (subpublishers).

Customary deals between U.S. publishers and foreign publishers grant the foreign firm the right to license and collect all monies arising from any and all sources, like record sales, originating in that country. The foreign publisher may issue the license through a mechanical-right society, such as MCPS in England, which might deduct as much as 10% for its services.

Should the recording gross $100 in mechanical royalties, the licensing agency pays 90% ($90) to the foreign publisher, whose agreement with the U.S. publisher allows it to retain, say, 25% or $22.50 ($90 x 25%). The foreign publisher then remits the balance ($67.50) to the U.S. publisher, who then pays the writer 50% of that ($33.75).

All other usages:
____% of all net sums received by the publisher for all other usages not otherwise specified in the agreement (*normally 50%*).

"Net sums" = all income received by the publisher after deduction of collection and administration fees from licensing agents, mechanical-right societies, and foreign subpublishers.

It is, perhaps, appropriate to point out here how advances received by the publisher from licensees should be treated in so far as the writer is concerned. Songwriters do not share in advances paid for the rights to license the publisher's catalog. There is no way to accurately project and prorate how much, if any, a particular song from the catalog will earn under the licensing agreement. Therefore, it is impractical for a writer to insist on a portion of a publisher's catalog advance.

However, when a publisher receives an advance for a specific work, then the writer customarily receives a proportionate share. For instance, the publisher might be paid an advance for the use of a song in a TV-marketed album. If the writer's contract calls for 50% of mechanical royalties, the writer would be entitled to 50% of the advance. Of course, if the writer owed unrecouped advances to the publisher, the writer's share of the advance would be applied to the unrecouped balance.

Professional copies:
No payments will be made to the writer for complimentary *professional* copies issued (and not sold or resold) for the purposes of promotion, public relations, and advertising.

Performance income:
Writer shall not share any monies received by publisher from any performing-right society that makes payments directly to writer.

Writers must become members of one of the performing-right societies, BMI, ASCAP, or SESAC. The societies distribute performance royalties directly to their members.

ACCOUNTINGS

Accounting procedures must be specified, either in the body of the agreement, or in an attached *exhibit*.

Timing of royalty statements is the first item. As discussed above in the section on negotiable terms, this is normally twice yearly for the periods ending 30 June and 31 December. The publisher agrees to provide royalty statements, along with payment for any monies due, within (*30, 45, 60, or 90*) days of the end of each accounting period.

This clause should also clarify that royalties due

for the period shall be applied to any advance outstanding. The table below demonstrates how much two writers will actually get paid when both owe advances of $200, but one earns royalties of $500 while the other only earns $100.

Writer A		Writer B	
Royalties earned:	$100	Royalties earned:	$500
Advance owed:	-$200	Advance owed:	-$200
Balance due writer:	($100)	Balance due writer:	$300
Remaining advance:	$100	Remaining advance:	- 0 -

The contract may further provide that if royalties payable for the period amount to less than a certain sum (say, $10), payment will be deferred until a future accounting period when accumulated royalties are greater than that sum.

There is usually a disclaimer that unless the writer objects to a rendered statement in writing within six months of receipt of the statement, the statement will be considered accepted as rendered.

Writer's right to audit publisher:

Upon written advance notice from the writer, the publisher will allow the writer or the writer's representative to examine at the publisher's place of business during normal business hours all books, records, documents, licenses, statements, accountings, and other instruments relating to the song, for the purpose of verifying royalty statements rendered or delinquent under the terms of the agreement.

Many publishers permit audits only once a year in order to prevent nuisance audits. They may also require the audit to be done by a certified public accountant (CPA) to prevent time-wasting by individuals who don't understand accounting procedures.

Some agreements require the publisher to pay for the audit if an underpayment of, say, 5% or more is revealed. In all fairness, a writer shouldn't have to pay a CPA's hefty fee in order to recover money legitimately owed by the publisher. On the other hand, a publisher who accounts accurately shouldn't be unfairly penalized by having to pay the writer's CPA for an audit that confirms everything is in order.

PERFORMANCE CLAUSE

If the writer successfully negotiates a performance clause, this section details that condition of assignment whereby the publisher shall perform, or cause to perform, the specified act or acts within a specified period of time. As discussed above (see negotiable terms), typical performance obligations include one or more of the following:

• Publisher guarantees to have the song recorded and released on record within one year of the agreement's date,
• Publisher guarantees to have the song published in sheet music form,
• Publisher guarantees to license the song for use in a feature film, or television production, or advertising jingle,
• Publisher guarantees to pay an additional advance (amount specified) as a condition of retaining rights to the song.

If the publisher fails to perform as stipulated within the allotted time, the writer can issue, by certified mail, a written demand that the failure be cured within 30 days. If the publisher fails to remedy the default within 30 days of receiving the demand, the writer may recapture all rights to the song.

DEFAULTS

In addition to a failure by the publisher to meet milestone performance obligations, the failure to perform other contractual obligations (such as proper and timely accounting of royalties) can result in the writer recapturing the work. Normally, default clauses state that in order for the writer to recapture the song, the writer must first send a written demand by certified mail. Only if the failure is not then remedied by the publisher within 30 days can the writer recapture the song.

The publisher usually manages to limit liability for recapture with a sentence worded something to the effect that if any one section of the agreement is found to be invalid in a court of law, that section shall not affect the validity of any other section of the agreement. A further publisher's hedge may be a contractual provision stating that the writer must act to issue a written demand to cure within X days of becoming aware of the publisher's failure.

The writer can retain options to later recapture the copyright by insisting on contractual wording stating that any failure to demand a fault be cured shall not affect the writer's right to later insist that any other faults or failures be cured.

CREATIVE CONTROL

The writer will agree to any changes, edits, translations, arrangements, adaptations, dramatizations, etc. that the publisher considers necessary to commercially exploit the song. This may include a change of title, setting new lyrics to the music, or new music to the lyrics. The publisher may instruct the writer to make the changes, or, at its own discretion, may commission others to do so.

If the song is an instrumental, the publisher will have the right to commission another writer to write lyrics (not subject to the composer's approval), and the composer shall then be entitled to only one-half the royalties otherwise due.

As the one who invests time and money in the song and asserts an expertise in knowing how best to achieve commercial success, the publisher usually insists on final creative control over the song. This clause tends to aggravate songwriters, and it is not often acted upon by the publisher in reality. Nevertheless, the publisher should retain the final say.

Some writers may fairly demand the right to at least attempt such changes in the song (new lyrics, adaptations, etc.) as directed by the publisher. But, as publisher, you will want to maintain the right of subjective approval of their changes and the subsequent right to assign others to make changes if the writer's attempts are commercially unsatisfactory in your opinion.

RIGHT TO PUBLICIZE NAME AND LIKENESS

The publisher, his successors and assigns, will be permitted to use the writers' name and likeness on the cover or label of any recording, folio, piano copy, etc., and to otherwise use or authorize others to use the name and likeness to promote and advertise the song.

RECOUPMENT OF EXPENSES

In order to promote the song, it's essential to produce a demonstration recording, or *demo*. Some publishers consider demos an ordinary business expense and don't charge the costs to the writer. Other publishers do charge these costs to the writer, or at least a portion of the costs, and recoup them from the writer's royalties. In effect, charged demo costs constitute another form of advance.

There are also other expenses some publishers charge back to the writer, including copyright registration fees, lead sheets, copying, and advertising. If you do charge any type of expenses to writers, the policy should be clearly set forth in the agreement, and each category of expense should be specified.

THIRD-PARTY LEGAL ACTIONS

The publisher will, at his own expense, initiate and prosecute any legal action against alleged infringers of the copyrighted song. All monies won as a result of such legal actions are usually divided 50/50 between publisher and writers after deduction of legal costs incurred by the publisher.

If another party alleges that the song infringes another copyright, the publisher will notify the writer in writing of the claim, and shall have the right to defend, settle or otherwise dispose of the claim in whatever manner he decides. Until such a claim is settled, the publisher shall hold in escrow all royalties accumulating to the writer for the song.

If the allegation is settled in favor of the claimant, any monies paid to the claimant by the publisher, along with all legal costs incurred by the publisher, may be deducted from any and all monies due the writer from the publisher, whether or not such monies were due before or after the claim was settled.

The writer may be allowed to put up a bond to indemnify the publisher against losses arising from an infringement claim, rather than have the publisher hold royalties in escrow pending settlement of a claim.

POWER OF ATTORNEY

The writer irrevocably gives the publisher the right to execute, sign, make, transfer, acknowledge, and deliver any instrument necessary to vest in the publisher any and all of the rights referred to in the agreement. The publisher may in turn authorize others to execute, sign, make, transfer, acknowledge, and deliver any such instrument on behalf of himself or the writer.

RIGHT OF ASSIGNMENT

The publisher reserves the right to assign the agreement (including his obligations to the writer thereunder), or to sell, license, transfer, or otherwise dispose of all or part of his rights and obligations arising from the agreement, to any individual, firm, or corporation. Any such transfer of rights carries with it the obligation by the assignee to pay royalties to writer as stipulated in the agreement.

JURISDICTION

This agreement shall be construed under the laws of (the *state* of _____ if in the USA, or name of *country*, or *province* if not in the USA.).

NATURE OF AGREEMENT CLARIFIED

This agreement does not constitute a partnership or joint venture between the parties hereto.

CLOSING BOILERPLATE STATEMENTS

If any part of this agreement is adjudged invalid or unenforceable, the balance of this agreement shall not be affected.

This agreement represents the entire understanding between the parties and shall be binding upon and shall inure to the benefit of the parties hereto and their respective heirs, assigns, legal representatives, and successors in interest.

IN WITNESS WHEREOF, the parties hereto have affixed their signatures and seals the day and year first above written.

Analyzing exclusive songwriter agreements

Since a publisher's stock in trade is songs, it is desirable to have reliable sources of quality songwriting talent to provide new material. Writers who consistently produce commercial songs are eagerly sought after by publishers wanting to sign them to *exclusive songwriter agreements.*

All songs written during the term of an exclusive agreement are automatically assigned to the publisher. Exclusivity means the writer may not use his craft for, or assign any of his works to any other publisher during the term of agreement. In most exclusive agreements, writers also assign all songs written to-date not already assigned to other publishers, including those not previously published, as well as copyrights recaptured from other publishers.

Exclusive agreements typically contain the same provisions discussed above regarding individual or single-song agreements, except that exclusive contracts cover *all works* written during the term of the agreement. Since most if not all of the songs have not been written at the time the agreement is signed, the writer agrees to execute a supplemental *acknowledgment letter* for each song, as and when it is delivered (see below). For existing songs in the writer's catalog that are assigned at the date of the agreement, a schedule of titles is attached to the contract.

Exclusive songwriter agreements typically contain provisions that differ from single-song contracts in the following respects:

DURATION OF SERVICES

Exclusive songwriter agreements are *personal service contracts* in which the songwriter agrees to provide services (songwriting) to the publisher during the term agreed. Service contracts can't be open-ended; there must be a cut-off date where the service provider is free to renegotiate or take his or her services elsewhere.

Most exclusive songwriter contracts bind writers to an initial one-year term, with options to extend the agreement. The number of options is usually limited to between two and four additional one-year terms. Some states invalidate personal service contracts that extend beyond a set number of years. California, for instance, caps personal service contracts at seven years. New York's limit is ten years.

Aside from limiting the time a writer can be exclusively bound to a publisher, some states also require publishers to guarantee writers a minimum level of income during each year of an agreement, otherwise the contract may be invalidated. This means the publisher must provide an annual advance equal to at least the minimum income required by the state in the event royalty revenue does not meet the statutory threshold.

The legal motivation of these statutes is to protect the service provider's ability to earn a livelihood. Since the writer has in effect become the publisher's exclusive property, he or she is ostensibly prohibited from earning a living through the exercise of his or her craft for anyone other than the publisher during the term of agreement. In addition, since most exclusive writer agreements require the writer to assign all works in his or her back catalog that have not been previously published, the writer is further restricted from pursuing outside opportunities to earn money from his or her work.

California courts have ruled personal service contracts unenforceable when the writer's annual income from the publisher falls short of $9,000. So, for an exclusive songwriter agreement to be enforceable in California, the publisher must cap the duration of agreement at seven years and guarantee the writer will receive at least $9,000 in each year. The monetary guarantee can, of course, be in the form of a nonreturnable advance, recoupable from royalty earnings.

Options

Most exclusive agreements bind the writer for an initial one-year term with options for the publisher to renew the agreement for further one-year periods (i.e., four one-year options, making the contract a five-year-agreement, if all options are exercised). Structuring a contract by one-year options is to the publisher's advantage. The publisher has an "out" if the writer's services prove to be unprofitable to the company. Rather than locking in a commitment to pay the writer advances over, say, a five-year period, the publisher can simply not pick up its options and cut its losses.

Options to extend the original term are rarely available to the writer. The publisher usually has the prerogative to exercise an option whether the writer wishes it or not, providing the publisher has fulfilled all its obligations during the preceding term.

There are two contractual methods by which a publisher can exercise an option: *passive* and *active.* In the passive method, the option is automatically picked up unless the publisher notifies the writer prior to 30, 60, or 90 days (or whatever) of the current term's end that it does not intend to pick up the option. If the publisher wishes to continue the relationship, it takes no overt action. But if the contract's option provision is active, the publisher must serve written notice to the writer at least 30, 60, or 90 days prior to the end of each current term that the option will be exercised.

DURATION OF COPYRIGHT ASSIGNMENT

This section deals with the period of time, or *duration*, that the publisher owns or controls copyrights created during the writer's contract term. A songwriter in a strong negotiating position may be able to recapture all works at the end of the contract term itself, subject to certain *retention* provisions (see below). Some agreements may allow the writer to only regain works that were not commercially released during the contract term, and some contracts may allow recapture after a relatively short period of time, such as five or ten years.

Employee for hire

Many exclusive agreements, however, term the writer as an *employee for hire*. As such, the writer is not entitled to reclaim the rights to any of the songs written under the agreement (the publisher retains all songs for life of copyright). If this is the case, the contract must make clear that songs written under the agreement are construed as *works for hire*, and the copyrights thereto shall be totally owned by, and in the name of, the *employer*.

Though the copyright to a work for hire is in the name of the publisher, the songwriter receives full songwriting credit on all label copy, sheet music, film credits, registrations, licenses, etc., and the songwriter's share of royalty and fee income is not normally affected when a song is a work for hire. So what's the difference?

Remember, when a song is written, the creator is automatically vested with copyright ownership. The writer can assign copyright interest to a publisher but still be eligible to recapture the copyright under conditions previously discussed in the chapter on *Copyright* (i.e., after a lapse of the prerequisite number of years, and/or other conditions of assignment between the writer and publisher).

Under a work for hire agreement, the writer has no vested interest in the copyright. The writer was hired or commissioned to write the song *prior* to actually writing it. The writer is never eligible to recapture the copyright, because he never had it in the first place. If the employer or commissioner fails to meet all obligations laid down in the contract, the writer's only recourse is to sue for damages (although such a suit might include a demand that the copyright be assigned to the writer).

Commission to write vs. employee for hire

A copyright can be a work for hire in one of two ways. In typical exclusive songwriter agreements, the writer is "hired" (an employee for hire) to create songs *within the scope of his or her employment.* Officially, this means there must be a continuing business relationship during the creative process in which the employer guides, supervises, and oversees the writer and/or provides facilities, equipment, and materials.

The other approach is when the employer *commissions* the writer to create works for a specific use, such as a film or television production, a jingle, translation, or adaptation, etc. Once the commissioned work is completed, the relationship officially ends. The commissioned material is a *work for hire*, though the creator is not an employee, since there is no ongoing relationship.

Retention period

Where the writer is not an employee for hire, the writer can reclaim the copyrights after 35-40 years, as noted in the chapter on *Copyright*. But some agreements allow writers to recapture songs sooner (i.e., five or ten years from the contract expiration date). Other agreements may only assign the songs to the publisher for the actual term of agreement (the writer recaptures the works upon the contract's expiration).

In such cases, the publisher should retain rights to any songs commercially released during the last one or two years of the agreement. This *right of retention* is usually for a further period of at least one year.

A *retention period* allows the publisher to fully benefit from exploitation efforts made as the contract nears its end. Without rights of retention, publishers would be reluctant to invest time and money working songs in a contract's final year, as there wouldn't be sufficient time remaining to profit from their efforts.

Derivative works

Aside from a retention period, publishers should argue for the right to collect monies arising from *derivative works* (i.e., licenses issued before the expiration of the agreement for records, sheet music, synchronizations, etc.). The argument may not succeed, but the rationale is simple: The publisher should be able to continue to profit from its exploitative efforts undertaken during the agreement term. (See "publisher's right after termination" in the chapter on *Copyright*).

ADVANCES

Songwriters obviously need some type of inducement to enter into an exclusive contract. The most common inducements are monetary advances, recouped by the publisher from royalties earned by the writer's works. Advances may be made either as a lump cash payment upon signing, or as a draw (i.e., periodic payments prorated weekly, monthly, quarterly, or annually). They might also be triggered by milestone events, such as achievement of certain income levels, release of albums, marking an anniversary of the contract's signing date, exercise of options, delivery of commercially acceptable songs, chart placings, etc.

Advances for exclusive songwriters are always *cross-collateralized* to cover all songs written during the term. They are also usually cross-collateralized with any songs written under previous agreements and/or future agreements with the publisher.

Writers with significant bargaining power may receive cash inducements that are not recoupable (signing bonuses). And some inducements may be nonmonetary, such as a recording contract with the publisher's affiliated record company.

The agreement should specify the amount of advances paid to the writer during term and the dates or timing of payments. For example, $5,000 upon signing, and $5,000 at the end of each succeeding quarter; or $250 each week, payable biweekly, etc. The amount of any advances paid during each option period must also be specified. Will it be the same as during the initial term, or will the amounts increase during each option period? See the chapter on *Acquisitions* for detailed discussion of advances.

ACKNOWLEDGMENT LETTERS

The writer should agree to promptly execute an *acknowledgment letter* for each song written under the agreement. These letters serve to document each song written, and the writer's acknowledgment that the particular song is assigned to the publisher as per terms of the agreement. A sample acknowledgment letter is shown below.

Sample Acknowledgment Letter

To: *[name of publisher]*   Date:_____
    [publishers address]

Re: Exclusive Songwriter Agreement dated _____
by and between *[name of songwriter]* and *[name of publisher]*.

Gentlemen:

I hereby acknowledge that the following musical composition(s) was/were written by the undersigned and assigned to you as per the terms of the above referenced Exclusive Songwriter Agreement:

TITLE(S)   OTHER WRITER(S)   MY SHARE (%)

_____
WRITER'S SIGNATURE

PERFORMANCE CLAUSES

Obligations contractually imposed on the publisher may include performance clauses such as those discussed previously in the section on individual song contracts. But since an exclusive agreement covers all the writer's output, a performance clause that guarantees a recorded release would reference a guaranteed *minimum number* of songs commercially released during each option period. Other performance clause provisions may guarantee that the writer's earnings during each period reach a certain level, or that the earnings are sufficient to cancel any outstanding advances.

Writer's obligations

But performance obligations can cut both ways. Since exclusive agreements are ongoing (i.e., covering the writer's output during each option period), the songwriter may be required to meet certain milestone achievements as well.

The most common obligation imposed on a writer is to submit a minimum number of new songs during the term. The songs must meet the publisher's standards of commercial quality. Requiring songs to be acceptable by the publisher is to prevent disgruntled writers from fulfilling delivery commitments with junk.

Just as a publisher's performance obligations may include the commercial release of a certain number of songs during the term, the tables may well be turned on writers who are also producers or artists. These types of writers are usually signed in expectation that their collateral work will generate commercially released material assigned to the publisher. In such situations, advances may be payable as and when songs are actually released.

If performance requirements are imposed on a writer for delivery of songs or commercial releases, the number of songs accepted as fulfilling the requirement are prorated to reflect the percentage of authorship. For example, the writer's percentage of a co-written song should count toward the commitment in relation to the percentage belonging to other co-writers (i.e., a half or a quarter of one song).

LEGALITIES

Any contract can be as creative as need be to accomplish the goals of the parties entering into it. There is no concrete set of terms. There are, however, certain follow-the-dot terms and provisions that are required to (a) protect both parties and (b) make the contract a legally enforceable instrument. Most of these provisions are summarized in the table below, but, in the beginning, you should take legal advice during negotiations, and have your contracts drafted by an experienced music business attorney.

Legal fees can be saved by having an attorney supply you with a generic agreement, which you can tailor to suit each deal. If you agree to any terms or provisions that are slightly creative, have the attorney check your agreement before the final signing.

Summary

In this examination of what is involved in single-song contracts and exclusive songwriter agreements, we have generally presented the basic terms from the publisher's side of the desk. Writers with track records or songs you desperately want to acquire may be able to nit-pick and narrow some of the clauses more in their favor.

Obviously, you should fully understand the import of each clause before deciding what is negotiable and what is not. Reread each of the clauses and think through the reasons they are worded as they are and the ramifications of each change a writer wants to make.

Just as you should understand the short- and long-term implications of the agreement, so should the writer. If you're dealing with an inexperienced writer, it is not only ethical but prudent that you advise the writer to seek independent legal advice before signing.

This is especially important when negotiating exclusive songwriter agreements. There have been cases where writers have had agreements (or portions of agreements) nullified in court because, at the time of signing, the writer was "inexperienced and ill-advised" and therefore "unduly taken advantage of" by the proverbial cigar-chomping, fast-talking, publishing shark. Though it may be tedious haggling with a lawyer to get an agreement signed, the exercise can prevent more severe pain later on.

Summary of songwriter contract terms

- Nature of rights assigned
- Warrant of exclusivity
- Title(s) of work(s) assigned
- Exclusions
- Duration of agreement
- Options
- Duration of copyright assignment
- Territory
- Advances
- Timing of advance payments
- Cross-collateralization
- Recoupment of expenses
- Royalties
- Method of calculating royalties
- Accounting period
- Performance clauses

CHAPTER 7

Co-Publishing

Co-publishing (or *split publishing*) is when two or more publishers share ownership of a copyright. Every active publisher's catalog contains split copyrights, and negotiating co-publishing arrangements is a common occurrence, although it's not always an easy one.

Co-publishing typically comes about when:
- two or more writers signed to different publishers collaborate on a song
- a record company, producer, or artist acquires a copyright interest in return for recording a song
- a film or television production company acquires interest in a copyright in return for using a song
- a small publisher splits copyrights with a full-service publisher in return for an advance or other financial consideration
- a small publisher splits copyrights with a full-service publisher who can handle promotion, administration, and licensing

Writer collaborations

When two or more writers signed to different firms collaborate on a song, their respective publishers automatically find themselves in a co-publishing situation. Some publishers contractually prohibit their writers from collaborating with songwriters signed to other publishers without first obtaining permission. In practice, writer collaborations are not only common, they are constructive and productive. A publisher who refuses to let a writer collaborate risks having 100 percent of nothing as opposed to 50% of a hit.

Some publishers even encourage collaboration, going so far as to arrange and pay for travel and lodging to bring writers together. The reason is quite sim-

ply that there is a beneficial synergy in the exchange of ideas. Creative people often are sparked by other creative people. A sharing of talents and perspectives, and mixing of personalities leads many times to inspiration for a work that is much more creative than one lone writer could achieve. Collaboration can help a writer out of a rut or overcome writer's block.

When collaborations occur, the percentage of publishing rights assigned to each publisher generally reflects the way the writers split their own shares. For instance, if both songwriters contribute equally to the work, the writers' royalties are split 50/50, and the publishers respectively share 50/50 as well. Or, if one writer's contribution is 15%, his publisher's share is also 15%.

Quite often as many as three, four, or five different writers contribute to a copyright's creation, and each writer is represented by a different publisher. The result is a three-, four-, or five-way split. This can further result in a very interesting discussion between the publishers as to which of them will act as the administrator. (See *Administration* later in this chapter.)

Incentive assignments

Some smaller publishers assign co-publishing rights as an incentive to get a copyright recorded or otherwise commercially exploited. For example, a small publisher might agree to assign co-publishing to a record company's publishing subsidiary to get a song released. Similarly, a writer or small publisher might give up an interest in a copyright to a major artist or producer who promises to cut a song.

Little publisher/big publisher

Small indie publishers sometimes need the administrative expertise, marketing clout, or cash injection a larger publisher can offer. It may be that the smaller publisher is essentially a one-man operation, perhaps a writer, artist, or producer. Or, the smaller publisher may be a copyright holding company owned by an investor, a studio, an indie record company, or film production company. Whatever the case, the copyright owner assigns co-publishing rights to an active, full-service publisher who will administer and promote the work.

Division of ownership rights

A co-published song is called a *split copyright*. The term *split* in co-publishing means shared ownership; it does not mean that the copyright itself is *divided*. Remember, there is always just *one* copyright in a work.

Although divisibility of rights is theoretically possible, there are only a few practical applications of this. One situation is when a lyricist adds lyrics to a composer's melody, and neither shares rights to the other's work. The lyricist's publisher then has rights to the lyrics only, while the composer's publisher has rights only to the melody. Usually, however, the contributing elements to a work are *merged* so that both collaborators (and their publishers) share equally in any income, whether arising from lyrics or music or both.

There are situations where an original publisher assigns a share of earnings from a specific source to another publisher. For instance, a producer may be assigned *X*% of mechanical royalties only, as an inducement to record a song. The producer only profits from record sales arising from his own production and doesn't share in any other earnings generated by the song. This is a division of income, not of copyright ownership. It is not co-publishing, but more properly called a "cut-in." (See the chapter on *Mechanical Right Licensing*.)

However, full co-publishing rights can be assigned on a short-term basis as an inducement to record a song. *Duration* of the co-publishing agreement may be limited to three years (or less), rather than life of copyright. This restricts a co-publisher to the immediate income arising directly from getting the copyright recorded. The producer (or artist, or label) is not entitled to any income that may materialize from other, unrelated usages in later years.

Administration of co-published works

In co-publishing situations, there is sometimes a bit of dickering over which publisher will *administer*, or manage, the copyright. The *administrator* has the sole right to license and collect all royalties and fees earned by the song on behalf of all co-publishers.

The administrator can make, or not make, deals for the song at his own discretion. Of course, the administrator must account to co-publishers for their share of royalties (including their respective writers' shares). But this might mean that the administering publisher retains monies due the other publishers and their writers until the normal semi-annual accounting period (June 30 and December 31). And, while retaining the other publisher's money, the administrator can earn interest on it. Some co-publishers may insist, therefore, that the administrator forward their share within ten days of receipt.

Justification for claiming full administrative rights arises where one publisher has a larger share of the copyright (i.e., one publisher has two writers in a three-way split and thus owns 66.66%); or, where one publisher is an established, full-service company, while the other is insufficiently staffed to properly administer and promote the work.

CO-PUBLISHING VS. ADMINISTRATION DEALS

When both parties are not equal (i.e., a start-up indie splits a song with a major publisher) the big dog usually does the administration. Still, if both parties share copyright ownership for the life of copyright, the term to describe the situation is *co-publishing*. If, however, the administrating party's rights terminate sooner (e.g., three years, after which the other party regains full copyright control), the situation is usually referred to as an *administration deal*.

LIMITATIONS ON ADMINISTRATOR'S CONTROL

In any type of deal, everything is negotiable. Thus, the administrating publisher may have certain limitations placed on its authority to issue licenses. Where nonstandard licenses or permissions are considered, such as reduced mechanical rates, or the size of a fee for a synchronization license, the nonadministering publisher may insist on right of approval.

Likewise, for *joint-administration* deals, there may be exceptions as to when one party or the other is allowed to issue a license without consultation with the other party. For instance, either party may unilaterally issue standard licenses (as long as the licensee is instructed to pay each party's share directly). But both parties must approve any nonstandard deal, such as those requiring negotiated licensing advances, fees, or royalties.

If special licensing circumstances are foreseen, the parties should work out how to handle them during contractual negotiations and spell them out in the co-publishing agreement. Examples of special licensing circumstances include cases where one party is an artist whose record deal calls for controlled composition rates, or where one party has print or foreign licenses already in place.

ADMINISTRATION FEES

The administering publisher sometimes charges an *administration fee*. The fee may be 5% or 10% or more. Depending upon how the co-publishing agreement is worded, the fee is either deducted from gross receipts, before any royalty distribution is made, or directly from the co-publisher's net share. There is really no difference.

Assume an agreement calls for a 10% administration fee charged to co-publisher's *net* share. If the song is split 50/50, the administrator takes $55 out of each $100 (his $50, plus 10% of the other publisher's $50), paying the other publisher $45. If, however, the administration fee comes off the top, then the administrator deducts $10 (10%) from the $100 and splits the $90 balance. Each publisher, then, technically receives $45—but in reality the administering publisher still gets $55.

Other administration fees

In addition to taking a percentage off the top as a catch-all administration fee, the administrator might also insist on recouping any *direct* costs. The catch-all administration fee ostensibly covers *indirect costs* (e.g., overhead, rent, salaries). Indirect costs can't be precisely attributed to any one copyright, whereas *direct costs* (e.g., copyright fees, lead sheets, demos, advertising, collection costs, etc.) can easily be itemized and allocated.

Agreements that call for recoupment of direct costs should state that the nonadministrative party must approve in advance any expenditure over $100 (or $500, or whatever). Without prior approval, the administrator must absorb the cost of any expenditure over this limit.

The administrator should not deduct from a co-publisher's share any expenses that are to be recouped from songwriter royalties. For instance, suppose a songwriter is to be charged 50% of demo costs, and a demo is produced for $1,000. And suppose the administrator pays for the demo under an agreement that calls for the two co-publishers to split expenses 50/50. The administrator should charge the songwriter's advance account $500. The nonadministrative publisher should be charged $250.

However, if the administrator is not contractually prohibited from doing so, it could try to charge the co-publisher $500 as 50% of the demo costs. Then it would charge the songwriter $500 as 50% of the demo costs. Thus, through "double-dipping," the administrator would avoid paying any of the demo costs.

JOINT-ADMINISTRATION

There are times when an impasse is reached over administrative control. Neither publisher wants to cede the rights to manage its own copyright interest. The solution can be a *joint-administration* agreement.

In a joint-administration agreement, each co-publisher controls its own interest. Such agreements are fairly straightforward and can be amicably managed. Performing- and mechanical-right societies are instructed to make payments directly to each co-publisher for their respective shares. Each publisher can issue *routine* mechanical licenses, as long as licensees are notified to pay each owner their shares directly.

But in joint-administration deals, each publisher should insist on being consulted before one of the other parties authorizes any *nonroutine* license. This provision prevents a co-owner from granting an affiliated record company a special, low mechanical rate, or otherwise licensing the work in a manner detrimental to the potential earnings or protection of the copyright. And where a significant advance is involved, such as in a synchronization license, the co-publishers should agree to the terms before a license is issued. However, neither party should be able to block a commercially fair license without demonstrating good cause.

JOINT COPYRIGHT REGISTRATION

Only one co-publisher needs to register the work's copyright claim with the Library of Congress. The registration should clearly indicate all parties to the claim. All copyright notices used with the work's publication should include the names of all co-claimants.

Example:
© 1999 by Smith Music and Jones Publishing Company

Each co-publisher should register the work with their respective performing- and mechanical-right societies. The co-publishers' names should be included on the registration forms along with their respective royalty shares.

FOREIGN ADMINISTRATION

The administrator usually has sole right to make overseas subpublishing deals. If not, all parties must agree to the terms under which a work is to be licensed to subpublishers.

Although joint-administration can be a simple procedure in the U.S., there may be problems regarding joint-administration of foreign rights. Many overseas performing- and mechanical-right societies allow any co-publisher to block licenses without cause. That means that if two co-publishers assign their respective foreign rights to two separate subpublishers in the same country, either of the subpublishers can block a deal the other wants to make.

Foreign rights are simpler to handle if parties to a joint-administration deal can agree that only one of them will license a work overseas. A compromise might be reached whereby the co-publishers divide overseas administrative rights. Subpublication rights may be granted to Publisher *A*'s licensee in Germany, and to Publisher *B*'s licensee in France, for example.

How do the co-publishers divide the world between themselves? Territorial divisions could be made on the basis of which publisher's licensee offers the most favorable terms in a particular territory. For instance, Publisher *A*'s German licensee may pay 80% of all net revenue, while Publisher *B*'s licensee there pays only 75%.

Analyzing a co-publishing contract

Like songwriter's contracts, co-publishing deals can be made for an individual song or an entire catalog. And assignment can be for life of copyright or for a more limited period, such as three to five years. All negotiable provisions applicable to songwriter contracts can apply to co-publishing contracts as well (i.e., territory, term, options, advance, royalties, accountings, performance clauses, etc.).

TYPICAL CO-PUBLISHING CONTRACT PROVISIONS

Each party warrants that by virtue of an agreement with its respective writer it owns an undivided *X*% in the copyright and in any claims or interests relating thereto now or in the future.

The agreement is concurrent with the respective parties' rights to the copyright to the extent the parties own or control the copyright throughout the world.

If one party acts as administrator
- The administrator is given clear *authority* to license all usages of the work.
- The administrator shall be responsible for all required *registrations* with the Library of Congress, and performing- and mechanical-right societies in the names of all claimants.
- The administrator agrees that all *copyright notices* will be made in the names of all claimants.

- The administrator agrees to account to the other parties for their shares of monies arising from all usages, and the amount of those shares are specified (e.g., 50% of all net sums received).
- Any *administrative fee* is specified, along with the method of calculation.
- The *dates of accounting* are specified (e.g., within 45 days of 30 June and 31 December).
- *Right to audit*: Upon written advance notice, the administering publisher will allow the co-publisher or his representative to examine at the administering publisher's place of business during normal business hours all books, records, documents, licenses, statements, accountings, and other instruments relating to the song, for the purpose of verifying royalty statements rendered or delinquent under the terms of the agreement.

  Some agreements require the administering publisher to pay for the audit if an underpayment of, say, 5% or more is revealed.
- Each party assumes *responsibility for paying royalties* due its own writers, and *absolves from liability* the other party if it fails to do so.

For joint-administration agreements
- Each party agrees to *consult* with the others before licensing the work.
- Each party shall *register the work* with its performing- and mechanical-right societies, confirming the distribution of royalties and copyright ownership as per the agreement.
- All licensees, performing- and mechanical-right societies, etc., will be instructed to make *payments directly to the respective parties* to the agreement.
- Each party confirms it will cause all *copyright notices* to include the names of all claimants.
- The *administration of foreign rights* is clarified:
  (a) one party is assigned all foreign administrative rights (subject to mutually agreed licensing terms, or consultation before licensing);

  or

  (b) the parties divide administrative rights by territory, in which case there should be a schedule of territories assigning such rights in each territory to one party or the other (with minimally acceptable subpublishing terms, if any);

  or

  (c) if the parties insist on joint-administrative rights overseas, each party agrees to notify its subpublishers to license and collect on its behalf only (e.g., Publisher *A* owns 50% of the song; he authorizes his German licensee to collect and account to him for only 50% of all royalties earned in Germany, while Publisher *B* notifies his licensee to do the same on his behalf.)

JURISDICTION

The agreement shall be construed according to the laws of (*state or country of one of the parties*) and shall be binding upon and inure to the benefit of each party or their respective heirs and assigns.

ASSIGNMENT

Either party may sell, transfer, or assign its rights to another company or individual.

Sometimes there is a prohibition against either party assigning the agreement to another company without notification and/or giving the other party first refusal to acquire the share.

In no case should an assignment be allowed unless the assignee undertakes to abide by the terms of agreement.

LITIGATION

All parties agree to share equally the costs of any litigation and damages arising from third-party claims of infringement, as well as sharing litigation expenses and awards resulting from actions against alleged infringers.

PERFORMANCE CLAUSE

If one party obtained an interest in the copyright by promising the song will be released on record (or whatever), the conditions should be spelled out, and there should be a provision to nullify the agreement if that party fails to perform as agreed by a specified date or within a certain time frame.

NATURE OF AGREEMENT

It should be clear that the agreement does not constitute a form of joint-venture or partnership between the parties.

CHAPTER 8

Mechanical-Right Licensing

The earliest technology for reproducing musical performances included player pianos, music boxes, and hand-cranked machines that played acoustically recorded cylinders and discs. This technology was mechanical, rather than electronic, and gave rise to the term *mechanical reproduction*. Logically, then, permission to reproduce song copyrights by mechanical means was called a *mechanical license*.

Though the technology to reproduce sound recordings has long since evolved from mechanical to electrical means, and from analog to digital, the permission to reproduce and sell sound recordings of songs is still called a mechanical license. Today, a reference to *mechanical income*, or *mechanical royalties*, usually refers to monies earned from the manufacture and sale of songs in the forms of vinyl records, compact discs, audio tapes, and videocassettes. Mechanical income and performance income are the two main sources of revenue for most publishers.

Statutory mechanical royalty for audio-only recordings

The *statutory rate* is the maximum royalty publishers can demand for mechanical reproductions, but licenses may be granted at lower rates at publishers' discretion. The rate is called *statutory*, because, unlike other types of royalties and fees, which are set by the marketplace and negotiations between copyright owners and users, the mechanical royalty rate is established by statute and incorporated into copyright law.

CRT AND CARP

Until 1993, the *statutory mechanical royalty rate* was set by the *Copyright Royalty Tribunal* (*CRT*) and periodically adjusted to reflect changes in the consumer price index (CPI). The Copyright Royalty Tribunal was abolished in 1993. The mechanical rate is now periodically adjusted by the *Copyright Arbitration Royalty Panel* (*CARP*), which is appointed by the Librarian of Congress.

The statutory mechanical royalty rate currently in effect (from January 1, 1996 until at least December 31, 1997) is 6.95¢ per song for each record, disc, or audio tape sold, *or* 1.30¢ per minute of playing time, whichever is greater. Thus, for a recorded song of average length (three minutes) released in America, the record company is obliged to pay the publisher 6.95¢ for each unit sold. A recorded version of, say, seven minutes—as commonly issued on 12-inch singles for the dance/clubs/disco market—would yield the publisher 9.10¢ per song for each unit sold.

The statutory rate applies to all recordings manufactured and distributed after January 1, 1996, regardless of when the license was issued or the recording first manufactured. So, if a recording was released on June 1, 1995, and licensed under the then rate (6.60¢), any new pressings made and distributed under that license after January 1, 1996, automatically increase to 6.95¢ per song.

WHAT A PUBLISHER NETS

The statutory rate of 6.95¢ is, of course, the gross amount due the publisher and includes the songwriter's share. Typical songwriter contracts call for publishers and songwriters to split mechanical royalties 50/50. So, the net publisher's share is 3.475¢ from each record sale, and the writer also nets 3.475¢. It is not uncommon, however, for sought-after writers to successfully negotiate for as much as 60% to 75% of mechanical royalties.

DISADVANTAGES OF U.S. ROYALTY RATE SYSTEM

The U.S. rate remains 6.95¢ per song or 1.30¢ per minute, no matter how much a commercial recording sells for. Nor does it matter whether the song is released as a single or an album cut or whether the release is a vinyl record, compact disc, or cassette tape.

RSP and PPD

Many U.S. publishers are unhappy with this royalty structure and envy publishers in other countries where statutory rates are more fairly calculated. Most other countries base the mechanical royalty rate on a percentage of either *RSP* (retail selling price) or *PPD* (published price to dealers). Under these systems, the royalty automatically increases with the price of a recording, without tinkering by a bureaucratic body, such as the Copyright Royalty Tribunal. Also, royalty increases take place in real time as the prices of recordings increase, not a year or two after the fact.

Another point of controversy about the U.S. royalty system is that royalties may not always keep pace with inflation within the music industry itself. If the U.S. consumer price index rises by 10% but prices of recordings shoot up 100%, publishers would receive a royalty rise of only one-tenth the value of the price increase. This anomaly doesn't happen in countries where a percentage of the selling price determines the royalty.

In Britain, the rate is now 8.5% of *PPD* (published price to dealers). The royalty is *prorated* (the total amount paid for all songs on the recording is divided by the number of songs). A "single" 45 rpm disc containing two songs pays 4.25% of the dealer price for each song. An album of ten songs pays 0.85% of PPD per song. Translated, a ten-song cassette selling to dealers in England for the equivalent of $9.00 pays 7.65¢ per song; a ten-song CD with a dealer price of $12.00 pays 10.2¢ per song.

In major Western European countries, like Germany, France, and the Netherlands, the rate is 9.306% of PPD. This means that a ten-song CD selling to dealers at $12.00 pays 11.1672¢ per song. And in Australia, the rate is 10.5% of PPD, so the same ten-song CD selling to dealers at $12.00 pays 12.6¢ per song.

In Japan, the rate is 6% of the *retail* selling price (RSP). Since Japanese retail prices of CDs are much higher than those in the U.S., Japanese publishers are in the enviable position of collecting more mechanical royalties than publishers anywhere else in the world, despite the fact that more units are actually sold in America.

Consider, for example, that U.S. retail prices of CDs are normally $15.98-$16.98. If a publisher controls all ten songs on a ten-song CD retailing for $16.98

and receives the full statutory royalty for each song, he would gross 69.5¢ for each album sold (10 x 6.95¢). This is just a little over 4% of the retail price. But in Japan, where the retail price might be, say, $20, the publisher would receive $1.20, or 12¢ a song. That's almost twice what a U.S. publisher would gross on the same album.

RSP and PPD benefit record companies, too

Basing mechanical royalties on a percentage of selling price also benefits record companies, because they can budget royalty costs without regard to how many songs are contained on an album. Under a percentage-based mechanical rate system, publishing royalties are constant; record companies pay the same in royalties whether an album contains 8, 10, 12, or more songs. In contrast, American record companies pay 55.6¢ to publishers if an album contains 8 songs, but their costs rise to 83.4¢ if an album contains 12 songs, and 97.3¢ on 14 songs.

The difference between royalties payable on 8 and 14 songs is significant. An 8-song CD that sells 100,000 units requires the record company to pay the publishers a total of $55,600. But 14 songs would cost the record company $97,300—a difference of $41,700. On a million units, the difference is $417,000! This encourages U.S. record companies to: limit the number of songs per album, pressure publishers to reduce mechanical rates, and/or insist on *controlled composition clauses* in artists' contracts (see following).

Controlled composition clause

Not only do U.S. publishers have to contend with one of the lowest statutory mechanical royalty rates in the world, many U.S. record companies manage to reduce their liability for mechanical royalties even further. They accomplish this by writing into their agreements with recording artists something known as a *Controlled Composition Clause*.

The controlled composition clause states that the mechanical rate on songs written or controlled by the artist will only be 75% of the statutory rate (i.e., 5.2125¢ per song, instead of 6.95¢). Some labels also manage to shave even more off their mechanical royalty payments by insisting that total mechanical royalties shall not exceed ten times the three-fourths statutory rate for all the songs on the album.

This means that if an album contains 12 songs, for which the normal, aggregate statutory royalty is 83.4¢ (12 x 6.95), the record company actually pays only 52.125¢ (6.95¢ x 75% x 10). Even worse, many new artists find they have to agree to 50% of statutory rate. And virtually all controlled composition clauses call for 50% of the statutory mechanical rate on record club and budget-priced releases.

Another variation of the controlled composition clause is when a record company requires royalties to be calculated as if every song is under five minutes in playing time, regardless of any song's actual length. Under the current rate of 1.30¢ per minute, if one track is ten minutes long, the statutory rate would be 10.3¢. But under this provision, the track would be calculated as if it were under five minutes, for which the statutory rate is 6.95¢. And, if the rate is further reduced to 75%, the royalty payable would only be 5.2125¢, or nearly 50% off the statutory requirement.

Still another record company ploy is to fix in stone the controlled composition rate as of the time of recording. That means that if the statutory rate goes up before the release date (or even before the date of manufacture), the royalty calculation is applied to the older, lower statutory rate.

WHAT IF PUBLISHERS REFUSE TO REDUCE RATES?

The controlled composition clause states that *additional mechanical royalties will be paid out of the artist's share of royalties.* This pressures artists to either reduce the number of songs on their albums, or pressure publishers of those songs they record to grant reduced rates to the record company.

Needless to say, writers and publishers don't think this practice very fair, but so far there has not been a unified protest with sufficient clout to make record companies see sweet reason. In the UK, controlled composition clauses were recently prohibited by the British Copyright Tribunal.

RATIONALE FOR CONTROLLED COMPOSITIONS

Unless an artist writes all the songs and is signed to the label's publishing subsidiary under terms that allow songwriting and artist royalties to be cross-collateralized, the record company has to pay publishing royalties on every unit sold, regardless of whether an album ever breaks even. Mechanical royalties are thus a drag on a label's ability to recoup, which is why they argue, with a straight face, that controlled compositions are necessary.

Of course, publishers not controlled by an artist are not obligated to reduce their rates. The discrepancy between the statutory rate and the limitations imposed by the controlled composition clause must be made up from the artist's royalty share. The artist either chooses to drop a song, or pay up.

NEGOTIATING TACTICS FOR ARTIST/PUBLISHERS

When an artist controls a song (e.g., as an artist/publisher), the only recourse is to accept the reduced rate, or try to lessen the effects of a controlled composition clause through negotiation. An artist/publisher should strive to negotiate an *escalating* royalty rate, either based on sales levels or follow-up releases. For example, the 75% rate might rise to 85% on sales above 500,000 and to 100% on sales above 1 million. *Or,* the 75% rate might rise to 85% on release number two, and to 100% on release number three.

The artist/publisher might argue that the record company would not pick up options to proceed with additional releases if earlier ones had not achieved sufficient sales to risk further investment. In any event, an artist/publisher should insist that controlled composition rates be calculated from the date of release, not the date of recording or manufacture.

Rate discounts, splits, cut-ins

Aside from controlled compositions, U.S. record companies frequently pressure publishers to issue mechanical licenses for less than the statutory rate of 6.95¢. Some producers and smaller record companies also demand *cut-ins* or *splits*.

RATES

Some record companies ask for a *rate* (a reduction of the statutory rate by 25%-50%) as inducement to release a song as an "A" side—or to even release it at all. Often this is a bluff, because the record company has already decided to release the song as an "A" side, but many smaller publishers agree to the reduced rate, fearing to call the bluff and risk lost income.

CUT-INS

A *cut-in* is when the publisher agrees to give a record company, artist, or producer a percentage of the mechanical royalties earned from sales of that particular release.

SPLITS

A *split* is when the publisher agrees to co-publish a song with the record company, artist, or producer, giving up a percentage of the copyright. This entitles the record company, artist, or producer to share in the song's income from any and all sources, now and forever.

In effect, rates, cut-ins, and splits amount to kickbacks, although they have so far been seen in law as merely a matter of wheeling and dealing. However, a record company employee who demands a cut-in or split for personal benefit without his employer's knowledge may be liable to prosecution for commercial bribery and dismissal from his job.

If you ever feel compelled to agree to a split in order to get a song released, be sure you include a clause in the agreement specifying that the split will be revoked if the company fails to release the song within a specified time (say, six months, or one year). Otherwise, even if the company never releases the song, they'll have a share in the song whenever anyone else releases it.

RECORD CLUBS

Reduced royalty rates are also sought from publishers by record clubs, such as BMG and Columbia Record Club, who sell over $500 million worth of records to some 6 million members each year. To achieve this volume, maintain membership, and recruit new members, the clubs offer discounts and free recordings as bonus incentives to members when they join or purchase a certain number of tapes or discs. The clubs therefore argue the need to discount royalties payable in order to hold down costs.

Publishers usually agree to accept a 25% discount in mechanical royalties from clubs (currently 6.95¢ - 25% = 5.2125¢). However, such reduced-rate agreements should provide that the clubs pay this rate on all units shipped to members, including those issued free as bonuses.

SPECIAL PRODUCTS

Other reduced-rate situations include TV marketed albums (e.g., CDs with 24 tracks selling for $19.95) and *premium* giveaways (e.g., albums used as incentive bonuses to purchasers of some other product, such as a tank of gas). Premium albums fall under a category called *special products*. Some major labels have special product divisions that package premium albums for other companies.

For example, Texaco may want to give away specially packaged albums as incentives or bonuses to customers who buy Texaco products. But, since Texaco has no expertise in packaging or manufacturing recorded product, it will approach the special products division of BMG or Sony. BMG or Sony would then license the tracks, design and print the covers, and manufacture the discs or tapes for Texaco.

Special product divisions of record companies (and other types of companies) also package *theme-oriented* albums to release on their own labels. This entails licensing masters from other labels and songs from a variety of publishers. Notable packagers who release theme-oriented albums under their own labels are Time-Life, Readers Digest, and K-Tel.

In some cases, special product packagers can pick and choose which songs to include on a theme-oriented album. For instance, albums with titles like *Soul Sounds of the Sixties, Ladies Sing the Blues, Going Country,* etc., give lots of scope for the titles included on them. The packagers can pick and choose from virtually *any* R&B song, blues song, or country song, which gives them latitude to exclude tracks or songs whose copyright owners refuse to grant reduced royalty rates.

On the other hand, if the package is geared to a specific selection, such as *All the Top 10 Hits of 1977,* the packager has no choice but to include all songs that reached the Top 10 that year. Knowing that gives the publisher leverage to demand a higher, or statutory rate.

TV and special products packagers generally pay advances to get reduced rates from publishers. Advances for TV albums typically range from $250 (which guarantees 5,000 unit sales at 5¢ a song) to $1,000 (20,000 units). A premium giveaway may warrant an advance of $5,000 for 100,000 units at 5¢ a song.

First use

Copyright owners have a virtual monopoly over their material. They control who uses the copyright, how and for how long it is to be used, and how much the user must pay for the privilege of using it. But there are some exceptions to this monopoly, and one of them is in the area of mechanical licensing.

The copyright owner's monopoly is secure as long as the copyright is not released commercially in any phonorecord format. Until it is released, the copyright owner can refuse to license anyone to record or release it or charge any mechanical royalty without regard to the statutory rate established by the compulsory licensing provision of the copyright law. Thus, the copyright owner has the right to determine and control the work's *first use.*

However, once a copyright is distributed to the public in recorded format, its owner cannot prevent others from using the material in phonorecords, as long as the user abides by the provisions of a *compulsory license.* A compulsory license compels the copyright owner to permit the use of a previously released musical work in a recorded, nondramatic performance.

Compulsory mechanical licenses

Once a song is commercially released, the copyright owner can not prevent others from releasing it, as long as users comply with the *compulsory licensing provision* of the 1976 Copyright Act. Anyone who wishes to record and release a song under the compulsory license provision must:

- serve a *notice of intention* on the copyright owner (before any recordings are distributed and within 30 days after recording the work)
- pay mechanical royalties at the statutory rate by the 20th of each month for all recordings sold in the preceding month
- make each monthly accounting sworn under oath
- make cumulative, annual statements, certified by a CPA

If monthly payments and annual accountings are not made on schedule and the default is not cured within 30 days of a written demand from the copyright owner, the compulsory license can be terminated.

If the notice of intention is not served, no compulsory license will be issued. Anyone who makes and distributes recordings of a copyrighted song without a license may be subject to prosecution for copyright infringement. But if the person wishing to make the recording cannot locate the copyright owner, and the Copyright Office is unable to provide a current address, notice of intention can be sent to the Copyright Office with a $6 filing fee.

If the copyright owner has not registered a claim to the work with the Library of Congress, no compulsory license is necessary, and there is no obligation to pay the owner. The owner can still register a claim and demand statutory compensation for all copies made and sold *after* registration, but cannot claim royalties on copies sold before registration.

It must be emphasized again that the compulsory licensing provisions do not apply to the first recording of a song. Copyright owners have full discretion over who may first record and release a song under the concept of *first use*. After a publisher authorizes the first recording's manufacture and distribution, anyone can record and distribute the work if the compulsory licensing provisions are followed.

Negotiated mechanical licenses

Compulsory licenses are cumbersome for users to comply with. However, the onerous compulsory licensing provisions are usually reserved for labels with histories of slow or no payment. Most publishers are happy to grant *negotiated mechanical licenses* to legitimate record companies.

KEY FEATURES OF NEGOTIATED LICENSES:
- Record companies are not required to serve notices of intention.
- Royalties are paid quarterly, rather than monthly.
- Accountings don't have to be under oath.
- Cumulative annual accountings certified by a CPA are not required.

- The royalty rate may be less than statutory, if the copyright owner agrees.

What a typical mechanical license contains

PRELIMINARIES
- Date of license
- Song title
- Name(s) of songwriter(s)
- Name(s) of publisher(s)
- Name of record label
- Name of recording artist
- Record, disc, or tape number
- Configuration (CD, DAT, 45 rpm, 33 rpm, cassette, etc.)

WARRANTIES, ACKNOWLEDGMENTS, REPRESENTATIONS
- Publisher declares it is the owner of the copyrighted work and/or is authorized to license the rights to manufacture and distribute the work in recorded form.
- Publisher acknowledges it has been notified that the record company wants to record, manufacture, and distribute the work under the compulsory license provisions of the 1976 U.S. Copyright Act.
- Publisher acknowledges that the record company shall have all rights granted to, and all obligations imposed upon, users of the work under the compulsory license provisions of the 1976 U.S. Copyright Act; *except that*:
  —The record company shall account and pay royalties to the publisher within 45 days of the end of each calendar quarter; and
  —Said accountings and royalties shall be on the basis of each recording manufactured and distributed; and
  —For each recording manufactured and distributed the royalty shall be the statutory rate effective at the time the records are manufactured (or, if the publisher has agreed to a rate less than the statutory rate, the amount is stated here); and
  —The record company is not obliged to serve notice of intention as required under the compulsory license provisions of the 1976 Copyright Act.
- Record company acknowledges that the license pertains only to the recording of the work by the artist identified in the license.
- The record company acknowledges that the license pertains only to the recording identified by the record, disc, or tape number in the license. If the record company intends to release the recording in different formats, such as 45 rpm, 33 rpm, cassette

tape, CD, or whatever, it must obtain a separate license for each format.

- The parties acknowledge that the license does not supersede nor otherwise affect any previous agreements concerning the work.
- Should the record company fail to account or pay royalties as provided, and further fails to account or pay within 30 days of receiving written demand to do so from the publisher, then the license is terminated, and any further manufacture or distribution of the work will subject the record company to prosecution for infringement and to all remedies provided by the 1976 U.S. Copyright Act.

RESERVES

The traditional method of selling recorded product is on consignment. A record company might fill an order from a regional distributor or chain for, say, 15,000 units, only to see 6,000 units ultimately returned unsold. For this reason, record companies normally withhold a portion of artist royalties as well as mechanical royalties to offset possible returns of unsold product, for which no royalties are payable. Withheld royalties are called *reserves.*

Reserves on artist royalties range from 25% to 50%. But mechanical royalty reserves generally run higher, from 50% to as much as 75%. Why? Record companies have other means of recouping royalty overpayments from artists, but not from publishers.

The record company can add the overage amount to the artist's advance account and cross-collateralize against other product by the artist. But, overpayments to publishers can't be cross-collateralized, because each mechanical license is applicable only to the one release of the one song.

Reserves have to be liquidated over a reasonable period of time. Different record companies use different declining balances, but eventually (usually within three or four quarterly accounting periods) all units that are actually sold and paid for must be accounted to the publisher.

Videocassettes

Home video is still a relatively new area of growth for publishers, but it does generate significant income, not only for the use of songs in movie soundtracks, but from songs used in special-interest videos, like aerobics and golf lessons, some of which sell 100,000 copies each.

Mechanical royalty rates for songs used in videocassettes vary, depending upon the type of video. In fact, the situation is still in flux and is largely negotiable. So publishers are wise to deal for royalties based on a percentage of the video's selling price rather than a fixed dollars-and-cents sum per unit.

On videos with content that primarily features music, rates can range from 7%-8% of the retail price, divided between all the songs on the tape, to 6¢-8¢ per song. One manufacturer of VCRs recently engaged BMG Special Products Division to package a ten-song video of country hits as a premium giveaway to purchasers of new VCRs. The company paid an advance of $10,000 per song, representing the manufacture and distribution of 100,000 videos at 10¢ a song.

For feature films rereleased in video form, rates often depend on whether or not the film is new. On older movies, the film studios sometimes locked publishers into broad licenses that covered later technological developments, but some licenses were specific enough to give publishers negotiating room for newer uses.

Song substitution sometimes results when publishers demand rates that film distributors regard as too high—the publisher's song is removed from the film. But that's an expensive process and not always workable, especially where the song is synchronized to a choreographed dance number.

BUY-OUTS VS. ROYALTIES

Distributors of some types of videos (including new feature films) may request a *buy-out,* or *flat fee,* ranging from $5,000-$20,000. Some publishers charge major motion picture producers video buy-out fees equal to 100%-200% more than what they received for the film's general-release synchronization license fee.

But publishers may ultimately be short-changed by a flat fee if the release is a big seller, which is why royalties are preferable. (Some feature films achieve video sales of 2 million units.) Publishers should accept a flat fee only for the first 50,000 copies or so, with additional fees, or royalties of 6-8¢ per unit, on incremental sales above that figure.

PROMOTIONAL VIDEOS

Record companies frequently produce videos of artists' performances as promotional vehicles to boost sales of discs and tapes. In these cases, record companies may rightly expect the publishers to waive any mechanical royalties, since the videos are used exclusively as *clips* to promote recordings. And publishers may agree, as long as the clips are provided for in-store projection or all-music channel television programming such as MTV, and are not offered for sale. In fact, publishers occasionally agree to help a record company finance a video production in order to stimulate a song's recorded sales.

Some record companies use the controlled composition clause to exclude any royalty payment on promotional video clips, which may be fair enough.

However, some labels also try to extend this to commercial video releases, which should be resisted.

On commercial video releases, the record company may attempt to get the publisher to accept a small buy-out fee of, say, $200-$300. The safer bet is to insist on a royalty rate, which is usually around 4% of the wholesale price, prorated among all songs contained on the release.

Mechanical-right licensing societies

Many publishers authorize *mechanical-right licensing societies* to license and collect mechanical royalties on their behalf. Societies use economies of scale to issue licenses, monitor payments and accountings, and periodically audit record companies to keep them honest. Since societies represent many publishers, they have more clout to ensure diligent performance of obligations assumed by record companies under the mechanical licenses.

THE HARRY FOX AGENCY

The Harry Fox Agency (HFA), operated by the *National Music Publishers Association* (NMPA), is the dominant mechanical-right society in the United States. As an illustration of the music publishing industry's expansion in recent years, the number of publishers affiliated with Fox jumped to over 14,000 in 1996 from 4,000 in 1984. Moreover, gross collections on behalf of members increased an average 26% each year between 1984 and 1994, from some $80 million to approximately $358 million. 1995 collections jumped again, to over $392 million.

The Fox Agency processed some 162,000 licenses on behalf of its members in 1995. During the first two quarters of 1996, Fox reported, it processed 17% more licenses than in the same period of 1995.

Fox is diligent in its pursuit of record pirates and defaulters, and they are vigilant in protecting its clients' rights under copyright laws. One benefit of licensing through Harry Fox is particularly evident when it comes to auditing record companies. Audits cost several thousands of dollars. It isn't usually cost-effective for one publisher to conduct an audit, because royalties collected may not cover the cost of the audit. However, by representing so many publishers, the Fox Agency can profitably conduct audits using economies of scale.

Fox bolsters its in-house auditing staff with the services of two outside auditing firms. Every record company is subject to audit by Fox. Each major record company is audited at least once every two years; smaller companies are audited at least once every one to three years depending on need. Fox's affiliated publishers frequently receive checks representing under-payments the agency has recovered. Audits by Fox resulted in distributions of more than $12 million to publishers in 1994.

The Harry Fox Agency charges publisher-clients 4.5% of gross mechanical royalties collected. When collections run ahead of projections, as they consistently have in recent years, Fox voluntarily reduces its commission fee. In 1994, the commission was reduced to 3.5%, and in 1995 the fee was further reduced to 2.75%.

Fox also advises clients, and/or negotiates on their behalf, regarding appropriate fees to charge users for synchronization and jingle licensing. For synchronization licenses, the Agency charges 5% of fees collected or $2,200, whichever is less. This fee is also reduced when collections outpace budgeted overhead needs. Thus, in 1995, the commission fee for synchronization licensing was reduced to 3%.

AMRA AND CMI

There are two other mechanical-right organizations in the U.S. worthy of note. AMRA (*American Mechanical Rights Association*) handles mechanical licensing for several foreign mechanical right societies, such as Germany's GEMA. AMRA's service charge is comparable to the Harry Fox Agency: 5% of gross collections.

There is also a Nashville-based company called CMI (*Copyright Music, Inc.*). CMI claims to currently collect the equivalent of 15% of all U.S. mechanical licensing revenue. But, apart from mechanical licensing, CMI provides clients the option of letting the company handle complete administrative services worldwide. Its administration package includes registering songs with the Copyright Office, filing clearances and cue sheets with performing-right societies, preparing and managing songwriter agreements, co-publishing contracts, synchronization licenses, and other related documents, contracts, and licenses, handling overseas collections, and preparation of royalty statements to songwriters.

CMI's service charge to clients is two-tier: 5% of gross collections for U.S. and Canadian mechanical licensing only, or 10% of gross collections for publishers who elect to use its complete, international administration package.

SONGWRITERS GUILD

For songwriters who don't have publishers, the Songwriters Guild issues mechanical licenses to record companies.

CMRRA

The Canadian Mechanical Rights Reproduction Agency (CMRRA) is the Canadian counterpart of the Harry Fox Agency. CMRRA charges publishers a 5% fee for mechanical collections and 10% for synchronization license fees. American publishers affiliated with Fox usually affiliate separately with CMRRA, but it is possible to affiliate with one agency and not the other.

Neither Fox nor CMRRA require publishers who use their mechanical licensing service to also use their synchronization services. However, the expertise of both agencies in the area of synchronization licensing is often worth their service fees when it comes to negotiating the most appropriate advances, fees, and licensing terms.

OVERSEAS MECHANICAL-RIGHT SOCIETIES

The Harry Fox Agency has reciprocal agreements with most overseas mechanical-right societies. This enables U.S. publishers to collect mechanical royalties through Harry Fox in countries where they don't have subpublishers. It also enables overseas publishers to collect U.S. mechanical royalties through their respective mechanical-right organizations, rather than relying on American subpublishers.

Overseas mechanical-right organizations deduct their own commissions before paying Fox, and Fox then deducts its fee before paying U.S. publishers. However, U.S. publishers can become associate members of certain overseas societies, thus eliminating double commissions (one to the foreign society and another to their own society), and lag times between collections and payments.

Major overseas mechanical-right licensing societies:

AMCOS	(Australia and New Zealand)
CMRRA	(Canada)
GEMA*	(Germany, Austria, Poland, Hungary, etc.)
JASRAC*	(Japan)
MCPS	(Great Britain and Ireland)
NCB	(Scandinavia)
SABAM*	(Belgium)
SDRM	(France and French-speaking African countries)
SGAE*	(Spain)
SODRAC	(Canada)
SIAE*	(Italy)
SPA*	(Portugal)
STEMRA	(Holland)
SUISA*	(Switzerland)
VAAP	(Russia and former U.S.S.R.-member countries)

* Indicates a society that licenses both *performance* and *mechanical rights*

Mechanical rights in cyberspace

Cyberspace may well be the mode of distributing musical product to consumers in the future. The term references information and entertainment forums on commercial online services like CompuServe and America Online, as well as electronic bulletin boards and individual information providers on the Internet or World Wide Web.

The linking of personal computers to databanks presents many challenges for copyright owners. The ease with which data stored in cyberspace forums can be accessed by anyone, anytime, anywhere risks loss of control over how copyrighted material might be used.

The prime concerns for copyright owners are copyright protection of material uploaded to cyberspace forums and establishing effective means of compensation for any resulting usages of the copyrighted material. There are three music licensing issues related to cyberspace: mechanical rights, performing rights, and synchronization rights. (See the chapter on *Miscellaneous Licensing Issues* for further discussion.)

In 1996, the Harry Fox Agency entered into a licensing agreement with CompuServe, which, for now, serves as a model for licensing mechanical rights to other commercial online services and information providers. Mechanical licenses for online transmission are substantially the same as those issued for phonorecords. The only difference is that instead of making and distributing copies via phonorecords, online licenses permit the licensee to transmit digital copies via commercial online services.

When a license request is received from an online service forum, Harry Fox issues a mechanical license on behalf of the song's publisher. The license permits the making and distribution of nondramatic, audio-only copies of a specific audio recording, via transmission of digital data. The licensed recording may then be uploaded and stored in the forum's database for downloading by subscribers.

Online mechanical licenses are issued at the statutory royalty rate in effect at the time of downloading and royalties are payable for each downloaded copy. As with negotiated mechanical licenses, the royalty rate may be lower than statutory if the publisher agrees.

CHAPTER 9

Performing-Right Licensing

Many publishers find that their largest and most consistent source of income is performance royalties. In the United States, $750 million is collected annually in performance royalties on behalf of publishers and songwriters. Worldwide, performance licenses generate over $2 billion each year, accounting for over 40% of all publisher/writer income.

A song that reaches number one on the *Billboard* Top 100 chart can earn performance royalties of between $100,000 and $200,000. In the *first year* alone. From *U.S. radio airplay* only. And that's just the *publisher's share*!

Radio performance royalties usually account for between 80% and 90% of all domestic performance royalties from a song that hits the Top 100. So, when you factor in performance royalties from television, jukeboxes, live venues, wired and other usages, and add the writer's share, the total U.S. *gross* on a number one hit could easily top $400,000, not counting mechanical, print, synchronization, foreign, and other income.

Hit songs in niche markets (e.g., country, R&B, easy listening) earn smaller amounts but generate significant performance royalties nevertheless. But if a song crosses over to hit number one on the pop, R&B, country, or adult contemporary charts as well, gross U.S. performance royalties from the first year could reach $600,000.

And it doesn't stop there. Foreign performance royalties can equal the U.S. earnings, assuming international success. Although performance royalties fall off substantially after the first couple of quarters of peak activity, a hit song might still be generating as much as 10% of its first year earnings in the 20th year of release.

First year U.S. performance royalties (publisher's share only)						
Chart Position	Pop Radio	Pop TV/Other	Pop TOTAL	Country Radio	Country TV/Other	Country TOTAL
#1 (Low)	$75,000	$18,750	**$93,750**	$60,000	$15,000	**$75,000**
(High)	$150,000	$37,500	**$187,500**	$100,000	$25,000	**$125,000**
#5 (Low)	$50,000	$12,500	**$62,500**	$40,000	$10,000	**$50,000**
(High)	$125,000	$31,250	**$156,250**	$65,250	$16,310	**$81,560**
#10 (Low)	$30,000	$7,250	**$37,250**	$25,000	$6,250	**$31,250**
(High)	$100,000	$25,000	**$125,000**	$55,000	$13,750	**$68,750**
#20 (Low)	$20,000	$5,000	**$25,000**	$16,000	$4,000	**$20,000**
(High)	$75,000	$18,750	**$93,750**	$45,000	$11,250	**$56,250**

Various types of performance uses

Each commercial performance requires the user to pay a royalty to the copyright owner and songwriter. Most of the royalties amount to just a few cents in each case, but it all adds up. There are many types of performance usages, and any song achieving commercial success inevitably earns income from several categories of performing-right users.

On any given day, one hit song may be:
- Broadcast on hundreds of radio and television stations across the country
- Performed live in nightclubs, concert halls, and arenas
- Played on countless jukeboxes in bars and cafes
- Played on tape decks in aerobic and dance studios, hair salons, and boutiques
- Used as background music in restaurants, elevators, malls, supermarkets, offices, and factories

Performing-right societies

It is simply not economical for any publisher to administer each performing-right license to each individual user. No individual publisher or songwriter has the capacity to monitor every performance and collect royalties due from thousands of users. By the same token, neither mom-and-pop operations nor giant corporations have the capacity to track down thousands of copyright owners in order to get permission and pay royalties for every song played or performed on their premises.

Since it is virtually impossible for publishers to economically and efficiently track the thousands of enterprises that perform or use music every day, there has to be a centralized, cost-effective entity to license performing rights and to collect and distribute performance royalties. *Performing-right societies* were formed to meet this necessity.

Every publisher and professional songwriter belongs to a performing-right society. Sheer numbers give the societies negotiating clout and economies of scale. The collective strength of thousands of members enables performing-right societies to negotiate blanket licenses to broadcasters and venues where music is used or performed and to effectively administer licenses and collect royalties on behalf of publishers and writers.

Performing-right societies in the United States

ASCAP AND BMI

ASCAP (Association of Composers, Authors & Publishers) and BMI (Broadcast Music, Inc.) are the two societies most publishers deal with most of the time. They are by far the largest and most important of the three societies and are the main focus of this chapter.

Founded in 1914, ASCAP is the oldest U.S. performing-right society and collects the most performance royalties, though BMI represents more writers and publishers. ASCAP collects some $400 million annually on behalf of over 60,000 writer/publisher *members*. BMI, which has *affiliates*, not "members," was founded in 1939. It now represents over 140,000 writers and publishers and collects over $300 million annually.

As non-profit organizations, ASCAP and BMI retain an average 18% of their gross collections for administrative overhead and distribute the balance to their members or affiliates. Together, ASCAP and BMI license the performing rights for approximately 99% of all song copyright repertoire in the United States.

SESAC

SESAC (Society of European Stage Authors & Composers), a for-profit corporation, was founded in 1930 and is now owned by a private investment group. Until 1992, it licensed mechanical and synchronization rights on behalf of members, as well as performance rights, but now it concentrates only on non-dramatic performance rights, like BMI and ASCAP.

Since it is privately owned, SESAC is not required to disclose operating expenses or profits. But, its estimated revenues are between $7 million and $11 million per year, of which about 50% is distributed to affiliated publishers and writers. SESAC claims its royalty payments are competitive with ASCAP and BMI. SESAC's repertoire is only about 1% of the total licensed for performing rights in the U.S. Though relatively small, SESAC does have its merits and is worth looking into.

Why U.S. publishers must form two or more companies

Because there is more than one performing-right society in the U.S., most publishers find it necessary to form at least two separate music publishing companies. Here's why: The societies demand exclusivity. Songwriters may only affiliate with one society. This means their songs must be registered with their respective society only. The entire repertoire of every writer is thus assigned to either ASCAP, BMI, or SESAC.

Likewise, a music publishing company may only be a member of one society. But, since a company is a legal entity, just like a person, one person or organization can own two (or three, or more) separate publishing companies, and each of these companies can belong to a different society.

The vast majority of American songwriters belong to either ASCAP or BMI. Therefore, publishers must form an ASCAP company to publish songs by ASCAP writers and a BMI company to publish songs by BMI writers. A SESAC company is also needed if SESAC writers are signed.

A songwriter affiliated with, say, BMI as a writer *and* as a publisher, may form another publishing company for membership in ASCAP in order to publish songs written by ASCAP writers. The BMI writer-publisher cannot, of course, assign his own writer's share of any collaborative works to the ASCAP company.

Collaboration between writers belonging to different societies

There is no problem when ASCAP, BMI, and SESAC writers collaborate on a song. The writers' respective shares are assigned to their respective performing-right societies. The publishing shares must match the writers' shares and be assigned to the same society.

But if all three writers are signed to the same publishing company, the company has to be structured as three separate entities, each belonging to a different society to accommodate each writer's performing-right affiliation. That means, in effect, the publisher co-publishes the collaborative work with itself. The ASCAP writer's share is assigned to the publisher's ASCAP company, the BMI writer's share is assigned to the publisher's BMI company, and the SESAC's writer's share is assigned to the publisher's SESAC company.

The following publishing companies are examples of separately structured entities owned by the same parent company in order to affiliate with the two major performing right societies:
• EMI-April Music ASCAP and EMI-Blackwood BMI
• WB Music ASCAP and Warner Tamerlane BMI
• Almo Music ASCAP and Irving Music BMI
• Chappell Music ASCAP and Unichappell BMI

How performance royalties are divided between publishers and writers

The societies consider royalties payable to writers and publishers as a single unit equal to 200%. Writer royalties = 100%; publisher royalties = 100%. Normally, this is distributed 100% to writers and 100% to publishers.

However, the writer's share can exceed 100%; the publisher's share cannot. Thus, a writer may successfully negotiate a contract with a publisher to receive 75% of all performance royalties (actually 150%: 100% of writer royalties and 50% of publisher royalties). But a publisher cannot receive more than 50% of all performance royalties (or 100% of the 200% that represents both the writer's and publisher's share). If a writer has not assigned performing-rights to a publisher, the writer can receive the entire 200%.

Publishers don't collect writer's performance royalties

Each performing-right society pays its members directly. That is, publishers receive performance royalties *net* from their affiliated society. The writer share has already been deducted and paid directly to the writer by the society. Co-publishers also receive performance royalties directly.

However, if a publisher pays an advance to a writer or co-publisher that is inclusive of anticipated performance royalties, then the publisher can have the recipient of the advance assign performance royalties to the publisher. The society will then pay the writer's (or co-publisher's) share directly to the publisher until the advance is recouped.

Administering performing-rights licenses

Performing-right societies issue *blanket licenses* to broadcasters and venues where music is used or performed. Blanket licenses permit licensees to use or perform any work in the society's repertoire, so that the user doesn't have to seek individual permissions for each and every title.

The societies monitor licensees to ensure compliance with the licensing provisions and to ascertain what songs are actually being performed. Performances are randomly—but scientifically—logged by song title and weighted by formulas designed to calculate the nearest approximate number of performances for each song during the monitoring period. Then the societies distribute performance royalties accordingly to publishers and songwriters each calendar quarter.

BMI tracks radio station airplay by requiring radio stations to submit programming logs on a rotating basis. Each station is notified by BMI when to start and stop the compilation of its log, so that every station is monitored for at least one week out of each year. The logs detail every song title played during the monitoring period.

ASCAP hires independent contractors to monitor radio airplay. The tracking is done without notification to the stations being monitored. The contractors actually listen to, and tape record each station for a designated period each year. A log of all titles played is then compiled and used to extrapolate a statistical assessment of national radio airplay during the quarter.

Hitherto, BMI and ASCAP radio airplay monitoring has, of necessity, been on a rotating, or spot basis. No station has been monitored 24 hours a day, 7 days a week, 52 weeks a year. However, the introduction of *Billboard*'s Broadcast Data System (BDS) opens up the possibility that every station can be monitored 100% of the time. With its capacity to monitor every song played, BDS may ultimately provide a logging system that more accurately reflects actual airplay than the statistical projections used heretofore.

As for television performances, networks and stations are required to submit *cue sheets* to ASCAP and BMI. Cue sheets detail every song used in every program. The details include title, length or duration of performance, type of use (theme, incidental, instrumental background, visual vocal, etc.). ASCAP and BMI allocate set dollar payments for each type of use, factoring in such variables as duration, population reach of the broadcasting outlet, whether usage was local or network, etc.

How performance royalties are calculated

Royalties are determined by the types of performances given. For example, full-length, featured performances on network television earn higher royalties than partial plays on local radio. Live performances at large concert halls earn more than taped background music played in neighborhood bars.

Performance royalties are determined by:
- types of use (feature, background, theme, live, jingle)
- duration (lengths of performance in minutes and seconds)
- size and type of venue

BMI'S BROADCASTING RATES:

BMI broadcast media rates	Royalty per performance
Local radio:	
Radio 1 (large market)	12¢
Radio 2 (small market)	6¢
Network radio	12¢ multiplied by number of stations broadcasting
Local TV	$1.50
Network TV:	
Between 7 p.m. and 2 a.m.	$9.00 multiplied by number of stations broadcasting
Between 2 a.m. and 7 p.m.	$5.00 multiplied by number of stations broadcasting

NOTE: These are BMI's minimum rates; because the organization is nonprofit, BMI distributes all income less operating costs, so payments are often voluntarily increased.

In addition, BMI pays *bonuses* after a song has received a certain number of broadcasting plays. The bonus formula ranges from 1.5 times base rate for works receiving 25,000 plays to 4 times base rate when a work has achieved 1 million plays.

Thus, when a song has achieved 1 million plays, it thereafter receives 48¢ for each radio play on a large-market station, and $36 on network TV multiplied by the number of stations carrying the broadcast. (One TV network prime time play of a 1-million-bonus-award work, on a program carried by 100 stations, earns $3,600.)

ASCAP PAYMENT SYSTEM

ASCAP payments to members are based on *credits*. Each surveyed work is assigned a number of credits representing the kind of usage and the medium in which it is used. Credits are *weighted* to reflect the value of the performance, ranging from a low of 2% of one credit for some usages of copyrighted arrangements of PD works to 100% of one credit for a full-feature vocal performance on primetime network television.

ASCAP also makes bonus payments for significant numbers of radio performances. For instance, a song that logs more than 5,000 feature radio performances in any one quarter receives an *award* that amounts to roughly an additional 44%. For example, if the credit for that quarter is $4.00, the award would amount to roughly $1.75.

ASCAP divides performances into several classifications, each of which is subdivided into *weights* (or

Music Publishing: The Real Road to Music Business Success

percentages of one full credit) according to duration, medium, and nature of performance. At the end of each distribution period, the number of ASCAP works surveyed, times the number of credits assigned to each performance, are divided into the gross amount of collections available for distribution (i.e., total collections less administrative costs).

This calculation provides the dollar amount of each credit for the distribution period. The total number of credits received by each member's catalog is then multiplied by the dollar amount of each credit. The resulting amount represents how much performance income each member receives for the distribution period.

For example, suppose $80 million is available for distribution at the end of one quarter, half of which is available for publisher members. And suppose there are 10 million credits earned by all publishers. $40 million ÷ 10 million credits = $4 per credit. A publisher that earned 20,000 credits during the quarter is then due $80,000.

TIMING OF ASCAP AND BMI ROYALTY DISTRIBUTIONS

Both ASCAP and BMI distribute royalties from U.S. collections every three months. ASCAP pays publishers six months in arrears. That is, earnings during a three-month period are calculated and paid out six months after the end of the quarter in which the royalties were collected. ASCAP pays writers seven and a half months after the end of each calendar quarter. BMI pays both publishers and writers simultaneously, eight months after the end of each calendar quarter.

For foreign collections, ASCAP pays both writers and publishers tri-annually, each April, August, and December. BMI distributes foreign royalties semi-annually, each July and December.

ASCAP Publisher (U.S.) distributions	ASCAP Publisher (foreign) distributions	BMI Publisher (U.S) distributions	BMI Publisher (foreign) distributions
March	April	February	July
June	August	May	
September		August	
December	December	November	December

BMI pays both writers and publishers the full amount due for each quarter (*current amount basis*). ASCAP also pays publishers on a current amount basis, but writers can elect to either receive the full, current amount, or to be paid on what's called the *four funds basis*.

ASCAP's four funds basis spreads payments as follows:

- 20% of the payment represents an aggregate of credits from the writer's most recent 4 quarters.
- 40% of the payment represents an aggregate of credits from the writer's most recent 20 quarters (5 years).
- 20% of the payment represents an aggregate of credits from the writer's *recognized works* over the most recent 20 quarters (5 years). "Recognized works" are songs that show up in ASCAP performance surveys 4 quarters from the date of first appearing in a survey.
- 20% of the payment represents an aggregate of credits from the writer's *recognized works* over the most recent 40 quarters (10 years) *and* the aggregate credits from *all* the writer's works since inception of the writer's ASCAP agreement, up to a maximum of 168 quarters (42 years).

The four funds accounting method averages a writer's income over the years. Thus, some writers elect this payment plan for two reasons: (1) it spreads tax liability, and (2) it provides a steadier income flow, which can be helpful in later life after writing activities cease or levels of success decline.

In addition to the regularly scheduled distributions of domestic and foreign performance income, ASCAP and BMI make *special distributions* from time to time representing retroactive payments collected as the result of litigation, arbitration, and settlements.

All in all, the payment structures and credit calculations used by BMI and ASCAP are very complex and can be confusing. Both societies provide complete explanations of payments to affiliates or members, and continually provide updates when adjustments are made, as they continually are.

SESAC'S ROYALTY SYSTEM

Unlike BMI and ASCAP, SESAC's royalty payment system has not traditionally relied on monitoring radio broadcasts. Instead, it has had a structure of *release money* payments that are made whenever a song is commercially released in any format that receives public performance.

There are additional preset payments whenever a song appears on the charts published by nationally recognized trade papers, like *Billboard, Cash Box, Radio & Records, The Gavin Report*, and *College Music Journal (CMJ)*. Rather than using weighting systems like the larger societies, SESAC payments are based on the song's success, which is determined by noting the highest chart positions attained in those publications.

For instance, a song reaching Number 50 on the country singles chart would receive a set amount distributed equally over four quarters. Thereafter, declining payments are made over following quarters for what SESAC calls *post chart payments*. Besides using singles chart positions for a payment formula, SESAC treats nationally distributed album cuts in a similar fashion.

SESAC augments chart data with verifiable performance data from affiliates, as well as radio playlists obtained from program syndicators. SESAC also recently entered into a trial agreement with BDS to log specific radio plays in certain markets so that payments on a *pay-per-play* basis could be made. As BDS covers more stations and markets, assuming the computerized surveys generate satisfactory results, it is likely SESAC and the other performing-right societies will make more extensive use of actual pay-per-play.

As for television performances, SESAC checks network and cable programming service logs, *TV Guide*, cue sheets supplied by affiliates, the Nielsen Report on Syndicated Television Programs, *TV Data*, and does spot monitoring of networks and local television stations.

SESAC also factors other data into determining the amount of royalties it pays. Affiliates are paid more or less depending upon seniority of SESAC affiliation, their catalog size, the number of copyrights licensed for recording and synchronization, and the affiliate's level of current activity in catalog promotion, acquisitions, and diversity.

Like ASCAP and BMI, SESAC has reciprocal agreements with overseas performing-right societies to collect foreign performance earnings of its writer and publisher clients.

Jukeboxes

ASCAP, BMI, and SESAC also license jukeboxes. Until the Copyright Act of 1976, jukebox operators were exempt from paying royalties to publishers whose works were played on the boxes. The 1976 act required operators to license and pay an annual fee to the performing-right societies for distribution to members.

Initially, the fee was $8.00 for each jukebox in operation. The Copyright Royalty Tribunal was authorized to review and escalate the fee periodically. By 1990 the fee had increased to $63.00 per box, and ASCAP, BMI, and SESAC collected more than $14 million for their members on an estimated 225,000 jukeboxes in the U.S..

Presently, jukeboxes are covered by blanket licenses from the *Jukebox License Office (JLO)* to cover repertoire from all three performing right societies. The JLO is a panel of members comprising appointees from each of the performing-right societies and the *Amusement and Music Operators Association* (AMOA).

Performing-right society membership requirements

Because BMI and ASCAP hold a virtual lock on collecting performance income in the United States, they cannot exclude anyone wishing to do business as a publisher. Both societies operate under judicial consent decrees that require them to be quite liberal about membership acceptance.

BMI and ASCAP extend membership to any applicant "actively engaged" in the music publishing business. Proof of activity can be demonstrated by distribution of at least one song in sheet music or recorded format. Officially, the song must have been in distribution at least one year, but both BMI and ASCAP normally waive this requirement and admit applicants promptly.

ASCAP requires an annual $50 membership fee from publishers. BMI has no annual or recurring fee, but does charge a $50 application fee upon joining the society.

SOCAN

Until 1990, Canada's BMI affiliated performing-right society was PROCAN; ASCAP's Canadian affiliate was CAPAC. But the two organizations have now merged into the *Society of Composers, Authors, & Music Publishers of Canada* (SOCAN). Now, virtually all countries, other than the U.S., have only one performing-right society.

Overseas performing-right societies

All foreign societies have reciprocal agreements with ASCAP, BMI, and SESAC to collect royalties on behalf of their members. Although BMI and ASCAP collect foreign royalties for their members, they deduct commissions for doing so. BMI charges 5%; ASCAP charges 3.5%. There can also be a lag between the time a foreign society allocates royalties to ASCAP, BMI, or SESAC and the time the American societies distribute those royalties to their respective members.

Many foreign societies accept U.S. publishers as associate members, so royalties can be collected directly without the double commissions or lag time in payments. If you have not assigned performing-rights to a subpublisher in a country where you have become an associate member, the local society will pay you directly. This eliminates the commission to your own society and the lag time before your society would ordinarily distribute foreign royalties to you.

Major overseas performing-right societies:

APRA	(Australia)
BUMA	(Holland)
GEMA*	(Germany)
IMRO	(Ireland)
JASRAC*	(Japan)
KODA	(Denmark)
PRS	(Great Britain)
RAIS	(Russia)
SABAM*	(Belgium)
SACEM	(France)
SACM	(Mexico)
SAMRO	(South Africa)
SGAE*	(Spain)
SIAE*	(Italy)
SOCAN	(Canada)
SPA*	(Portugal)
STIM	(Sweden)
SUISA*	(Switzerland)
TONO	(Norway)

* Indicates a society that licenses both *performance* and *mechanical rights*

THE BLACK BOX

If a foreign society cannot identify a song's owner, royalties earned by the work are considered unclaimed and are put into what is known as the *black box*. Monies accumulated in the black box are eventually distributed to that society's own members. This potential loss of foreign income adds an incentive to make subpublishing deals in major territories to ensure that all your works are properly registered with the local societies.

ISWC

Recently, a new method for identifying music copyrights has been worked out to ensure that copyright owners receive fast, accurate, and efficient distribution of royalties earned by their songs throughout the world. Upon registration of a work with a performing-right society, the society will issue an ISWC (International Standard Work Code) number that is unique to the song.

The ISWC works like the ISBN number (International Standard Book Number) given to each book that is published. The ISWC number identifies the song itself, rather than relying on secondary identifiers, such as names of songwriters and publishers. (Record companies will simultaneously begin using ISRC [International Standard Recording Code] numbers to identify recordings, rather than relying on secondary information, such as names of artists and record companies.)

The ISWC is a nine-digit number sandwiched between the letter *T* and a single check digit, which confirms a work has been correctly numbered.

Example:
ISWC T-034.275.981-1

The society with which a work is first registered assigns the ISWC and links the number to the international *WorksNet* database in New York. Then, any rights agency or society anywhere in the world can identify the work by plugging the ISWC number into the database, thereby locating the proper copyright owner.

ISWC numbers should slash administrative costs for mechanical- and performing-right societies, while increasing copyright protection for copyright owners. Any society in any country can access the WorksNet database in order to unlock ownership information and ensure royalties are distributed in timely and accurate fashion.

As the universally recognized copyright identification tool, all publishers should quote a song's ISWC number in all correspondence, licenses, and dealings with all rights societies, subpublishers, co-publishers, and music users.

Performing rights in cyberspace

Cyberspace is that fabled *information superhighway* linking personal computers to online services, electronic bulletin boards, and individual information providers on the Internet or World Wide Web. The electronic transmission of data through personal computers presents many challenges for copyright owners. Specifically, the ease of access to data stored in cyberspace forums risks loss of control by copyright owners over who might receive, copy, and download copyrighted material.

Copyright owners are primarily concerned with copyright protection of material uploaded to cyberspace forums and with effective means of being compensated for any copyright usages that result from the material being made available. There are three music licensing issues related to cyberspace: mechanical rights, performing rights, and synchronization rights. (See the chapter on *Miscellaneous Licensing Issues* for further discussion.)

The transmittal of music through cyberspace constitutes a "public performance," like broadcasting a work over television or radio. Thus, online providers must be licensed by, and pay performance royalties to, performing-right societies on behalf of copyright owners. ASCAP and BMI have been actively working to establish online licensing precedents.

ASCAP currently issues a blanket performing-right license called *The ASCAP Experimental Agreement for Computer Online Services, Electronic Bulletin Boards, Internet Sites, and Similar Operations*. The license grants online service operators permission to publicly perform (by means of electronic transmissions) all songs in ASCAP's repertory.

The online service provider pays ASCAP a licensing fee commensurate with the site's gross revenue, its total music revenue, and its total ASCAP-related music revenue. The minimum annual licensing fee is currently $500 per year per site. BMI uses a similar type of blanket license to cover performances of works in its repertory.

ASCAP vs. BMI

Publishers generally tend to place the bulk of their catalog with either BMI or ASCAP, using an affiliate company to place songs in the other society only when they acquire songs written by a writer belonging to that society. So, which society should you favor, BMI or ASCAP (or SESAC)? The debate has raged for years between the societies themselves and between writers and publishers.

Both BMI and ASCAP have venerable histories and repertoires. Both have reason to proclaim their merits. Both offer a wealth of information to back their claims to your preference. So, your decision will have to be made after you have requested membership applications and digested the information they send you, and after, perhaps, you have had experience with the personnel and workings of both societies. And sometimes it may well come down to the personal relationships the societies' representatives establish with you. Of course, a further determination may be that your most important writers belong to one society or the other, which means you must register the writers' works with the society they belong to.

Addresses of all three performing-right societies are listed in the Appendix. Contact them directly for current information on membership, payment schedules, registration procedures, etc.

CHAPTER 10

Synchronization Right Licensing

In music publishing, the term *synchronization* refers to integrating music with visual images to produce an audiovisual work. (*Audiovisual*, of course, is the term used to describe sound and sight combined.) A *synchronization license*, therefore, is the authorization given by publishers to audiovisual producers to include music in their product.

Synchronization licenses are issued for movies, television productions, training films, travelogues, documentaries, promotional clips, advertising, how-to videos, electronic games, etc. New technologies have fueled a rapid expansion of visual media in recent years, so that licensing music for audiovisual works is an increasingly important source of music publishing revenue.

Different types of synchronization licenses

There are at least six different types of synchronization licenses:
1. Theatrical
2. Television
3. Videogram
4. Commercial advertising
5. Promotional music video
6. Nontheatrical/noncommercial

Each of these licenses differs from the others in how the copyright owner is compensated, and in the scope of permission granted to the user, including the term, territory, method of distribution, and options available.

Other licenses needed for audiovisual works

In addition to synchronization rights, licensing music used for audiovisual works usually involves two other types of rights: *performance* and *mechanical*. Performance licenses permit the exhibition (or public showing) of music in audiovisual formats. Mechanical licenses authorize the manufacture, distribution, and sale of copies of audiovisual productions in various consumer-friendly formats, like videos, laser discs, CD-ROMs, etc.

Some synchronization licenses incorporate performing- and mechanical-right provisions allowing users to perform and make copies. But when synchronization licenses don't include these provisions, the user must obtain separate performance and mechanical licenses if public showings are intended or if copies are going to be made and sold.

Before an audiovisual work can be offered for exhibition, or reproduced for the home video market, however, music must be *synchronized* to the visual action on the film. So, first things first, the audiovisual producer must get a synchronization license from the music copyright owner.

Theatrical synchronization licenses (music in movies)

Motion picture producers must obtain synchronization licenses *and* performance licenses from copyright owners of any music used in their productions. Performance rights are licensed separately from synchronization rights in the United States, because

U.S. court decisions prevent ASCAP and BMI from requiring U.S. movie theaters to obtain blanket performance licenses for theatrical exhibitions. Authorization to exhibit a film with music included must, therefore, be obtained by the film's producer or distributor directly from the copyright owner.

Film producers do not need performance licenses for television broadcasts of movies. Television stations and networks are responsible for clearing performance rights for all broadcasts, which they do through blanket performance licenses with the performing-right societies.

Motion picture producers must also obtain mechanical licenses in order to distribute and sell videos and laser discs for home consumption. Frequently, motion picture producers will attempt to negotiate a very inclusive synchronization license to take into account plans to rent or sell the film in all media, domestically as well as overseas.

ORIGINAL MUSIC FOR MOVIE SOUNDTRACKS

The musical score underlying a movie soundtrack is usually *commissioned* by the film production company. This is most often done directly between producers and composers, bypassing music publishers. Composers work as *employees for hire*, and the final score is a *work for hire*, with the copyright owned by the film company.

In cases where a big-name composer is engaged to do the score, the composer (or his publisher) might successfully negotiate partial copyright ownership. Sometimes, a composer is commissioned to do the background score, and a big-name songwriter is commissioned to write one or more songs to be featured as the title track and/or as a recurring theme.

PREEXISTING COPYRIGHTS IN MOVIE SOUNDTRACKS

Commissioned soundtracks are frequently augmented by previously written songs licensed from music publishers. Film producers seeking a certain atmosphere will "drop" a song into the soundtrack. A well-known hit, for instance, might serve as a backdrop to a specific scene in order to evoke a nostalgic mood or establish a time frame.

A hit song might also be licensed to play behind the title or closing credits, for use as a running theme throughout the film, or featured as a performance by a character on screen. For a drop-in of a preexisting work, the publisher retains full copyright and issues the film production company a synchronization license to use the song in that particular production.

THEATRICAL SYNCHRONIZATION FEES

A theatrical synchronization license usually provides a one-time synchronization fee to the copyright owner. The size of a synchronization fee depends upon the importance of the song generally and its importance to the film specifically. If the song is essential to the film, such as providing the film title, storyline, or theme, the fee can be substantially more.

Theatrical synchronization fees for motion pictures typically range as follows:

- **$5,000-$13,000** for a few seconds background use of a new or unknown song
- **$10,000-$20,000** for a few seconds background use of a well-known or established copyright
- **$50,000-$100,000** (or more) for important copyrights used as themes or featured performances

More money to come
The theatrical synchronization fee may be just a curtain raiser for much more income earned over the years as a direct result of a film project. Derivatives and spin-offs from an original film can include:

- broadcast performance royalties
- mechanical royalties (soundtrack albums, singles, covers, and compilations)
- rebroadcasts and syndications
- overseas theatrical performance royalties
- printed edition sales
- lyric reprints
- commercials
- games, toys, karaoke, etc.

NEGOTIATING THEATRICAL SYNCHRONIZATION FEES

Although theatrical synchronization fees are generally quite handsome, it doesn't pay to price a song out of a film producer's range. Be flexible in negotiating synchronization fees, because the potential follow-up income may be much, much greater. Without giving away the store, the publisher's strategy should always be to get his work included in any film that has potential for commercial success.

Nature of use
Among other things, the size of the fee depends on *how* a song is used. A featured performance is worth much more than an incidental moment of background mood. The terminology for the nature of use is:

- title theme
- closing theme
- visual vocal (featured onscreen performance)
- visual instrumental (featured onscreen performance)
- background vocal (nonfeatured use)
- background instrumental (nonfeatured use)

- incidental (segues, transitions, scene intros and closers, etc.)

Length of performance

The *duration* (length) of the performance is also vitally important to the size of the fee. Obviously, the fee is much greater when a song is used in its entirety, rather than for just a few seconds.

Combining duration and nature of use, it should be obvious that a visual vocal performance of three minutes duration warrants a substantially higher fee than does ten seconds of incidental, instrumental background use.

Star power

Star power is another consideration when negotiating synchronization fees. Film producers sometimes view the performance of a well-known recording artist as a box office attraction. The stature of the recording artist may be more important to the producer than the song itself. The producer may opt to drop a song for which the publisher demands a high synchronization fee in favor of a less expensive song performed by the same artist.

Importance of the song

By the same token, a well-known hit can be sought after by a film producer because the song is important to the film in some way. Again, the inclusion of the hit may be considered as the producer's desire to buy star power.

No matter how important the song is to the film, the *song's importance as a copyright* should always be a factor in determining the size of the fee. Any song that has become a major hit is a major copyright. It will be sought after for many types of usages in years to come. Don't devalue it by accepting the same size fee as you would for a song that has never sold a single record.

Most favored nations clause

On the other hand, be careful not to inflate the importance of a song, because, in most cases, producers can find suitable substitutes if the fee is too high. The publisher has a careful balancing act when it comes to negotiating a fee: not too high, not too low. Some publishers fall back on naming a fee with the stipulation that it is subject to a *most favored nations clause.*

A most favored nations clause requires the producer to pay no less a fee than the highest fee granted to any other publisher for the use of another song in the same production. So, if you quote a fee of, say, $15,000, and another publisher then successfully negotiates a fee of $20,000, the producer is obliged to also pay you $20,000.

This can be difficult for a producer to accept, because not all songs are equally important to the film, and not all songs will be used in the same way or with the same amount of playing time. For a most favored nations clause to be fair, it would have to apply to songs that are exactly alike in usage, duration, and significance both as a copyright and to the film itself.

Soundtrack album guarantee

A reduction in the size of the synchronization fee might be considered if the producer guarantees the song's inclusion in a soundtrack album. Soundtrack albums issued in conjunction with a film's release mean additional income to the publisher from mechanical and performance royalties. A soundtrack album, and publicity surrounding the film's release, might also generate special sheet music editions.

Soundtrack albums recorded by established artists can generate significant spin-off income. When a song from a successful movie is issued as an 'A' side, the payback can be huge. So, if a soundtrack album is guaranteed and you gauge the project to have box office appeal, consider the potential extra income as a factor in the size of the fee. Especially when a name artist is performing the song, and even more especially if an 'A' side release is guaranteed.

Film producer's budget

Although production budgets for many modern feature films are astronomical, allocations for the music are usually relatively small by comparison. Despite music's importance to a film's final quality and box office appeal, it is still pretty much an afterthought in the film producer's scheme of things. And, as an afterthought, it often happens that music is the area where a panicky producer tries to economize after going over budget on the production.

If the publisher can determine the size of the budget for music in relation to the overall production budget (vis à vis the number of other songs for which the producer must pay synchronization fees), it's easier to gauge how much to charge.

But, again, the fee also depends on the importance of the song to the film. If the song is interchangeable (i.e., used to create background ambiance for a scene simply requiring a "country song"), the producer may easily drop from consideration any work whose publisher demands too high a fee. But, if the song provides a theme, storyline, title track, etc., the producer is more or less forced to pay accordingly and economize elsewhere.

Number of uses

Another determining factor in the size of a fee is whether there are multiple or recurring uses of a song in a film. Each use requires a fee. But that doesn't necessarily mean that if you charge $ X for one use, you would charge the producer three times X for using the song three times.

You might, instead, formulate a fee scale where:
a) $ X = one use,
b) $ $X + (X \times 75\%) = 2$ uses, and
c) $ $X + (X \times 75\%) + (X \times 50\%) = 3$ uses.

Translated, this might work out to, say:
a) $10,000 for one use,
b) $17,500 for two uses, and
c) $22,500 for three uses.

Of course, this assumes all three uses are relatively equal in terms of duration and type of use.

Lyric changes

Film producers sometimes request changes in lyrics to suit a scene or character. Proposed lyric changes must always be considered carefully. First consideration has to be whether the songwriter's contract requires approval of any changes. Even if it doesn't, the prudent publisher will allow the writer to approve or reject proposed changes, in order to keep relationships smooth.

More importantly, proposed changes must be considered from the standpoint of what it does to the song's future value as a copyright. The changes might make a mockery of the song or turn it into an off-color joke or spoof. If so, and the film (or TV show) achieves widespread popularity, the new version may supersede the original version in the way the song is identified by the public.

In any event, if lyrics changes are allowed, the publisher must retain full copyright of the song, including the altered lyrics. The screenwriter, or whoever it is that makes the changes, should not share in the copyright. Normally, when lyric changes are permitted, the publisher is able to raise the synchronization fee as a trade-off.

Exclusivity

Film producers sometimes seek to prohibit the licensing of a song for use in other movies. Exclusivity may be requested when a song is vital to a film, such as usage as a title track or recurring theme, or when the film itself is based on the song's title or storyline.

A producer should certainly expect to pay a hefty synchronization fee to obtain exclusivity. However, publishers can never afford to shut all doors forever and thereby diminish a copyright's value. So,

exclusivity should be restricted to two to three years from the film's release date or two to three years from the time the license is issued, whichever comes first.

Holds

Sometimes a *hold* is requested, even though no decision has yet been reached as to whether the song will make the final cut. Requests for holds should be treated similarly to requests for exclusivity. A song may be so important to a film project that the producer requests the publisher not to license it for any other film until either his film is released, or until X months (or years) after the release date.

The publisher doesn't want to jeopardize having the song not used at all, but neither does he want to forego other opportunities that might arise in the meantime. Especially if the song might be ultimately left on the cutting-room floor. It is the same dilemma publishers face when record producers or labels request holds on songs considered for recording projects. Happily, however, film producers are usually willing to pay for the privilege of putting a hold on a song (unlike record producers and labels).

In effect, the film producer takes an *option* on the song, so the publisher will hold it until either usage is confirmed or the song is dropped from the project. The option may require the producer to pay the publisher a percentage of the ultimate synchronization fee as a nonreturnable advance. (Which means the synchronization fee must first be agreed between the publisher and producer.) If the song is not used after all, the publisher does not have to return the advance.

Alternatively, a publisher may insist on an option payment as a *fee*, rather than an advance. The fee pays for the privilege of holding the song without regard to the amount paid for the full synchronization fee. Option payments made as fees may not be deducted from the ultimate synchronization fee.

Option fees may range from $1,000 to $5,000 for a six-month hold. The producer might be given the option to renew the option for additional six-month periods upon payment of equal amounts. It is wise to limit the number of renewable options so as not to tie the song up forever.

Package deals

A publisher may be persuaded to lower the synchronization fee if more than one song from his catalog is used in a film. A fee scale might be agreed similar to the one cited above where there are recurring uses of one song in the same film.

Also, a publisher with an extensive catalog might be able to forge an agreement with a film production company whereby the company agrees to use X number of songs in various productions within a stated period of time. Again, a sliding fee scale might be set up, so that fee discounts graduate according to the number of songs ultimately used. For instance, the full fee is paid for song number one; a 15% discount on songs two through four; a 20% discount on songs five through eight, and so on.

Be careful, however, that any package deal involves apples and apples, rather than apples and oranges. Each song must be comparable to the others in importance as a copyright; each type of usage must be similar; and the duration (playing time) of all uses must be roughly equivalent.

Alternative quotes

Movie producers sometimes try to wheedle little deals with publishers when negotiating synchronization fees. They may ask for an *alternative quote*, in return for including the song in a spin-off, such as a sound-track album.

In other words, the publisher is asked to quote two fees: one for use in the film only, and a 10%-15% reduction in the size of the fee if the song is included in a spin-off. A publisher has to judge whether mechanical royalties will likely offset a reduced fee and whether or not the producer will actually keep the song off the soundtrack release if a reduced fee is not given.

Cut-ins, splits

Another producer ploy is to seek partial publishing on a preexisting copyright. As with some record producers and labels, there will occasionally be film producers who promise to include a song in a film *if* the publisher agrees to either a cut-in on certain types of income or assign an interest in copyright ownership. Before even entertaining the idea of such a deal, the publisher has to consider the importance of the copyright as it now stands, the potential value of the copyright if it is used in the film, and its anticipated value if it is not used.

If the song has already been a hit and is an important income-generating copyright, no such deal should be considered. But if the song is new, or has been dormant awhile, and the film's box office potential will likely activate the work to an important level, cut-ins or splits might be considered under the right conditions.

Assuming a song has nothing else exciting looming for it on the horizon, a split might be worth it. Seventy-five percent (or 50%) of something is certainly better than 100% of nothing. However, a cut-in is always preferable to a split.

A split involves the sharing of copyright ownership and division of all income received from all sources. A cut-in limits the other party to income sharing only (not ownership) and restricts the sources of income to specific derivative usages arising directly from the film.

For instance, a cut-in might allow the producer to share in mechanical royalties generated by the soundtrack album, print sales of a folio edition based on the film's release, overseas box office performance royalties, and performance royalties arising directly from television showings of the film.

If a major production might revive a sleeping copyright (as opposed to an active standard) and/or if you believe the producer will substitute another song, the producer might be given a cut-in for, say, 25% of the mechanical royalties arising from the soundtrack album only. Even so, the cut-in should not be in perpetuity. There should be a cut-off date of somewhere between three and ten years, either from the film's release date or the soundtrack album's release, whichever comes first.

Obviously, all these points and more are matters for negotiation. But, in any event, a producer should expect to pay a synchronization fee commensurate with any special terms.

Performing-rights for synchronized usages

Although U.S. theaters don't pay performance royalties for music used in films, copyright owners do receive performance royalties when films are shown on American TV. Since U.S. theaters are exempted from having to pay performance fees, a flat performance fee for U.S. theatrical exhibition is included in the synchronization license, to be paid by the film production company. The performance fee is normally equal to the synchronization fee, though some publishers request up to 200% of the size of the synchronization fee.

However, performing-right societies in most other countries do collect performance royalties for theatrical showings. For films that do well overseas, performance royalties can be significant. In Europe, theaters must pay performing-right societies a percentage of box office receipts (usually from 1%-2%). So, the bigger the film is as a box office hit, the more money copyright owners of the music receive.

SYNCHRONIZATION LICENSE PROVISIONS

- The work is identified by title and writer(s).
- Duration of the license is defined:
  —Usually in perpetuity for feature films; lesser periods for other types of uses
  —Generally concurrent with the publisher's right to the work during the remaining life of the copyright

NOTE: In many cases, a publisher only has a few years left on the copyright assignment from a writer. For instance, an established writer may have made a ten-year agreement, after which the writer recaptures all rights to the work.

—Theatrical synchronization licenses are most often requested in perpetuity. If the publisher is not able to grant a license in perpetuity, the film producer may very likely seek another song to substitute, and the publisher loses a financial opportunity.

—Of course, this means the songwriter also loses a lucrative income opportunity. The solution is for the publisher to convince the writer to authorize the publisher (in writing) to grant the license in perpetuity.

- The producer agrees that the work may only be used in the one motion picture production, which is then identified by title.
- The amount of the synchronization fee is stated.

—This is sometimes referred to as a recording-right license fee, and the agreement is conditional upon its being paid to the publisher by the motion picture producer.

- The publisher gives the producer *nonexclusive* permission to record the work and to make "copies" (of the film containing the recording of the song) for import into any country covered by the agreement, subject to the terms of the agreement.
- The nature of the use is stated.

—Examples: partial length featured vocal performance (partial visual vocal), full length featured vocal performance (full visual vocal), background instrumental, etc.

- The number of such uses is stated.

—That is, how many times the work will be used within the production, and the duration in minutes and seconds of each use.

- The territories covered by the license are named.

—Usually "the world," although the word "universe" is becoming used more often by licensers who realize the time may not be far off when copyrights will be used to entertain and edify humans (or others) beyond the confines of earth.

- The amount of the performing-right fee to be paid is stated.

—As noted above, performance fees from exhibition of films in European theaters are collected by European performing-right societies; movies shown on U.S. television result in performance fees to the publishers, which are collected by BMI, ASCAP, and SESAC. But U.S. theaters are exempted from paying such fees to BMI or ASCAP, so a flat performance fee for U.S. theatrical exhibition is included in the synchronization license.

- In return for payment of the performance fee, the publisher gives the producer *nonexclusive* permission to perform or authorize others to perform the work as recorded in the motion picture, and in radio, television, and theatrical advertisements for the production.
- Permission for public performance of the work is limited to places of public entertainment where motion pictures are commonly exhibited, including television, and the production may only be exhibited on television stations or networks that have valid licenses from a performing-right society with authority to license and collect performance fees on the publisher's behalf.
- The producer promises to furnish the publisher a *cue sheet* within 30 days of the production's release to the general public.

—The publisher must file copies of the cue sheet with his performing-right society, and, through his subpublishers, with overseas performing-right societies in order to ensure proper payment of performance royalties.

- The producer may not alter the lyrics or melody of the work in any way that changes the character of the work (unless permission has otherwise been negotiated and granted by the publisher).
- The producer may not use the lyrics or title of the work in the story of the motion picture (unless permission has otherwise been negotiated and granted by the publisher).
- The publisher reserves all rights to the work not specifically granted to the producer in the license.

—This precludes the producer from using the work in videocassettes or other new methods of delivering the film to the public without renegotiating for the right to use the music when doing so.

—In addition to theatrical synchronization licenses, movie producers and distributors must obtain videogram synchronization licenses (or include provisions for video release in the theatrical synchronization license).

Nontheatrical synchronization licenses

Many large corporations and government agencies make audiovisual programs for training, informational, and business-to-business promotional purposes. No commercial use is intended, insofar as exhibition to the paying public or sale of videograms.

Synchronization licenses for these types of productions are generally issued for a flat fee ($1,000-$2,500) and for a limited period (one to five years). Distribution of the work is usually restricted to in-house screenings or closed circuit video-conferencing. If the user desires to make videocassettes for distribution to employees, trainees, or prospective clients, an additional fee is charged, usually based on the number of copies to be made.

Videogram synchronization licenses

VCRs are becoming as ubiquitous as radios and home stereos, which means the sale of home videos, or videograms, is increasingly an important source of income for music copyright owners. The term *videogram* includes home videocassettes and videodiscs.

Under copyright law, any type of videogram (whether promotional clip, music video, how-to, feature film, etc.) is defined as an *audiovisual work*, and producers of any audiovisual work are required to obtain synchronization licenses from the music copyright owners or their agents.

MECHANICAL RIGHTS FOR VIDEOGRAMS

In addition to a synchronization license, video manufacturers or distributors must get *mechanical licenses* from owners of music copyrights in order to make, distribute, and sell copies of audiovisual works (e.g., videos, laser discs, CD-ROMs). As in the case of phonorecords, mechanical licenses for audiovisual works may be handled by a publisher's mechanical-right society, such as the Harry Fox Agency.

Compensation to music copyright owners for phonorecords is limited to a maximum statutory mechanical rate, but compensation for videogram mechanical rights is negotiated, rather than statutory. Negotiations between video distributors and music publishers may result in mechanical rights being paid for in one of three ways:

1. **per unit royalty** for each video sold (usually 6¢ to 12¢ per song)
2. **buy-outs** (a one time payment, no matter how many videos are ultimately sold)
3. **rollover advances** (a set, nonreturnable sum representing an advance on X number of units sold, with further nonreturnable advances in the same amount as additional sales levels are reached)

☞ *For instance, a $5,000 advance may be paid for sales up to 50,000 units. When and if 50,000 units are sold, a further $5,000 is due to cover a further 50,000 sales, and so on, with continuing $5,000 advances each time another 50,000 unit plateau is reached.*

NOTE: It is more common than not for movie production companies to insist on buy-outs rather than agreeing to per-unit royalties. This is the policy laid down by all major film distributors, leaving no room for negotiation. If you don't agree to a buy-out, your song will probably not be used in the video and very

possibly will be dropped from the theatrical version as well. In this case, the only negotiating room is with regard to the size of the buy-out fee.

PERFORMANCE RIGHTS FOR VIDEOGRAMS

As for *performance rights* to music used in videos, the exhibitioner (who shows, or "performs" the work to the public) is required to obtain a performance license from the music copyright owner. In practice, permission to perform or show videos is obtained from performing-right societies under blanket licenses issued to the venue or broadcaster that exhibits, performs, or transmits the video.

VIDEOGRAM SYNCHRONIZATION LICENSE PROVISIONS

Typical videogram synchronization licenses contain provisions similar to those found in a theatrical synchronization licenses, with the following differences:

- The license is granted for a stated, limited term of years, rather than full term of copyright, and all rights granted to the producer terminate at the expiration of the stated term.
- The producer is given permission to copy, sell, and distribute for sale the song as contained in the videogram, as identified by title of the film and videogram number.
- The license is not valid for rental of videograms. A producer wishing to rent videograms containing the work must first negotiate an agreed compensation with the publisher, which will be based on rental receipts.
- The producer promises to pay the publisher a royalty of $X\%$ of the retail price for each copy of each videocassette sold and paid for in the licensed territory. This may be stated as a certain sum, rather than as a percentage.
- A royalty of $X\%$ of the retail price for each copy of each videodisc sold and paid for in the licensed territory. This may be stated as a certain sum, rather than as a percentage. For discussion of what the royalties may be in the above two provisions, see the section on videocassettes in the chapter on *Mechanical Licenses*.
- Producer shall account to the publisher within (30, 45, 60, or 90) days of the end of each calendar quarter for each videogram sold and paid for and shall pay publisher accordingly all royalties then due.
- Publisher has the right, upon written notice, to inspect producer's books relating to the sale of said videogram, during normal business hours at the producer's place of business.
- Producer may not assign or transfer the rights granted by the publisher without consent of the publisher.

Promotional video clips

Promo video clips are produced by record companies to promote sales of singles and albums. Record companies must obtain synchronization licenses from the publishers of songs used in such clips.

Video production costs can easily exceed recording costs for the album itself. Publishers are generally willing to issue free licenses for songs used in promo clips, though some publishers insist on token license fees (e.g., $100). But, remember, the publisher and record company are on the same side. Both want to promote the release and make the song/album a hit.

The licensed territory is normally for the world, because both publisher and record company want international affiliates to use the clip to promote the work. However, licenses should ideally be limited to one to two years, with options on the publisher's part to renew for further periods. The publisher should insist on this option as a trap door clause to terminate the license if the publisher is unhappy with the record company's use of the song in the clip.

Publishers should insist on licensing provisions that prohibit the record company from charging any fees for use of the clip. Licenses for promo clips should be narrowly drawn, so that if the clip is at some point released commercially, or combined with other clips for commercial release, the publisher will be paid for each unit sold. Commercial use should compensate the publisher either on a fixed royalty per unit (i.e., *X¢*), or on a prorated percentage of the wholesale or retail price of the video (i.e., *Y%* of retail ÷ the number of songs included on the video).

Television synchronization licenses

Synchronization licenses for television productions are usually limited to five years (as opposed to movie synchronization licenses, which are normally granted *in perpetuity*). *Short-term* licenses may be requested for topical programs that aren't expected to be syndicated or rerun extensively. Short term licenses are usually for one-year terms with options for one- or two-year renewals.

TYPICAL FEES FOR FIVE-YEAR LICENSES

- **$500-$1,000** for a few seconds background use of a new or unknown song
- **$5,000-$13,000** for the same usage in a made-for-television motion picture
- **$1,000-$5,000** for a few seconds background use of an established copyright
- **$10,000-$20,000** for the same usage in a made-for-television motion picture

- **$50,000-$100,000+** for important copyrights used as themes or featured performances
- **Reduced fees** are usually expected for *short-term* licenses. Additional fees are paid upon exercising any options to extend synchronization licenses beyond the original term

FREE TELEVISION SYNCHRONIZATION LICENSES

Don't be alarmed when a TV producer's music supervisor requests a *free television synchronization license*. The license isn't actually free in the sense that you don't get paid for the usage. The term simply means that the producer can sell or license the program to any network, syndicator, or television station during the license term without additional payment to you, as long as the ensuing *broadcasts are carried free to viewers* (not pay-per-view). In other words, the term applies to "free television," which is not the same thing as a "free license."

"Free television" refers to programs viewers can get without charge, broadcast over media licensed by performing-right societies. In the main, free television includes the networks (ABC, CBS, Fox, NBC, and their local affiliates), independent local stations, and syndicated programs broadcast by local stations.

When considering what fee to charge for a free television synchronization license, the usual conditions must be defined:
- importance of the copyright
- duration of performance
- type of performance (background, feature, instrumental, etc.)
- term of license
- territory requested
- whether lyrics will be changed
- recurring or single use
- number of other songs in relation to the budget allocated for music
- options for derivative uses, such as home video, pay-per-view, cable, public television, nontelevision uses, and theatrical showings.

FREE TELEVISION SYNCHRONIZATION FEES
- **$800-$1,500** for a 5-year license
- **$1,500-$4,500** for a 10-15 year license
- **$3,000-$9,000** for a life of copyright license

These fees may not sound like much compared to movie synchronization fees, but performance royalties from televised broadcasts can be substantial. Just one featured broadcast performance on a network primetime program typically pays $1,800 net to the publisher (and $1,800 to the writer). Also, a copyright's value is almost always enhanced by such usage.

The publisher also gets performance royalties of

around $750 each time a song is broadcast on a network as a theme, and $500 for each network background usage of three minutes duration. Considering the number of repeats and syndicated showings that might follow the original broadcast during the term of the license, the synchronization fee is likely to be a lot less than the ultimate earnings potential. So, the publisher's strategy is to be reasonable when negotiating television synchronization fees in order to reap follow-on performance royalties and enhance the copyright's value.

OPTIONS

Television producers frequently request options in free television synchronization licenses to cover contingent uses. Typical options requested include:

Renewals (if the original term is less than copyright)

To renew a five-year-term for a further five years, a license may call for an additional payment equal to the original fee plus 25%-33%.

Life of copyright

In the event the producer wants to exercise an option to extend the license for life of copyright, the option fee might be equal to four or five times the amount charged for the initial five-year term (e.g., $1,000 for five years plus $5,000 if the option for life of copyright is exercised).

All television or all media

Producers frequently request an option to distribute a program to pay TV and subscription channels.

Subscription television includes optional cable offerings, such as HBO, Cinemax, Showtime, and Disney, as opposed to basic cable, which includes USA, TNN, and MTV.

Option payments for All Media might range from an additional $3,500 for five years to $7,500 for life of copyright. Often, instead of renewal options, producers seek All Media licenses for life of copyright, in which case the fees might range from $5,000 to $10,000.

Title of the program

The right to use a song's title as the title for an episode in a series can boost a synchronization fee by 50% to 200%, depending on the extent of the song's usage as a recurring theme or background element, as well as the importance of the copyright.

Promo spots

The right to use a song as a promo spot, that is, to tout the TV program in which the song is used, usually warrants an additional $350 to $750.

Bumpers

Generally, the same fee charged for promos is charged for the right to use a song as a bumper (lead in to, or out from, a commercial break).

Right to change lyrics

Lyric changes must be considered carefully, as per reasons cited above in the discussion on movie synchronization licenses.

Home video rights

It is not uncommon for television programs to be packaged for sale as home videos. Whereas home video releases of feature films usually call for synchronization licenses in perpetuity, videogram licenses for television programming is more normally restricted to 5-15 years.

Television producers may seek options to package programs for home video either through a one-time buy-out or through payments on a per unit royalty basis.

Royalties may be offered as a penny rate of between 6¢ and 12¢ per song per unit sold, or as a percentage of between 5%-10% of the wholesale price of the video. If the royalty is percentage based, the percentage will be prorated either on:
- number of songs included in the program or
- duration in seconds vis à vis total seconds of all songs combined or
- duration in seconds vis à vis the program's total running time

When royalties are offered, as opposed to a buy-out, an advance is usually warranted. Royalty advances are calculated either on estimates of potential sales, or on a rollover basis.

With a rollover, the advance equals the agreed royalty rate times a certain level of sales, with another like sum advanced each time that sales plateau is reached. For instance, a rollover advance on 15,000 unit sales at 6¢ per song would be $900 (6¢ x 15,000 units). When 15,000 units are sold, an additional $900 is paid; then, a further $900 is paid when the next 15,000 units are sold, and so on.

There is a trend by major TV producers to insist on one-time buy-outs. This relieves producers of having to make periodic accountings and royalty payments. To exercise a buy-out option, the license might call for payment of an additional $3,000-$10,000. The exact size of the fee within that range depends upon the nature of the use (background, featured performance, theme, recurring usage, etc.) and other factors already cited.

Theatrical distribution

An option to show the program to theater audiences is usually confined to overseas. The fee to exercise such an option is normally equal to the fee for a home video buy-out, though it can be more, depending on the nature of the use.

Foreign theatrical distribution is more akin to a movie synchronization license, in that it is usually for life of copyright. Remember: overseas theatrical showings generate performance royalties from box office receipts, unlike U.S. theatrical usage, which does not.

REDUCED FEES FOR TV LICENSES

Like film producers and record labels, television producers frequently ask for specially reduced synchronization fees. There are numerous situations when such a request may be justified.

Short-term licenses

As mentioned above, synchronization fees are usually reduced for short-term licenses of one-year's duration. Types of programs where short-term licenses are the norm include chat shows, interview programs, news magazines, and news specials—in other words, topical programs that lose immediacy and are not normally repeated or syndicated beyond the first year. However, additional fees are paid upon exercising any options to extend these licenses beyond the original term.

Partial use

Using just a brief snatch of a song doesn't necessarily warrant a reduced fee, especially if a work is vital to setting a scene or mood. But there are some types of programs where dozens of songs are used in 10-20 second bites, and, because of the sheer number of works involved, the producer must get reduced fees in order to afford all the music required. As an example, some game shows use brief portions of recognizable songs as part of a quiz (name the title, artist, or composer). Fee reductions are generally expected, and given, in such cases.

Program budget vis à vis number of songs used

Some shows have set budgets for music from which the music supervisor must obtain licenses to use varying lengths of 20, 30, or more songs. The publisher can choose to hold out for the standard fee and invariably see his song dropped, or agree to a reduced license fee based on a formula the supervisor has already worked out.

The formula likely will entail the total budget divided by the aggregate playing times of all songs. Depending on the budget and the number of songs involved, the fee may range from $50 for 15 seconds to as much as $400 for over 2 minutes but less than the full length of a song.

The publisher will be careful to establish whether the use is more prominent than other songs, that is, more vital to the production. If 25 songs are used in brief 15-20 second bites, and yours is featured as an on-camera vocal performance for two minutes, it should be worth close to the standard fee rather than falling within the reduced formula. Still, the publisher has to consider that, even at a reduced rate, the song will generate significant performance royalties and enjoy increased value as a copyright from televised usage.

Recurring use

Another reduced fee situation might arise when a song is used several times in one program. Although the normal fee is charged for the first use, subsequent uses in the same program are licensed at reduced rates.

For example, the first use might be $900 with three additional uses licensed for $300 each. There is no hard rule on this; some publishers consider up to three minutes constituting one use, so that three 60-second uses are licensed as one, and each additional three minutes aggregate use, or portion thereof, is charged the same as the first use.

In this way, a television program might use bits and pieces of the same song some 10 or 15 times. What counts is the total duration, not the number of usages. To illustrate, the fee for seven minutes aggregate use might total $3,000 as follows:

- First three minutes aggregate = $1,000
- Second three minutes aggregate = $1,000
- Seventh minute = $1,000

Noncommercial broadcasts

Though not exactly a "reduced fee" situation, in the sense that the producer asks for and receives a smaller fee than otherwise, synchronization fees for noncommercial, "public" television are limited to a statutory maximum rate. Public Broadcasting System (PBS) is a partially taxpayer funded, nonprofit operation. As such, it is entitled under the Copyright Act to use copyrighted material upon payment of preset fees, as opposed to market-oriented rates negotiated between the performing-right societies and commercial broadcasters.

PBS, in fact, is one of four licensing areas for which the Copyright Act provides compulsory licenses. (The other three compulsory licensing provisions apply to mechanical licenses for phonorecords, jukeboxes, and basic cable rebroadcasts of television programming originating on "free television" networks and local stations.) In other words, PBS and regional public television stations can compel copyright owners to issue licenses at set fees, provided the broadcast is aired only over the noncommercial network or its affiliated local public stations.

PBS licensing fees are determined by CARP (Copyright Arbitration Royalty Panel). These fees are currently as follows (through December 31, 1997):

- $99.85 for each featured performance
- $50.46 for each background performance
- $50.46 for a theme of a one-off program
- $50.46 for themes in the first episode of a series.
- $20.48 for a theme used in each successive episode
- $29.98 *per minute* for use in a concert performance

PBS licenses are limited to three years. Additional three-year renewals can be made upon payment of 50% of the original fee, and second three-year renewals can be made upon payment of an additional 25% of the original fee. Alternatively, the producer can opt for an indefinite license by paying an amount equal to 100% of the original fee before the first three-year term expires.

Cable television rebroadcasts

As mentioned above, compulsory licensing also applies to basic cable distribution of free television programming. The reasoning is that cable is the only means of television reception for some households, particularly in rural areas. As long as the cable program is not pay-per-view or a subscription channel like HBO, cable companies can rebroadcast, transmit, or distribute programming by television stations and networks upon payment of specified fees.

Movies and television shows based on existing songs

Occasionally, a song's title, lyrics, or storyline sparks an idea on which to base a movie, teleplay, made-for-television movie, or series. In such cases, the film or television producer will probably seek exclusive rights to use the song as the basis for the production.

In setting a value on granting exclusive rights to use a song in this manner, the publisher assesses many of the same criteria discussed for all licensing situations, including:

- how central the song is to the project
- the importance of the copyright
- the possibility that other opportunities must be declined

PARTICIPATION

The size of the fee (when a production is based on a song) is also determined by other terms the producer may want to include in the license. When a program revolves around a song, the song takes on additional importance. If the program is a success, it propels the earnings of the song through derivatives and spin-offs. The producer will be mindful of this and try to negotiate the right to participate in some of the rewards generated by the film or television show. Participation may include cut-ins on mechanical royalties from soundtrack albums, or overseas performance royalties from box office receipts, etc.

However, participation should cut both ways. Since the song inspired the project, and is therefore the germ of the producer's success, the publisher may insist on participating in some of that success. For example, the publisher may insist upon receiving any or all of the following:

- a percentage of the producer's profits from film distributors, home video sales, television networks or syndicators
- a percentage of merchandising rights
- a percentage of net profits from sequels or derivative programming

OPTIONS

After agreeing on a synchronization fee, as well as the terms of any participation provisions, the producer and publisher usually then negotiate an *option price*. The producer won't want to incur liabilities for acquisition fees if the project never materializes, but he will want protect exclusivity *prior* to going ahead with the project. This means, of course, the producer will not put up the full acquisition purchase price for the exclusive rights until the production is a go, hence the option.

An option basically allows the producer time to finance the project, confirm distribution, line up casting and a director, etc. If the producer is unable to put together all these pieces, the project is scrubbed and the rights revert to the publisher.

The option fee is a percentage of the acquisition price. Typically, this might be 5%, for a period ranging from 6-18 months. Longer option periods call for a higher option price (10%-15%). Of course, the producer may insist on the right to renew the option upon payment of an additional sum and may also be given the right to extend the option if serious negotiations are underway for financing and distribution at the time the option period comes to an end.

Synchronization rights in cyberspace

The terms *cyberspace, information superhighway, Internet,* and *World Wide Web* all refer to electronic transmission of data through personal computers. There are three music licensing issues related to cyberspace: mechanical rights, performing rights, and synchronization rights. (See the chapter on *Miscellaneous Licensing Issues* for further discussion.)

Mechanical licenses for cyberspace are subject to statutory royalty rates, and performances are covered through blanket licenses from performing-right societies. However, copyright owners must negotiate synchronization licenses directly with program producers on a case by case basis. As with any synchronization situation, each case has its own parameters. Fees and other terms must be arrived at after careful analysis of each licensing issue (e.g., nature of use, duration of use, duration of license, etc.). Cyberspace synchronization licenses must be granted for the *world*, since the medium has no borders.

Producers of audiovisual programming for online distribution are also required to distribute the program only via Web sites with valid performing-right licenses, because transmitting the program constitutes a public performance. Mechanical licenses are also required before consumers can be allowed to download copies of the programs.

This is an emerging technology, so copyright owners must narrowly define and limit the scope of rights granted. The duration of any synchronization license should be restricted to as short a term as possible. Options to renew the license at the publisher's discretion can be granted, but the point is not to commit long-term to licenses that may become outmoded as the technology develops.

Synchronization licenses for commercial advertising

Synchronization licenses are also needed to integrate music with visual images in television or other types of video-related commercial advertising. This is quite a lucrative area for copyright owners. Fees can range from $25,000 to upwards of $500,000 (or more for truly important standards) for just one year's usage on a national scale for television commercials. Proportionately smaller fees are paid for shorter periods (less than a year) and/or in regional or local markets rather than national. (See the chapter on *Licensing Songs for Commercials Advertising* for further discussion.)

Publisher's follow-through after licenses are issued

There are at least three follow-through steps publishers should take once a synchronization license has been issued for a film or television broadcast.

CUE SHEETS

Once the program or film editing is complete, a cue sheet must be obtained from the film or television production company. A cue sheet identifies the film or program by name, shows how the song was used (featured, background, theme, etc.) and the duration of each use.

Cue sheets should be examined carefully by the publisher to determine if the usage cited reflects the licensing terms. The cue sheet should also be compared with the broadcast or film version to insure that it accurately reflects the actual usage. Any discrepancies should be immediately resolved with the producers, and the cue sheet should be corrected accordingly.

NOTIFICATIONS

After confirming their accuracy, copies of cue sheets should be immediately forwarded to your performing-right society and overseas subpublishers. Cue sheets are used by performing-right societies to establish how much performance royalties are due the writers and publishers. Overseas subpublishers must be advised of the inclusion of songs in synchronizations so they can ensure proper credits are being picked up by their local performing-right societies.

By the same token, if a subpublisher issues a synchronization license on your behalf to a foreign television producer, you should receive a cue sheet from your licensee. Subpublishers generally have the right to license your works to television producers in their countries. The subpublisher negotiates and collects the synchronization fee and forwards your share as set forth in your contract. In turn, you pay your writers their share (or apply it to their advance account).

If the overseas television producer licenses the program for broadcast in your own country, you will not be able to collect a second synchronization fee from the domestic broadcaster, assuming the overseas producer obtained a worldwide license. You do, however collect performance royalties directly from BMI, SESAC, or ASCAP for showings in the U.S., and you must submit a cue sheet in order to do so.

RENEWAL REMINDERS

Publishers must maintain good *management information systems.* One of the purposes of an MIS is to provide a memory tickler to keep track of important dates and deadlines. You need to be alerted in plenty of time to take needed action *before* any deadline is reached. When a synchronization license is about to expire, you need sufficient time to send the producer a renewal notice so that the option can be exercised and your fee paid.

CHAPTER 11

Foreign Licensing

Because the United States is such a huge market, some American indie publishers tend to overlook the importance of overseas licensing. Although publishers should concentrate foremost on their home market, overseas royalties and advances are significant revenue sources. Indeed, publishers who aggressively pursue foreign deals might receive almost as much income from overseas as they do from domestic revenues. At minimum, a publisher with a broadly-based catalog can add 20%-30% to U.S. earnings through good international representation.

The percentage of a publisher's foreign income vis à vis total revenue depends upon the nature of the catalog. Pop and rock music are fairly universal, for instance. R&B-oriented dance music often does well overseas. Historically, country music has done less well than R&B, but that is changing.

Music publishers in English-speaking countries have a great advantage when seeking overseas deals. Not only is English more widely understood than any other language, American and British influences have become the *lingua franca* of popular music. Of course, countless international megahits have originated from non-English speaking countries (Sweden has given us Abba and Ace of Base, for instance), but these are usually produced in English in order to appeal to the widest possible audience.

Worldwide publishing revenues were over $5.83 billion in 1994. The breakdown of income by country reveals the United States as far and away the largest market, in terms of revenue generated. Japan is now the second largest market, followed by Germany, France, and Great Britain.

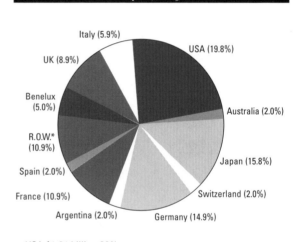

Worldwide music publishing revenues - 1994

- USA $1.24 billion-20%
- Japan $922.82 million-16%
- Germany $875.07 million-15%
- France $643.66 million-11%
- United Kingdom $503 million-9%
- Italy $328.05 million-6%
- Benelux $310.72 million-5%
- Spain $112.38 million-2%
- Argentina $105.46 million-2%
- Switzerland $97.78 million-2%
- Australia $92 million-2%
- R.O.W.* $599 million-11%

* R.O.W. = "Rest of World" (48 other countries)

(*Source - N.M.P.A.*)

Subpublishing

The process of licensing copyrights overseas is called *subpublishing*. When a foreign publisher licenses exclusive publishing rights to a song or catalog for its territory, it becomes the de facto publisher in the territory. The term *subpublisher* applies to a company that has full publishing rights under license from the original copyright owner.

Subpublishing agreements can cover an entire catalog or one or more specific songs only. There are, in fact, several types of subpublishing deals, including:

- *Blanket catalog agreement* with one subpublisher for the world, excluding the original publisher's home territory
- *Blanket catalog agreements* with one or more subpublishers for specific territories
- *Blanket catalog agreements* covering the works of one or more specific writers
- *Specific song agreements* covering one or more designated songs
- *Collection agreements* (either blanket catalog or specific song agreements) whereby the subpublisher collects overseas earnings but does not actively promote the licensed copyrights

DO YOU REALLY NEED SUBPUBLISHERS?

It is not necessary to have a subpublisher in every country. Performing- and mechanical-right societies in all countries have reciprocal agreements to collect royalties due each other's members.

For example: Smith Music, an American BMI company, has a hit in England. The British performing right society, PRS, collects the performance royalties and pays them to BMI, who then pays Smith in due course. And, since Smith uses the Harry Fox Agency to collect mechanical and synchronization royalties in America, the MCPS in London collects these royalties in the UK and pays them to the Fox Agency, who then pays Smith.

It is usually not an efficient use of time to negotiate specific subpublishing deals for countries where your type of music is not particularly commercial, or where there is a small population base. Countries like Ghana, Honduras, or Libya will hardly generate enough income to make the effort worthwhile. Reciprocal agreements between your performing- and mechanical-right societies with local societies may be all that's needed.

Alternatively, a major international publisher could provide *collection deals* covering certain geographical areas, such as "Central America." It is also common to make subpublishing deals with publishers in major markets that include smaller, neighboring countries where the culture or language is similar.

Particular examples are deals with German publishers that cover Germany, Austria, and Switzerland, or agreements with Swedish publishers covering Scandinavia (Norway, Sweden, Denmark, Iceland, and Finland). Other examples include the Benelux territories (Belgium, the Netherlands, and Luxembourg), and France plus the French-speaking countries of Africa.

Many overseas mechanical- and performing-right societies allow publishers from other countries to affiliate as *associate members*. An associate member receives income directly from the society that collected it. This eliminates a double commission fee (one to the overseas society, and one to the society in the publisher's own country). It also cuts out the lag time that occurs when a publisher must wait for foreign royalties to be paid to its local society by an overseas society.

But relying on associate membership in *major* foreign territories, rather than making subpublishing deals, is often a false economy. There are distinct advantages in licensing subpublishing rights. Even though subpublishers take a percentage of your foreign income, your earnings might not reach full potential without subpublishers in place.

Subpublishers are on the spot to:

- Promote local releases of recordings originating in your country
- Obtain *cover* releases by local artists
- Initiate printed editions in the local territory
- License local television/radio commercials, themes, etc.
- Coordinate local tours by artists who record your works
- Generate local press coverage on artists who record your works
- Generally promote your copyrights in other ways
- Identify and take action against local infringers
- Register works with local rights societies, so royalties don't disappear into the *black box*

COLLECTION DEALS

In some cases, an indie publisher might only need or want a *collection deal* in a particular overseas territory. For instance, an artist/publisher's catalog might be virtually limited to the artist's own output. Since the songs involved are released overseas by the U.S. record company's affiliates, the artist doesn't consider it important to have full bore catalog promotion. The only concern is ensuring that foreign mechanical and performing rights are properly administered and all royalties collected.

In a collection agreement, the subpublisher retains anywhere from 5%-15% of all revenue and remits the balance to the original publisher. The sub-publisher does not provide catalog exploitation, and advances to the original publisher are either nominal, or (more likely) not offered at all.

But even small artist/publisher operations should realize their catalogs might contain songs that could be exploited to local artists or be otherwise promoted overseas. A good subpublisher can seize local opportunities to increase a catalog's foreign income and ultimately enhance the value of the copyrights.

PROS & CONS OF EXCLUSIVE CATALOG DEALS

In making overseas deals, some smaller publishers prefer to license works on a song-by-song basis, rather than doing exclusive catalog agreements with subpublishers. Their reasoning is as follows:

They can often obtain more in advances. For instance, suppose a British publisher offers an advance of $25,000 to acquire UK subpublishing rights for an entire catalog. With an exclusive catalog agreement, just one hit song from that catalog might bring an offer for $10,000 in the UK, leaving the publisher free to make similar deals as other songs achieve hit status. This way, the publisher may be able to make, say, three $10,000 deals for three songs alone. The total ($30,000) would thus be $5,000 more than the publisher might have gotten for licensing the entire catalog in the first place.

The publisher may also feel that an advance for one particular song demonstrates a subpublisher's faith in that song's commercial potential. This makes it more likely the subpublisher will concentrate full promotional efforts on the song, if only to recoup the advance.

On the other hand, it's not realistic to expect a subpublisher to feel as strongly about each and every song in an entire catalog. Not every song will receive adequate promotional attention. Therefore, the reasoning goes, each song should be individually licensed to a subpublisher who demonstrates full commitment.

There are merits to the above arguments. But there are also drawbacks. A closer relationship exists between the original publisher and the subpublisher when the whole catalog is involved. The subpublisher has more of a stake in the original publisher's overall success.

There are many cases where a subpublisher has taken an obscure song from a catalog and made it a hit in his territory, even though the song previously had no success in the country of origin.

Also, there will hopefully come a time when a publisher's growth requires a full-time subpublisher in a particular territory to look after the entire catalog; or a time when it makes financial sense to set up a wholly-owned publishing company in the territory. In either case, it could be inconvenient to have the rights to several of the publisher's most important works floating around among diverse subpublishers, under different contractual terms.

Further, if a publisher decides to sell the catalog at some point, the fact that various rights belong to different subpublishers for varied lengths of time makes the catalog somewhat less attractive to a buyer, and that will be reflected in any price offered.

REPERTOIRE COVERED BY EXCLUSIVE AGREEMENTS

Most exclusive subpublishing agreements are dynamic rather than static. The subpublisher not only licenses the catalog as it exists on the date the agreement is signed, but all acquisitions made by the original publisher "in the normal course of business," during the term of the agreement, also fall within the scope of the subpublishing contract.

Acquisitions made in the normal course of business

Acquisitions made in the normal course of business include new songs written by writers under contract at the outset of the subpublishing agreement, as well as works by new writers signed during the term, and purchases of individual copyrights. But the agreement should not include major acquisitions made by the original publisher *outside* the normal course of business.

Acquisitions made outside the normal course of business

An acquisition outside the normal course of business would be the purchase of another copyright catalog that significantly increases the original publisher's revenue stream. Major acquisitions that skew the dynamics of the original deal should be subject to new and separate negotiations as and when they arise. Such acquisitions shouldn't change the original catalog agreement, which remains in effect. The subpublisher can negotiate to represent the acquisition, which might mean paying an additional advance, or the subpublisher might be content to represent only the catalog currently under contract.

For instance, ABC Publishers makes a subpublishing deal with DEF Ltd. in London. ABC then purchases XYZ Music, thereby doubling its catalog size and annual revenues. The original subpublishing agreement with DEF was negotiated without considering the infusion of income and activity the addition of XYZ would make.

ABC would then approach DEF and offer to add the XYZ catalog to the subpublishing deal in return for an additional advance commensurate with the value of the acquisition. If DEF passes on the offer,

ABC can then license XYZ to another subpublisher. Of course, ethics and common courtesy require ABC to at least give DEF first refusal.

European Union

In recent years, there have been changes in Europe that may affect the nature of some subpublishing deals. Most Western European countries belong to the *European Union* (EU), or *Common Market*. Member nations are eliminating trade barriers so that Western Europe will, for all practical purposes, be one commercial entity. The model is the United States, where companies in different states can do business with each other without cross-border red tape inhibiting the free movement of funds or goods.

Ultimately, then, the mechanical-right society in, say, Great Britain (MCPS) can license and collect mechanical royalties for a recording released anywhere within the EU. This would mean an American publisher could conceivably make a blanket European deal with a British publisher (or Dutch, or German, etc.), who would then be able to handle the American catalog throughout the EU without having to sublicense their rights in turn to publishers in other countries.

Indeed, under the *Treaty of Rome*, there is a general prohibition of territorial agreements that prevent free circulation of goods and services across borders within the European Union. However, the European Court recognizes special problems with intellectual properties such as copyrights. And since copyright laws vary among individual European countries at this time, the Court so far seems to have taken the view that it is expedient to continue exclusive territorial agreements for now.

However, as copyright laws are harmonized throughout the European Union during the next few years, as they surely will be, there will be less inclination to allow exclusive territorial arrangements. And as economies of scale become evident in European-wide licensing and administration of copyrights, there'll be more deals with a single subpublisher to cover the entire European Union.

Already, major record companies like Warner Bros. and PolyGram are taking central mechanical licenses for Europe, and there is a definite trend towards a centralized record industry. Centralized publishing is moving more slowly towards realization, however. Major publishers still fragment by territories and do their collections and administration on a territorial basis. But no one should bet that publishers will not follow the record companies' lead towards centralization over the next few years.

Although it may be more feasible to deal with only one subpublisher for collections and licensing throughout the EU (instead of doing deals in each individual EU country), there are still advantages for making separate territorial agreements. Cultural differences remain (languages, local artists who appeal to one country but not others, etc.), and on-the-scene knowledge of local markets is essential for effective promotion.

Foreign taxes on overseas earnings

If you receive a $50,000 advance from a British music publisher, the Inland Revenue (Britain's equivalent to the IRS) would require the British company to withhold British income taxes from the advance. And even though you're paying taxes to Great Britain, the IRS would require you to pay income tax on the balance of the money that you actually receive here. This is *double taxation.*

But the United States has reciprocal treaties with Great Britain and most other major foreign countries to protect citizens of the member countries from being subject to double taxation. As long as you don't maintain a permanent base or branch of operations in a country where foreign earnings originate, you can file a refund claim with that country's tax authority if part of your earnings are withheld for payment of local taxes.

However, dealing with bureaucracies, foreign or domestic, is time consuming and inconvenient. Instead of trying to get money back that you really aren't obligated to pay in the first place, you can file *alien tax-exemption certificates* with tax authorities in countries where you're likely to earn royalties, declaring your nonresident status so that payments can be made to you without deductions of foreign taxes.

To speed your way through local bureaucratic mazes, request (or make it a contractual requirement) that your subpublishers help you obtain and file the proper *nonresident* tax-exemption certificates. At the same time, you can get help and information from the IRS regarding the paperwork and procedures required for obtaining exemptions in those countries that have reciprocal tax treaties with the United States.

Dealing with unpredictable currency exchange rates

Always be mindful of fluctuating currency exchange rates between countries when entering into overseas deals. Consider, for example, the rate of exchange between Great Britain and the United States. In mid-1980, one British pound (£1.00) was equal to $2.40.

This meant that if, in 1980, a British publisher agreed to pay you a £10,000 advance for the British rights to your catalog, you would have received the equivalent of $24,000.

But by early 1985, £1.00 was only worth $1.10. If the British publisher's contract provided for an automatic renewal after five years upon payment of another £10,000, he could have so renewed in 1985 upon payment to you of just $11,000, the then-equivalent of £10,000. You would have lost $13,000 on the exchange rate difference that occurred in the years between the time you entered into the contract and the time for renewal.

You could have protected yourself from this loss by making the advances payable in dollars, so that you received $24,000 no matter what happened to the exchange rate. Of course, from the British publisher's point of view, he would have had to pay £10,000 in 1980 (£10,000 x $2.40 = $24,000) but would then have found himself having to pay £21,818 in 1985 (£21,818 x $1.10 = $24,000).

In such circumstances, the British publisher might conclude that renewing the deal is unprofitable, since his cost (in his own currency) has more than doubled, although your advance in dollars remains constant.

However, requiring payments to be made in your own currency doesn't protect you from unfavorable exchange rates when receiving royalties. Royalties are always computed in the currency of the country of sale, even though they may be converted into your currency for payment.

Consider: If your 1980 royalty share in Great Britain was £10,000, the British publisher converted that to dollars and paid you $24,000. But if, in 1985, your British royalties again totaled £10,000, you would have only received $11,000 after conversion to dollars.

Exchange rates are subject to many national and international forces, and there isn't much you can really do about them. However, you might consider setting up an interest-bearing bank account in the country where you're earning foreign royalties and instruct your licensee to deposit the royalties (in the local currency) into that account if the exchange rate is unfavorable.

You then simply wait it out until the exchange rate turns again in your favor, at which time you convert your account to dollars and withdraw it. Or, you might have your royalties deposited (in the local currency) in a local bank account and use the funds to buy locally produced goods for import and resale. Or, you could use the funds to pay advances to local publishers in return for the subpublishing rights to their catalogs for your own territory.

Licensing foreign catalogs

Though the focus of this chapter is on licensing your copyrights overseas, don't overlook foreign publishers as a source of valuable copyrights to represent in your own country. Although you may have to pay advances or guarantee certain milestone achievements, the negotiating process is much the same used for acquiring copyrights or songwriters at home.

The difference, of course, is that your foreign acquisitions will be limited to the territory where you're active, and the duration of the rights you acquire will be limited to the term provided for in your agreement. But any advance you pay will discount these limitations.

You will have to scramble to compete with larger, more well-heeled publishers for copyrights that have already proven themselves to be commercial successes in other countries, but that's part of the fun. On the other hand, there are often some real nuggets available, which other publishers overlook, that may have real potential in your country though they have yet to make a mark in their country of origin.

Establishing contacts with overseas publishers

Licensing your catalog overseas, as well as locating and acquiring foreign copyrights for representation in your own country, requires knocking on doors. But international contacts are not hard to make and sustain in this age of faxes, e-mail, the Internet, overnight delivery, and jet travel. International relations are not much different than cementing working relationships with other companies at home. Business revolves around establishing rapport and trust.

There are numerous directories listing overseas publishers and their contact addresses. The *Billboard International Buyers' Guide* is a good example. You can establish areas of interest with these contacts using faxes and mail as an introduction. Ultimately, the optimum way to make contacts and build on relationships is face-to-face, so the most efficient method of personal contact is to attend international trade shows and expos such as MIDEM in France and POP-KOMM in Germany. These essential marketplaces are explored further in the chapters on *Exploitation* and *Marketing*.

Maintaining good working relationships with subpublishers

Large music publishers usually have an international department, or at least one person whose only job is international affairs. Smaller publishers should appoint someone within the company to be the liaison for overseas contacts, even if it means that person wears more than one hat. A good working relationship with subpublishers is ultra-important, for administrative as well as promotional purposes. Cultivating a successful international relationship requires consistent exchanges of information.

Subpublishers must be provided the following details for every new copyright acquisition:

- Writers' names, percentages, performing-right affiliations, and duration of your rights to the work, including any retention period
- Co-publishers, percentages, performing-right affiliations, and duration of your rights to the work, including any retention period
- Copyright notice information (copyright date and names of all copyright owners)
- Names, addresses, and percentages of any subpublishers collecting on behalf of co-publishers in the territory (if you don't have full administration rights in that territory)
- Record release information (artist, label, record number, release date)
- Details of all synchronization licenses (with cue sheets)
- The ISWC (International Standard Work Code) number of each song

In addition, subpublishers must be supplied with copies of the following:
- Lead sheets, lyrics
- Cue sheets
- Demos
- Press releases
- Commercially released recordings
- Printed editions
- Promotional video clips
- Tour dates
- Charts, reviews, and press clippings (from other territories in addition to those of your own country)

Analyzing subpublishing agreements

Every subpublishing agreement is tailored to meet the objectives of the parties involved and the unique qualities of their catalogs. The outcome of every deal depends upon the negotiating strengths and talents the parties bring to the table. However, all subpublishing contracts contain certain fairly standard provisions, which are addressed as follows:

RECITALS
The original publisher warrants that it is the sole proprietor of the licensed copyright(s), free of all claims and encumbrances for a period of time not less than the term being entered into with the subpublisher.

TERRITORIES
The original publisher assigns the following rights to the subpublisher for the territory of (*name of licensed countries*):

Subpublishing agreements restrict the assignment of rights to either the country where the subpublisher is based or a group of countries where the subpublisher is active. The country or countries where the assignment is made is called *the territory*.

Typical territorial assignments include:
- *Australasia* (Australia and New Zealand)
- *Benelux* (Belgium, Netherlands, Luxembourg)
- Brazil
- France and French-speaking territories of Africa
- *GAS* (Germany, Austria, Switzerland)
- Italy
- Japan
- Mexico and Central America
- *Scandinavia* (Sweden, Norway, Denmark, Iceland, Finland)
- Singapore and the Far East
- South America (less Brazil)
- Southern Africa
- Spain & Portugal
- United Kingdom and Republic of Ireland
- United States and Canada
- *ROW* ("Rest of World")

ROW is a catch-all designation for relatively minor markets. Some subpublishing deals may be made with major publishers like EMI or Warner-Chappel for specific major territories and include ROW to cover the multitude of relatively minor territories like Israel or Greece where earnings will be minimal. Territories have also emerged for subpublishing purposes since the Soviet Union's fall. Such former Eastern bloc countries as Hungary, the Czech Republic, Poland, and Russia may be grouped into the ROW designation.

NATURE OF RIGHTS ASSIGNED

▼

*Subpublishing doesn't bestow a
share in copyright ownership*

The assignment grants the subpublisher the exclusive rights to license songs locally for any and all commercial, nondramatic uses.

A subpublishing deal is merely a *temporary* assignment of rights, limited to the subpublisher's territory for the duration of the agreement. Subpublishers are not granted any share of copyright ownership. Subpublishing contracts should identify the specific rights that are licensed under the agreement and state that any rights not identified are reserved by the original publisher.

Rights usually assigned by the original publisher include:

- The exclusive right to print, publish, sell, and license others to print, publish, and sell, copies of the work(s) in the licensed territory.
- The exclusive right of public performance and broadcasting in the licensed territory.
- The exclusive right to issue mechanical licenses in the licensed territory.
- The *non*exclusive right to issue *non*exclusive worldwide synchronization licenses for motion picture and television productions produced in the licensed territory.
- The original publisher retains the exclusive right throughout the world, including the licensed territory, to issue synchronization licenses for motion picture, television, and other audiovisual productions produced outside the licensed territory and exported to the licensed territory; the subpublisher is not entitled to any royalties or fees arising from use of such productions within the licensed territory except for performance royalties payable to the performing-right society in the licensed territory, for which the subpublisher shares as per the provision in the subpublishing contract relating to performance royalties.
- The *non*exclusive right to make translations of the lyrics, to make adaptations or other new arrangements of the music, to provide new lyrics, and to change the title to make the work more commercially marketable in the licensed territory. But any or all such changes, additions, or adaptations become the sole property of the original publisher, and there is no obligation or liability on the part of the original publisher to account for or pay royalties to the authors or composers of such changes, additions, or adaptations, unless otherwise consented to and approved in writing beforehand by

the original publisher.
—Who owns the copyright to a translation commissioned by a subpublisher? Especially if the translator is one of the subpublisher's exclusive writers? Original publishers should resist letting a subpublisher acquire any sort of permanent retention of copyright. All translations, adaptations, and arrangements should become the original publisher's property.

—Otherwise, when the subpublishing agreement comes to an end, the new version will remain partly owned by the subpublisher. The subpublisher can either veto or share income from all future licenses in the territory.

—Remember, a translation will likely have a new title in a different language. Ensure that any translations are properly registered with rights societies with appropriate credits to the original writers and yourself as original publisher. Also, demand the right to approve translations, as well as any other adaptations and changes.

—Who pays for the translation or adaptation? Because the subpublisher generally receives a larger percentage from local covers, the translator or local arranger should be paid from the subpublisher's share of income earned by the local version. Further, insist on contractual language that restricts payments due translators or adapters to income arising from the translated or adapted works only; they should not also be entitled to income arising from the work in its original form.

—Also, if the subpublisher's agreement does allow the subpublisher to retain a higher percentage from translated works, make sure your contract is clear that the higher percentage pertains only to the translated version. Otherwise, a subpublisher could commission a translation of your hit, then collect the higher percentage off your original version as well as the translation, even though the original version may be the only significant earner in the territory.

RIGHTS *NOT* ASSIGNED

Subpublishers are rarely granted *grand rights* or the right to authorize dramatizations. The original publisher normally retains the exclusive right throughout the world, including the licensed territory, to license grand rights, dramatizations, literary adaptations, and any and all rights not specifically granted to the subpublisher.

SAMPLES

The subpublisher shall provide the publisher, without charge, one copy of each recording and one copy of each printed edition issued in the licensed territory (the number of copies to be provided is always negotiable).

The original publisher shall provide the subpublisher without charge one lead sheet copy, one copy of each recording, and one copy of each printed edition of each work covered in the agreement upon availability.

COPYRIGHT NOTICE

The subpublisher agrees to cause all copyright notices on each and every printed edition to read:

Copyright [*year*] by [*name of publisher*]

All Rights Reserved

Authorized for sale in [*name of territory*] only

The original publisher retains full ownership in and to the copyright(s) throughout the world, including the licensed territory.

DURATION

The term of agreement shall be for (*number of years*) from the date of the agreement.

Subpublishing agreements usually vary in duration from three years upwards. Most have an initial one-year term with renewal options for additional one-year periods. Options are normally at the subpublisher's discretion. But it is common to require subpublishers to meet certain conditions before they can pick up options.

Many European mechanical- and performing-right societies won't recognize subpublishing agreements with durations of less than three years, because of the administrative expenses involved in registration changes. However, the societies will accept non-performance or default by a subpublisher as valid reasons to nullify subpublishing agreements before the term otherwise ends.

Conditions of renewal may include payment of additional advances upon renewal, or renewal may be conditional upon the catalog achieving a certain earnings threshold. There may also be performance clauses requiring the subpublisher to obtain a minimum number of local covers.

Subpublishers naturally seek to acquire rights for as many years as possible, but original publishers will want to limit the duration periods so that they're not locked into long-term deals with subpublishers who perform unsatisfactorily. Therefore, from the original publisher's point of view, an optimum duration would be three to five years at maximum.

RETENTION PERIOD

Upon termination of the agreement (except when the subpublisher fails to perform as agreed), the subpublisher retains rights to all recorded works released in the territory for a further period of *X* years.

The normal retention period ranges from one to two years, especially in the case of local covers. In all fairness, the reason for retentions is that subpublishers should be able to benefit from efforts expended to secure and promote local releases. Otherwise, as an agreement nears its end, a subpublisher won't consider such promotional efforts to be commercially viable.

Retention rights may also be extended to works the subpublisher gets included in a film, TV production, or local TV commercial.

Pipeline income

Sometimes retention is limited to *pipeline income*. Money in the "pipeline" is income earned during the agreement which has not yet been received by the subpublisher at time of termination. The right to collect pipeline income is usually limited to 6-18 months from the date of termination. Sometimes, however, pipeline income is collected by the new subpublisher, who is obligated to then pay the old subpublisher. In this case, the new subpublisher takes only an administration fee (5%-10%) of the pipeline collections.

A pipeline situation could arise where the original publisher guaranteed that a certain number of songs would be released in the subpublisher's territory. The subpublisher might have been induced to enter into a deal because the original publisher's writers have producer or artist deals with release commitments in the territory. Suppose a number of these guaranteed releases don't occur until the last six months of the term. Technically, the original publisher meets the release guarantee, but, in reality, the subpublisher cannot profit in the time remaining in the agreement.

The solution is for the subpublisher to have retention rights to any guaranteed release issued within the final year of the agreement. The retention period might reasonably be 6-12 months from the date of release, or from the date of termination, whichever is later.

Limiting retention rights

The original publisher may be able to limit the subpublisher's retention rights only to cover songs that achieve specified milestones. The rights retained apply only to cover recordings that are successful by some identifiable yardstick, such as chart positions, sales levels, or income generation, etc.

Some contracts allow the subpublisher to retain

the entire catalog if advances have not been recouped at the end of the term. This may help clinch a deal if you offer it, but don't be open-ended. You may not want to renew the deal because you feel the subpublisher didn't aggressively promote your catalog; you may feel the advance wasn't recouped *because* of the subpublisher's incompetence.

If you only allow catalog retention for a period limited to, say, 6-18 months, you are protected from rewarding the subpublisher's incompetence in perpetuity. But, bear in mind that allowing retention in the event an advance is not recouped detracts from the value of your catalog when negotiating a new deal. Your entire catalog remains with the old subpublisher until the retention period ends. Meanwhile, a new subpublisher can only license copyrights created after the old subpublishing agreement's termination date.

PERFORMANCE OBLIGATIONS

As discussed earlier, some songwriter contracts require publishers to perform certain milestone achievements. Subpublishers might also have to contractually agree to meet certain objectives when the original publisher has sufficient negotiating clout.

Typical performance obligations include
any or all of the following:
- a guaranteed number of local cover record releases
- a certain number of printed editions issued during the term
- catalog earnings reach or exceed a specified level
- advances paid by certain dates

Performance obligations can cut both ways. The original publisher might contractually guarantee that a certain number of songs will be released in the territory during the term by virtue of artist or producer deals the publisher's writers have. In the event the catalog does not generate the guaranteed number of local releases, the original publisher may have to allow the subpublisher to extend the agreement until such time as all advances have been recouped. Alternatively, the original publisher may be obligated to repay the outstanding balance of any unrecouped advance.

COMPENSATION

Advances

Upon execution of the agreement, the subpublisher shall pay to the original publisher a nonreturnable advance in the amount of X. Said advance shall be fully recoupable from any and all income due the original publisher under terms of the agreement. (If the subpublisher is required to make more than one advance payment during the term, a schedule of payments is set forth detailing the amounts and dates due, including any amounts due upon exercising renewal options.)

Aggressive overseas publishers are eager to license good catalogs and will pay advances for subpublishing rights. Obviously, the amount of any advance you're able to negotiate depends on many factors, including the size of the territory, the popularity of your style of music there, and competition from other subpublishers for the rights.

A nonadvance deal essentially is a *collection deal,* and it would be hard for a subpublisher to justify retaining more than 10% of all revenue generated (15% at most).

Advances can be structured in several ways:
- *One lump sum* payment on signing
- *Annual installments*
- *Specified sums triggered upon local release* of records by the catalog's major acts (i.e., $X per album where the original publisher controls 100% of the songs, proportionally reduced for each track not controlled by the original publisher)
- *Specified sums triggered by recoupment* of previous advances (i.e., $X paid upon recoupment of 75%-100% of outstanding advance)
- *Specified sums triggered upon local chart showings* (i.e., $X per album and $Y per single reaching Top 20, an additional $XX per album and $YY per single if the release reaches Top 10, and an additional $XXX per album and $YYY per single if the release reaches Number One)

The amount of an advance is determined by the respective negotiating strengths of the parties involved and other factors, including:
- *Importance of the catalog*
- *Size of the catalog*
- *Number of local releases the catalog is expected to generate*
- *Size of the territory:* The size of the territory is only as important as the marketability of the music in that particular culture. For instance, an Australian subpublisher would probably pay more for an American catalog than would a Brazilian subpublisher, although Brazil dwarfs Australia in population.
- *Catalog's earnings history:* Established catalogs have earnings-histories in each territory upon which advances can be negotiated. Otherwise, offers are based on commercial judgments of how successful the catalog will be in the local markets.

A new publishing company is obviously at a disadvantage trying to negotiate advances for subpublishing deals, since there is no earnings history the subpublisher can use to structure an offer. But that does not preclude subpublishers from offering good advances if knowledge of the company's management and writers indicates strong commercial potential, or if the new publisher has a hit the subpublisher expects will enjoy similar success in his country.

• *Subpublisher's share of income:* Typically, subpublishers remit 75% of all income to the original publisher —except for local cover recordings, in which case subpublishers usually retain 50%. Splits of 70/30 in favor of original publishers are also common (with 60/40 on local covers). But, generally, the higher percentage a subpublisher can negotiate for himself, the higher the advance he is willing to pay. And the higher advance a subpublisher pays, the more incentive he has to promote the catalog.

For collection deals, as noted previously, the subpublisher retains a rather minimal percentage of all revenue. Typically, 10% is the subpublisher's share in a collection deal, though some may retain as low as 5%, others as much as 15%.

Royalties

The royalty divisions are contractually spelled out as follows:

• *X*% of the retail price for each printed edition (except collective works) sold and paid for (this usually ranges 10%-12%).

• *X*% of the retail price of each book, folio, or collection of works, divided by the number of songs contained therein, sold and paid for (If a folio of ten works containing one work belonging to the original publisher earns $100 in royalties, the original publisher's share is $100 ÷ 10 = $10).

▼

Insist that your royalties be prorated among royalty-bearing songs only!

• Subpublisher shall pay original publisher *X*% of all other income actually received by the subpublisher, except in the case of local covers, in which case subpublisher shall pay original publisher *X*%. (A typical agreement may call for the subpublisher to pay 75% of all other income, except for local covers, in which case the percentage might be 50%).

Performance royalties

Some subpublishers try to negotiate a larger share of performance royalties than on other types of income. The reason is that the subpublisher collects 100% of gross earnings from all sources *except* performance royalties. Performance royalties are collected 100% by the local performing-right society who pays the subpublisher *only* the gross publisher's share; the performing-right society pays the writer's share directly.

Thus, where the subpublisher's share is 25%, the subpublisher keeps 25¢ out of every dollar of mechanical income. On performance income, however, the subpublisher's performing-right society pays the subpublisher *only* the gross publisher's share, which would normally be 50% of every performing-right dollar generated. And if the subpublisher is then entitled to only 25% of all collections, it is in essence only receiving 12.5¢ out of every performing-right dollar generated.

So, the subpublisher may argue, it should be entitled to 50% of the publisher's performing-right royalties, which works out to 25¢ of every performing-right dollar generated. The success of the subpublisher's argument should come down to whoever gets the upper hand in contract negotiations. Ideally, the original publisher will get the idea scrapped, unless the subpublisher is willing to pay an advance high enough to make this concession attractive.

Performance royalties on local covers

A similar problem might arise on local covers (not local releases of recordings originating outside the territory), where the subpublisher is entitled to a higher percentage. Performing-right societies account by title and writer only. There is no distinction as to whether broadcasts were of a local cover or an original recording. So how can the subpublisher distinguish whether performance royalties were earned by local covers or original recordings when accounting to you?

One solution is to base the percentage of performance royalties on an approximate ratio of mechanical income received for a song. Thus, if a cover generates one dollar in mechanical royalties and the original recording earns $10.00, it may be reasonable to assume that 10% of the performance royalties were generated by the cover recording.

But this is reasonable only if both versions are released in similar formats (i.e., both versions are either 'A' sides, 'B' sides, or album tracks). When one version is an 'A' side, and the other is an album track, the 'A' side would likely generate a higher percentage of total performance income. The only solution then is to contractually limit the subpublisher to a higher percentage of performance royalties only in cases where the local cover is released as an 'A' side.

However, even this can present a problem when both versions are 'A' sides, and one version is clearly more successful than the other. For instance, the original version might reach the Top 10 in the territory, while the local cover languishes. Though negotiating royalty breakdowns to account for every eventuality might seem like nitpicking, there could ultimately be a lot of money involved.

So, either the subpublisher is restricted to a higher percentage on local covers released as 'A' sides *and* achieving some verifiable success level (such as chart entry or unit sales), or there has to be good faith negotiations between both parties to work out fair royalty divisions on a case by case basis.

Mechanical royalties on local covers

Distinguishing mechanical royalties earned by cover records from royalties earned by other releases is a fairly simple matter. Sources of mechanical income can be pinpointed as to how much each version earns, because record company royalty statements are itemized by record number, artist, and units sold.

For local cover recordings, subpublishers usually retain 50% of mechanical royalties, though splits of 60/40 in favor of original publishers are also common.

Don't allow subpublishers to collect a higher percentage on *all* mechanical earnings of a particular song once a local cover is achieved. The subpublisher should be entitled to the higher percentage on earnings from *local covers only*.

Otherwise, once a local cover has been achieved, the subpublisher receives 50% of all income from that song, even if most of the income stems from record releases the subpublisher did not initiate.

Unscrupulous subpublishers can use the local-cover provision to take unfair advantage of original publishers.

Here's how:

Smith Music gets a song called "I Love You" recorded by Sammy Superstar in America, which then becomes a huge hit. The American record by Sammy Superstar subsequently becomes a hit in Germany as well. German publishing royalties from Sammy Superstar's version amount to $60,000.

Smith's German subpublisher, Schlock Musik, is entitled to 25% of income from German record sales of songs owned by Smith, including Sammy Superstar's version of "I Love You." But Schlock isn't content with 25% ($15,000, in this case). The subpublishing agreement states that he is entitled to 50% of *all* income from songs that have local covers in Germany.

So, Herr Schlock pops down to a neighborhood Ratskeller and hires a drunken accordion player to record a solo instrumental version of "I Love You," and then releases 50 copies of this version on his own label.

Technically, Schlock has gotten a *local cover*. He is therefore entitled to 50% ($30,000) of the income from the hit version by Sammy Superstar, although he had nothing to do with its success. The extra $15,000 Schlock picks up should go to Smith, by all rights.

When the subpublishing deal was being negotiated, Smith should have insisted the contract specify that Schlock get 50% of mechanical earnings from *local covers only*. That way, Schlock would be entitled to 50% of the drunken accordion player's version, but only 25% of Sammy Superstar's version.

ACCOUNTINGS

Subpublisher shall provide original publisher with statements of earnings together with any payment due less advances within __ days of the end of each 30 June and 31 December.

Accountings are normally made by the subpublisher *twice yearly*, within 30, 45, 60, or 90 (whatever you negotiate) days of 30 June and 31 December, with statements accompanied by payment of royalties due, less advances.

Subpublishers' statements should be itemized by records issued and sold (listing recordings by song title and name of artist, label, and record number), and a breakdown of royalties received from the local performing-right society, from sales of printed editions, and from all other sources.

Statements should show the gross amounts the subpublisher received from each of these sources, and the net amount due the original publisher, less any outstanding advances.

The original publisher may also require photocopies of all statements received by the subpublisher from its licensees and mechanical- and performing-right societies relating to the work(s) in order to verify the accuracy of the statement.

Royalty payments should be made in the original publisher's native currency at the rate of exchange prevailing on the date due.

Some countries may have restrictions on transfer of funds overseas or may require documentation supporting your status for tax purposes. The agreement should therefore take note of any governmental restrictions or requirements regarding transfer of funds and should require the subpublisher to make every effort to comply with governmental regulations in a timely manner, so that the royalties can be paid as and when due without unnecessary complications or delay.

AUDITS

Upon written advance notice, the subpublisher will allow the original publisher or his representative to examine at the subpublisher's place of business during normal business hours all books, records, documents, licenses, statements, accountings, and other instruments relating to the original publisher's catalog, for the purpose of verifying royalty statements rendered or delinquent under the terms of the agreement.

Some agreements require the subpublisher to pay for the audit if an underpayment of, say, 5% or more is revealed.

It would be best to hire a local accounting firm in the subpublisher's country if it becomes necessary to conduct an audit.

DEFAULTS

It shall be considered a default should the subpublisher fail to render statements and account for royalties as and when due. If the subpublisher fails to cure the default within 30 days of receiving a written demand from the original publisher, the agreement will terminate and all rights will revert to the original publisher without further notice.

If subpublisher fails to perform milestone achievements as provided, the failure shall constitute a default. And if the subpublisher further fails to cure the default within 30 days of receiving a written demand from the original publisher, the agreement will terminate and all rights will revert to the original publisher without further notice.

Termination for whatever reason does not absolve the subpublisher from the obligation to account to and pay the original publisher any monies earned or accrued by the copyright(s) while the agreement was in force.

RIGHT OF ASSIGNMENT

The subpublisher has the right to assign any of the rights granted in the agreement to any subsidiary or affiliated company in the licensed territory, *provided that*:

- The subpublisher notifies the original publisher within 30 days of the assignment.
- The subpublisher notifies the original publisher of the terms of such assignment.
- The assignee agrees in writing to abide by all terms of the agreement between the original publisher and subpublisher and to assume all obligations of the subpublisher within the assignee's territory.
- Notwithstanding anything in the assignment or in the original publisher's agreement to it, the subpublisher shall ultimately remain liable for fulfillment of all terms and obligations of the subpublishing agreement, including payment of all royalties as and when due.
- The assignee shall account directly to the original publisher.
- The assignee shall calculate and pay royalties to the original publisher based on income earned *at source* (i.e., in the assignee's territory).

- No royalties payable to original publisher shall be in any way reduced as a result of such assignment.

At source

Some foreign publishers acquire subpublishing rights for neighboring territories where they don't actually have offices, by virtue of a contractual clause allowing them to assign or *sublicense* their rights to other subpublishers in specific countries. When negotiating deals covering more than one country, always insist that:

- You're paid on royalties calculated *at source* (i.e., your split is based on income generated in each country included in the overall territory).
- Your royalties are not in any way to be reduced by such assignment.
- Assignees pay you directly within a specified number of days from the periods ending 30 June or 31 December in which your works generated income. Otherwise, the subpublisher must first collect from the assignee, which delays your payments.

These three points are very important! Without them, you can be taken advantage of by an unscrupulous subpublisher, as illustrated by the following scenario.

You make a deal with Shifty Music of Sweden covering the Scandinavian territories (Sweden, Norway, Denmark, Finland, and Iceland). Mr. Shifty has set up subsidiary companies in each of these countries.

Here's what he can do:

His Swedish company assigns the rights for Norway, Denmark, Finland, and Iceland to his *Icelandic* company. His Icelandic company assigns the rights for Norway, Denmark, and Finland to his *Norwegian* company. His Norwegian company assigns the rights for Finland and Denmark to the *Finnish* company. His Finnish company assigns the rights for Denmark to the *Danish* company.

Now, you have a huge hit in America. It's released in Denmark and is a hit there as well, grossing $10,000 in publishing royalties. Your Scandinavian deal calls for Shifty to get 25%, since this is not a local cover. So Shifty's Danish company takes its 25% ($2,500) and remits the balance of $7,500 to the Finnish company. The Finnish company withholds $1,875 (25% x $7,500) and sends the $5,625 balance to the Norwegian company. The Norwegian company deducts $1,406.25 (25% x $5,625) and sends the balance of $4,218.75 to the Icelandic company. The Icelandic company takes $1,054.69 (25% x $4,218.75) and remits $3,164.06 to the Swedish company. Mr. Shifty then takes a further $791.02 (25% x $3,164.06) and sends you $2,373.04 instead of the $7,500 you should have been entitled to for the Danish earnings.

You have just been legally deprived of $5,126.96. And, instead of the $2,500 you thought Mr. Shifty would get out of the $10,000 Danish earnings, he has pocketed $7,626.96, which is more than the $7,500 you might have expected to receive yourself!

But Mr. Shifty adds insult to injury. Each of his subsidiary companies pays royalties 90 days from the period ending 30 June or 31 December. So the Danish company receives the royalties earned from your hit on January 15, 1998. It therefore pays the Finnish company on 30 September—90 days after 30 June. The Finnish company pays the Norwegian company on 31 March, 1999!—90 days after 31 December. The Norwegian company pays the Icelandic company on 30 September—90 days after 30 June. The Icelandic company pays the Swedish company on 31 March, 2000!!—90 days after 31 December. Mr. Shifty sends what's left of your little share on 30 September, 2000.

Thus, you not only receive less than one-third of what you properly should have gotten from the Danish hit, it also takes you over two and a half years to get paid at all!

If you really want a nightmare, suppose your contract allows Mr. Shifty 50% of *all* earnings from a song that achieves a local cover—like the German deal with Schlock Musik—and Mr. Shifty then presses 50 records of a Danish folksinger warbling a solo version of your song.

Upshot of all this: you wait well over two and a half years to get $1,186.52, instead of getting $7,500 within three or four months, while Mr. Shifty gets $8,813.48 instead of $2,500, plus he earns interest on your $1,186.52 for nearly three years.

So (it is worth repeating) your subpublishing agreements should clearly state that:
- You are paid on royalties calculated at source of earnings.
- Any assignee accounts to and pays you directly within the specified number of days from the period ending either 30 June or 31 December in which monies for your works were received so that your money is not floating around earning interest for someone else, long past the time it should have been in your bank account.
- Your royalties are not in any way to be reduced by assignment.
- The subpublisher gets 50% of earnings from local covers only, not 50% of all income from a song once it has had a local cover.

LEGAL EMPOWERMENT

The subpublisher shall be empowered to protect all rights in and to the copyright(s) in the licensed territory and may take whatever action necessary to enforce those rights in the name of the original publisher. The subpublisher may initiate prosecution against any alleged infringer or defend any claims of infringement in the licensed territory, and the subpublisher may settle or dispose of any such claim or action as it sees fit, as long as such settlement does not in any way diminish the original publisher's rights in and to the copyright(s).

Any damages or recoveries received by the subpublisher from actions taken against alleged infringers in the licensed territory shall be divided equally with the original publisher after deducting reasonable costs and legal expenses of such actions.

TERMINATION

The agreement can be terminated by the original publisher should the subpublisher go into bankruptcy, compulsory liquidation, or be forced to make assignment of assets to the benefit of creditors.

MORE BOILERPLATE RECITALS

The agreement between the parties does not constitute a partnership or joint-venture. The agreement constitutes the entire understanding between the parties and will be binding upon them, their heirs, successors, and assigns. There should be a declaration as to which country (or state, or province within a country) shall have jurisdiction if a dispute between the parties needs judicial arbitration.

The original publisher should suggest the jurisdiction of his own country, because of the time, expense, and distance involved in prosecuting actions overseas. However, subpublishers may insist, with reason, that alleged defaults, having taken place in their own country, should be interpreted according to the laws of their own country. So jurisdiction is a matter of negotiation at the time the agreement is made with arguments for both sides holding weight; but the matter must be resolved and clarified in the final agreement.

For catalog agreements, an attached schedule lists works covered as of the effective date of the contract (titles, writers, co-publishers, percentages, record release information, ISWC numbers, etc.). The original publisher agrees to promptly advise the subpublisher of all new works acquired during the term of the agreement.

CHAPTER 12

Licensing Print Rights

Sheet music was the principal format in which songs were marketed to the public during the late 19th and early 20th centuries. The mass market consisted of amateur musicians who regularly bought new sheet music to play at home. Before the advent of records and radio, the method of popularizing a song was to get it performed by popular entertainers, which built consumer demand for the sheet music.

Tin Pan Alley publishers in London and New York employed *songpluggers* to demonstrate new songs to impresarios, bandleaders, vaudeville acts, and popular singers. Songpluggers often used foot-in-the-door tactics and bribery. They'd buy drinks, pass out cigars, or slip someone a fiver or two to gain a favorable audience. The songplugger's demonstration invariably involved pounding a piano while belting out a song with more gusto, perhaps, than talent. (Irving Berlin started as a songplugger, but was embarrassed by the quality of material given him to promote—so he started writing himself.)

Teddy Holmes rose from teenaged songplugger to managing director of the oldest and largest publisher in the world, Chappell Music (now Warner/Chappell). Holmes recalled the early days in London when sheet music was sold on barrows in street markets: "One of a songplugger's duties was to go round to Soho, tip over barrows belonging to rival publishers, and dump their music into wet, muddy gutters." So much for the genteel age of music before rock & roll!

Today, most publishers don't print their own sheet music at all. They license print rights to specialist companies, such as Columbia Pictures Publications, FJH Music, Cherry Lane Music, Consolidated Music Sales, Hal Leonard Publications, Warner/Chappell, and Plymouth Music. Though print sales no longer dominate the music publishing business, sheet music remains a potentially lucrative supplement to a publisher's income. Overall, this segment of the business now accounts for around 11% of worldwide publishing revenues and brings in about $300 million annually in America.

Back when sheet music was the prime method of delivering music to consumers, hit songs easily sold a million and more piano copies, but today's big hits only manage to sell 30,000-100,000 single-song piano copies. Folios containing several hits sell as much as 100,000 copies.

However, most songs issued in sheet music don't sell enough copies to warrant a second printing (minimum first printings are usually 1,000). And certain categories of songs—rap, for example—are not generally considered worth printing at all.

Printed music formats

There are some 30-50 different formats in which a single song can be published in print. Hits usually appear in several formats simultaneously, thus adding to potential print income. For instance, a song could be printed as:
- **Piano copy** (single song editions, unbound)
- **Marching-band arrangement**
- **Combo arrangement for dance band**
- **Educational or method books**
- **Arrangements for specific instruments** (guitar, accordion, organ, etc.)
- **Choral arrangement**
- **Stage band arrangement**
- **Brass band arrangement**
- **String orchestra arrangement**
- **Concept folios editions** (e.g. *Top Country Hits of 1999*)

- **Mixed folios** (songs by different writers, popularized by different artists)
- **Fake books** (top lines with chord notations and lyrics)
- **Personality folios** (focus on a particular artist or songwriter, which generally requires an additional royalty of around 5% to be paid to the personality for use of his/her name and likeness)
- **Matching folios** (issued in conjunction with a specific album release, reproducing the album cover on the folio cover, and including all the songs contained on the album)

▼

One single song can be published in some 30-50 different formats within the broad categories listed above.

AVERAGE SHEET MUSIC RETAIL PRICES
- $2.95-$3.50 for a single song, piano copy
- $9.95 for a 15-20 song folio
- $35.00 for a marching band arrangement
- $75.00 or more for a full orchestral arrangement
- There are also more expensive, deluxe, hardbound editions

Royalties to copyright owners

Publishers usually receive from 12%-20% of the retail price of printed editions from licensees. Although contracts may be offered specifying royalty payments in cents (e.g., 60¢ for each piano copy sold), copyright owners should insist on a *percentage* of the retail price so that if and when prices rise the royalty payable increases automatically.

Where a song is included in a folio or book of collected works, the royalty is prorated (the total royalty is divided by the number of songs included in the publication). So, if your song is one of 25 in an edition selling for $9.95, and the royalty rate is 12% of the retail price, your actual gross royalty per edition would be just under 5¢.

$$\$9.95 \times 12\% = \$1.194 \div 25 = 0.04776$$

Your gross royalty *rate* would be just under one-half of one percent of the selling price.

$$12\% \div 25 = .48\%$$

Songwriters customarily receive 50% of what their publishers earn from licensed print-rights. So, assuming your writer receives the standard 50% of gross royalties received from print licensees, your *net royalty rate* is .24%, and your *net dollar amount* is just over 2¢ (2.388¢).

There are also situations where the copyright owner, or original publisher, elects to incur all preparation and printing costs but to distribute the printed editions via an established sheet music publisher, or selling agent. This is similar to a P&D (Pressing and Distribution) agreement an indie label might have with a major label. Typically, the selling agent would handle all warehousing, selling, distribution, shipping, invoicing, and collections in return for 20% of gross sales. All inventory belongs to the original music publisher.

Exclusion of public domain works

When you negotiate a print-licensing deal, keep in mind that your songs earn on a prorated basis (royalties payable per song divided by the total number of songs in the collection). But licensees may often include your songs in a collection mixed with works in *public domain*. Why? Because no royalties are payable on PD works. But it is usually the copyrighted works (e.g., your songs) that have achieved recent hit status that make the printed edition commercially viable.

So why should PD works dilute royalties payable to you? They shouldn't. Therefore, insist your royalties be prorated by the number of royalty-bearing songs in the edition rather than the total number of songs, which may include several PD works.

Consider again the above example of a 25-song collection selling for $9.95, at a prorated royalty rate of 12%. Suppose 10 of the songs are PD. The print publisher would actually only have to pay royalties on 15 songs, which effectively means paying only 7.2% (15 x .48%) instead of 12%. But, when PD songs are excluded from the calculation, each of the 15 copyrighted songs receives 7.96¢ gross instead of 4.776¢ (or .8% instead of .48%).

However, copyrighted arrangements of PD material may be allowed to fall within the prorated number of songs used. If copyrighted arrangements of PD songs are included, the print publisher must pay royalties just as if the works were still in copyright. This legality may encourage some print publishers to commission arrangements of PD works. The print publishers then own the copyrighted arrangements prorated with the total number of songs in the edition, thereby reducing cash outlay for royalty payments to third-party copyright owners.

Reserves

Print publishers generally distribute printed editions to retailers with return privileges. They therefore usually hold a percentage of royalties in *reserve* to avoid paying royalties on product that is subsequently returned unsold. Copyright owners should insist that reserves are depleted within the next couple of accounting periods. A typical reserve provision might enable the print distributor to withhold as much as 50% for the first quarterly accounting period, diminishing to 25% in the second quarter, 15% in the third quarter, and none thereafter.

Term of agreement and sell-off period

Agreements to license print rights usually range in terms from one to five years. Automatic annual extensions are normally given to the licensee until one party or the other issues written notice to terminate the agreement. Upon termination, the licensee will generally retain the nonexclusive right to sell off inventory for another 6-18 months, conditional upon payment of previously agreed royalties.

Similar to a record label distribution agreement, inventory (in this case sheet music) that remains unsold at the end of the sell-off period must either be destroyed or turned over to the licensor. Usually, destruction, verified by affidavit, is the method.

Licensees may resist having to destroy folios and books, because they are more costly to produce, and try not to have a limited sell-off period. This means they end up with rights to sell existing inventory until it is gone, which could take years. If there is no limited sell-off period, the original publisher should make sure the licensee does not *stockpile* inventory by printing large numbers of new inventory just before the agreement ends.

Your contract should restrict the licensee from printing more inventory than needed during the remainder of the term, which should be justified by established sales patterns. If there is to be a limited sell-off period, the original publisher should ensure that the licensee sells remaining stock at prevailing wholesale prices through the normal retail system. This to make sure the licensee does not *dump* unsold product at *distress sale* prices.

Catalog agreements vs. single-song agreements

Publishers usually receive advances from sheet music distributors in return for licensing their works. Licensing may be done on a song-by-song basis (with the publisher shopping around for the highest advance each time he licenses a song), or by blanket agreements whereby the distributor gets the print rights to all the publisher's catalog for a fixed period.

Some publishers prefer dealing on a song-by-song basis, to maximize advances on songs as they become hits, but blanket catalog deals tend to be better for the publisher's overall catalog. After all, a distributor who pays a large advance for an entire catalog has an incentive to quickly recoup that advance by publishing more of the publisher's copyrights. The distributor will be more inclined to take numerous, lesser-known works, which otherwise might never get into print, and put them into folios, educational editions, marching band arrangements, etc.

If you license print rights to a song on a nonexclusive basis, or on a song-by-song basis, remember to narrow the license to a specific use, preferably identifiable by title of the folio or publication number. Otherwise, the print publisher may be entitled by default to use the song in numerous formats and additional folios without having to pay an additional advance or seek further permission.

By narrowly defining specific uses in each license, your negotiating position is strengthened. The user always has to come back to you for a new license (or amendment to an old license) for every new use, and you can demand additional compensation if you determine the new use warrants it.

Where you do see the advantage of entering into an exclusive catalog print arrangement, it would be to your benefit to insist on retaining the right to license songs to other print publishers on a one-off, nonexclusive basis for inclusion in folios with works owned by other publishers. If your catalog contains a well-known hit, you'll be approached by several print publishers who wish to use it in theme-type folios, such as *Country Love Songs* or *Top Dance Hits of 1999*, or whatever. Your exclusive licensee may rightly insist on *first use* in a folio, and *exclusive use* for sheet music (piano copies), but should otherwise allow secondary uses for compilation folios issued by other print publishers.

Lyric reprint licenses

When negotiating an exclusive print agreement, it is important that you retain the right to license the lyrics separately (without the music) to other companies for other usages. Publishers are frequently asked to license song lyrics for publication in books, magazines, newspapers, greeting cards, print advertisements, etc.

Permission to reprint lyrics are most often granted individually on a *per use, nonexclusive* basis. Publishers normally receive one-off fees for these licenses, rather than royalties, although greeting cards may either be a royalty or a set fee based on the number of cards printed.

PERIODICALS

There are a number of mass-circulation magazines that feature collections of lyrics from the latest hits. Some of these magazines are devoted to pop music, while others concentrate on country, rock, or R&B songs. Charlton Publications of Connecticut is perhaps the most prominent publisher in this field, with a number of lyric-magazine titles under their imprint.

Licenses issued to periodicals usually are limited to one year. Average reprint fees for periodicals range from $25-$50 (for newspapers or small circulation magazines not dedicated to lyric reprints), and $100-$350 (for major magazines and magazines featuring lyrics as primary content). If a work reaches the upper Top 20 of a recognized Top 100 chart (such as *Billboard*) additional payments of, say, $50, may be chargeable.

Generally, when a royalty-based license is used, an advance is paid on either the expected number of sales or the number of paid subscribers. For instance, if the magazine's cover price is $1.50, the total royalty may be 18¢. If there are 30 songs contained in the issue, each song earns 6/10 of one cent. If the magazine has a circulation of 100,000, the advance would be $600 (100,000 x .006).

There are also magazines that contain sheet music (the music is printed along with the lyrics). Licenses for these types of magazines may be offered on a royalty basis of around 12.5% of the cover price prorated among the number of songs included in the issue.

BOOKS

Book publishers often seek reprint licenses to use lyrics in educational works, anthologies, sociological treatises, novels, short story collections, etc. Fees can range from $50 to several thousand dollars, depending upon the number of works included in the book, whether the book is issued in paperback, hardback, or both, the importance of the work to the book, and whether all of the lyrics are used. Generally, the greater the number of songs used in the book, the less the book publisher is willing or able to pay.

Larger fees are warranted when:

- lyrics further a novel's plot (especially when all the lyrics are used)
- the book title is derived from the song's title, refrain, or lyrics
- the song's storyline forms the basis of the plot
- the song's storyline inspires the creation of a character or the book

In any event, reprint licenses for books should be clear about the type of edition (hardback, paperback, book club), and the territories in which the license applies (U.S. and Canada only, the world, or whatever).

The broader the license is, and the more importance the lyrics are to the theme of the book, the higher the fee should be. Some publishers may also require additional payments for additional printings beyond a certain ceiling, such as 100,000. And, generally, reprint licenses are restricted to the language of the first edition, so that any translations require additional licenses.

Without these restrictions, a book publisher could sublicense the work around the world for printing into numerous foreign language editions and formats, abridgments, and adaptations without any recourse or further advance payments to the copyright owner.

Any reprint license should require the licensee to affix the correct copyright notice, either on the same page with the lyrics or in the acknowledgments section.

Print advertisements

For print advertisements, fees can range from $2,500 for regional campaigns to $5,000 to $10,000 for a national campaign duration of one year or less. (See the chapter on *Licensing Songs for Commercial Advertising* for further discussion.)

Greeting cards

Royalties for lyrics reprinted on greeting cards may be based on either the wholesale or retail price of the card. However, the policy of some greeting card companies is to pay a set fee based on the number of cards printed (such as $1,000 for 50,000 cards).

Typical royalties range from 5% of wholesale to 5% of retail, which translates to approximately 2¢ per card upwards. The size of the royalty or fee (or advance) depends upon the number of lines used, whether lyrics are used on the face as well as the inside of the card, the territory granted, etc. Most licenses are limited to one to three years or to a specific number of cards.

Publishers generally retain the right to approve the design of the card in order to protect the integrity of the lyric in so far as it is used. And, of course, proper copyright notice should be printed on the card.

Games

Lyrics are used in various types of computer and board games, often as answers to trivia-type questions. Again, the size of any advance, fee, or royalty depends upon the number of lines used, the aggregate number of song lyrics used in the game, the territory, the duration, the number of games manufactured, etc.

Royalties may range from as low as 1¢ per game to as high as 7¢. Advances or fees may be set at, say, $200, based on 5,000-10,000 games being manufactured. (Additional fees or advances become due when additional games are manufactured.)

In computer games, it is common to play a snatch of the melody, in which case a mechanical license is in order. Be aware that some greeting cards also have an audio feature akin to a music box, whereby a bit of melody is played when the card is opened. This usage would also fall under a mechanical license usage.

Where mechanical licenses are needed for games and cards, a reduced rate (rather than statutory) is appropriate, since the duration of the performance is usually limited to a few seconds. The amount of any advance, fee, or royalty depends on many of the negotiating factors discussed above, which are found in virtually all licensing agreements:

- duration of performance
- number of other works included in the case of games
- territories covered by the license
- all the other usual licensing considerations

Album covers and inserts

The right to reprint lyrics on album covers or album inserts is normally given *gratis* to record companies, since the use in essence further promotes the songs contained on the album for which the record company is paying mechanical royalties. Permission should be coupled with a requirement that the record company acknowledge the publisher with appropriate copyright notice (e.g., Reprinted by permission, © 1999 by You, Inc.).

CHAPTER 13

Grand Rights and Dramatic Rights

Mechanical, performance, print, and synchronization rights are collectively called *small rights*. The term *grand rights* applies to *dramatico-musical* works created for and performed on the *living stage*.

The living stage refers to *live* theatrical productions of musicals, operas, operettas, and ballets. This does not include dramatizations that are recorded, filmed, or broadcast.

Grand rights are administered differently than small rights. For instance, mechanical- and performing-right societies do not license grand rights, but music incorporated into a grand right can be extracted and licensed as a small right. For example, the song "Don't Cry for Me, Argentina" from the musical *Evita* has been licensed for records (mechanical rights), played on radio (performance rights), and sold as sheet music (print rights).

Key characteristics of grand rights

A *grand right* applies to a collective work in its entirety. This means that the literary content of a musical play, opera, operetta, or ballet is combined with the music as a copyrightable whole, or single work. (*Literary content* is the book, libretto, script, choreographic directions, dialogue, and/or lyrics.) The entire work is covered under a single grand right. No single element of the work has a grand right in and of itself, and every element is essential to the whole.

For a song to be included in a grand right, it must be woven into the storyline as an integral element of the plot. It must further the action and be every bit as essential as the dialogue, either lyrically (as in operas, operettas, and musicals), or instrumentally (as in ballets).

Distinction between grand rights and dramatic rights

A *dramatic performance* is not the same as a grand right. A song can be taken out of context from a musical play and rendered a dramatic performance with scenery, costumes, and acting out of the storyline. This can apply to a song not specifically created as a dramatic work but dramatized when performed. For instance, a theatrical troupe might dramatize the Dolly Parton-penned Whitney Houston hit "I Will Always Love You." Or, a dramatist might take the song "Memories" from *Cats* and write a new script that has nothing to do with the original play itself.

A song can also be taken out of context from a musical play and performed as a *nondramatic* small right. *Nondramatic* is the performance of a song *as a song*. For instance, the song "Memories" from *Cats* is covered under a performing-right blanket license as a nondramatic performance when Peter Pianoman plays it in a Holiday Inn lounge or WZIT-FM plays a recorded version by Barry Manilow.

Venue does not dictate whether or not a performance falls within the scope of grand rights; grand rights could cover a musical play performed in a nightclub. But grand rights do not apply to live, stand-alone performances in the course of a revue, concert, or club act. A Broadway *revue* of songs loosely connected by a theme, but not individually essential to a central storyline, would constitute small rights.

Nor does a grand right necessarily apply to music in every type of dramatic production. *Incidental music* used for opening and closing themes and background ambiance is outside the scope of grand rights when it occurs in *nonmusical plays* and *plays with music*.

Nonmusical plays are productions where the music is commissioned after the play is written. *Plays with music* are dramatic plays that use music to set the atmosphere, but not to develop the action of the story. In both types of productions, the music is incidental to the story. It enhances the performance, but is not essential.

Licensing grand rights and dramatic rights

Performing-right societies are only authorized to license *nondramatic* performances of music, such as the broadcast of a song from a cast album. They cannot license dramatic performances of songs, nor can they license the grand rights of dramatico-musical works.

Copyright owners of dramatico-musical works license performances directly or through a theatrical agency. So when a semipro theatrical company in, say, Bangor, Maine wants to stage a play, permission must be obtained from the copyright owner or its agent.

But if an ersatz Liberace performs a song from a musical in a piano bar somewhere, the copyright owners are compensated under the bar's blanket license with the relevant performing-right society. If, however, the bar's owner stages a scene from a musical with costumes, scenery, and dialogue, an infringement of copyright occurs, unless a license for this type of performance is first obtained from the copyright owners. Dramatic renditions are not covered under blanket performing-right licenses.

When a publisher licenses dramatic rights to an agency, the agent sublicenses subsidiary dramatic rights to users, such as stock and amateur theatrical companies. Leading agents for dramatic rights include Tams-Witmark, Rodgers and Hammerstein, Samuel French, and Music Theater International.

WHAT CONSTITUTES A DRAMATIC PERFORMANCE?

Controversies often arise as to whether a performance is dramatic or not. Sometimes a copyright owner contends it does, the performer disagrees, and a judge has to decide. A song performed with costumes, scenery, and "acting out" of the lyrics doesn't necessarily constitute a "dramatic performance" in the strictest sense. If a song created specifically for a musical play is performed with costumes, scenery, and lead-in dialogue that is *not from the play for which it was created*, grand rights do not apply.

But the song might still be considered a dramatic performance if it is integrated into a plot or action or storyline and the overall production is diminished by eliminating the song. This also apples to songs not specifically created for the living stage but incorporated later into dramatic productions.

Grand rights and dramatic performance rights and copyright owners

Small rights apply when a song is interchangeable with other songs in a manner that doesn't affect the context of an overall performance. For instance, a radio station broadcast of 15 unrelated records by different artists is clearly a program of interchangeable parts. So, too, is a concert or revue, even with interconnecting dialogue and introductions.

But if a song is woven into the plot of a storyline, it becomes an integral part of a whole. When a song "furthers the action," or develops the story, it is not so easy to substitute or eliminate it from the overall performance. The impact of the performance would be affected, which raises the importance of the song to the larger work.

PERFORMING-RIGHT SOCIETIES DON'T LICENSE DRAMATIC RIGHTS

Each dramatic production must be licensed separately under terms specifically applicable to the production. The more essential a song is to a performance, the greater the license fee it can command. This is why copyright owners do not grant the right to license dramatic performances to performing-right societies.

It is impractical for publishers to monitor the millions of small right performances (radio, TV, clubs, concerts, etc.), so they rely on performing-right societies to do it for them. Performing-right societies grade and weigh small rights performances according to the venues or methods of use (e.g., seating capacity, time of broadcast, size of station, duration of performance, regional or national broadcast), but statistically contrived formulas are not so easily applicable to dramatic performances.

It is beyond the mandate of performing-rights societies to distinguish the relative importance of a particular dramatic performance as perceived by the copyright owner. The copyright owner must judge each dramatic rendering on its merits, decide how essential the song is to the performance, and, by extension, how much the license fee should be.

Who owns grand rights?

The author of the literary content shares an undivided interest in the play's copyright with the composer and lyricist. This doesn't prevent the composer and lyricist from copyrighting the music separately from the playwright's work.

Music used in a dramatic production is ordinarily commissioned by the show's producer. Composers and lyricists are paid upfront fees, plus a royalty based on a percentage of box office receipts. Writers retain all rights to the music but assign limited rights to the producer, including the right to stage the dramatization and participate financially in certain subsidiary rights.

Subsidiary, or *ancillary*, rights may include the small rights born from the original theatrical production. Examples include synchronization licenses for television productions and feature films and mechanical licenses for original-cast recordings. Other subsidiary rights include licensing the grand rights to amateur, semipro, and professional theatrical groups for performances in schools and provincial theaters.

Theatrical producers do not always participate in the small rights when songs are extracted from a production and licensed for records, sheet music, and nondramatic performances. Whether or not producers do share in small rights, and to what extent, or under what conditions, depends upon the negotiating strength of the parties to their agreement.

Financial aspects

While most theatrical presentations fail to recoup production costs before closing, a box office smash generates a fortune for owners of the music performed in the show. Broadway, off-Broadway, and *road shows* by professional touring companies generate nearly $1 billion a year in box office receipts. Recent trends show about two-thirds of the gross box office is earned on the road and the other third directly from Broadway runs.

For a major Broadway production (as well as when the show is taken on the road), song royalties range from 4.5%-6% of box office receipts, prorated among all the songs included in the production. For a smash, long-running show, this can translate into anywhere from $250,000 to several million dollars annually. Any royalty agreement, of course, requires the music copyright owners to join with the producer in speculation. Should the play flop, it will close without generating much income for the copyright owners.

Alternatively, the producers and music copyright owners may agree to a flat weekly fee per song. This guarantees music copyright owners a set income as long as the play is in production, whether or not

many theater seats are occupied. Such fees range from $200-$500 per song per week. Thus, a production containing 15 songs and paying $500 per song, which runs for 52 weeks, pays out $390,000 to the owners of the music.

But consider this: megahit musicals generate several hundred thousand dollars per week. At a 6% royalty of box office receipts on a play grossing an average $700,000 weekly, the writers will net $42,000 per week, or $2,184,000 over the course of a year. And while this isn't the result for most productions, there have been some that earned even more.

DRAMATISTS' GUILD

Most composers and lyricists active in musical theater belong to the *Dramatists' Guild*, which has set minimum benchmark terms for contracts with producers. The terms cover the following essential points:

- **First option**—$18,000 prorated between the writers to secure a one-year exclusive option to stage the production
- **Second option**—$9,000 to extend the option for a second year
- **Third option**—$900 per month for up to 12 months to extend the option beyond the second year

Once a play goes into production, additional advance payments are called for, which are based on what is called *capitalization* (i.e., the amount of money the producer secures from investors and lenders to stage the work). Writers' advances equal 2% of the total capitalization up to a maximum of $60,000.

All advances and option payments are recoupable from a maximum of 50% of the royalties that later accrue to the writers, and those royalties become due only after the production's costs are themselves recouped. However, all Broadway productions first undergo regional tryouts. Only after this test marketing exercise has gotten the kinks out and demonstrated audience approval does the Broadway debut occur. During tryout performances, writers receive guaranteed compensation plus a royalty when and if the production recoups its costs. These pre-Broadway fees include:

- $4,500 per week minimum for up to 12 weeks of performances
- 4.5% of gross box office receipts for weeks 13 and thereafter until either the play opens on Broadway or costs are recouped (whichever comes first)
- 6% of gross box office receipts once the costs are recouped

ANCILLARY INCOME

The primary source of income is, of course, the show itself. But this isn't necessarily where most of the writer's earnings ultimately come from. When a production proves successful, numerous secondary income generators open up for the music owners.

In addition to licensing professional road companies who take the show on tour, licenses are issued to stock, semipro, and amateur theatrical production companies to perform the work in the hinterlands as well as overseas. Small rights are also licensed for cast albums, sheet music, folios, cover recordings, synchronization licenses for theatrical and home video film productions, performance royalties for television and radio broadcasts of excerpts and recordings. There are further licensing opportunities for commercials, background music, etc.

But even a relatively unsuccessful theatrical venture can generate fortunes for copyright owners through subsidiary rights. This occurs when certain songs rise above a show's lack of public acceptance and establish a market appeal on their own. And remember, even after a successful show closes, the music continues to earn for years through subsidiary rights.

Music publishers and grand rights

The financial risks of developing and staging most Broadway musicals are so enormous that only well-connected pros need apply. Upfront costs of several million dollars are now the norm for a new Broadway production, with several hundred thousand dollars needed for weekly overhead to take the play through to the break-even point. The overhead includes cast, choreographers, musicians, designers, staff and crew salaries, royalties, guarantees, advertising, publicity, venue expenses, insurance, and taxes.

Since grand rights usually stem from works commissioned by a theatrical producer, the primary use of the material is covered by agreement between the producer and the writers. The music publisher comes into the picture only when the material is exploited to media requiring the licensing of small rights. However, most successful Broadway composers and lyricists have the savvy and wherewithal to set up their own music publishing companies for this purpose.

And, since the music is normally commissioned and created specifically for a theatrical production, this is not an area where usual songplugging activity by a music publisher is likely to succeed. However, there are many cases where a theatrical concept involves staging a revue that includes material previously written. In such cases, publishers with older hits in their catalogs may delight in finding their copyrights revitalized through a hit stage production.

PREEXISTING SONGS USED IN PLAYS AND REVUES

Songs not created specifically for the living stage, but which are later incorporated into a play or revue, do not become part of the new work's grand right. Rather, they would be licensed directly by the copyright owners as a *living stage performance.* Licensing fees in such cases are based on:

- size (seating capacity) of theater
- location of theater
- nature of use (*featured performance, incidental, etc.*)

For a feature use in a small off-Broadway theater (less than 100 seats), a standard license fee is $5 per performance. This escalates to $100 per performance week in theaters of 100-500 seats. If the song's featured performance lasts over four minutes, the license fee could approach $350 per performance week.

When a song is used in a Broadway theater, fees range from $150 per performance week to $500 for works with longer performance times. Alternatively, a royalty might be agreed, based on 5% of box office gross prorated with other songs used in the production.

CHAPTER 14

Licensing Songs for Commercial Advertising

Whether the product is beer, banking, cars, insurance, or cereal, most consumer product manufacturers and service companies employ advertising agencies to create marketing concepts for their products or services. When devising ads for the broadcast media, agencies come up with an angle to sell the product, create a script, then procure music to fit the concept. Although music might be the last element chosen for an ad, it is no less important than any other part of the package. In fact, music can make or break television and radio advertising campaigns.

There are two ways an advertising agency procures music for a client's campaign. One is to *commission original music*; the other is to *license an existing song*. Either way, since the concept is created first, the music must meet preconceived criteria to form the atmosphere desired for selling a particular product. It must fit the marketing concept and make the product or service memorable with a catchy, melodic hook.

Commissioned jingles

The term *jingle* is commonly applied to music written specifically for an advertisement. Many large ad agencies employ staff writers to create jingles for clients. But, frequently, jingles are commissioned from independent songwriters and jingle production companies.

When commissioning music from third parties, advertising agencies generally work with a select group of experienced jingle writers or jingle producers who can work fast and provide complete turnkey packages at one inclusive price. Jingle production companies often own their own studio facilities and have producers, songwriters, lyricists, musicians, singers, and arrangers on tap.

Some music publishers set up jingle production companies as separate profit centers to obtain jingle commissions for staff writers. Music publishers cultivate contacts at ad agencies in order to be given opportunities to submit ideas for jingles.

Ad agencies generally present a storyline and suggest a musical genre to several writers, jingle producers, or publishers, and invite them to submit demo ideas. Commissioning fees to creators of the winning idea range from the low $100s for local radio spots to $10,000 or more for national television commercials containing as little as 30 seconds of music. Superstar writers may command even higher fees, ranging upwards to $100,000 for a full-scale nationwide television ad campaign.

Typically, a production company's finished jingle can cost an agency anywhere from $5,000-$10,000 for a 30-second local or regional spot to $20,000-$50,000 for a nationally run commercial. Remember, though, the fee paid to a production company includes studio costs, musicians, singers, arrangers, etc.

Occasionally, original jingles have been rewritten, recorded, and released as pop records with chart success. For instance, British jingle-writer Lord David Dundas had a number one single with "Jeans On," which he'd originally written and performed as a television jingle for an apparel company. Another instance was "I'd Like to Teach the World to Sing," which was a Coca-Cola jingle and also a hit record.

The ad agency, or its client, normally holds the copyright to the finished jingle, since it is a commissioned *work for hire*. But, contracts have been negotiated whereby the writer (or publisher) owns the copyright to a rewritten version released on record. In such cases, the ad agency might share in the new version's mechanical royalty revenue.

And even where the jingle's copyright is held by the employer, the performing rights often remain with the writer, publisher, or jingle production company. In this situation, the contract must make clear that performing rights are reserved by the writer (or publisher or production company).

Also, the synchronization license must be conditional on all broadcast media using the jingle being duly licensed by the publisher's performing-right society. Further, the license must not state that broadcasting rights are "bought out" by the agency (or any other party), that these rights remain the exclusive property of the publisher, and that they are licensed exclusively through the publisher's performing-right society.

When the writer is signed to a music publisher, the publisher participates in the commissioning fee and any performance income resulting from broadcasts of the commercial.

Licensing existing songs for commercials

Ad agencies find value in licensing existing songs to drive home marketing concepts. A song that has previously achieved hit status possesses proven public appeal. An agency hopes some measure of this appeal will transfer to the product being advertised, and they look for songs that hopefully will arouse subliminal or nostalgic impulses that cause consumers to react favorably to the product.

When an ad agency licenses an existing song, the publisher retains full copyright. When an ad agency commissions new lyrics to an existing song, however, the copyright to the new lyrics usually resides with either the agency or its client.

If lyric changes are requested, the publisher should have the right to approve (and ideally should extend the right to the songwriter, whether or not the writer's contract requires it). Agencies generally expect to pay a higher fee in order to secure the right to alter lyrics. A word of caution about authorizing lyric changes: A jingle that gains widespread recognition might forever change the way the public identifies the song.

For publishers with catalogs containing established hits, advertising licenses are significant revenue centers. United Airlines paid $250,000 to use "Rhapsody in Blue" for one year, and a large insurance company reportedly paid $500,000 to use another major copyright. When licensing a hit song for a commercial, the ad agency is buying a "celebrity" to advertise the product.

In order to generate licensing interest in existing copyrights, publishers frequently circulate sampler CDs and catalog lists to ad agencies containing highlights of major works in their catalog. These are accompanied by brochures categorizing songs by titles and subject matter. For instance, songs may be categorized by:

colors: "Red Roses for a Blue Lady," "Yellow Rose of Texas," "Blue Monday"
jewelry: "Little Band of Gold," "A String of Pearls"
location: "I Left My Heart in San Francisco," "Way Down Yonder in New Orleans"
seasons: "Summertime," "Autumn Leaves," "April in Paris," "Memphis in June"
vehicles: "Slow Boat to China," "Mustang Sally," "Up, Up and Away"
animals: "A Horse With No Name," "Walking the Dog," "Rockin' Robin"
foods: "Mashed Potatoes," "Cherry Pie," "Sugar Sugar"

The usefulness of categorized information is obvious. Ad agencies are constantly trying to come up with advertising concepts for clients. Their job is somewhat easier when sampler CDs and catalogs are available to resource musical ideas relating to whatever their clients are selling, be it jewelry, clothing, cars, vacation packages, or whatever.

Considerations for licensing commercials

Before even discussing licensing terms with an agency for an existing copyright, the publisher should consider the song's significance in terms of past and current popularity. It goes without saying that a licensing fee should be commensurate with the copyright's importance. The publisher may welcome a licensing request if it is felt the use will reactivate a dormant song. A possible by-product of the commercial could be that the song's popularity will be reactivated, leading to increased income from many sources.

On the other hand, consideration must be given as to whether such use might oversaturate a song with the public for a period of time. Other potential users may shy away from licensing a song that has become too closely identified with a particular product.

Some publishers and songwriters refuse to license certain venerable works for commercial advertising uses. Irving Berlin, for example, refused to allow any of his songs to be used this way. And there was controversy when ATV Music (owned by Michael Jackson) licensed a song by John Lennon and Paul McCartney for a commercial. Some fans regarded the use as a sacrilege.

NEGOTIATING FACTORS

There are so many variants in licensing terms for commercials that it is hard to say what a "normal" range of fees might be, but negotiations start with the usual guidelines applicable to other types of licenses:

- the importance of the copyright (for preexisting works)
- whether the use is for television, radio, or both
- whether the scale of usage is national, regional, or local
- duration of playing time (30 seconds, 45 seconds, 1 minute, etc.)
- duration of license (brief test period, six months, one year, etc.)
- options (for wider territories or longer licensing periods, etc.)
- new lyrics, original lyrics, instrumental version only
- exclusivity (licenses not issued for products in same category)

Fees for existing copyrights used in national television commercials might range from $25,000 for a one-year license to as much as $500,000 for truly important standards. A typical one year, national television license for a major song falls within the $100,000-$200,000 range.

Fees are proportionally reduced for licenses of less than one year's duration, and/or for licenses confined to regional or local use. For regional or major metropolitan areas, reaching approximately 10% of the national population, a one-year license for a major song might be prorated to $10,000-$20,000.

For shorter term licenses, fees are generally prorated vis à vis what the publisher would charge for a one year license, plus 10%-15%. For instance, if the publisher's fee to use a particular song for one year is $100,000, a three-month license might have a prorated fee of $27,500 ($100,000 x 25% = $25,000 + 10%). Alternatively, the publisher might charge somewhere between $500 and $1,500 per week, depending upon the size of the broadcast area.

LICENSING PERIOD

Though most commercial licenses are issued for one year, shorter periods are common. But, music publishers should avoid licensing commercial rights for periods of longer than one year, especially for a national usage. If a work becomes firmly identified with a single product, other users might be reluctant to consider it, thereby diminishing the copyright's value.

Requests for licenses of longer than one year should be countered with proposals for renewal options after an initial one-year term. Options give the publisher a trap door clause to terminate the license if it seems the song's long-term value is being diminished. If a renewal option is extended, the licensee should pay a renewal fee equal to the original fee plus 10%-20%.

EXCLUSIVITY

In many cases, an ad agency will request—or even insist—on a license that excludes the publisher from licensing commercials for similar products. This is not an unreasonable request when an advertiser pays a substantial fee for the right to use a song nationally. In fact, agencies normally require that a song not be licensed to advertise similar or directly competing products during the license term.

Sometimes, however, agencies ask for *total* exclusivity (i.e., the song must not be licensed to advertise *any* other product during the term). The advertiser should expect to pay for the privilege of total exclusivity. A substantial fee must be charged to make it worth the publisher's while to shut the door on other licensing opportunities. The additional fee should be at least equal to the nonexclusive fee. In other words, if your fee for a nonexclusive one-year nationwide license is $100,000, you should charge $200,000 for an exclusive one-year nationwide license.

Exclusivity is another matter when it comes to requests for local and regional advertisements. Publishers should be very careful about issuing exclusive licenses on a regional or local basis, because potential opportunities for national commercials from other advertisers would then have to be turned down.

The use of a song in other commercials, even though not directly competing with the product of an agency's client, may make an agency hesitant to use a song. Agencies naturally prefer all components of an advertisement to build a unique identity for their clients' products. So, if an agency expresses interest in a song that is currently being used or has been recently used (within the last couple of years), the publisher is ethically bound to disclose the fact.

TERRITORY

Although the typical commercial license is limited to one country, it is common to include neighboring countries where the product is also sold (e.g., U.S., Canada, and Mexico; or Belgium, Netherlands, and Luxembourg). Obviously, the more widespread the usage, the higher the fee. Sometimes, options are requested to add additional territories or regions within a specified period of time upon payment of additional, specified fees.

AD TESTING

Before rolling out an expensive, nationwide campaign, ad agencies often prefer to test an advertisement in order to gauge its effectiveness. The agency will then request a license limited to the region and duration of the test, with an option for a national usage in the event the test proves successful. There are two different types of tests that might be licensed. One is a *regional (or local) test*. The other is an *off-air test*.

Regional (or local) test

Prior to a national or widespread regional campaign, a two or three month license may be requested for one locality, perhaps one small region, or even two cities in different parts of the country. If the ad works in theses tests, the full license option is taken and the commercial is rolled out nationally. Regional or local test licenses range from $2,500 to $20,000, depending on the stature of the copyright, the duration (1 minute, 30 seconds, 15 seconds) and length of time requested (one, two, or three months).

One major restriction should be placed on regional or local tests. The area covered should not reach more than $X\%$ of the national population. For example, if the test fee is $10,000, and the full roll out fee is $100,000, then the test market area should not contain or reach more than 10% of the national population.

Be careful, too, when issuing regional test licenses, that the media selected does not bleed over into larger markets. For instance, if the test area is Long Island, there is a possibility that stations broadcasting the commercials might be watched or listened to in New York City, Newark, or Philadelphia. This warning also applies to nontest licenses ostensibly confined to regional or local markets, which spill over into areas with greater population densities.

Off-air test

The second type of test is *off-air*. Rather than running the test on television or radio in selected test markets, the agency uses focus groups. Nonbroadcast tests may be for periods of one, two, or three months, with fees ranging anywhere from $1,000 to $12,500.

PUBLIC SERVICE ANNOUNCEMENTS

Public Service Announcements, or *PSAs*, are made by nonprofit organizations and government agencies. They have many of the same characteristics as commercial advertisements in that they often are accompanied by musical jingles to reinforce their message.

Many PSAs are of an informative nature, giving the public access to telephone numbers and addresses of organizations set up to deal with specific areas of concern, such as recognizing symptoms of diabetes or heart problems, or finding help with social security benefits or prenatal care. Some PSAs are like advertisements in that they recommend taking action (e.g., see your Army recruiter, give blood, volunteer for the Peace Corps).

Since PSAs are produced by nonprofit groups, they are broadcast by radio and television stations during unsold commercial time. The broadcasting stations contribute to "the public service" by running these spots free. Obviously, in such noncommercial, nonprofit situations, music publishers are called on to contribute as well, meaning that songs are most often licensed at token rates of $100-$500, with limited periods of use (i.e., six months to one year).

For new songs, or dormant copyrights, publishers may be willing to license PSAs at lower rates and be satisfied with performance royalties that arise from the usage. But publishers certainly aren't obligated to license works at reduced rates for PSAs. Some PSAs might be aired nationally, as often as some big budget commercial advertisements. Any song too closely identified with a widespread PSA campaign would probably not be considered for use by a commercial advertiser. Therefore, music publishers should be wary of licensing major copyrights for PSAs, because the usage may shut the door on other, more lucrative near-term opportunities.

Radio commercials

Television commercials require synchronization licenses because music is synchronized with visual images. Obviously, radio commercials have no visual component, so permission to use a music copyright is called an *electrical transcription license*. The fee charged advertisers to use a song in a radio commercial is called a *transcription fee*.

An important copyright used in a one-year national radio commercial should fetch a transcription fee of between $25,000 to $75,000. Shorter-term licenses for regional or local radio use are best licensed on a weekly rate, which might be anywhere from $250 to $1,000 per week, depending on the size of the population in the market covered.

Print advertising

An ad agency may conceive a marketing campaign that ties in broadcast and print media with a unified theme. They might then want the lyrics of a song used in the broadcast commercial to be reprinted in newspaper and magazine advertisements. The print rights might be obtained either through an additional provision in the synchronization/transcription license or through a separately negotiated print license. Usually, the print license's duration is concurrent with the synchronization or transcription license.

There is no hard rule on what fee to charge for the use of lyrics. Depending upon the scope of the license (i.e., local, regional, or national), the fee should be proportionate to the synchronization license fee. The typical considerations apply (i.e., duration, amount of lyrics used, importance of the copyright, etc.). Fees of $5,000-$10,000 have been paid for the right to use just a few lines from well-known songs in national publications during the course of one year.

CHAPTER 15

Miscellaneous Licensing Issues

Special use permits and permissions

Previous chapters detailed the most common types of music publishing licenses, notably: mechanical, performance, print, synchronization, dramatic, commercials, and foreign subpublishing. This chapter addresses licensing issues that arise less frequently, and which, in some cases, apply to newer technologies where clear precedents have yet to be established.

The terms *special use permits* and *permissions* are sometimes applied to licensing songs for use in new media, greeting cards, games, dolls, toys, etc. Before examining specific types of licenses and permissions in more detail, it might be useful to recap some of the principles of licensing already pointed out in previous chapters.

General licensing principles

Perhaps the most important thing to remember when drafting a license is to *always narrowly define the scope* of the permission being granted. A broad, vague, or generally worded license may be construed to grant permission to use a work in ways the licensor didn't foresee or in formats not yet devised. No one can possibly say what the future holds. Licenses must therefore be very specific about how, where, when, and under what conditions copyrights can be used.

As an example, publishers always restrict mechanical licenses to a specific release number and configuration, rather than to the master number of the recording. This requires the user to come back and negotiate additional licenses and compensation to use the work for other formats or releases. Otherwise, a licensee could freely use the work for any number of releases in any number of formats under terms of the original license, which may not adequately compensate the publisher for the newer uses.

Another principle to remember is that if a song is particularly unique or of such vital importance to a project that no other song will suffice, the publisher can usually demand a substantially higher fee. If, however, a number of other songs can easily be substituted, the user is in the enviable position of successfully negotiating a lower fee.

For example, if a movie producer wants to use the song "Blue Moon" as the title theme to a film called *Blue Moon*, the publisher can rightfully expect a higher fee. On the other hand, if a movie producer wants to use "Blue Moon" merely to set the mood of a scene in which countless other songs can be used to the same effect, the publisher must accept a lower fee or risk having the song dropped from the film.

Similarly, suppose an advertiser requests a well-known song for a television commercial. If the song is apt to be closely identified with the product, the advertiser may ask that the song not be licensed to advertise a competing product. In such cases, the publisher is always right to demand a substantially higher fee to offset shutting the door on other potential licensing opportunities.

Every type of license grants permission to use a copyright under certain conditions and with certain limitations. Each of these conditions and limitations affects the size of the fee a licensee might reasonably be expected to pay. So, when negotiating fees, copyright owners must always consider the following factors:
- *Nature of usage* (performance, mechanical reproduction, audiovisual, print, etc.)
- *Type of performance* (feature, background, instrumental, vocal, title, incidental)

- *Uniqueness of the work* (can another work be easily substituted?)
- *Importance of the copyright* (is it a valuable standard or brand new work?)
- *Exclusivity* (does this license limit future licensing opportunities?)
- *Territory*
- *Duration of license term*
- *Options* (to extend the license term or use the copyright in other formats)
- *Duration of performance* (playing time)
- *Extent of usage* (lyrics only, instrumental version only, partial or full usage?)
- *Nature of product* (politically, socially acceptable? high ticket item?)
- *Restrictions* on publisher's right to license (does writer demand approval?)
- *Impact on future income* (does usage enhance or diminish copyright value?)
- *Conflicts* with other licenses or rights previously granted
- *Number of other works* included in the project (including PD works) relative to user's budget for music and/or potential pool of income to be allocated among all songs used

Negotiating tips

The following tips help lead to successful outcomes when negotiating contracts as well as nonroutine licenses:

- Negotiate only with those in authority to agree to your requests.
- Have a prioritized agenda. Start with the most incontestable items and work downwards to the stickiest points.
- Put yourself in your opponent's place and structure your arguments to address his or her concerns.
- Don't directly challenge your opponent's opinions.
- Don't issue ultimatums.
- Never concede a point, however small, without winning a comparable concession in return.
- Take notes and verbally summarize each point agreed before you move on to the next so that there's no misunderstanding.
- Follow up negotiations with a memo or letter summarizing what was agreed, and ask for a written response within so many days or hours if any points are disputed. Make necessary corrections right away, in writing. This reduces the agreement to writing and helps lock in the results. It is cheaper, less time-consuming, and less frustrating to fix a misunderstanding before it is drafted by lawyers into a license or contract.
- Make your opponent feel good about the outcome.

- Never brag about how you "won" or "put one over" on your opponent. If this gets back to him or her (and it could), it will either poison the outcome or make it that much harder to win again, or both.

Parodies

A *parody* is a take-off or comic slant given to an existing work for the purpose of spoofing or making fun either of the work itself or of some currently newsworthy event or person. A parody necessarily involves changing lyrics or in some other way altering the work, which requires special permission from the copyright owner. In other words, if the parody is to be a recorded performance, compulsory mechanical licensing does not apply.

Parodies are usually requested only for songs that are instantly recognizable. This means the song has previously achieved hit status and is thus an important copyright. If a publisher allows such usage, full ownership of the copyright in new lyrics is usually vested in the publisher, but not always. Sometimes, the adapter may successfully negotiate partial ownership of the new work.

Because the new lyrics are copyrightable by the new lyricist, the original songwriter's share is reduced, which may be a problem if the original songwriter has right of approval on any changes. The songwriter might then approve of the adaptation as long as the publisher absorbs any dilution in royalties from its own share. All things are negotiable.

In any event, it has previously been pointed out that publishers must always weigh carefully any request to change lyrics, parody or not. If the new version supersedes the original version in the public consciousness, the nature of the song is forever changed. This change affects the ultimate value of the copyright, and publishers must always strive to enhance, not diminish, the integrity of their copyrights.

Medleys

A *medley* is two or more songs tied together into one performance. A recorded medley might not necessarily require special permission if the user is prepared to pay the statutory rate, but this is usually not economically feasible from the user's standpoint.

For example, a mechanical license for one song at the current statutory rate is 6.95¢. If an artist combines four songs into one medley performance, the record company would owe royalties totaling 27.8¢ for one track, assuming the performance is under five minutes in playing time. Much more would be due if the recorded performance exceeded five minutes.

This is clearly not financially practical for a record company.

So, a medley may pose licensing problems unless the respective copyright owners agree to reduced rates. Normally, publishers involved agree to prorate their royalty shares. In the above case, where there are four separate songs involved, each publisher would receive 1.7375¢ per unit sold (6.95¢ ÷ 4).

However, some publishers insist on more than a strictly prorated share. While agreeing to some rate reduction, they may insist on no less than 25%, 33.33%, or even 50% of the normal statutory rate, no matter how many songs are included in the medley.

Other publishers may be willing to consider a prorated share only if all other publishers concerned receive a like amount. Otherwise, a *most favored nation* provision is required, whereby the publisher receives a royalty rate equal to the highest rate received by any other publisher.

Thus, if you agree to a rate of 1.7375¢ with a most favored nations clause, and another publisher wrangles a 3.5¢ rate, you will receive 3.5¢ as well. And, if publishers three and four also require most favored nations treatment, every publisher receives 3.5 ¢ and the record company must pay a total mechanical royalty of 14¢ for the one track.

An alternative method of royalty allocation, which is more practical from a record company standpoint, is a maximum royalty equal to the full statutory rate prorated by the length of playing time for each song. Using this method, if the total playing time is five minutes, there are four songs, and the duration of your copyright is one and a half minutes, you would be paid 30% of the statutory rate.

The formula used to work out the rate for each component part of the medley is to divide the total number of seconds of playing time by the total number of seconds of duration of each copyright. In the above example, then, a five minute track = 300 seconds (5 x 60). Your song's usage, which is 90 seconds, works out to 30% of the total (90 ÷ 300). Therefore, your royalty share is 2.085¢ (6.95¢ x 30%).

Sampling

In a sense, *sampling* is akin to a medley in that the end-product consists of components of previously created works. The difference, however, is that the sampled product is composed of exact copies of an original work, rather than a newly arranged performance of other works.

Digital technology has made possible the isolation of specific instruments and voices from existing, mixed recordings, which can then be copied, edited, and used in entirely new recordings. This has led to a plethora of new releases containing digitalized, sampled bits and pieces of older records by different artists.

There are two separate copyright issues involved in sampling: the original recording and the song. Generally, the record company that released the original recording owns the copyright to the sound recording; the music publisher owns the copyright to the song performed in the recording. Producers of sampled recordings must therefore obtain separate licenses from both the publisher of the sampled song and the record company from which the previously recorded sample was taken. In either case, sampling without permission is copyright infringement, subject to various civil and criminal remedies and penalties under the law.

Compulsory licensing provisions of the Copyright Act do not apply to samples, so each mechanical license must be negotiated, and the publisher can refuse to issue a license. Before a publisher can be in a position to intelligently negotiate licensing terms, the first step is to review a copy of the sampled work.

In some cases, copyright owners refuse approval due to the nature of the usage (protecting the integrity of the copyright). But, once the usage itself is approved, the issue becomes the terms of the license. The publisher holds the upper hand in the negotiations when the recording has already been made. (It would be hard to approve a usage unless you can hear how it would be used, which means the sampling must first take place). However, if the publisher does approve the usage subject to the right terms, negotiations should proceed in good faith to facilitate the sampled work's release, so that the publisher can reap any potential income.

Negotiating points for sampled product center around:
- duration —how much of the original work is contained in the new sampling
- how many other sampled works are included
- how important is the sampled work to the new creation

There are no clearly established precedents or set fees for compensation to the copyright owners of sampled product. Licensing sampled material is often a play-it-by-ear situation, negotiated on a case-by-case basis. Depending upon the extent of usage and the publisher's negotiating ability, compensation could be buy-out fees, royalties, advances plus royalties, or part copyright ownership in the newly created work.

For a brief few seconds of sampled music, a publisher might get a buy-out fee ranging from $1,000-$5,000. However, if the usage is more lengthy, repeated, or significant to the new recording, such as being part of a hook or refrain or catch phrase, the publisher might insist on royalty participation ranging from 10%-50% of the statutory mechanical rate and/or a copyright share to the new song.

Depending on how significant the sampling is, the original publisher can wind up with 10%-50% of the new copyright plus joint administration. With a share of the copyright to the new work, the publisher gets a percentage of all mechanical, performance, and other royalties that are generated by the new use and any derivative uses.

It is not unusual to treat a sampled work as you would a medley. In both cases, the preexisting songs are inseparable from the new work. Therefore, the copyright to the new work should be shared with owners of the original copyrights. If the publisher does participate in the copyright to the new composite work, that participation should include full right of approval for all derivative uses, such as movies, commercials, print, etc. Of course, full credits must be attributed to the writers and publishers of the original work as co-writers and co-publishers of the new entity. It must be stressed that the producer of the new composite work does not share in the copyright to the *original* work that was sampled.

Even where a publisher of a sampled work receives a copyright share in a new composite work, the publisher might also insist on an advance or one-off fee in addition to a percentage of all royalties. Some publishers require a *rollover advance* whereby, say, $1,000 is advanced upon release, and an additional $1,000 is paid for each 25,000 units sold.

New media

The term *new media* is broadly applied to newer technologies, such as MIDI, CD-ROMs, video games, karaoke, etc. Many of these technologies are still evolving as far as licensing parameters are concerned, and, as with sampling, there are not always clearly established precedents for compensation to copyright owners. So, licensing copyrights for new media is approached on a case-by-case basis with compensation depending upon the extent and nature of usage, and the publisher's negotiating ability.

MIDI SOFTWARE
The term *MIDI* is an acronym for *Musical Instrument Digital Interface.* It is an international standard for exchanging musical information on a computer. It has evolved into a widely available, relatively inexpensive technology used by many professional musicians, producers, and artists to enhance recording projects.

MIDI software stores digitalized sound so that it can be reproduced with virtually no loss of quality. A *MIDI sequence* is a computer data file of one particular MIDI data recording capable of playback through a computer.

MIDI rights license
Permission to use a composition in a MIDI sequence is given in a *MIDI rights license.* The license permits the user to make and distribute copies of a MIDI sequence program in what is called the *MIDI sequence market.* Specifically, this refers to the sale, lease, license, use or other distribution of MIDI sequences directly or indirectly to individuals for playback through a hardware sequencer or personal computer connected to a MIDI capable synthesizer using MIDI software or any similar devices.

Since MIDI software reproduces copyrights for sale in tangible form, a per unit royalty based on sales is paid, much like a mechanical license. However, the compulsory licensing provision of the Copyright Act does not apply to MIDI as in the case of phonorecords. So, each licensing situation is negotiated between the copyright owner and user.

Because of the various uses MIDI files are capable of, publishers must carefully analyze requests to use works in MIDI software, and they must be careful to strictly define and limit the rights granted in any licenses. Since this is still an emerging technology with licensing provisions being threshed out, a MIDI rights license should state that "no provisions of the license shall be binding upon or prejudicial to any position taken by the copyright owner subsequent to the expiration date of the license." Further, the copyright owner should make clear in the license that it reserves all rights of every kind not specifically authorized or granted to the user in the license.

Rights granted
A typical MIDI rights license grants the user permission to arrange, orchestrate, record, and rerecord the musical composition for use in a MIDI sequence, and to make and distribute copies of the MIDI sequence program throughout the territory, provided (a) the MIDI sequence does not exceed X minutes and Y seconds and (b) the composition is recorded as a nondramatic background, vocal, or instrumental.

Obligations of user
As a condition of the license, the licensee is required to place prominently on the packaging and, where practical, on every MIDI sequence copy the following notice:

It is a violation of Federal Copyright Law to synchronize this MIDI Sequence with video tape or film, or to print this MIDI Sequence in the form of standard music notation without the express written permission of the copyright owner.

The licensee is further required to make quarterly royalty payments accompanied by a detailed accounting statement listing units sold. The licensee may be permitted to maintain a reserve for returns in an amount not exceeding 20% of the number of the MIDI Sequences sold in any accounting period, providing this reserve is liquidated quarterly over three quarters from the end of the accounting period in which the reserve was maintained.

Prohibitions

Normally, MIDI rights licenses expressly prohibit the user to do the following:

- parody the lyrics and/or music or in any way alter the fundamental character of the composition
- print sheet music or program into the MIDI sequence the capability of making any use of the work not specifically authorized
- rent copies of the MIDI sequence or permit purchasers or others to do so
- use the storyline or lyrics or any other portion of the work for dramatic purposes in any way
- broadcast or transmit the work in any manner
- make, sell, lease, rent, or distribute phonorecords except for demonstration purposes
- use the work in any sound recording or audiovisual recording not owned and separately licensed by the copyright owner
- publicly perform the work; any public performance of the MIDI sequence program is strictly limited to performers or places of performance holding a current performing-rights license from the designated performing-rights society of the copyright owner

Compensation

Per unit royalties are usually calculated at around 5% of the software's retail price, which is prorated. The number of songs prorated should include only those works that are in copyright and are royalty-bearing (as opposed to PD works). Alternatively, a specific amount may be required of around 50¢ per song per

unit. Advances are usually offered in the $250 range, representing a guarantee of approximately 500 unit sales.

MULTIMEDIA AND INTERACTIVE MEDIA

The term *multimedia* covers technologies that combine other existing technologies, usually in an interactive format. For example, music, text, photographs, drawings, recorded voice-overs, and movies may be combined on a CD-ROM, which users can manipulate on home computers to produce information or entertainment tailored to specific tastes or needs.

Multimedia products can include software used for entertainment, education, research, and business. Examples include electronic, or interactive encyclopedias, anthologies, almanacs, discographies, and self-instruction programs dealing with a vast array of subjects. Multimedia products are also often referred to as *interactive media.*

In addition to CD-ROMs described above, the *interactive compact disk* (CD-I) is available on most new home computer systems. CD-Is containing games, educational instruction, and informational resources allow users to call up music and information selectively and manipulate it by changing the sequence, altering the sound, and blending music or spoken word with visual images, etc.

Licensing arrangements vary. Compensation ranges from upfront one-off fees (buy-outs) for a specific number of units (with additional or graduated payments due upon additional manufacture) to royalties per unit. Rollover advances are also often due upon renewal of a short-term license or recoupment of an initial advance. Many licenses for multimedia or interactive-media products contain wording and provisions similar to licenses granted for videos and laser disks.

As previously noted, publishers should narrowly define the scope of a license and limit its duration as much as possible. Restricting the time a license is to run is especially important because this is a new technology. As the medium matures, the economic ramifications will be clearer and licensing practices will become more or less standardized. Meanwhile, you should not be locked into long-term licenses that ultimately prove unfavorable. With short-term licenses, you can monitor the progress of this medium and ensure that terms of renewals keep pace with reality.

Licensing provisions for multimedia products are essentially the same as applied to MIDI software discussed above. The same basic prohibitions apply with regards to public performances, unauthorized copying, rental, changing the nature of the work, etc.

For many multi- or interactive-media products, royalties for music range around 5% of retail, which is prorated among all songs included, or 50¢ per song. Advances are usually offered in the $150-$2,500 range.

However, where there are hundreds, even thousands of songs included (e.g., an electronic encyclopedia), logic must prevail. It is obviously financially impractical for a licensee to pay, say, 50¢ per song per unit if 500 songs are included on a product selling at $40 per unit. A prorated percentage, on the other hand, reduces the royalty to fractions of a cent, which makes inclusion feasible, though not exactly lucrative to the copyright owner.

In such situations, the question might then arise of whether it is even worthwhile for copyright owners to grant a license. Usually it is, unless, for some discernible reason, the use of the work diminishes its value. Inclusion generally enhances a copyright's value, since the more a copyright is used and kept in the public's awareness, the more the copyright remains alive for other uses, and the more value it ultimately accrues.

This is especially true where the work is used in reference works (encyclopedias, anthologies, discographies, educational aids, training programs). The mere fact that a work is included denotes a copyright's importance as representative of an era or genre. This, then, enhances not only the prestige of the work, but increases the likelihood that potential music users, in the course of research, will be made aware of the work and perhaps want to license it.

The key to setting a fee or royalty scale is also relative to the uniqueness of the work as it relates to the product being licensed. We come back again to the question: can the song be easily replaced? If the work is one of hundreds of alternatives available for an anthology of, say, popular mid-1960s soul classics, it would behoove the copyright owner to license the song. Inclusion in such a work helps etch in stone the song's importance. If, however, the song is more crucial to the intended product (e.g., *Number One Pop Songs of 1975*), it cannot be substituted. The licensee is then under the gun to pay a higher fee or royalty in order to use it.

KARAOKE

Karaoke machines play audio tapes and/or videos containing musical tracks with no lead vocal. The machines are placed in public commercial establishments such as nightclubs, skating rinks, amusement arcades, etc., where customers take the stage and sing along with the music. Karaoke machines are also sold, along with instrumental tracks of hit songs, for home use.

Obviously, the appeal of karaoke rests with using well-known songs members of the public enjoy singing. That means virtually all music produced for karaoke must be licensed, rather than being created especially for the format.

Licenses for karaoke sing-along tapes and discs are akin to mechanical licenses, with the statutory mechanical rate paid for each copy distributed. However, the appeal of karaoke is sing-along, which means the customer base needs access to the lyrics of each song. So, in addition to the statutory mechanical rate, the licensor pays an additional 2¢-6¢ per copy when lyrics are printed or displayed electronically in conjunction with the music. A video version may pay as much as 10¢-12¢ per copy.

Karaoke synchronization licenses

Karaoke video booths are attractions at carnivals, theme parks, arcades, malls, etc. Here customers can have video clips made of their sing-along performances. This raises the question of whether a synchronization license is needed, since customers' vocal performances are synchronized with their visual images. This is often covered with a *fixing fee* of around $200-$300. Typically, publishers are paid a 50¢ royalty per video clip sold to customers.

Videos produced for use in karaoke machines are called *programs*. Licenses for music used in karaoke recordings are called *karaoke synchronization licenses*.

In a typical karaoke synchronization license, the publisher assigns to the producer the nonexclusive, limited right to create and use arrangements of, and to record and re-record, the named composition in synchronization or timed relation with the identified program. Generally, the producer is granted the following rights:

- to use the title of the composition on the program
- to display the original lyrics of the composition on the program
- to manufacture, distribute, advertise, rent, and sell copies of the program solely for use in karaoke machines, *provided that* the machines are sold strictly for home use, for the public to sing along with the program, and/or for the public to record vocal performances on the instrumental track and purchase one-off copies of such performances.

Term

Karaoke licenses are usually granted for a term of seven years. Renewal options may be granted upon payment of additional advances. It would be more prudent, however, to not include a renewal option. Remember, in emerging technologies and new media, it is best to issue a license for as short a term as possible. Users that want to renew will ask to do so at the appropriate time, and you won't be locked into terms that may ultimately prove unfavorable in a changing world.

Performance rights

The publisher reserves all rights not expressly granted to the karaoke producer, including but not limited to the performing rights in the composition. Establishments where members of the public sing along or record their vocal performance must hold a valid performing-rights license from the publisher's performing-rights society.

Copyright to arrangements

Since the karaoke producer must record an instrumental version of the composition, all arrangements of the composition must be created as *works for hire*. The license requires that the publisher be deemed the *author* of the arrangement for copyright purposes, and all rights to the arrangement belong to the publisher. The producer must obtain and deliver to the publisher a written *work for hire agreement*, executed by the arranger, before copies of the program can be distributed.

Compensation

The publisher's compensation may include advances, fixing fees, and royalties.

Fixing fee:
A *fixing fee* is usually paid to the publisher within ten days after the composition had been recorded for use in the program. This fee is not an advance and is therefore not recouped from royalties. It is normally a rather nominal sum of around $200-$300.

Advance:
At the same time as the fixing fee is paid, a nonreturnable payment of around $200-$300 is made to the publisher as an advance against royalties.

Royalties:
Royalties may arise from either the sale or rental of copies of the program to commercial establishments and from the sale or rental of copies for home use.

Under normal circumstances, a royalty of 10¢ is paid for each copy distributed during the term. However, many publishers require an escalating royalty, either based on surpassing a sales plateau or lapse of time. For instance, with a seven-year license, the royalty may be 10¢ for each copy distributed during the first half of the term (42 months), escalating to 12¢ for each copy distributed in the final 42 months of the license term.

Where video programs are produced for synchronization of performances by members of the public, copies of which are then sold to the public, a substantially higher royalty of around 50¢ may be paid.

Most favored nations clause:
Many publishers insist on a most favored nations clause. As described earlier, this clause insures that if, during the term of the license, the producer agrees to pay any other publisher a higher fixing fee and/or royalty rate than that prescribed, then that higher fee and/or royalty rate shall also apply to the composition in question, and that higher fee and/or royalty rate shall be retroactive to the date of the license. In such event, the producer shall immediately pay the publisher the difference between the original fee and/or royalty with regards to past sales, and the producer must continue to pay the publisher at the higher royalty rate for all copies distributed thereafter.

Rollover advance:
Since the fixing fee and royalty advance for most karaoke licenses are rather nominal, it is common practice for publishers to insist on a *rollover advance*. In such cases, the license usually requires the producer to make a further advance against royalties in the amount of $150 at the end of each six-month period in which all previous advances have been recouped. In other words, the publisher is perpetually in the red to the producer in the amount of $150 or whatever the rollover advance is. However, the license may provide that no rollover advance be made for the final six-month period prior to the expiration date of the license.

Accountings, payments, and audits:
As with all licenses and contracts, the producer is obligated to keep accurate accounts, which may be inspected upon reasonable notice by the publisher. The producer is further obligated to issue statements of account each quarter (every 3 months) together with payment for any royalties due for the period just ending. Generally, the statements and payments are due within 45 days following the end of each calendar quarter from the date the first commercial sale or rental of the program takes place.

VIDEO GAMES

Video games, like those manufactured by Sega, Nintendo, et al., are a form of multimedia product. Licenses usually provide compensation on a per unit royalty basis, as discussed, along with a *fixation* or *fixing fee*. And normally an advance against royalties is provided, ranging from the low hundreds to the low thousands. Where numerous works are included in the software, a buy-out or a prorated royalty may be offered.

Video arcades

Video games enjoy popularity in arcades where pinball machines once ruled supreme. Software for arcade games is obviously not a mass market item, though users who play the games do constitute a mass market. Game machines cost arcade operators upwards of $3,000 each.

Royalties to copyright owners are calculated against the cost of the machine, and usually range from ½%-1% of the price ($150-$300). Or, a prorated royalty of between $10-$15 per song per unit might be considered. In either case, a fixation or synchronization fee is usually required, which might be anywhere from $150 to $600.

The use of music in video arcades amounts to a public performance. The license issued to the machine manufacturer does not include the right of public performance, but it requires the machine to be authorized for use only to arcade operators who have valid blanket licenses from the performing-right societies.

MUSIC LICENSING IN CYBERSPACE

The terms *cyberspace, information superhighway, Internet,* and *World Wide Web* interchangeably refer to electronic transmission of information through personal computers. The convenience of digital transmission via PC links may make online databank services the preferred mode of music distribution to consumers in the not too distant future.

Already, commercial online services like CompuServe and America Online reach an estimated 10 million subscribers throughout the United States. In addition, some 60,000 bulletin board operators link between 15 and 20 million PC users nationwide. But cyberspace has no borders. PC users in Prague and Pretoria can access the same data at the same time as someone in Peoria.

That means a record company in Peoria can sell its product to consumers in Prague and Pretoria via cyberspace, eliminating the manufacturing process, as well as costs of shipping and cuts by middlemen (distributors, retailers, overseas licensees, etc.). Consumers benefit from being able to acquire music of their choice 24 hours a day, seven days a week. They don't have to wait until stores open, fight traffic, find a parking space, or face disappointment when product is out of stock.

The rapid development of cyberspace technologies for distributing information and entertainment has caused a scramble among copyright owners to upgrade international standards of copyright protection. The ability to upload, store, and download music affects copyright owners of sound recordings as well as owners of the underlying musical works con-

tained on the recordings.

There are three licensing issues related to the use of music online. First, transmission of the music is a "public performance" and therefore subject to a *performing-right license*. Second, downloading transmitted music constitutes "copying" and is thereby subject to a *mechanical license*. And, third, combining music with visual images for transmission falls within the scope of a *synchronization license*.

While cyberspace presents new marketing opportunities, there are great challenges as well. Though things are very much in flux and are likely to remain so for some time, steps are being taken to solve some of the problems. Copyright owners are working to establish clear legal precedents and effective methods for licensing musical works on terms commensurate with the nature of their use.

Online mechanical licenses

In January 1996, the Harry Fox Agency and CompuServe entered into a licensing agreement that will likely serve as the standard for licensing mechanical rights to other commercial online services. Mechanical licenses for online transmission are substantially the same as those issued for phonorecords. The only difference is that instead of making and distributing copies via phonorecords, online licenses permit the licensee to transmit digital copies via commercial online services.

When a license request is received from an online service forum, Harry Fox issues a mechanical license on behalf of the song's publisher. The license permits the making and distribution of nondramatic, audio-only copies of a specific audio recording, via transmission of digital data. The licensed recording may then be uploaded and stored in the forum's database for downloading by subscribers.

Online mechanical licenses are issued at the statutory royalty rate in effect at the time of downloading, and royalties are payable for each downloaded copy. As with negotiated mechanical licenses, the royalty rate may be lower than statutory if the publisher agrees.

Online performing-right licenses

ASCAP and BMI have also been actively working to establish online licensing precedents. Whereas downloading song copyrights may be equivalent to "making and distributing copies" and subject to mechanical licenses, the online transmittal of music is a "public performance," like broadcasting a work over television or radio airwaves. Therefore, online providers must be licensed by, and pay performance royalties to, performing-right societies on behalf of copyright owners.

ASCAP currently issues a blanket performing-right license called *The ASCAP Experimental Agreement for Computer Online Services, Electronic Bulletin Boards, Internet Sites, and Similar Operations.* The license grants online service operators permission to publicly perform (by means of electronic transmissions) all songs in ASCAP's repertory.

The online service provider pays ASCAP a licensing fee commensurate with the site's gross revenue, its total music revenue, and its total ASCAP-related music revenue. The minimum annual licensing fee is currently $500 per year per site. BMI uses a similar type of blanket license to cover performances of works in its repertory.

Online synchronization licenses

Synchronization is the third licensing issue related to transmitting music in cyberspace. Undoubtedly, there will be *made-for-cyberspace* movies and other types of audiovisual programming produced for online distribution that will require synchronization licenses. In addition to a synchronization fee, a producer must agree to distribute the program only via Web sites with valid performing-right licenses, because transmitting the program constitutes a public performance. Mechanical licenses similar to the one worked out between the Harry Fox Agency and CompuServe would also be needed to enable consumers to download copies of the programs.

Whereas mechanical licenses for cyberspace are subject to statutory royalty rates, and performances are covered through blanket licenses from performing-right societies, copyright owners must negotiate synchronization licenses directly with program producers on a case by case basis. Each situation is unique. Fees and other terms must be arrived at after careful analysis of each licensing issue (e.g., nature of use, duration of use, duration of license, etc.). Obviously, a cyberspace synchronization license would have to be granted for the *world*, since the medium has no borders.

Since this is very much an emerging technology, copyright owners should narrowly define and limit the scope of rights granted. In particular, the duration of a synchronization license should be restricted to as short a term as possible. Renewal options can be included (to be exercised at the publisher's discretion), but the key is to not get locked into licenses that prove unfavorable over the long-term. Limited duration gives the publisher a trap-door mechanism when terms of a license become outmoded.

Electrical transcription licenses

The term *electrical transcription* is used to describe the recording of music specifically for broadcast or performance to the public. Examples include production of recorded programs for radio syndication, radio advertisements, in-flight entertainment on airlines, and background music used in commercial establishments.

An *electrical transcription license* differs from a mechanical license in that the latter permits the making of copies of a recording for sale to the public, whereas the former permits only the public performance of the recording, *not* the sale. Unlike mechanical licenses, electrical transcription licenses are not subject to the compulsory licensing provision of the Copyright Act. Each license must be negotiated directly between the user and the publisher, or the publisher's agent.

Transcription licenses combine aspects of performance licenses as well as mechanical licenses, because they involve the reproduction and the public performance of music. However, most transcription licenses do not include the right to perform the music, only the right to record it for the purpose of performing or rebroadcast.

BACKGROUND MUSIC

Music heard in elevators, shopping malls, banks, restaurants, etc. are provided either on tape or through broadcasts transmitted via FM, cable, or special phone lines. It is sometimes called *piped music*, and is used to enhance the atmosphere of an establishment as opposed to entertainment. Background music service firms, such as Muzak, usually obtain a master or *block* license from the performing-rights societies.

Most block licenses from performing-right societies call for annual fees based on the number of franchised establishments where the transcribed programs are used. In licenses that combine both mechanical and performance rights, a specified royalty is paid per composition for each program sold or rented to users. These licenses usually break down the royalty as 40% representing payment for mechanical right usage and 60% for the performance right. Thus, if the stated royalty were 5¢ per song per copy, 2¢ would cover the mechanical right and 3¢ the performance right.

RADIO

In addition to programs produced for radio syndication, some publishers produce *recorded music libraries* containing music suitable for themes, background, intros, and segues. Transcription licenses for syndicated programs and library services are obtained directly from music publishers or their agents (e.g., Harry Fox), which cover the mechanical rights only. Transcription licenses for syndicated radio programs usually pay $75 per song. Music publishers who own libraries generally issue transcription licenses *gratis* for radio use. Actual performance of the transcriptions (for both syndicated programs and recorded music libraries) are paid for by the radio stations through blanket performance licenses with the performing-right societies.

When a song is used in a television commercial, a *synchronization license* is required, because the music is synchronized with visual images. For radio commercials, however, transcription licenses are required, since no synchronization with visual images is involved.

An important copyright used on a national scale in a one-year radio commercial should fetch a transcription fee of between $25,000 to $75,000. Shorter-term licenses for regional or local radio use are best licensed on a weekly rate, which might be anywhere from $250 to $1,000 per week, depending upon the population of the market covered.

IN-FLIGHT PROGRAMMING

Airlines provide music for passengers to listen to on headsets. The nature of the usage more closely resembles syndicated radio programs than background music, because it is intended for entertainment rather than mood enhancement. Therefore, transcription licenses issued for airline music programming are similar to those issued to radio syndicators, as opposed to background music services. The transcription license is akin to a mechanical license that authorizes the packager to duplicate the work, and it is issued by the publisher or the publisher's mechanical-right society. Rights to perform songs on the transcribed program are obtained from performing-right societies.

Consumer products

Consumer product licensing refers to permitting the use of compositions in a variety of traditional products where music enhances the nature of the product. In some cases, the music itself may be key to the product's desirability by the consumer. In other cases, the capability of the product to replicate music is the result of new or emerging technologies, like the microchip.

One of the oldest technologies for reproducing music is the music box, which predates phonograph records by a couple of centuries. In general, consumer product licenses, particularly music boxes, might be considered mechanical reproduction. A licensor might then attempt to secure a mechanical license at the statutory rate, regardless of the product's selling price.

But many music boxes sell for sums substantially higher than a CD or tape. Should a copyright owner then be satisfied with a statutory rate of 6.95¢ on a music box selling for $100? Especially if the music used is arguably and indisputably a key element of the item being sold? The same question applies to dolls, toys, greeting cards, musical cigarette lighters, and other products or novelty items that use microchips to play music.

The best tack for the publisher is to insist on a royalty of around 5% of retail per unit, with an advance ranging from $250 to $2,500. If the manufacturer insists on using the compulsory mechanical licensing provision of the current copyright law (thereby paying only the statutory mechanical rate), the publisher can then demand the manufacturer's compliance with the onerous provisions of the law (i.e., monthly audited statements and payments for each unit manufactured).

DART

Home taping for personal consumption is not copyright infringement. You can buy a CD and make a cassette copy to play on your Walkman while jogging. Of course, if you give away, sell, or rent your cassette copy, you are then infringing the copyrights in the sound recording and the songs. Problem: How is it possible to police what millions do with home copies? Ever since the advent of tape recorders, the music industry has struggled to find a workable solution that prevents abuse of home taping and compensates copyright owners for lost revenues.

Several countries have enacted legislation that puts a levy or tax on every tape recorder (of whatever kind) and blank audiotape. Revenues collected go into a pool that is distributed periodically to copyright owners. Just as the U.S. belatedly amended its copyright laws to extend the term of copyright protection and bring mechanical royalties into line with the rest of the world (albeit not quite, as discussed previously), Congress has attempted to address the home taping issue with an act referred to by its acronym *DART*, which stands for *Digital Audio Recorders and Tape*.

And, just as the U.S. legislative approach to mechanical royalties has left many publishers dissatisfied, DART, too, leaves much to be desired. It goes only half way. It applies to only *digital* recordings. That means analog tape recordings can still be made at home without any regard to copyright owners. At least there is now a method of compensating copyright owners when home digital recordings are made. And, no doubt, digital recordings will entirely replace analog within a few years, just as vinyl records have gone the way of the old wax cylinder.

The DART act provides:
- a 3% tax on the wholesale price of blank digital audiotapes
- a 2% tax on the wholesale price of non-professional digital recorders
- a *Serial Copyright Management System* (SCMS) encoded on every digital recorder so that copies can't be made of copies.

ALLOCATION OF DART REVENUES
Taxes collected from sales of digital recorders and blank tapes are allocated as follows:
- two-thirds to copyright owners of the sound recording (record companies) and performers (artists)
- one-third to copyright owners of the music (publishers) and writers

Of the one-third share allocated to the music copyright, 50% goes to the music publisher, and 50% to the songwriter. In other words, for every $1.00 collected under DART, music publishers and songwriters each get 16.66¢.

The Harry Fox Agency collects the music publishers' share of DART income. Performing-right societies collect the songwriters' share, and pay the writers directly.

Revenues collected under DART are paid to copyright owners, writers, and artists by Harry Fox, BMI, and ASCAP in proportion to their respective percentages of all other income collected by the rights organizations. For example, a publisher whose percentage of income from BMI is equal to .001% of all BMI collections, will receive approximately .001% of all DART money collected by BMI during the period.

CHAPTER 16

Exploitation

Exploitation is usually defined as "selfishly, unethically, or unfairly taking advantage of someone, something, or a situation." Novice songwriters may thus be alarmed to hear publishers talk of "exploiting songs." But when music publishers use the term *exploitation*, they are talking about the process of marketing copyrights.

Market targeting

The market for music is obviously universal, but the market for your particular type of music probably isn't. However much we want every living soul to love and buy what we do, that's an impossible dream. Tastes and cultures are as wide ranging as they are conflicting.

So, while it may be interesting to try to persuade hardcore Dixieland jazz aficionados to buy gangsta rap, any marketing dollars spent doing so will likely be wasted. Logic and budgetary constraints dictate that you concentrate marketing resources where they'll be most effective, which means you must first identify your true audience. That relatively small segment of humanity is your *target market*.

You have to be attuned to your market's tastes, needs, and desires in order to develop product they want and to know how to best make them aware of its existence. The characteristics of your target market (age, income range, lifestyle, etc.) influence your choices of product acquisition and development, packaging, distribution, advertising, and promotion.

Market research

ONLINE DATABASES

With a computer and modem, you can reach a variety of databases to quickly access marketing data. Electronic bulletin boards and the Internet allow music business professionals to exchange e-mail, synth programs, and information relating to numerous music business issues. You can also develop new contacts and solidify professional relationships.

Four database services operated by *Billboard* magazine are particularly useful for ongoing research. These services, Billboard Online, BDS, Soundscan, and BIN, are available by subscription, and are accessed with a PC and modem. *Billboard* supplies software packages containing user manuals, installation disks, customer support hotlines, and novice-friendly technical help.

Billboard Online

Billboard Online provides access to text and chart data from past and current issues of *Billboard* magazine. You can scroll through headlines to find subjects you're interested in. More efficiently, you can type in a key word, such as the name of a company, artist, industry issue, or product, and the system will search its archives to find the relevant information. In seconds, it generates a list of references on your computer screen. Select the specific articles or charts you want with a simple keystroke or click of your mouse, and the data is displayed. Save the full text or charts in your PC's memory, then read it later or print it out on your printer.

Specific information offered includes 15 categories of singles charts, 7 album charts, 5 video charts, and 2 European charts, all covering airplay and sales.

You can search RIAA statistics and consumer profile information, and find all gold and platinum RIAA certified audio and video releases since 1958.

Also available are box office and touring data, regional breakout charts (searchable by artist, title, label), and creative and production credits for music videos. The text archives go back to the beginning of 1991, and the charts go back to 1985. The archives are updated weekly. New editions of *Billboard* are available electronically each Friday prior to newsstand distribution. This service is an ideal one-stop research resource, since *Billboard* extensively covers everything to do with the music business.

Broadcast Data Systems (BDS)

Billboard's Broadcast Data System (BDS) monitors radio, TV, and cable broadcasts nationally and instantaneously updates its central databank as songs, records, videos, and commercials are aired. Through this service, labels, publishers, managers, producers, and others associated with a particular release can get the details of each play.

BDS generates reports that include specific stations playing a song, their locations, the size of the listening audience, the dates and times of each play, and even the record's ranking on each station's playlist during the reporting period. You get a summary of stations adding a release during the current period, the number of stations dropping it from their playlists, the total number of stations playing it, and the total number of plays it received.

Because the airplay reports are 100% accurate and up-to-the-minute, they can be used to find out exactly what's being played where and when. Thus, informed decisions can be made about deployment of promotion and marketing resources with maximum effect, and the results of those promotion and marketing efforts can be quickly evaluated.

You can order a variety of individually tailored reports, including:
• Song Activity Report
• Song by Station Report
• Song by Daypart Report
• Station Logs
• Station Playlists
• Video Logs
• Video Playlists
• National Airplay Chart
• Hot 40 Markets Report
• Market Activity Report
• Artist Activity Report

BDS is already having an impact on the way labels use independent promoters to get records added to radio station playlists. Because BDS reports the exact date and time of each play on over 550 radio stations in more than 100 markets (with more being added), label executives can monitor and verify the results of promoters' efforts. Accordingly, some labels now pay promoters by the number of actual *plays*, rather than by the number of *adds*.

Airplay Monitor

BDS also offers hard copy weekly reports through *Airplay Monitor*, a magazine format publication. Actually, there are several versions of *Airplay Monitor*, each of them dedicated to a specific market segment (R&B, Top 40, country, etc.).

Soundscan

Soundscan, another *Billboard* service, monitors actual sales at over 600 stores (with more being frequently added). When a compact disc or cassette is purchased, its bar code is scanned and the sale is reported to Soundscan's databank. Subscribers can track sales by searching the database by title, label, catalog number, or artist. You can tailor individual reports by artist, title, label, store, region, sales rankings, and comparisons with previous totals, etc. Like BDS, Soundscan's information provides vital feedback for evaluating sales, marketing, advertising, and promotional efforts.

Billboard Information Network (BIN)

Billboard Information Network (BIN) is the fourth *Billboard* database service. Its online information includes radio playlists, a weekly electronic newsletter, advanced sight of all *Billboard* U.S. and European charts the Friday before newsstand distribution of the magazine, availability of territorial music publishing rights to all charted songs, national and regional sales, rental, club, and airplay activity on audio and video releases, and chart share reports for labels and artists.

TRADE ASSOCIATIONS

Trade associations also provide excellent marketing research sources. Depending upon the type of product you're concentrating on, you might approach NARAS, NAIRD, NARM, NMPA, RIAA, or CMA, et al., and request a copy of their latest market research material.

Most trade associations can provide demographic breakdowns of the market (by age, sex, region, education, income), as well as overseas markets and opportunities. Plus, you'll learn how many radio stations across the country (and overseas) now program your type of music, how many cable customers watch TNN, CMT, MTV, VH-1, BET, or whatever. This arms you with much vital information for marketing your product. And, if you're raising money for your company, such information is useful ammunition to convince investors of the market potential for your product.

TRADE MAGAZINES AND DIRECTORIES
Magazines and newsletters dedicated to your trade provide essential information for business planning, decisions, and actions. Trade magazines are a source for new contacts and ideas for marketing campaigns. They also keep you informed about market changes that affect your future. In addition to news and views about your industry, most trade magazines also publish directories filled with contact information for potential users of your product.

Some of the trades you need to read regularly are: *Billboard, Cash Box, Gavin Report, Radio & Records, New on the Charts, SongLink Int'l, Hollywood Reporter,* and *Variety*. More are listed in the Appendix.

CONSUMER PRESS
There are hundreds of newsletters and magazines dedicated to music fans generally and aficionados of the market you're targeting specifically. These publications represent *vox populi*, and shouldn't be discounted just because they're aimed at the general public rather than at you, the sophisticated music biz pro.

The consumer publications listed in the Appendix are presented as just a sample of what's available. Magazine racks at large newsstands and bookstores offer a vast array other consumer publications directed towards specific genres (rap, country, rock, jazz, classical, etc.). They'll keep you up to date about what's hot and what's not among the hoi polloi.

Songplugging
Most indie publishers concentrate marketing efforts on getting songs recorded and released, which is the conventional way to establish a song as a hit. This involves promoting copyrights to recording artists, producers, and record companies. Traditionally, this exercise has been called *songplugging* and the task is assigned to a *songplugger*.

Many publishers these days give songpluggers other titles, such as *catalog manager, professional manager,* or *creative manager*. In addition to promoting, or plugging songs, the position might also include other duties, such as scouting, signing, and developing talent, producing demos, and acting as a liaison with licensees.

Songpluggers must be alert for all opportunities to promote their catalogs. In addition to establishing relationships with producers, artists' managers, and record labels, they have to maintain contacts with music supervisors at film and television production companies and a host of other potential users.

▼

Successful exploitation requires song-casting expertise, initiative, and people skills.

Contacts and relationships are important, because one of the keys to songplugging success is information. Songpluggers need to know when artists are planning recording sessions and what types of songs are needed. Armed with such information, a songplugger then must have the ability to *pitch* the right song to the right person at the right time. (*Pitching* is the term for *submitting* songs for a project.)

Hard sell won't induce an artist or producer to choose one publisher's song over another's. It all comes down to the artist's or producer's aesthetic taste and commercial instinct. The most a songplugger can do is be attuned to the producer's and artist's individual tastes, the current state of the market, and which songs in the catalog best match those criteria.

BACK CATALOG
Music publishing companies grow with the acquisition and promotion of new copyrights. But the lifeblood that gives a publishing company its ultimate value is its *back catalog*—songs that have been acquired over the years. A good back catalog generates steady cash flow as older songs are recycled through cover recordings, commercials, movies, videos, television shows, print editions, and live, background, and broadcast performances.

But in order to accumulate a catalog of copyrights that can be successfully promoted, publishers must always focus acquisition efforts on quality songs that hold up over the years. Publishers should also strive to build a catalog of diverse genres, in order to protect against cyclical shifts in consumer tastes.

HOLDS
A nightmare scenario for a record company is to invest money recording a song, schedule it as an 'A' side release, prepare promotional materials and a marketing campaign, then see some other label beat them to the punch with the same song. For this reason, labels and producers often ask publishers to place *holds* on songs they are considering before they actually record them.

Situations where holds can not be granted
Under the compulsory mechanical licensing provision of the Copyright Act, publishers can not prevent any-

one from recording and releasing a song once it has already been released. Obviously, therefore, a publisher can not place a hold on a song that has already been released. The best a publisher can do for a record company or producer wanting to record a previously released song is to promise not to actively plug it to other labels for a period of time. But for new, unreleased songs, the publisher has complete discretion over whether or not to issue a mechanical license.

Publisher's obligations when a hold is given

When a publisher grants a hold, it is promising not to plug the song to others, nor issue a mechanical license to anyone else, until such time as either the label decides not to use the song, the record is released, or the time period for the hold lapses without a definite decision by the label.

Record company's obligation when a hold is granted

Unlike situations where film producers request holds, it is not normal practice for record companies to pay for the privilege of putting holds on songs. There is no real onus on a label to follow through with actually recording a song for which a hold is granted, much less to release it as an 'A' side, or even to release it at all.

In fact, record companies should not be expected to guarantee an 'A' side release before a song is recorded. Rarely will a label invest in recording a song that does not have 'A' side potential, but neither can a label know for sure which songs will emerge from a session as 'A' side contenders until the session is complete.

Points to consider before granting a hold

Requests for holds should be considered very carefully. The publisher doesn't want to jeopardize having the song not used at all. But neither does he want to forego other opportunities that might arise in the meantime, especially if the song might be ultimately left in the can.

Once a publisher promises a hold, however, it must be maintained. Credibility is always important, and, as in any business, adhering to an agreement is vital. Although a hold is normally given verbally, it might be construed as a verbal contract.

Before granting a hold, the publisher should ascertain the following:

- the seriousness of intent to actually record the song
- the likely commercial potential of the release (a new artist on a no-name label without major distribution may not warrant giving a hold)
- whether others are currently expressing interest in the same song

Set time limits on holds

Realize that some A&R personnel and producers routinely ask for holds on all new material under consideration, even though no decision has been made as to what the final session line-up will be. So, a publisher should place a time limit on a hold.

At minimum, the cut-off date should be the approximate date of the recording session. Once a song is cut, the publisher can agree to extend the hold until such time as a decision is made on whether the song will be an 'A' side release. But the length of time given for the hold and any extensions must be clearly defined. The publisher should follow up a verbal hold with a letter restating the terms, to avoid any misunderstandings.

DEMOS

Songpluggers submit songs to potential users in the form of *demos* (demonstration recordings). Demo production is a vital function of the music publishing business. A demo needs to show off a song in the best light.

Always shoot for high quality demos

- The more a demo sounds like a hit record, the more likely it is that producers and record company execs will perceive the song itself as a hit.
- A demo may turn out so well that it can be licensed as a finished master, jingle track, movie theme, etc.
- Well-produced demos can showcase songwriters' talents as producers or artists and lead to production assignments or artist deals that open further opportunities to get more of the writers' repertoire cut.

Plan demo sessions carefully

Publishers should obviously take care to produce good demos, since they are, after all, *the* vehicle used to market the product. Demos needn't be expensive, but they require quality musicians and singers to perform them. If the songwriters aren't capable of performing and singing their own demos to professional standards, the publisher must hire suitable personnel.

Musicians' fees and studio costs can add up without careful planning and budgeting. A publisher must be very selective about which songs to demo. Not all songs are worthy of or are ready for demo production, despite a writer's opinion. Indiscriminate demo production is obviously costly. Demo costs can range from a few hundred dollars up into the thousands, depending upon the sophistication of the studio, equipment, and musical talent used.

In-house demo studios

Recent technological innovations have made relatively low cost, high quality recording equipment available, so that most active publishers find it economical to own their own demo studios. A publisher-owned demo studio eliminates many budgetary constraints. Without having to watch the clock, writers can spend more time experimenting and refining their demos, making the songs more commercial.

In-house demo studios also allow publishers more scope to develop writers into performing artists and producers. Since good demo recording equipment is now so affordable, in-house demo studios should only be a matter of securing suitable physical space in which to house them.

Allocating demo costs

Some publishers charge demo costs back to writers, as advances against the writers' future earnings. Other publishers split the costs, absorbing part of the expense and charging the balance to the writers' advance accounts. Still other publishers treat demos as a promotional cost of doing business and do not charge writers at all. The way demo expenses are treated often comes down to negotiation between the writers and publishers. In any case, songwriter contracts should clarify how demo costs are going to be handled to avoid serious misunderstandings at accounting time.

Who owns derivative rights to demos?

Many demos are produced to master quality. Some publishers license demos (or their musical tracks) as commercial recordings, jingles, movie or television themes, etc. Publishers who pay 100% of the recording costs own the demos, which usually gives them the right to license derivative usages.

Derivative usages provide publishers with synchronization fees, buy-out fees, and royalties for the use of the demo recording, in addition to fees and royalties from the use of the song itself. (Income arising from the use of the song is split with the writer, of course, but income from the use of the recording belongs solely to the publisher).

When a writer pays for a demo, however, there may be a question as to who has legal title to the recording itself. The publisher must obtain from the writer the right to license the recording and negotiate how any licensing fees or royalties will be split. Any compensation due the writer should be applicable to any outstanding advance balance the writer owes the publisher.

A further problem arises when the writer is also an artist. If the writer is signed to a record company and performs on the demo recording, the publisher naturally cannot license the demo recording without the record company's permission. If the writer performs on the demo but is not an artist, the publisher must obtain approval from the writer to license the performance.

Analyzing songplugging tactics

Songplugging frustrates many fledgling publishers, because their material meets with rejection more often than not. It may be small comfort to know that even major publishers working with top writers have the same problem. But if practically all your songplugging efforts are unsuccessful, you need to know why and what to do about it.

First, recognize that the real problem is not having your songs turned down. Rejection is the symptom of some other, underlying problem (or problems) that must be solved before you can succeed. Analyze your songplugging techniques to discover the real reasons you haven't had any "luck" with your catalog. And when you know the real reasons, the remedies will most likely be self-evident; you will see what to do, step by step.

Songplugging is marketing. Marketing is a matching process. You have to match the right product with the right customer at the right time. When your song is rejected, you failed to match it properly somewhere along the line. So you have to isolate, then analyze, each basic songplugging step until you uncover the root problem(s).

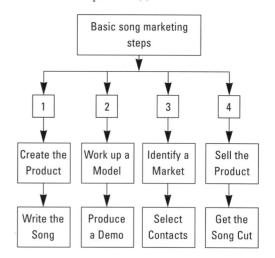

ANALYZING THE PRODUCT

You can't succeed unless step one—your product—is good. But what is a "good" song? Every hit has its detractors. Song quality is a matter of subjective opinion. The person to whom you submit a song judges it by a "feel" based on commercial and aesthetic instincts. You can't force someone to like a song.

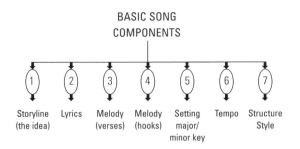

BASIC SONG
COMPONENTS

1. Storyline (the idea)
2. Lyrics
3. Melody (verses)
4. Melody (hooks)
5. Setting major/ minor key
6. Tempo
7. Structure Style

Maybe a song is well-constructed but lacks that magic sparkle that excites listeners. The person you submit it to doesn't like it, but is hard put to articulate the reason why. If the song is not well-constructed, however, the person you submit it to can say "bad lyrics," or "boring melody," or whatever.

It is hard to be dispassionate about the attributes of your own baby. But you must be as ruthless as you can to analyze your product objectively. Try to get feedback. Ask for it. Get friends to be honest with you. Better yet, ask enemies. If you get specific criticism on rejected songs, you have a starting point for correction.

If the lyrics cause the most adverse reaction, break them down into their components:
• Concept or storyline
• Choice of words used to convey the story
• Rhyme scheme
• Flow of the story from setting the scene to getting to the point
• Cadence of the syllables matching the melody and beat

If the melody is the problem, break it down into sections of verses and hooks:
• Is one of these sections too repetitious?
• Does it fit the mood of the lyric and story?
• Does it fit the other sections?
• Is it memorable?
• Is the range singable?
• Does it build?

When you identify a weakness in any of theses areas, work with the writer to get it corrected. If the writer can't seem to solve the problem with objective guidance, the remedy may be collaboration with a talented composer or lyricist. A collaborator's fresh approach might provide a synergistic effect that lifts a song off the ground.

Keeping the faith

Elvis failed an audition for the Grand Ole Opry. The Beatles were turned down by a record company that is now out of business. The lesson is that if your product is really good, you will find someone who recognizes its value, that is, if you persevere and target the right market. Many times a publisher's faith in a song pays off only after years of songplugging effort.

How can you maintain faith in a song after a series of initial rejections? You can only be prepared to do battle for each and every song in your catalog if you follow these two principles: (1) never sign a songwriter you don't believe in wholeheartedly; and (2) never market anything you consider substandard. When you and your organization are thoroughly committed, initial rejections won't defeat you.

Which is not to say you'll always be right and that the marketplace will ultimately agree with you. You can get emotionally involved with a song, especially after listening to it a thousand times. If you seem to be getting nowhere with a song, let it lie on the shelf for a period and concentrate on plugging other material.

After an interval (six months to a year, or more), listen to the song again. The cooling-off period should enable you to hear the song more objectively. Maybe you will now hear why it was repeatedly rejected. Perhaps you can hear what's needed to make it more commercial. Perhaps the market wasn't ready for it originally but is now. Or perhaps you'll conclude this song is simply not as good as you thought at first blush. You may have to accept you've been flogging a dead horse. If so, saddle up another animal and try again.

ANALYZING THE DEMO

Sometimes the product is good, but the working model doesn't demonstrate it attractively. Your chances are always improved by imaginative, well-produced demos with good production ideas. Try to imagine Ben E. King's "Stand by Me" without the distinctive bass line; or the Rolling Stones' "Satisfaction" without the driving guitar line. Creative instrumental arrangements helped make those songs hits.

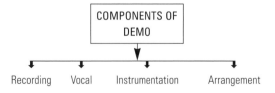

COMPONENTS OF DEMO

Recording   Vocal   Instrumentation   Arrangement

Pick your demos apart. If you discover failings, you discover, at the same time, what to do about them. Poor vocal? Find a decent singer who will interpret the song as it deserves. Poor arrangement? Call in some creative help; get better musicians with improvising skills. Poor recording? Get access to better equipment or a decent studio. The more your demo sounds like a hit record, the better chance you have of convincing someone that the song will make a hit record.

ANALYZING YOUR MARKET

No matter how good your songs are, you must know where and how to present them before you can succeed. Music publishers market songs *indirectly* to consumers. The publisher's *direct* market is music users: record companies, recording artists, record production companies, broadcasters, film producers, advertising agencies, etc.

Each user has a gatekeeper who may be in the guise of an A&R person, record producer, manager, music supervisor, etc. This gatekeeper is your *contact*, the person you must appeal to in order to get through the door. Take stock of your contacts and how you deal with them. Next to copyrights, contacts are your most important assets. They are your market.

Build a database of contacts

If you are weak in the area of contacts, you have to start building them. Make it a goal to add two new contacts to your database weekly. Where do you find them? Read trade magazines religiously. Study trade directories. Ring up record companies and ask who in the A&R department looks after a particular artist you're interested in. Network at industry functions, conventions, trade shows. Be like Sherlock Holmes, uncovering leads for your product, tracking down prospects.

▼

The more quality contacts you have, the more solid opportunities there are to get your songs into the consumer marketplace.

Keep your database current. Make note of staff changes at record and production companies. Be aware of new signings, address changes, new companies, new deals, new production assignments.

Your contact database should consist of three cross-referenced sections:
1. Contacts
2. Alphabetical listing of artists
3. Artists grouped by song categories

Use your database to stimulate exploitation ideas or quickly access marketing targets. For instance, if you have a particular artist in mind for one of your new works, you can look the artist up in your database and find the name, number, and address of the contact. Or, if you have a great new country song, you can screen your listing of country artists for prime targets.

A word about song categories: Catch-all designations like "country" and "pop" are very general, and each contains varying degrees of artistic expression. An R&B song that's perfect for Boyz II Men, for example, might not suit an act like Aretha Franklin. Similarly, a country song that's magic for Lorrie Morgan may not be right for Dwight Yoakam. You are advised to be very familiar with each artist's individual style before submitting material.

This business is very fluid. Personnel changes are frequent, as are producer assignments, label affiliations, and recording plans. So, use your database as a starting point to plan exploitation campaigns, then query the companies and contacts to make sure the timing and circumstances are ripe for your submission.

Nurture relationships with your contacts

Phone each of your contacts regularly to find out their current song needs. Don't be a nuisance and phone too often, but don't let too much time slip by, either. Your database should tell you the date you were last in touch and a suggested call-back date. Each contact has different needs at different times. Always ask when would be a good time to check back. A&R personnel at major record labels, who look after large rosters, may suggest you call monthly. Others may prefer a call every two or three months.

You'll frequently encounter problems getting through to a contact. They're often "in a meeting," "out of town," "in the studio," etc. Don't take it personally. Good contacts are busy people. But you have a job to do, and you've got to get information: who needs what kinds of songs to record. You can usually get this information from your contact's secretary or assistant.

It is therefore important to establish yourself with a contact's assistant. Get his or her name and note it in the contact's database entry. Whenever you phone a contact, make a point of saying hello to the secretary by name. Soon your name will become familiar. If you exhibit the friendly, charming personality you no doubt have, and the contact is unavailable, the secretary or assistant can usually either give you the info you need or call you back with it.

ALPHABETICAL ARTIST LISTING

ARTIST	CATEGORY	CONTACT	COMPANY
ABDUL, PAULA	DANCE/POP/R&B	CORFIELD, GEMMA	VIRGIN RECS [L.A.]
ADAMS, OLETA	R&B	ECKSTINE, ED	POLYGRAM [NYC]
ALABAMA	COUNTRY/ROCK	FUNDIS, GARTH	BMG [NASHVILLE]
ALLEN, DEBORAH	COUNTRY	PAYNE, MICHELLE	GIANT [NASHVILLE]
ASTLEY, RICK	POP/R&B	RAYMONDE, NICK	BMG [LONDON]
ATLANTIC STARR	R&B/DANCE	SINGLETON, EDDIE	WEA RECS [L.A.]

SONG CATEGORY LISTINGS—DANCE

ARTIST	CATEGORY	EMPHASIS	COMPANY
ABDUL, PAULA	DANCE	R&B/POP	VIRGIN RECS [LA.]
ATLANTIC STARR	DANCE	R&B	WEA RECS [L.A.]
BELLE, REGINA	DANCE	R&B	SONY RECORDS [NYC]
E., SHEILA	DANCE	R&B	WEA RECS [L.A.]
EASTON, SHEENA	DANCE	R&B/POP	MCA RECS [L.A.]
EN VOGUE	DANCE	R&B	EAST WEST [NYC]
FIVE STAR	DANCE	R&B	EPIC RECS [L.A.]

COMPANY LISTINGS

ELEKTRA RECS [L.A.]	345 Maple Dr., Beverly Hills, CA 90210, (310) 288-3800	
ARTIST	EMPHASIS	CONTACT
ELLIOTT, DAVID	R&B	NEWMAN, AMOS
FISCHER, LISA	R&B	NEWMAN, AMOS
LEWIS, HUEY	ROCK/POP	WISSERT, JOE
MENDES, SERGIO	LATIN/POP/JAZZ	CHILDS, CAROLE
PENDEGRASS, TEDDY	R&B	CHILDS, CAROLE

ELEKTRA RECS [NYC]	75 Rockefeller Plaza, New York, NY 10019, (212) 484-7200	
ARTIST	EMPHASIS	CONTACT
BAKER, ANITA	R&B/AC/CROSSOVER	LiPUMA, TOMMY
COLE, NATALIE	R&B/POP/CROSSOVER	LiPUMA. TOMMY
SNOW, PHOEBE	R&B/POP/JAZZ	LiPUMA, TOMMY
STEELE, JEVEETA	R&B/GOSPEL	LiPUMA, TOMMY

ELEKTRA [NASHVILLE]	1906 Acklen Ave., Nashville, TN 37212, (615) 292-7990	
ARTIST	EMPHASIS	CONTACT
CLARK, GUY	COUNTRY	CONDON, JOHN
HARRIS, EMMYLOU	COUNTRY	CONDON, JOHN

Gathering intelligence

Even a great song will be rejected if you mismatch it in the market place. Don't waste time shooting in the dark. Inform yourself before pitching material. Be sure every song you submit is tailored to the prospect's genre and current needs.

Listen carefully to what contacts tell you about their needs. You'll often be told they're looking for material reminiscent of a particular artist or song currently in vogue. Make a point of getting a copy of the recording referred to and listen to it for casting ideas.

Casting is key to the matching process. Who is your song *for*? A great song for Whitney Houston isn't necessarily a great song for Garth Brooks.

Note down anything you learn in small talk with a contact that might help you to solidify the relationship. If you find out his or her birthday, you might make a point of sending a card at the appropriate time, for instance. Jot down any information you might use to expand your relationship: hobbies, favorite football team, names of spouse and kids, where the contact likes to vacation. Soon you'll have an "intelligence file" detailing aspects of the contact's personality, whims, preferences, etc. Information is power.

Only strive to keep up with those artists and producers with whom you feel your product has an affinity. If you don't publish heavy metal, you won't need to keep up with the people on that side of the business. Choose your niche and learn as much about it as humanly possible.

ANALYZING THE SALES PROCESS

After you've done your best to perfect your product, demo, and contacts, you're faced with plugging the product via the demo into the marketplace.

Examine how you carry out each of these steps; they're all vital elements of the matching process.

Packaging

What attracts you to a new product on the shelf? What makes it stand out from similar products, makes it seem interesting, makes you want to try it? *Packaging*. Attractive packaging won't ensure that you'll like the product or that you'll even buy it after you've looked it over, but it will give that product an opportunity to sell itself to you.

Has packaging been a negative factor in getting your material listened to seriously? Were your cassettes accompanied by a neatly typed letter on printed letterhead, or a crude, handwritten note on the back of a grocery list? Assuming your writers spent sweat and tears writing a hit song and precious money on a demo, don't let them down by failing to have letterhead and labels printed so that your submissions look professional.

Every week, producers, A&R personnel, and managers get dozens of cassettes from publishers, as well as from hopeful songwriters. Most of these songs, they know, will be rubbish. But they sincerely want to find a gem among the dross. Their job depends on finding hit songs! However, they'll be predisposed to listen first to those cassettes they recognize as coming from pros. Don't let yourself down now. If you want to be given the same consideration as a pro, act like one, look like one, be one.

Timing

Timing is part of knowing your market—plugging into your contacts for essential information. Not only do you have to know where to send what kinds of songs, you also have to know *when*. It's no good FedExing that new ballad you're excited about to Sammy Superstar if he finished his album last week. Before you make a submission, phone your contact and find out if now is the time. If it isn't, rethink your market for that song. Who else will it be perfect for? Try them. Even if the product is great, rejection results if the timing is wrong.

Promotion

This is your sales effort, which is what you do when you submit a song for consideration. In reality, successful promotion is almost automatic if you've gotten all the preliminary steps right: excellent product, good demo, market correctly targeted, proper timing, and attractive packaging. All that remains is to ensure the person who makes the decision regarding your song gives it a fair listen. This will happen if you've gotten your contact right and found out how and when he or she wants to review your material.

The ideal way to pitch material varies from person to person and situation to situation. It is often a plus if you're able to personally play your songs to someone in a relaxed, convivial atmosphere—or right in the studio when pressure is on to find a song to complete a session.

Most of the time, however, it isn't possible to present your material in person. (Many producers will only listen when they're alone anyway.) You have to accommodate the whims of the person you are submitting your song to. If you try to force them to do it your way, you encounter built-in sales resistance before you even display your wares.

If you have to make your submission by mail, enclose a brief, literate letter, typed or neatly written on your printed notepaper, which tells the recipient these essentials: song title(s), for whom the material is to be considered, how to contact you for further information, and a "thank you" for taking time to review your material.

Be professional; don't waste time with extraneous details about how old the writer is or that he's an Afghan refugee recovering from leprosy. Superfluous background information will not make the song sound any better. And don't ask the listener to excuse a demo because the singer had double pneumonia, or the bassoonist hit a lot of wonky notes. (If you have to make excuses for it, don't send it.)

Narrow your sales pitch

Never submit more than three songs at a time. A cassette with five, six, or more songs on it will be put aside until the person you've submitted it to has more time to listen—and sometimes that time never comes.

Where, on a cassette with numerous songs, do you position your best one? If it's the first track on the tape, the person you've submitted it to may forget it by the time he's reached number six. If you put it as number six, he may be so jaded by your lesser material that the luster of your "hit" is considerably dulled by the time he reaches it. When you put more than three songs on a tape, you seem to be saying, "Look, I really don't know which of my songs is good for you . . . so, please, listen to them all." The gut reaction to that is: If you don't know your own best shots, why should anyone else?

The really ideal submission is one song only. You're then saying, "I am 100% positive this is the greatest song there is for your artist. I am so confident, I have not even bothered to submit any other songs as back-up."

Having said that, two or three songs will still be a good submission, as long as they're strictly within the guidelines you've been given for the artist and you're absolutely certain each of the songs is a blockbuster. If in doubt about a song, leave it out of your submission.

The closing

This is wrapping up the sale, clinching the deal. Salesmen have pat methods of closing. When they sense a prospect is interested but hasn't yet decided to buy, salesmen will say something like, "What color would you like this in?" or, "Would you like us to deliver?" They do this to get the customer to commit—to a color, to delivery, to something—without coming right out and saying, "Will you buy this product?"

This sort of closing might not fit the publishing business, but neither can you use hard-sell and expect to be welcomed back when you have another song to plug. Don't start ringing up daily to ask if your tape was received, what was thought about it, and so forth. Pros don't do that. They are too busy working on new projects. If your song is going to be recorded, you will be contacted. If not, you may or may not get it back with a rejection letter. Some contacts are courteous in this respect; others are too busy, understaffed, or simply too arrogant to bother.

If your follow-up sales efforts have included bugging someone with daily calls, you might consider that as a negative factor, one that will make that person less likely to listen to your next cassette with enthusiasm.

Remember that no amount of superselling will overcome weaknesses in the steps you've taken previous to the sales effort or promotion. You're only ready for the promotion and sales effort when you've done all you can to get the preliminary steps right.

Use promotion and closing to solidify your con-

Song activity worksheet

TITLE: *"What Happened to Our Love"*

DATE	SUBMITTED TO	FOR	REACTION	DATE
1/15/97	Joe Doe, XYZ Recs	Sammy Smith	Rejected No reason given	2/23/97
1/21/97	Sue Roe Magnum Records	The Crumbs	Rejected "Lyrics weak"	3/1/97
3/24/97	Shad Dash Krakatoa Records	Tom Dooley	Ask for hold!	4/10/97
4/30/97	" "	" "	Cutting May 10	
5/15/97	" "	" "	Picked as "A" Side Check June 1 for release date	
6/1/97	Shad Dash	Tom Dooley	Release date 7/15	

CONTACT: *Joe Doe, XYZ Records*

Address: *846 Fusion St., NYC 10019, 212 555-5555*

DATE	SUBMITTED TO	FOR	REACTION	DATE
1/15/97	What Happened to Our Love	Sammy Smith	Rejected No reason given	2/23/97
1/15/97	Our Love Got Lost	Sammy Smith	Rejected ditto	2/23/97
2/24/97	I Don't Care	Sammy Smith	Rejected "Hooks not catchy"	3/1/97
4/28/97	Trying Again	Sammy Smith	Asks for 60 day hold to consider for another artist	5/25/97
7/20/97	" "	Leon Noel	Will cut in Sept. Asks for hold until Oct. 1st	7/20/97
9/21/97	" "	Leon Noel	Cut!! Will be 'A' side Release Jan. 1st	

tact so that when you plug your next song it will be easier because you know more about the preferences and whims of your contact (learn from each sales effort), and your contact begins to know and respect you as a professional, whether or not he liked your material for this particular project.

TRACKING SUBMISSIONS

You need to keep a record of submissions. Keep a submission summary for each song title and another one for each contact. That way you can quickly review the activity generated for each song and keep track of submission efforts to each contact. Tailor these *Activity Worksheets* to your own needs.

Getting others to market your songs

If you're a songwriter or small indie publisher, you may think your songs will magically get recorded if and when you can find a big, successful publisher to do all the mundane marketing steps for you. A full-service publisher can free you from time-consuming marketing chores, so you can concentrate on creative aspects of the trade. But to get a full-service publisher interested in your work, you have to go through essentially the same process discussed here.

On the one hand, you have to sell producers or A&R men on the notion your songs will make hit records for their artists. On the other hand, you have

to convince a full-service publisher your copyrights will translate into hit records so he can likewise convince his record business contacts your work is hit material. Either way, you have to market yourself and your work. And, to do this successfully, you have to be able to analyze and understand the root cause(s) of why you may have had difficulty selling your work to date.

Analysis isn't all that hard, and it is the only way to accurately pinpoint any real problems you may be having so you can cure the disease and not the symptom. Everything discussed here is an ongoing process. The various steps may get easier with experience, but they can never be skipped.

Record production

Songplugging is no easy task. There is always fierce competition from other publishers vying to get established artists to cut their songs, and the whims and tastes of producers and label execs are often inexplicable. It is especially hard for new music publishers with little cash flow to sustain operations from the time a song is cut until the time royalties are collected.

Some publishers short-circuit the frustrating process of songplugging to third parties by setting up in-house record production companies. Through record production, music publishers sign artists directly, and then finance or produce masters of songs from their catalogs. This enables publishers to almost immediately activate any copyrights they feel strongly about.

Not only does record production directly activate songs in a publisher's catalog, it also generates income from production royalties on record sales. And, when finished masters are leased to record companies for distribution, it is common for the record company to advance the publisher, as owner of the master, a recoupable sum of money at least equal to the costs of production. Quite often these advances are for sums greater than the production costs.

Of course, once a master is produced, the next crucial step is to get the finished product into the marketplace. The publisher must either lease the master to a record company or set up an indie record label as an outlet for in-house productions. Many publishers form their own labels and enter into distribution deals with major labels. Before merging with EMI, SBK had a boutique label distributed by RCA; Nashville's Tree Music had a label distributed by Atlantic; and Atlanta's Lowery Music had a label imprint distributed by Capitol.

THE RISK FACTOR

Record production can be very expensive. Although recording costs can be reduced through careful planning and tight controls, full production of an album may be $25,000-$250,000, or more. Unless you've made an iron-clad agreement with a record company before you go into the studio, you can never be 100% certain of making a deal that will get your costs back.

Recording costs are always treated as recoupable advances against artists' royalties, but the production company has to fund the session up front. The production company can't recoup its investment if the master is not sold or leased to a record company. Or, if the publisher releases the master on its own label, there is the risk of not selling enough units to off-set recording costs, manufacturing, and promotion.

Reducing the risks

There are alternatives to risking the full costs of producing a complete album on spec. The publisher can instead produce high quality demos to showcase the artist's direction and song quality. If the demos arouse interest, a deal can be struck whereby a record company takes over production and finances a full-scale recording. This is, however, more properly *artist development* (discussed below), rather than record production.

Or, a publisher may elect to produce only two or three sides, rather than a full album. The finished sides showcase production quality as well as the artist and songs. The publisher then either shoots for a "sin-

gles" deal (with options for a completed album) or for an album deal the record company will finance. In either case, when options are exercised, the record company finances all follow-up singles and albums.

BENEFITS OF RECORD PRODUCTION

Though the risks must be carefully weighed, there is much to be said for committing part of a publishing company's budget to record production. Not only are songs in the catalog directly activated, generating mechanical and performance royalties, there is also income from production royalties on record sales. When a finished master is leased for distribution, the advance paid by the record company is normally more than the production costs, yielding an immediate return on investment.

To recap the benefits to publishers, record production:
- activates copyrights in the catalog
- advances careers of writer-artists and writer-producers signed to the company
- opens up another profit center (record sales in addition to publishing royalties)
- creates assets (finished masters), which can be depreciated for tax purposes and converted to cash at a later date by outright sale

And:
- recording costs can be recouped by advances from licensing masters to domestic and overseas record companies
- master-lease advances usually are greater than recording costs, ensuring profit whether or not the released masters are subsequently successful in the marketplace

RECORD PRODUCTION ROYALTIES

Royalties paid by the record company to the publisher for masters generally include royalties due the artist and producer, to whom the publisher is expected to account. A typical master-lease royalty might start at 12% of the record's retail price on 90% of all sales.

From this 12%, the publisher, as production company, pays the artist and the producer. The publisher negotiates these royalties directly with the artist and producer. Typically, the artist's royalty may be 6%, with 2%-4% due the producer. The publisher, as production company, retains the balance (2%-4%).

Often, master-lease royalties escalate. For instance, percentage points or half-points may be added incrementally for sales above a certain level (e.g., 12% for the first 500,000 units and .5% more for each 500,000 units thereafter up to an agreed maximum). Alternatively, 12% might be paid for the first album with incremental rises for each album option exercised by the record company.

Of course, the publishing company also receives mechanical royalties for each song contained on the record, and it receives performance royalties when the records are broadcast on radio and television.

☞ *The nuts and bolts of record production and master-licensing deals are outside the scope of this book, and the above royalty breakdowns are for illustrative purposes only. The art of negotiating and drafting artists contracts, distribution deals, and master licenses should be practiced only after careful study and with the help of an experienced music business attorney.*

Artist/producer development

Historically, publishers functioned as de facto talent scouts for record companies. This pivotal role of linking record companies with promising young artists and producers was profitable for all concerned but was not necessarily essential to a publisher's survival. Today, however, the proliferation of self-contained artists has considerably narrowed the field of song-plugging opportunities. As a result, aggressive publishers seek to sign writers who are also artists or producers, in order to increase the odds of getting songs cut. Thus, today's publishers are increasingly thrust into A&R and management roles, because so many artists now write their own material.

Signing writers who already have deals as artists or producers is not artist development, since the writer is already "developed" to the point of having a record deal. Writers with deals in place are usually more expensive to sign. There is more competition from other publishers, since the writers bring with them an assurance of copyright activity. The publisher doesn't have to secure a record deal or get songs cut by third parties. Thus, the publisher's role is rather passive. After paying an advance to sign the writer, the publisher banks on the in-place record deal to return a profit on its investment.

In an artist development deal, by contrast, the publisher grooms (develops) writers as artists or producers and then takes an active role in securing record deals. Many fledgling artists now see music publishers as a lifeline to getting a record deal. Major labels are more open to signing a new act that has been screened, groomed, and backed by a publisher. A publisher's backing demonstrates that a music business professional is convinced the artist has commercial potential, which might make a record company executive psychologically more inclined to consider signing the artist.

Publishers find budding artists much the way they find new songwriters. A demo arrives "over the transom," or a referral is made by a lawyer, manager, or some other music business contact, or the publisher catches a performance. The publisher believes the would-be artist is a diamond in the rough and offers to finance or produce an agreed number of demos to showcase the act to record labels. The publisher might directly negotiate record deals for the artist or it might team the artist with an artist-management firm to handle record company negotiations.

WHAT AN ARTIST DEVELOPMENT DEAL INCLUDES

As in all types of service contracts, artist development deals are tailored to meet specific objectives of the parties involved. The specifics are, of course, a matter of negotiation, but typical artist development deals cover the following points:

1. X number of songs will be produced to professional quality standard.
2. A budget specifying minimum and maximum amounts for each song recorded.

    The recording budget is treated as an advance. There are several ways the contract can deal with the subject of the recording budget: If the writer produces the sessions, a flat sum can be advanced to cover recording expenses (the writer is responsible for expenses over budget but may keep the difference if the sessions are completed under budget). The publisher can directly pay the studio, musicians, etc. The budget can be specified as one lump sum to cover all songs. The budget can be broken down per song times the total number of songs.
3. Recording session(s) will take place within a specified time frame. Usually within six months of signing.
4. Writer assigns X number of songs to the publisher during the term. If writer has less than 100% of a song, the writer's percentage will be prorated as to fulfillment of delivery requirement (e.g., 25% writer's share = delivery of one fourth of the song).
5. Publisher will advance X to writer during the term.

    The advance may be tied to milestone achievements (i.e., X on signing, Y on delivery of each song, and Z on delivery of each completed recording, and XYZ when a record deal is made).
6. Publisher undertakes to land a recording agreement for the writer within X months of signing, or Y months of delivery of last recording, whichever comes first (or last).
7. If a record deal is not made within the allotted time, the publisher shall have the option to renew the agreement for a period of X months upon

payment of an additional advance to the writer in the amount of $Y—*unless* negotiations with a record company are underway, in which case the publisher may extend the agreement, until either negotiations are successfully completed, negotiations are terminated for any reason, or X months have elapsed, whichever comes first.

8. If publisher fails to secure a recording deal after exerting all best efforts, and the development agreement comes to an end, publisher may elect to do one of the following:
   a) retain full publishing rights to songs delivered under the agreement upon payment of an additional advance in the amount of $X
   b) retain full publishing rights to *individual* songs delivered under the agreement upon payment of an additional advance in the amount of $Y per song
   c) return all rights to the writer upon writer's repayment of any outstanding advances

9. If publisher successfully secures a recording agreement for the writer, all songs written by the writer during the term of the recording deal and any extensions thereof shall be assigned to the publisher on terms specified in the development deal.

10. If publisher successfully secures a recording agreement for the writer, and the record company fails to pick up any options, the publisher shall have first refusal to reinstate the development deal and/or be given X number of months to secure another record deal.

11. The publisher shall have full authority to negotiate a record deal on the writer's behalf based on specific minimum terms with regards to:
    a) number of albums
    b) royalty rate
    c) advances
    d) recording fund
    e) number of guaranteed releases
    f) number of option periods

12. If publisher secures a recording deal meeting the minimum requirements and the writer refuses to sign the deal for whatever reason, the publisher may elect to do one of the following:
    a) extend the time allowed to secure another recording deal
    b) retain copyright to songs assigned under development deal without further obligation on its part to secure a recording deal
    c) demand repayment in full of all advances and recording expenses from writer in return for reassigning to writer the songs assigned under the development deal

Video production

Production of visual programming is another way for publishers to exploit catalog. This activity may range from music-content short-form and long-form videocassettes, to television programming, to full-length motion pictures.

As previously discussed, new television stations, networks, satellite and cable systems are popping up all over the world, and they all need programming. Well-produced music programs can always find outlets.

However, developing and producing visual programming is expensive. Audiovisual production is therefore very risky. Risks can be eliminated, however, by preselling programs to sponsors, video distributors, and broadcasting outlets. Successfully sold audiovisual programming can pay off considerably, not only from publishing royalties, but also from income derived as copyright owner and producer of the program.

Promo videos

As discussed in the chapter on *Mechanical Licensing*, record companies produce video clips to promote new releases. Publishers normally cooperate with record companies by issuing free licenses for use of their songs in promo clips, since the publisher and record company both want to make the song/record a hit. Some publishers even agree to help labels finance promo videos.

In the case of artist development, publishers might even finance videos to showcase artists to record companies. In that event, video production costs would be treated as an advance to the writer/artist, and the specifics of the production should be included in the artist development contract in the same manner as recording sessions.

Getting songs into television programs and movies

There are well over 100 television production companies in the U.S. that regularly license music for programs ranging from sitcoms, made-for-TV movies, dramatic series, soaps, variety shows, specials, etc. It is estimated that between 350 and 450 television shows are in some stage of production every day. In addition, there are approximately 500 new movies produced each year in the U.S. Since virtually every television program and movie requires music, audiovisual productions offer a wealth of catalog exploitation opportunities and a very lucrative source of revenue for music publishers.

Television and film production houses usually employ *music supervisors* to coordinate when, how, and what types of music are used in each project. A music supervisor's role often includes tracking down owners of music copyrights and negotiating licenses. Some producers use specialized *music clearance companies* or *clearing houses* to obtain necessary licenses. Others assign the task to law firms. Frequently, producers simply request licenses through the Harry Fox Agency. (For affiliated publishers who wish it, Fox negotiates licensing terms and fees in return for a nominal fee. See the chapter on *Mechanical-Right Licensing*.)

As noted in the chapter on *Synchronization Right Licensing*, there are several types of licenses required for audiovisual programming, including worldwide synchronization for theatrical and television broadcast (free television, basic cable, pay and subscription), home video production, promotional *trailers* or *coming attraction previews*, and performing rights.

Publishers who successfully promote songs for use in movies and television establish good working relationships with music supervisors and production houses. Obviously, it is easier to cultivate the right contacts when a publisher is located in or near centers of film and television production, such as New York and Los Angeles. But location shouldn't prevent aggressive publishers from establishing and making use of the right contacts.

Sourcebooks of contact information:
International Television & Video Almanac
Samuel French Theater & Film Bookshops
7623 Sunset Blvd., Hollywood, CA 90046
Tel: (213) 876-0570, (800) 822-8669

Film Producers, Studios, Agents, & Casting Directors Guide
Samuel French Theater & Film Bookshops
7623 Sunset Blvd., Hollywood, CA 90046
Tel: (213) 876-0570, (800) 822-8669

Film & TV Music Supervisor's List
S.R.S. Publishing
8491 Sunset Blvd., Suite 771, Los Angeles, CA 90069
Tel: (213) 850-8946

The optimum approach to any kind of catalog promotion is to be forewarned of your contacts' needs. The best time to make a submission is before a production gets underway. Know what is being planned so that you can be in a position to make intelligent submissions, before other songs are settled on. Regularly survey contacts to see what is in the pipeline and what types of music are needed. Read trade magazines like *Variety* and *Hollywood Reporter,* which give news about projects in various stages of development, production, and postproduction.

Contact relevant music supervisors or studio music department directors and try to get copies of scripts, plot synopses, or project scenarios. The more you know about a project, the better able you are to make submissions that are on the mark. Zero in on specific ideas to submit. Success is more likely when you can make specific suggestions (one or two titles that really fit the bill) rather than overwhelming the producer or supervisor with dozens of titles to wade through.

Theme commissioning

Composers and publishers can earn substantial fees for songs used as themes to motion pictures and television programs. In addition to upfront fees, lucrative performance royalties are earned from television themes, especially when the program is a long-running network series.

Film and television producers usually commission themes from a select group of composers who tend to specialize in this work. A few major publishers with film-studio connections (such as Warner Bros. and MCA) are well-placed to introduce newer composers into this select group.

Independent publishers must cultivate contacts within the television and film industry to get commissioning contracts. To further your writers' careers via theme writing, it often comes down to working your way into an old-boy network.

When themes are commissioned directly from composers, the composers generally work as *employees for hire*, and the producers own the copyright of the themes. Of course, if the writer is under an exclusive publishing contract, the publisher must approve any commissioning arrangement.

Unless the writer's publishing contract permits commissioned works outside the scope of the exclusive publishing agreement, the publisher is entitled to some form of compensation. This is usually a percentage of whatever the writer receives. A publisher that is instrumental in getting the commissioning deal normally receives a share equal to whatever the songwriter's publishing contract calls for in the section dealing with "all other income" or "all other usages."

Producers of visual programming sometimes seek out established singer-songwriters to write themes in order to capitalize on a star's name value. Naturally, star power adds to the importance of the theme as perceived by both the producer and the publisher, thereby increasing the size of the commissioning fee.

Producers may also want to use an established song, or standard, as a theme in order to tie in with the subject matter of the program or film or to add to box-office draw. This would require a synchronization license rather than a theme commissioning fee. Again, the relative importance of the copyright, as well as the nature of its use, impacts on the value of the synchronization fee. (See the chapter on *Synchronization Right Licensing.*)

COMMISSIONING FEES FOR THEATRICAL RELEASES

One song

Typical commissioning fees for one song in a feature film range anywhere from $5,000-$10,000, sometimes less, sometimes more. In addition to the fee, the songwriter can look forward to the usual royalties for extraneous usages (performance royalties for broadcast and overseas theatrical performances, mechanical royalties for soundtrack and cover recordings, print royalties from sheet music, etc.).

Prudent film producers insist on the right to reject a commissioned work that doesn't meet expectations. When producers maintain a right of rejection, they usually make an upfront deposit payment of 10%-20% of the agreed commissioning fee plus demo costs. If the song is ultimately not used, the writer keeps the deposit and also recovers all rights to the work.

Scores

The background music in a movie is called a *score*. The score may also be referred to as an *underscore*, since it is used to underline, enhance, and emphasize while remaining underneath the dialog. Occasionally, a unique type of film comes along that uses dozens of hits from a previous era strung together as the entire background ambiance and mood setter. In most cases, however, scores for movies are almost always commissioned. Composers are needed to write original music, unified perhaps by variations on a recurring theme.

For movies produced for theatrical release, score commissioning fees range from $10,000 for low-budget films to over $300,000 for major-name composers and big-budget films. Recording costs and other expenses (travel, orchestrations, etc.) are paid by the producer.

COMMISSIONING FEES FOR TELEVISION PRODUCTIONS

Name composers are in a position to retain a piece of the publishing on works commissioned for television. Lesser lights are usually forced to work as employees for hire. The commissioned material is then a work

for hire, and all copyright in the material belongs to the music publishing affiliate of the television producer.

Made-for-television movie scores pay commissioning fees of around $20,000-$40,000. Scores for one program in a series pay commissioning fees of about $1,000-$5,000 per half hour episode, and $3,000-$7,000 for hour long shows. Commissioned television themes for a series are very lucrative, ranging from around $10,000 to $30,000 (or more for name writers).

Television scores and themes also pay off handsomely in performance royalties. Royalties are earned every time a show is broadcast, including reruns and syndications.

Turnkey package deals

Television production companies sometimes contract with composers for *turnkey package deals,* which include the composer's fee plus all recording costs. Turnkey packages range from $5,000-$8,000 for half-hour shows, to $10,000-$20,000 for hour long programs, to $20,000-$50,000 for made-for-television movies.

Composers that go over budget must eat the excess costs. So, package deals should be carefully negotiated to stipulate that if rescoring is requested or demanded by the producer for reasons that have nothing to do with the composer (e.g., the director decides to add or change a scene or mood), the additional costs should be borne by the producer. Producers should also bear all technical costs, such as fees to a music editor, sound recording transfer to film, and *sidelining* (sidelining is the term used when actors or musicians are paid to appear on film in the act of performing the music).

Bluebirds, standards, and evergreens

Songs that achieve hit status and are then covered, or rerecorded, by other artists over time become the backbone of a catalog. These are the songs you hear everywhere: on elevators, in department stores. They become instantly recognizable and are known as *standards* or *evergreens.*

A happy by-product of having standards in the catalog is that they tend to perpetuate their own momentum in the marketplace. Ad agencies, artists, record producers, and audiovisual producers frequently decide to use one of these works on their own initiative, without any marketing effort by the publisher. When this happens, some publishers call these unexpected but welcome usages *bluebirds*. They are like the bluebirds in the old Disney film "Song of the South" that land, unbidden, on Uncle Remus' shoulder.

Generic catalog marketing

A song rarely becomes a standard accidentally. A publishing company's real value over time depends on the number of standards in the catalog, those songs that have multiple uses each year. So, in addition to pitching new songs, songpluggers must also consistently work back catalog. That means not only being alert for specific opportunities to pitch individual songs, but also catalog marketing on a generic basis.

When pitching material for specific projects, songplugging works best by submitting a narrow choice of ideas—ideally, one to three songs. But generic marketing involves touting the company's catalog to potential users for nonspecific projects. A&R personnel, advertising agencies, and film and television producers frequently stockpile songs for possible use in as yet unidentified future projects. This stockpile constitutes a reference library from which users can generate ideas.

It is important for a publisher to maintain a high profile. You want your telephone number prominently marked in a producer's Rolodex, so that when he or she needs material for a specific project you are sure to be called upon to submit ideas. But you also want your catalog included in potential users' reference libraries.

For this purpose, any publisher that has accumulated a catalog of quality songs needs to compile marketing tools to expose the songs to potential users. In order to spark licensing interest in existing copyrights, publishers frequently compile, produce, and circulate sampler CDs and catalog lists containing highlights of major works in their catalogs. Samplers and catalogs are effective marketing tools to generically promote a publisher's copyrights.

Samplers and catalogs are often effective when they are accompanied by brochures cross-indexing songs by titles and subject matter. In the chapter on *Licensing Songs for Commercial Advertising* some of the following categorized titles were used as examples:

colors: "Red Roses for a Blue Lady," "Yellow Rose of Texas," "Blue Monday"
jewelry: "Diamonds and Pearls," "A String of Pearls"
location: "I Left My Heart in San Francisco," "Way Down Yonder in New Orleans"
seasons: "Summertime," "Autumn Leaves," "April in Paris," "Memphis in June"
vehicles: "Slow Boat to China," "Mustang Sally," "Rocket 88"
animals: "A Horse With No Name," "Walking the Dog," "Rockin' Robin"
foods: "Mashed Potatoes," "Cherry Pie," "Sugar Sugar"
time: "Day by Day," "Now Is the Hour," "Sixty Minute Man"

Categorized information helps users zero in on songs that match specific projects. Ad agencies and audiovisual music supervisors constantly resource musical ideas relating to whatever project they're working on, so keep them updated with your catalog additions.

PACKAGE DEALS

Publishers with extensive catalogs might be able to forge package deal agreements with film or television production companies. Package deals are incentives for producers to use more songs from your catalog.

If a production company agrees to use X number of songs in various productions within a stated period of time, a discount is offered on the synchronization fee. A sliding fee scale might be agreed, whereby discounts escalate depending upon the number of songs ultimately used. For instance, a fee of $\$X$ is established for the use of one song. But a 15% discount on that fee is given for each song when two to four songs are used. If five to eight songs are used, the fee for each song might be discounted by 20%, and so on.

Package deals are entered into under *blanket synchronization licenses*, which establish parameters of the deals up front. Producers then know, when planning music, that they can shave production costs and time by drawing songs from your catalog under preagreed terms.

As noted in the chapter on *Synchronization Rights Licensing*, however, you must be careful that a package deal involves songs used in similar circumstances. Each song must be comparable to the others in importance as a copyright; each type of usage must be similar; and the duration (playing time) of all uses must be roughly equivalent.

Boosting performance royalties

Performance income is one of the two most important revenue sources (mechanical income is the other). To increase performance income, publishers often use the methods that follow (some of which have already been discussed).

RADIO

The most direct form of marketing to boost performance royalties is that of promoting record airplay on radio stations. However, this is usually done by record companies promoting their product. Occasionally, publishers hire independent promotion men to augment a record company's promotion efforts. (See the chapter entitled *Marketing 101* for further discussion.)

COMPILATION ALBUMS

A rather more indirect form of radio promotion is pressing promotional albums containing the publisher's "greatest hits" for free distribution to radio programmers who play tracks as "golden oldies." This generates performance-royalty income and stimulates further catalog activity by keeping songs alive in the public consciousness. Of course, compilation samplers are also useful as a generic form of songplugging to record, film, and television producers.

Promotional compilations often require the use of masters containing performances by various artists originally released by several different record companies. The publisher compiling a promo album must therefore negotiate licensing arrangements with each record company in order to use the masters. Since the compilation is for promotional purposes only and will not be sold, record companies usually grant these licenses for token fees.

RECORDED MUSIC LIBRARIES

Building up an active recorded music library can generate performance royalty income as well as licensing fees.

ORCHESTRAL ARRANGEMENTS

Performance royalties can be augmented by commissioning arrangements of songs for marching bands and orchestras. The arrangements are distributed to universities and high schools to generate live performances at concerts, football games, etc. This generates print income as well as performance royalties.

TELEVISION

Performance income from television broadcasts can be very lucrative and requires courting television producers and music supervisors to get songs performed, featured, or used as title themes and/or background music. Remember, cue sheets for commercials, movies, and television programs should be promptly lodged with the relevant performing-right society to ensure accurate royalty accounting.

PROMO VIDEO CLIPS

As discussed above, publishers might agree to help record companies finance the production of promotional video clips on new releases in order to create important television exposure. Almost always, publishers are called upon to forego any synchronization fees, because video clips help promote the recording of their copyrights and generate performance royalties when played on television. Some publishers may even fund promo clips on their own initiative when they feel a strong promotional push provides measurable long-term benefits for a writer/artist or writer/producer.

JINGLES AND COMMERCIALS

In addition to upfront fees, important jingle commissions are good sources of performance income. To successfully tap this revenue source requires courting advertising agencies to get commissions, and/or existing copyrights licensed. Cue sheets should be promptly lodged with the relevant performing right society.

LIVE PERFORMANCES

ASCAP, SESAC, and BMI log titles performed at major concerts (ASCAP currently surveys the 100 largest concert tours in the U.S.), but many performances go unreported. Publishers with working bands and performing songwriters must ensure that all concerts and tour plans are lodged with the appropriate society so that live performances can be properly credited.

Recorded music libraries

Some publishers invest in the production of *recorded music libraries* to generate income from performance royalties and transcription fees. Normally, these libraries consist of specially written instrumental material, as opposed to the inclusion of existing songs from a catalog.

Typical libraries contain prerecorded instrumental themes and musical fragments capturing a range of moods useful for production of documentaries, radio programming, and advertising. Albums containing 20 or more tracks are distributed free to likely users who pay licensing fees for any musical segments they subsequently use in their productions.

Each album focuses on a specific type of music. For example, one album might feature synthesized music conjuring up visions of outer space. Another might offer lush orchestrations of romantic themes, and still another album could provide music that builds suspense, tension, and fear.

This is a specialized market for a publisher to enter. Libraries require considerable investment for recording and album manufacture, not to mention the time required to build up a useful variety of selections. Much time and marketing energy must also be invested to build up contacts who use this type of product and to cater to their specialized needs.

A recorded music library is certainly not the fastest way to fame and fortune in music publishing because of the investment needed in time and money and the relatively low return. But a recorded music library provides a new profit center for a publisher. A sizable library, marketed well, can be a steady income generator.

Promoting copyrights overseas

As discussed in the chapter on *Foreign Licensing*, promoting your catalog overseas requires knocking on doors. International contacts are not hard to make and sustain in this age of faxes, e-mail, the Internet, overnight delivery, and jet travel. The process is not much different than working with contacts at home. Business revolves around establishing rapport and trust.

Though you can establish initial contact with potential licensees through listings found in directories such as *Billboard International Buyers Guide,* the optimum way to make deals and solidify relationships is face-to-face. Plan to attend trade shows and expos such as MIDEM, SXSW, NMS, POPKOMM, etc. At these marketplaces, product is played, displayed, and offered, and a range of marketing opportunities abound under one roof. For the price of one trip, you get to meet hundreds of contacts from dozens of countries.

Trade shows, expos, conventions, and seminars are places to show the flag, display your wares, establish new contacts, solidify existing relationships, pick up new product, find licensees and distributors for your product, check out the competition, gain insights into the business, keep abreast of changes, and, above all, sell your product!

There are many reasons to attend as many of these events as you can, and many goals to accomplish while there but don't hop on a plane without planning. Before you go, list all the things you hope to accomplish, rate them in importance, then plan what to do hour by hour once you get there. Try to line up appointments with people you need to see before you arrive, because everyone gets solidly booked up fast. Immediately upon arrival, track down those you couldn't reach beforehand and arrange to meet them ASAP.

Don't squander precious time meeting with people from your own hometown. If you're from New York and you're attending MIDEM in Cannes, meet with other New Yorkers when you're back home. Concentrate on seeing international contacts first, and contacts from other parts of the country second. Make every minute count and make every minute pay.

Taking a stand

Once your business is established, it may be worthwhile renting a stand or booth at an international trade fair, like MIDEM––but only after you've been to a few of these events and noted what works and what doesn't. Your presentation must stand out, be consistent with your message, and portray your company as solid, one that others will want to do business with.

You'll need professionally produced materials: brochures, catalogs, business cards, fliers, backdrops, signs, perhaps novelty giveaways (like T-shirts), and plenty of product samples. You'll need good sound equipment to present your product and review product offered to you. You should place a nice ad in the event's directory, which attendees usually hang on to for future reference.

The most important factor about your success (or failure) is how you staff your booth. Whoever is on hand to greet and talk to people must be presentable, personable, and knowledgeable, and you must have the booth staffed at all times with someone who meets all these requisites. Suppose all your key people are gone to lunch or away meeting others when someone of potentially major importance to your future happens by. If your booth is temporarily closed or staffed by some gofer who can't answer questions knowledgeably, you may lose a deal that could make your future.

CHAPTER 17

Marketing 101

The chapter entitled *Exploitation* explores numerous methods of generating catalog activity, but it is important to have a holistic understanding of marketing in order to achieve lasting success in any business. This chapter, therefore, examines time-tested marketing concepts and techniques, with particular focus on how they apply to music publishing.

What is marketing?

Anything that exposes your company and product to the public is marketing. Whether you're conscious of it or not, marketing starts the moment you begin to put into practice the fundamental concept you have of your company. The end result of all your marketing efforts is how your company is perceived by consumers, business associates, competitors, employees, the community, and the world at large.

To ensure the public perception of your company matches the message you wish to project, keep your concept and your marketing plan simple and work it consistently. There are innumerable messages and products out there clamoring for attention, so yours must cut through distractions like a laser beam.

It is imperative to integrate a marketing focus throughout your organization. Each person in the company must be indoctrinated to carry out their functions with the marketing concept foremost in mind. This includes:

- knowledge of what your target market needs or wants
- orchestrated efforts to fulfill those needs or wants
- orchestrated efforts to successfully meet your company's goals

Marketing consistency

It is important to market consistently at all levels. This means your marketing efforts must be consistent with your concept, and you must *never stop marketing*. Repeat those words to yourself every day as a mantra. If you ever stop marketing, you stop selling, you stop making money, and you come to a complete stop!

If you're ever forced to cut overhead, slash everything you can except marketing, or you'll be slashing your own wrists. Doing nothing ensures nothing happens. Instead of the safest way out of a tight spot, it is the surest way of tightening a noose around the neck of your business.

MARKETING IS AN ETERNAL PROCESS
Memories are short
People forget. They're exposed to literally thousands of messages a day. A recent survey found that 80% of viewers who saw one TV spot several times a day for three months had completely forgotten it two months after the ad stopped running.

The moving parade
People lose interest in some things as they mature; others become interested in those same things as they mature. People move out, others move in. People die, others are born. Your market is in flux, and new opportunities are constantly evolving.

The tortoise and the hare
Remember the fable? The fleet-footed hare took frequent rest stops, but the plodding tortoise never stopped competing, no matter how far behind he seemed to fall. And who was it that won the race? Never stop marketing!

Oxygen to breathe

Overhead is your company's oxygen: salaries, rent, utilities. If you can't pay overhead, you're forced to close the doors, you're dead! Where do you get oxygen for your business? Sales. How do you sell? Marketing. When the oxygen supply is cut off, so are the lights.

Marketing plans

Marketing takes time and money, two precious commodities you must not squander. It is unlikely you can match the marketing muscle of the dominant, major companies in your field, so you have to find ways to maximize every dollar and every minute you spend on marketing. Since you can't afford mistakes, it is necessary to carefully craft marketing plans that efficiently and economically motivate people to buy your product.

▼

Marketing is carried out on two levels:
Strategic Macromarketing
and
Tactical Micromarketing

MACROMARKETING

▼

Macromarketing is one grand, never-ending strategy
to promote your company and product-line as a
whole.

Macromarketing integrates your business concept into a *grand strategy* designed to create a desired identity for your company. Through macromarketing, for example, you may establish a public perception of your company as a young, dynamic, hip, fun enterprise.

Macromarketing includes your choice of company name and logo, the way you decorate your office, and how you speak on the phone or relate to people in person. And since everything you do sends a message about your company, all your activities must consistently conform to your business concept so that you don't send mixed or confusing signals.

The *macromarketing plan* defines the *strategies* by which you position your product so it can be seen, heard, and bought. It lays down principle guidelines without all the nuts-and-bolts details.

MICROMARKETING

▼

Micromarketing is a series of finite exercises
you must go through with each and every product
you introduce.

A written *micromarketing plan* can be quite comprehensive, and might run 10-20 pages or more. It elaborates on specific marketing tools and media used, frequency of use, costs, milestones, and objectives.

Micromarketing concerns the *tactical* functions of moving individual products, ideas, and services through channels of distribution into the marketplace. These tactical exercises include pricing, placing, and promoting product in order to create a demand that results in sales. It is not so much force-feeding the customer as it is tailoring the presentation of the product to match consumers' desires or needs so that they want to purchase it.

When formulating marketing plans, concentrate on:
- how you want to position your company in the marketplace
- how you want to expose your product to the public
- the image or message you want to project about your company and product
- the mechanics of projecting that image or message
- how you actually sell your product

Once you've settled on a plan, it is important to stick with it. You may have to fine-tune here or there, but consistent application is the key. Always be marketing-conscious. Treat marketing expenditure as a long-term investment. You may not always see instant results from every marketing exercise, but a solid plan followed religiously is the difference between success and failure.

Professional consultants

Since marketing is such an important component of success, many indie publishers hire professional help to devise marketing plans, either for their entire product line or to carry out certain functions for specific projects. Even the majors frequently use outside specialists for promotion, press, graphics design, and advertising.

You don't have to spend a fortune. With creativity, innovation, and plain hard work you can maximize sales while minimizing costs. But do not scrimp on the wrong things. You wouldn't advance $100,000 to sign a recording artist if you weren't also prepared to spend money for qualified producers, engineers, studio facilities, and musicians. And if you need expert medical, legal, or accounting advice, you go to a doctor, lawyer, or CPA.

You also need experts to develop your advertising and marketing materials. Putting together a good advertisement takes several skills: copywriting, graphics, design, artwork, photography. You may be capable of doing some or all of these things yourself, but it's self-defeating if you're not experienced. You not only waste valuable time, the results can really backfire. Positioning product in the media and marketplace requires expertise.

Hiring real talent should be looked upon as a money-making investment, because *real talent produces bankable results*. That's why NFL and NBA teams bid so high to recruit the best athletes. If you're obsessed with hiring the cheapest studio, musicians, producers, artists, designers, advertising and marketing consultants, etc., you stand a good chance of getting mediocre (or worse) results. Without paying over the top, it pays to get the best. After all, you're in business to generate profits, not slash overhead.

Getting the most bang for your bucks

Ultimately, there are two kinds of marketing: expensive and inexpensive. A campaign that costs $100 and grosses $101 is dearly expensive. However, if you spend $100,000 and gross $1 million, the money is well spent; the marketing was inexpensive in proportion to the results.

One trick of the trade for cutting ad production costs is to pay a top-notch, highly professional designer to do a generic layout for you. Thereafter, instruct a less expensive designer to follow the same, generic format tailored to specific projects. You then get a series of polished, expensive-looking ads that cost a fraction of what the original designer would have charged for each one but which are based on an original format that is far superior to what the less expensive designer might have created.

Similarly, hire a real marketing whiz to formulate generic creative and media plans that you can use and reuse, with minor tinkering, to cover almost all your projects for the immediate future. You might then retain the services of a less expensive consultant to customize or modify the plans as needed for each project.

As for your company's overall, master marketing plan, develop it with the assistance of the best marketing mind you can find. For a small retainer or preagreed fee, have the expert remain available for follow-up consultations until all kinks are ironed out and the plan proves to work for you.

Once you've gotten your strategic marketing plan right, stick with it. Unlike creative and media plans (tactical components of the strategic marketing plan), which change with circumstances and time, the strategic marketing plan becomes almost etched in stone.

Managing consultants

When using consultants, remember that you are the best and final judge of what you want to convey about your company and its product. Plans created with professional assistance should conform closely to your concept. Retain creative control and don't allow experts' egos to confuse your message.

Consultants work for you, not the other way around. Listen, learn, and absorb, but accept only those ideas and advice that mesh with your goals. Don't be talked into anything you're uncomfortable with, because the consequences of failure will be yours, long after consultants have pocketed their fees and moved on.

Projecting your message

Ultimately, the public forms a perception of your company. You want to ensure that perception matches the image you intend to project.

Your company message should be visually reinforced by the choice of colors, graphics, typefaces, and language used in all your advertising, stationery, labels, album covers, posters, brochures, business cards, etc. They should all reflect the stylistic genre of your product so you don't send mixed messages or confuse anyone about who you are or what your product offers.

COMPANY NAME

Sooner or later, your company's name comes to represent a certain image in the minds of people who have any kind of experience with you or your product. But from the very start, before anyone knows anything about you, your company's name can be used to project the image you want. Try to choose a name that's unique, memorable, or captures the essence of the message you want to convey.

LOGO

Your logo is also very important, and having it professionally designed can be well worth the money. Use your logo consistently and prominently on all marketing materials and product. Establish it as synonymous with the type of music or company-style people can expect.

Both your logo and company name can directly appeal to your target market's characteristic profile. You can convey a sense of fun, dignity, class, rebellion, eccentricity, youth, maturity, ethnicity, musical genre, or a particular lifestyle.

Protecting your trade name and logo

Choosing a company name and logo are among the most important and difficult decisions faced when launching a new venture. It's imperative to establish legal protection for your name and logo. The best way to do this is through *active trading* and *branding*. Trademarks and trade-name protection are weighted in favor of those who establish *first use*. An established *brand* is therefore the best defense against others adopting names or logos that might be mistaken for yours.

BRAND RECOGNITION

Build a strong *brand recognition*. Thus, when your company name is mentioned or its logo is seen, a subconscious recognition of the image you want to convey is achieved. (If you're into management or production as well, build brand recognition for each of your artists for the same reasons.)

Branding establishes a market identity. When your company becomes associated with quality in a certain genre, it is easier for consumers to accept new product from you based on perceptions they've formed from previous experience with your product. You build a loyal customer base, encouraging repeat sales.

Different brands can be created for different market targets or niches. For instance, MCA Records reactivated the brand name Decca for product coming out of Nashville. Similarly, Capitol Records "brands" country product through its Nashville-based label Liberty Records. Chrysalis Records uses the Cooltempo label for its dance/R&B-oriented product, Ichiban Records releases rap artists on the Wrap label, and Motown uses the MoJazz label for jazz.

Branding also enhances company value. A company that establishes its name through brand recognition builds into its *book value* a certain amount of *good will*, which is a valuable asset.

Brand Extension

Once brand recognition is achieved, it makes sense to extend the value of the brand to new product lines or profit centers to avoid starting from square one when launching a new product or service. For example, Virgin Records chose the label name Virgin Classics when it launched a classical division. Warner Brothers created Warner Western for traditional western and cowboy music. A new, boutique label distributed or partly owned and financed by a major label can benefit from having the established brand extended in split fashion (i.e., Epic/Pyramid).

Examples of brand extensions in other industries include Coca-Cola's Diet Coke and Cherry Coke and Miller Beer's Miller Lite. In fact, Motown's jazz label, MoJazz, is a subtle form of brand extension.

ARTWORK AND PACKAGING

Album and folio covers are very important marketing tools. Resist whims of recording artists and songwriters to dictate packaging, unless you agree their ideas enhance the product's salability. All too often, designs done by the artists themselves (or their friends or relatives) are amateurish, enigmatic, or downright obscure. Cover art must relate to the music, be informative, and be visually attractive. It must stand out from competing product in retail bins. Lavish, multipage inserts and other artist ego-builders are usually unnecessary expenses that don't help sales.

DEFINING YOUR MESSAGE

Most conventional products are positioned to appeal to customers on more than one level. Consumers consider such factors as price, profit-making opportunities, practicality, convenience, security, health, fashion, and feelings. Music almost entirely appeals to feelings or emotions. Define what you want people to feel about your product, then drive that message home, indirectly, directly, blatantly, and subliminally, in all your marketing and sales exercises.

How to focus your company and product:

- How do you want the public to *feel* about your product?
- What *message* reinforces this?
- What message do you send with your *company name*?
- What message do you send with your company's *logo*?
- What message do you send with *album titles*?
- If you have a company *slogan*, what message does it send?
- What *key words* in your marketing materials drive home your message?
- What *graphics, designs, and images* do you consistently use for album artwork, posters, advertising, brochures, catalogs, trade show displays, etc., to drive home your message?

Sales

Sales is the object of the marketing process.

Sales is a component of marketing, but it is a specific function that requires its own plan. The sales process involves actions asking potential customers to actually buy the product.

It's surprising how many deals are lost simply because the target wasn't urged to action. Never make the mistake of thinking a beautiful presentation is all you need. You'll never again have the customer as receptive, so follow through and close while the iron is hot.

For most music publishers, a "sale" is getting a song cut or used in a film, commercial, television production, etc. This is the responsibility of songpluggers, who are, in effect, the publishing company's sales force. However, major licensing deals with subpublishers, print distributors, et al., which are usually made on a more senior management level, is also selling.

Every member of your organization must be aware of basic salesmanship. Integrate a customer focus throughout the organization. Educate all personnel to be market driven. Any company, no matter its size, can have opportunities killed by rudeness, arrogance, indifference, ignorance, or insensitivity shown to potential customers by anyone in the organization, from receptionists to senior executives.

To restate what should by now be obvious: Everything and everyone connected with your business reflects upon your company and affects your success. Attitude and behavior are components of public relations, which is a component of marketing, and marketing is salesmanship.

THE SALES PROCESS

Marketing positions your product so you can take direct actions needed to actually sell it. The sales process might involve selectively targeted direct-mail shots to likely music users, telephone solicitations for leads, and networking with personal contacts. It can also include direct-response offers to consumers via mail or over the airwaves, or simply putting a "For Sale" sign next to a stack of CDs on a table set up at a gig.

The sales process includes the nature of your sales presentations and sales calls and the quotas or goals you expect from sales efforts. Specific steps in the sales process can include a combination of two or more of the following exercises:

- *Cold calls*. Contacting potential song users you don't know without knowing whether they're interested in your product.
- *Getting leads*. A *lead* is a potential buyer you have reason to think may be interested in your product. Leads come from referrals and people who respond to surveys, direct mailings, or coupons. They may also come from tip sheets, like *SongLink International, Songplugger, Lead Sheet, Songs Wanted, New on the Charts*, etc.
- *Following up leads*. The sequel to getting leads is the sales presentation, or pitching material, which is done by mail, telephone, or in person.
- *Fulfillment*. Once you've made a "sale," you have to deliver the product. Fulfillment includes the turnaround time from receipt of an order to the customer's receipt of the product. It also includes the

turnaround time it takes you to prepare and deliver a contract or licensing agreement.

- *After sales follow-up*. After a logical interval, always follow up a sale to see if the customer is satisfied. This can lead to still more sales. People who buy your product or use your services are obvious targets for future sales.
- *Productivity*. Make efficient use of the time and money it takes to close each sale. Productivity is a major factor of profitability. You're in trouble if it takes $200 in sales-related expenses to close a deal worth $100. Know how much time and money it realistically takes to close each sale so you can gauge whether your sales efforts are productive.
- *Goals or quotas*. To meet your projections, each songplugger has to reach certain goals, which should be set by the size of the target market and the productivity factor you've established. But it's not enough to achieve a preset sales volume. It's entirely possible to sell a million dollars worth of product by spending $2 million in the process. Effective marketing, obviously, has to be profitable.
- *Training*. True salesmanship is an art practiced on different levels depending upon the sophistication of the product and/or the customer. Ensure your people are trained to accomplish your goals.
- *Compensation*. Decide how your sales people are paid (salary, commission, or a combination thereof), and what incentives you offer to spur sales (bonuses, awards, stock, gifts, etc.). Give bonuses when warranted, as often as you can afford it. In fact, if bonuses are based on results, you'll be able to afford it. Structure bonuses on points earned for each unit sold above set quotas.
- *Credibility*. When you promise a *hold*, an in-store promotion, bonus, POP materials (or whatever), deliver exactly what you pledged and exactly on time. Make sure everything you tell songpluggers or promotion people (about airplay or sales, for instance) is 100% accurate. They must always be able to count on the tools you give them to do their jobs.

Sales management is a never-ending exercise. Songpluggers can get burned out. Watch for signs of sagging enthusiasm, lagging attention, slipping quotas, excuses, absenteeism. Encourage songpluggers, as salesmen, to continually study their craft. And remember, both negativism and enthusiasm are contagious. Exude enthusiasm about your product and demonstrate that you expect professionalism and success. Motivate your team; fire them with enthusiasm about your product.

Make sure your songpluggers and promotion people know your product inside out. Update them with the latest reviews, charts, tour dates, airplay data, and sales information, with anything and everything they can use for ammunition to sell your product and promote your company.

Reporting is essential. Operating budgets rely on sales projections. If sales slip under projections, your budgeting is skewered and you're heading for big trouble. Unmet quotas are red flags, warning you to take corrective action somewhere: in promotion, advertising, marketing, sales management, or at the product level itself. It is vital to know, at the end of every month at least, how actual sales compare with projections. Set up a reporting system that provides you complete, up-to-date sales information regularly and punctually.

The marketing mix

Marketing involves a mix of four ingredients called the four Ps: product, price, place, promotion. The quality and quantity of each of these ingredients, and the method of mixing them, can influence demand for the product. Even superb product fails to sell if the price is too steep, the product is not placed where consumers can find it, or promotion is dismal. Conversely, inferior product might sell well with low pricing, widespread availability, and superb promotion.

The marketing task is to find the right recipe to mix the four ingredients for best results. Sometimes, a midstream adjustment to the mix can turn failure into success (lowering the price, changing the mode of distribution, or shifting promotional tactics).

Variables within the marketing mix			
PRODUCT	PLACE	PRICE	PROMOTION
Quality	Distribution	Retail	Radio airplay
Genre	Chain stores	Wholesale	TV airplay
Features	Mom & pops	Discounts	P-O-P displays
Packaging	Mail order	Credit	Publicity
Branding	Record club	Allowances	Advertising
Bundling	Racks	Advances	a. Copy
Quantity	Allocations	Royalty rate	b. Media
Services	Shipping		c. Timing
	Jukeboxes		d. Frequency
	Venues		e. Size/duration
			Sales
			Live performances

PRODUCT

The key to success is the *customer's* perception of the product, *as opposed to the company's perception.* Product development and marketing decisions must be made with this in mind. Even if you're offering a service that has no tangible attributes, the manner in which the service is offered can take on a tangible attribute in the customer's mind (e.g., "service with a smile").

Product development should conform to the company's business strategy and overall marketing concept. If the strategy and concept is sound and firmly rooted, product development can be an intuitive rather than a scientific process.

PRODUCT LIFE CYCLE

Like human beings, recorded products have a recognizable life cycle. Song copyrights generally follow a similar pattern, but can more easily be reborn and enjoy new life through remakes and covers long after the original cycle.

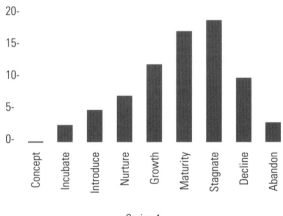

Series 1

Stages of a product's life cycle:
- *Conception.* The idea for the product is generated and evaluated. A cost analysis and sales forecast are required to justify committing funds for development.
- *Incubation.* Once the idea is accepted as viable, funds are committed and development begins. Expenses might include advances, demos, preproduction, recording, mixing, mastering, artwork, and manufacturing. Simultaneously, marketing plans are finalized, a release date set, and prerelease promotion and publicity begin in accordance with a marketing calendar. At this stage, much money is invested with no opportunity for sales.
- *Introduction.* With the product's launch into the marketplace, costs continue to rise as initial marketing steps are executed. Testing begins in earnest, and orders may trickle in, but sales aren't sufficient to recoup investment.

- *Nurturing*. The product is still in its infancy. Positive feedback from testing is used to nurture the product by pyramiding initial successes throughout the marketplace. Further promotion and marketing costs are incurred, still out of proportion to return, but in line with the amount of positive results demonstrated thus far. (Don't get too far ahead of the curve by committing heavy marketing expenses until the concept is proven valid.)
- *Growth*. Now the product begins to fulfill its promise with positive sales results, so that full-scale marketing can be committed with confidence. The rising line of sales income closes in on the line of product expenditures.
- *Maturity*. The product has become established and is profitable. It may still be possible to reenter the growth phase if more marketing resources are committed, but only if careful analysis shows further growth potential is great enough to justify additional expense.
- *Saturation*. Sales reach a plateau as the marketplace is saturated. The product has gone as far as it can. Further marketing expenditures are not justified, because the product has peaked. New investment would only reduce return on investment and will spur additional sales.
- *Decline*. The product has reached old age, sales are rapidly falling off, ultimately to a trickle. The product is maintained mainly as a catalog item.
- *Abandonment*. The product has died. Inventory maintenance costs more than it's worth, and the product is shelved, or (in the case of recorded product) deleted from the catalog, scrapped, or sold as cut-outs.

Good product management involves allocating marketing resources to prolong a product's lifespan for maximum sales and profit. You need instant access to up-to-date financials for each song or songwriter's catalog. You need to know how much has been spent vis à vis how much income has been generated, so that an evaluation can be made of actual performance versus projections during each stage of the life cycle. This data is essential for calculating whether further investment is warranted. Will additional marketing increase sales without eating into profits?

▼

Life cycles apply not only to individual products but also to entire lines of product (or song catalogs), as well as to artists, songwriters, rosters, and companies.

The 80/20 Rule

At any given time, you'll likely see 80% of your sales coming from just 20% of your catalog or songwriting roster. Some of your product (or writers or artists) will be in one of the embryonic stages (conception, development, introduction, nurturing), while others are in the declining stages. Still others may never have reached the growth stage at all (still-births). This leaves approximately 20% of your catalog generating 80% of your sales in either the growth stage, the maturity level, or at the saturation stage. It behooves you to recognize each product's status in order to properly allocate resources so that as the top 20% start down, others are geared to move up and sustain your business.

Stars, cows, kids, and dogs

Back in the '70s, the Boston Consulting Group devised a system of classifying product into four categories:
- *Star*. This is a product that rises rapidly, an undeniable hit. It doesn't flame out before yielding a good return over a satisfactory life cycle.
- *Cash Cow*. This may be a product (songwriter or artist) that was formerly a Star, but has now settled into a pattern of returning unspectacular but satisfactory profits. Or, it may be a product that never actually achieved star status but generated solid profits and continues to bring a steady return on investment.
- *Problem Child*. Here's a product that hasn't performed as hoped yet has managed to get a foothold. It is worth continued work because it may yet prove profitable as a Cash Cow, even if it never reaches Star status.
- *Dog*. In this case, the product either fell on its face at the outset, or has had its day. There's no point in expending further time or money.

Resurrecting a Dog

Although unprofitable, a Dog might still add a worthwhile degree of prestige to the company, enhancing brand recognition, perhaps even attracting future stars. Perhaps a publisher offers a full range of product (e.g., record production, jingle production, recorded music library, administrative services to smaller publishers, etc.), and one of those areas is now a Dog. Instead of shutting that division down, the company wants to maintain its image as a well-rounded company. So energies are directed towards correcting the decline and turning the Dog into a Problem Child, with the aim of converting it into a Cash Cow if not a Star.

While decline and abandonment are inevitable and can leave a song or master a virtual Dog for a time, anything that's a hit today generally becomes worth something as someone's nostalgia tomorrow. Meaning, the product can see a second life, albeit in reduced proportions, as a Cash Cow or Problem Child catalog item in the future.

PLACE

The second of the Marketing Mix's four Ps, *place*, deals with the channels of distribution linking your product with end users. This starts with the source of your product and includes shipping as well as intermediaries who funnel the product down the line to the consumer (record producers, record companies, sheet music publishers, wholesalers, rack jobbers, and retailers).

Ultimately, there is, or should be, a close relationship between a music publisher and the various links in its distribution system. All are mutually interested in successfully marketing the product, and all must contribute their own strengths and expertise to the process. While the onus is always on the user (e.g., record company or sheet music publisher) to motivate consumers to buy, aggressive publishers co-operate, where practical, to make the process work.

The distribution system for recorded product has been going through a series of shakeups in the United States, and there are an increasing number of opportunities for labels to by-pass the traditional system by using direct-response sales pitches on TV and mail-order. The future may well see digital transmission of music to consumers' homes via central databanks or libraries of recorded music.

These changes may also provide opportunities for music publishers to produce and market music directly to consumers. But, for the near-term, the traditional distribution system must be utilized, albeit with ever-changing entities involved. The flow chart below demonstrates current channels of distribution used by record companies to reach consumers.

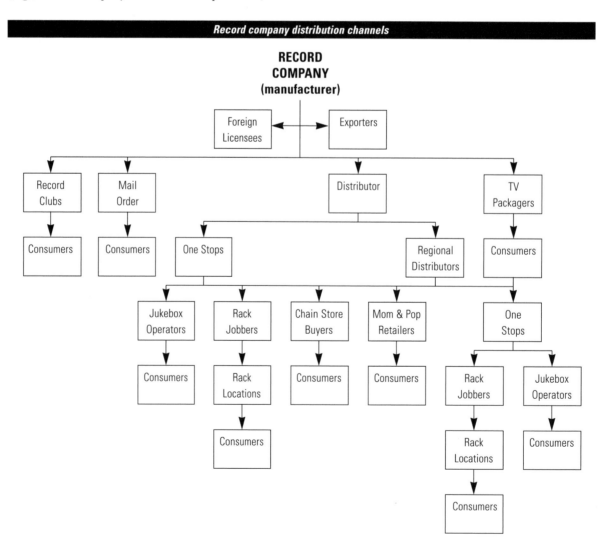

Record company distribution channels

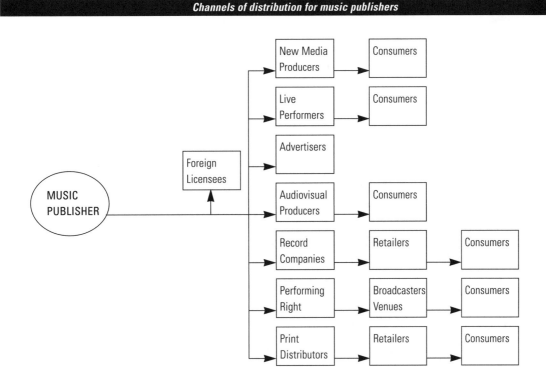

Distribution levels

There are three basic distribution levels for any product:

1. **Intensive** is the usual choice for recorded product. The product is made available through any retailer or wholesaler willing to accept the company's terms. Recorded product might then be found in Wal-Marts as well as mom & pop stores and even in truck stops, drug stores, convenience stores, book stores, etc.

2. **Elective** is when a product is made available to certain types of outlets only, such as specialist shops, where it's important to maintain a particular image. You wouldn't normally find Rolex watches on sale in convenience stores, for instance.

3. **Selective** distribution limits a product's exposure to area franchises, or exclusive territories. An example is the Big Mac, which you can only find at McDonald's; you can find Cokes available just about everywhere (intensive distribution).

Integration

One of the obvious factors about how you "place" your product is that the more functions or links you control in the distribution system (source of product, manufacturing, shipping, wholesaling, retailing), the larger the share of the product's retail price you get to keep.

Backward Integration

If a record label buys a music publishing company, studio, mastering facilities, and manufacturing plant in order to increase control over raw product, it is *integrating backwards*, towards its sources of product supply.

Forward Integration

If a music publisher establishes a record label and sets up a wholesale distributorship and retail outlets, it engages in *forward integration*, towards the sources of demand (the buyers).

Vertical Integration

If a publisher manages to get control of all elements (backwards to the source of supply as well as forward to the source of demand), it then becomes a *vertically integrated* company.

Risks of Integration

On the surface, it appears that if a company integrates backward, forward, or vertically, profits will be greater since middlemen and their cuts for services rendered are eliminated. However, integration should only be made after careful cost analysis. Each function in the distribution chain is highly specialized and can only be efficiently carried out with expertise and economies of scale.

Shipping, for instance, can be done through UPS or any one of dozens of freightlines at a minuscule fraction of the cost it would take for a record label to maintain its own fleet of trucks. Nor would it make sense to buy or build a state-of-the-art CD and cassette manufacturing plant unless enough product is required to keep the plant operating at full capacity. Whether the choice is additional staff or capital investment in facilities and equipment, integration is only practical if the company can do the job better and cheaper than existing entities available for the work on a contract basis.

PRICE

Pricing policies can be used to differentiate product or service, but price flexibility faces constraints of the marketplace and the type of product you offer. For instance, mechanical royalties have a ceiling under the compulsory licensing section of the Copyright Act (though nothing prevents a publisher from licensing copyrights lower than the statutory rate).

Labels can charge wholesalers anything they want for CDs or cassettes, but it makes little sense to be too far out of line with prevailing industry practices. However, it can make sense for labels to set different wholesale prices for different categories of product (front-line artists versus catalog reissues or budget-priced compilations.) And, of course, there's wide latitude for pricing licensing fees and advances.

Pricing policies

Premium. Compared with similar products, premium pricing is used to create a perception of higher quality or value. You'd expect to pay more for a Cadillac than a Chevrolet, and you'd assume that a lawyer commanding a fee of $300 per hour has more clout and ability than does one who charges $50. You might suppose that a studio with hourly rates of $175 offers better facilities, equipment, and personnel than one that charges $75.

To demand and receive a premium price takes more than just attaching a high price tag, however. Extra value, quality, and pizzazz must be added to the commodity in order to prevent customer resistance.

Fair. If you demonstrate your publishing catalog earned $10,000 in Japan over the past three years, it would be seen as "fair" to ask for an advance of $10,000 from a Japanese subpublisher seeking a three-year license. Fair pricing is arrived at from market research and/or historical earning patterns. It would also be fair to boost the price by an amount based on demonstrably reasonable assumptions of increased future earnings over historical patterns.

Penetration. The pile 'em high, sell 'em low concept is penetration pricing. Profit through high volume is the aim, as well as attempts to grab market share. An example might include package deals offered to television and film producers whereby synchronization fees are discounted when additional songs from your catalog are used in the producers' projects.

Parity. If you're not concerned with differentiating your product or service from competitors' offerings by pricing, you set rates on a par with competitors. Back to the example of music publishing royalties, or the wholesale price of CDs, there is a general parity within the industry for certain products.

Cost-plus. If the concern is merely return on investment, the price might be factored to yield a certain level of profit (e.g., expenses plus 20%). Cost-plus pricing isn't always realistic, since strict adherence means neither the marketplace (customers) nor competition is taken into account when setting prices.

Pricing policies should be consistent. Favored treatment to one account can bring unhappy repercussions from others who receive less favorable terms. Favored treatment should only be based upon performance, such as quantities bought, conditions of payment, limited returns, etc. These special considerations must be made available to all buyers within each class. In that way, any account can take advantage of your special rates if they match your requirements.

PROMOTION

In addition to getting records played on the air, promotion covers a broad area, including advertising, PR, publicity, and sales. Each of these areas is discussed further in the section on *marketing tools* below.

There are two basic promotion concepts: the *push strategy* and the *pull strategy*. The push strategy promotes product to *indirect* customers who then assume the sales function to the end user or consumer. Music publishers promote songs to record companies using the push strategy, for instance, and record companies then promote the recorded songs on to consumers, usually with the pull strategy.

The pull strategy involves creating a consumer demand for the product so that buyers request the record from retailers. Sensing the demand, retailers then order the record from wholesalers; and the wholesalers, in turn, order product from the label.

Thus, in the first example, the product is *pushed* by the originator through the pipeline to the consumer; and, in the second example, the product is *pulled* by consumer demand through the pipeline from the originator.

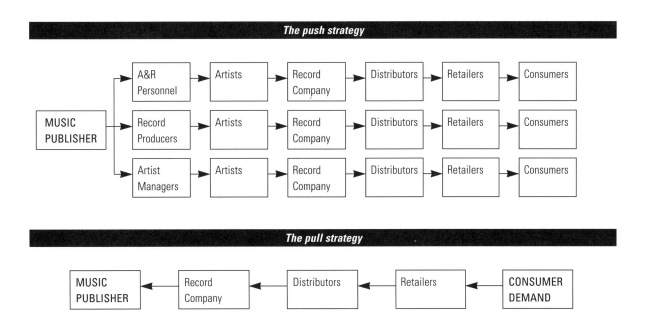

The pull strategy

Marketing tools

Once you've defined your message, you must choose the most appropriate tools for getting it into the marketplace. Which tools you employ and how often you use them depends upon what you want to accomplish and whether you're aiming your product directly at consumers or intermediate users. Record labels must spend and do more than music publishers, because recorded product is aimed at consumers in their thousands, plus hundreds of intermediaries (deejays and reviewers) and indirect customers (distributors, one-stops, rack jobbers, and retailers).

Marketing tools include publicity, advertising, networking, promotion, merchandising, and public relations. They all cost money and time, so you can't afford to misuse any of them. Each tool must be considered from the standpoints of *fit, affordability, mix, and repetition.*

Fit. How and where a marketing tool is used must *fit* the message you're trying to send and fit the targeted market. You wouldn't, for instance, advertise rap music in a country fanzine, nor would you use Old English type-face to denote *dash* and *youth*.

Affordability. Strive to maximize the potential results expected from marketing expenditures. A full page ad in *Billboard* may be good for the ego, but if you're marketing product to a limited niche audience, such as barbershop quartet fans, you'd be better off spending the money on more specifically targeted vehicles, such as direct-mail shots to known aficionados of barbershop quartets.

Mix. Use more than one vehicle to reach your customers so that your message is reinforced and those who miss your message from one source can get it from another.

Repetition. People are busy, distracted by many things, so your message needs to be driven home again and again to really be effective.

RECORD PROMOTION

Record promotion centers around radio to a great degree, but it also includes coordination with sales and other marketing functions. The old image of a promotion man as a jive-talking huckster, to whatever extent it was true, must give way to a disciplined, knowledgeable professional doing a demanding job under a great deal of pressure. If he doesn't deliver, he's out of a job.

The successful promotion man knows every aspect of his product: the artist, the audience targeted, sales and airplay momentum to date, etc. However, he's thoroughly informed about his competitors' product as well.

His job is not only to supply information to radio programmers, he also has to supply enthusiasm. Although your music is the key to enthusiasm on the emotional level, you've also got to bolster the promotion man's enthusiasm on an intellectual level with the very latest tracking sheets, airplay reports, sales reports, copies of picks, reviews, marketing materials, tour dates, merchandising campaigns, etc.

Credibility is a prerequisite for successful promotion. There's no excuse today for incomplete or incorrect information. Even one-man publishers and record labels now have access to precisely pinpointed sales/airplay data because of services like Soundscan, BDS, Billboard Online, and BIN.

Being credible also means (surprise!) telling the truth. Never hype a promotion man. If he supplies erroneous information, his credibility is tarnished, and his effectiveness is diminished. He can't tell a radio station PD in Buffalo that your release is getting heavy rotation in Cleveland unless the Buffalo PD can call his Cleveland counterpart for verification.

You have to be in the business of establishing careers, not exploiting quick, one-shot hits. For newer artists, personal appearances and video clips are extremely important roads to building a customer base. Promotion must be informative, imaginative, and persistent to be effective. If you cut corners to get a hit at the expense of credibility, you damage the prospects for an artist's long term career.

Adds

With so much competition for air time and with stations restricting playlists as a result of their own competitive situations, the onus on promotion men to deliver *adds* grows greater. That's why you should use only the most highly professional, credible promotion people and back them up with accurate data, not to mention great product. Check references before you hire an independent promotion man. (There are still some jive-talking hucksters around.)

Paying indie promo men

Until recently, promotion men were hired on retainer, with a specified minimum number of weeks committed to working a release. The amount of the retainer varied according to how many stations and/or cities the promoter covered (and, of course, according to the promoter's stature).

Recently, labels have begun paying independent promoters *per add*, rather than by weekly retainer. (Top 40 format promoters receive about $700 per add on major market stations and between $300 and $400 per add in midsize markets.)

The reasoning is that promoters should earn their fees by results. In the past, paying per add opened temptations for abuse. Promoters could induce certain program directors to report adds on records that never really received airplay at all, resulting in meaningless *paper adds*.

But with the advent of BDS, labels and publishers can monitor and verify the results of promoters' efforts. Because BDS reports the exact date and time of each play on over 550 radio stations in more than 100 markets (with more still being added), there may now be a move to pay promoters by the number of actual plays, rather than by the number of adds or by weekly retainer.

Managing promotion personnel

Cut the bureaucratic layers promotion personnel have to go through. Don't distract them from being where they should be and doing what they need to do, by having them report to too many people. Promotion works best one on one. They should deal with one point person at your company only and be encouraged to call that person anytime of the day or night.

Maximizing record promotion

Set up a systematic reporting procedure whereby promotion personnel regularly and punctually provide news of anything and everything pertaining to your release. Update and recycle that information to other promotion people in the field.

The essence of promotion is to get records played, get them in the stores, and report back the sales and airplay data, so that any success generated can be built upon to stimulate further play and sales. When you get movement in one town, spread it to adjoining areas in similar market profiles, then expand the success outward from there until the product is generating money you can reinvest to go all out.

Radio, once the do-or-die factor of a record's success, has become harder to crack. Record labels compete heavily for airplay, and, because of the huge number of new releases every week, air time is very limited. Radio programming is becoming increasingly sophisticated, with centralization, syndication, market surveys, focus groups, and *burn-out* computer tracking reports. (This latter phenomenon tracks the number of times a record receives airplay in a particular market, so that programmers can determine when to reduce airplay before listeners get burned out and tune out or turn off.)

With such heavily restricted playlists, it seems you can't get a record added unless it's already playlisted somewhere else. Catch 22. Key, power stations in major markets are not likely to add a new artist's record until it has demonstrated audience appeal at secondary stations. But even secondary stations are difficult to crack these days. You may have to start a grassroots movement, instead.

Work backwards to see which secondary stations influence a major station to add a record. Then trace further down market to determine which of the still smaller stations influence those secondary stations. You'll find these so-called marginal stations include college stations, public service stations, and small-town stations, or even some secondaries whose deejays have more latitude about what they can play late at night, after midnight, and weekends. Attack these more accessible stations with a vengeance and work upwards.

Promptly service all stations that express interest in your product, no matter insignificant their status. And keep servicing them with new product. Treat each of them as if they were the *numero uno* station in New York or L.A. They'll not only appreciate your attention (having been ignored or overlooked by the majors), but, often, personnel from these stations are youngsters who move up to bigger and better things. They'll remember the respect you showed them in their dark, difficult days of breaking into the business.

When you get heavy rotation and brisk sales in a city of 40,000, you can use that as ammunition to snare airplay in a neighboring city of 100,000. And success in this second city can lead you up the ladder to a city of a half million, and so on. Success in one city can be parlayed into mirrored success in several cities of similar size. From there, you can pyramid airplay into other regions of the country and ultimately achieve national breakthrough.

Crossing over

There is much specialization in the music industry, with tightly segmented playlists for Top 40, dance, rap, contemporary R&B, AOR, soft rock, hard rock, alternative, heavy metal, easy listening, country, third world, new age, jazz, blues, etc. If you're able break a record in one particular category, the path to really great success comes when you can cross it over into other market segments. Proven audience appeal in one sector provides promotional ammunition to attack other logically selected targets.

Testing

Testing is vital to successful marketing. You can't tell the marketplace what it wants; the marketplace tells you. But you want it to tell you before you squander your entire budget trying to force an unvalidated concept on an unenthusiastic public.

Testing doesn't mean trying one thing one time. Edison tried 10,000 different elements before he got the light bulb right (and said that if the 10,000th try hadn't worked, he would have tried 10,001, then 10,002, and so on). Although you may have to accept defeat at some point, keep knocking on different doors with different presentations until the marketplace convinces you to quit.

Test ads by trying different presentations to determine the most effective headlines, copy, layout, etc. Use focus groups to determine which album track to concentrate on as the 'A' side. Testing tells you if your product, marketing materials, advertising copy, and promotional tactics are honed to do the job necessary to bring a record home.

Regional testing

Test various propositions on a small scale, fine-tuning until it's clear you have a winner. Do regional testing before committing to an expensive, national campaign. The best test region is usually your own home base, or that of the artist or songwriter you're promoting. This is where you have some assets in place, a degree of proven market identity or acceptance, and where you have the most knowledge of, and personal access to, media outlets and other marketing opportunities.

If your marketing doesn't succeed within the home region, you have either failed to get your marketing concept properly focused or you have a product failure. Either case is a red flag, indicating barriers to success on a national level. Never roll out big bucks for a full-scale marketing campaign until you've proven there's definite commercial acceptance of the product.

PERSISTENCE

Stories abound of publishers refusing to give up on a song after initial rejections, and having their faith rewarded after persistent songplugging efforts, and there are cases where labels' persistence paid off after months of working and nursing albums to hit status.

Persistence requires concentration. Your release schedule or catalog must not expand beyond your ability to marshal sufficient marketing resources behind each record or song. Throwing product against the wall to see what sticks is shortsighted and expensive, especially for a young company.

A major record company might put out 20 to 30 releases in one month, and if seven or eight hit, the success ratio is very good. But smaller companies can't afford to play the law of averages. When you're releasing one or two albums a month, you can't deal in percentages; each release has to count. You don't have the financial resources of a major, so you must work each and every release to the hilt.

Assuming you would never sign an artist or songwriter you didn't believe in wholeheartedly or market anything you consider substandard, each and every song or release is something you and your organization should be thoroughly committed to fight for. With faith comes persistence. You won't always be right, but you must be prepared to fully test each release until the market place gives you a resounding no.

Trade Shows

Trade shows, expos, and seminars are discussed in the chapters on *Foreign Licensing* and *Exploitation*. They are also an important element of the marketing mix in your own country. As previously noted, these events offer economical and efficient platforms for you to show the flag, display your wares, establish new contacts, solidify existing relationships, reestablish old relationships, pick up new product, find licensees and distributors for your product, check out the competition, gain insights into the business, keep abreast of changes and portending changes, and, above all, sell your product!

Advertising

Although music publishers don't usually advertise in consumer media, there are occasions when they do contribute to marketing campaigns employed by music users, as well as occasions when advertising in trade media makes sense. Advertising campaigns must be planned with the following criteria in mind:

- **Reach**. How many potential customers will receive the message?
- **Demography**. Who, exactly, do you want to reach, and how will you tailor the message to get their attention?
- **Geography**. What area are you targeting?
- **Frequency**. How often will the message be repeated?
- **Duration**. How long is the message (broadcast media)?
- **Size**. How large is the ad (print media)?
- **Impact**. Does the message cut through the clutter of competing messages to make the audience aware, interested, and/or reminded of the product?
- **Cost**. For each message delivered, how efficient is the use of your advertising dollars in terms of the number of people reached?

COST ANALYSIS

Before you do any sort of advertising, back out the costs. Calculate how many records (or whatever it is you're selling) you need to sell to recoup the expenditure; then judge whether the ad can actually increase sales enough to make it worthwhile.

Consider: if an ad for an album release costs $5,000, and your net per unit—after all costs and royalties—is in the range of $1.50, the ad must increase sales by 3,333 units just to pay for itself. If your stake in the album is limited to mechanical royalties, and your combined net mechanical royalties is 20¢ (after all royalty payments), your $5,000 ad has to pull in an additional 25,000 sales for you to get your money back.

Could that $5,000 be more effectively spent on independent promotion and press? Could you get better mileage out of much smaller ads repeated several times? (Rather than one full-page ad, you could get, perhaps, six eighth-page ads, or ten sixteenth-page ads. You could get three 15-second spots rather than one 60-second spot.)

CPM formula

Advertising that reaches the most people is not always the most effective. Consider a $10,000 full-page ad in a sports magazine with 2 million readers. Officially, the ad costs one-half cent per reader. But how many of those people are actually interested in your product? How many half-cents are you wasting?

If, instead, you spend $2,000 for a full-page ad in a small trade magazine read by 20,000 people in your precise target market, your cost per reader is 10¢, twenty times the per person cost of the sports magazine ad. But it is obvious which ad is more cost-effective.

Publications and broadcast media provide potential advertisers with demographic information along with circulation or viewer/listener numbers. This data tells you not only how many people a particular media outlet reaches, but what kinds of people.

For instance, a magazine's circulation research might show that, say, 66% of its readers are college educated, 59% have annual incomes over $75,000, 71% are male, 68% are in managerial or professional occupations, etc. From this, you can deduce whether the magazine fits your targeted market segment. If you're aiming at upper middle class, male execs, it looks like a good vehicle, but if you're marketing grunge, rap, or alternative rock, it doesn't.

When faced with a choice between advertising in one media outlet or another, use the *CPM formula* (cost per thousand) to assess the most effective use of your advertising dollars. Assuming all other factors are relatively equal (the audience reached by each media outlet option fits your demographic target), the CPM Formula is:

$$\frac{\text{Cost of advertising}}{\text{Audience in 1000s}} = \text{Cost per person} \times 1,000 = \text{CPM}$$

CPM media analysis				
	Media A	Media B	Media C	Media D
Cost of Advertisement	$5,000	$7,500	$10,000	$40,000
Audience (in 1000s)	75,000	125,000	350,000	900,000

Media A

$$\frac{\$5,000}{75,000} = \$0.0667 \times 1,000 = \$66.70 \text{ (CPM)}$$

Media B

$$\frac{\$7,500}{125,000} = \$0.0600 \times 1,000 = \$60.00 \text{ (CPM)}$$

Media C

$$\frac{\$10,000}{350,000} = \$0.0286 \times 1,000 = \$28.60 \text{ (CPM)}$$

Media D

$$\frac{\$40,000}{900,000} = \$0.0444 \times 1,000 = \$44.40 \text{ (CPM)}$$

From this analysis, we see that Media Outlet _C_ presents the most efficient use of advertising dollars ($28.60 per thousand people reached), even though Media _D_ reaches 2.57 as many people (but costs 1.55 times as much per thousand). Perhaps, however, you'd prefer to spend over 1.5 times per thousand in order to reach over 2.5 times as many people. At least you're now able to make such decisions on a cost-effective basis.

When considering the type of media to use, consider the factors in the following chart:

MEDIA TYPE	AUDIENCE REACH	IMPACT	COST	SELECTIVITY	LEAD TIME
TRADE MAGAZINES	Medium/ Low	Medium/ High	Medium/ High	High	Medium/ Short
TRADE DIRECTORIES	Medium/ Low	Medium/ High	Medium/ High	High	Long
FANZINES	Medium/ Low	High	Medium/ Low	High	Medium/ Short
MAGAZINES	Medium/ High	Medium/ High	Medium/ High	High	Long
NEWSPAPERS	Low/ High	Medium/ High	Medium/ Low	Medium/ Low	Short
RADIO	Low/ High	Medium/ Low	Medium/ Low	High	Short
TELEVISION	Very High	High	High	Low	Short
CABLE TV	High	High	Medium/ High	Medium	Short
DIRECT MAIL	Low/ High	Medium/ Low	High	High	Medium/ Long
P.O.P.	Low	Medium/ High	Medium/ Low	High	Short
BILLBOARDS	Low/ High	Medium/ Low	Low	Low	Long
SPECIALTIES	Medium/ Low	Medium/ High	Medium/ Low	Medium/ High	Long

THE PURPOSE OF ADVERTISING

Advertising works when done right. Ads done badly waste money and can actually harm your product. Confusing ad copy, poor layout, amateurism, all defeat your purpose. And beware of artsy, cutesy ads that say more for the pretensions of the ad designer than they do for your product.

The purpose of advertising is to sell. You want people to notice and remember your product, not the ad itself. Make your product the compelling factor about the ad, not its graphics or pictures or artistic merit (or lack thereof).

▼

Two precepts of successful advertising
are simplicity and repetition.

Essentials of successful ad copywriting

- *Keep the message short and easy to grasp.*
- *Start by announcing to the audience what you're going to tell them.*
- *Then tell them.*
- *Then remind them what you've just told them.*
- *End with a call to action (e.g., "Buy Now!").*

POSITIONING

An old real-estate saw says the three most important things about property value are location, location, and location. This applies to marketing as well. The success of any proposition depends on *position, position, and position.*

- *In advertising,* that means placing an ad where it's most likely to be seen or heard by your target market.
- *In merchandising,* it means displaying the product in a manner and place where your target market is most likely to see it.
- *In making a business proposal,* it means presenting a deal in the right way to the right person at the right time.
- And *in business, generally,* it means positioning your product or service to differentiate it from the competition in ways that appeal to a significant segment of your market.

The prime space positions for print advertising are the back cover, the first page, and the inside front and back covers. These are also the most expensive. If you don't want to pay the premium for such a prominent position, the better spots are generally on right-hand pages and either in the section your targeted readers are most interested in or as close to the front of the issue as possible.

For radio and TV spots, the most effective times to advertise are *drive time* (radio) and *prime time* (TV), and during the most watched or listened to pro-grams. These are the most popular times sold by stations and are therefore the most expensive.

HEADLINES

A headline is an advertisement for your advertisement. Your message must be immediately obvious. How many people, after all, read magazines or watch TV for the ads? Not many, if any. Make your audience stop, look, and listen to what you've got to say. You do this with your headline.

Headlines are said to account for the success or failure of an ad by a factor of 80%. Headlines are essential in all areas of marketing. The first thing you say to someone on the phone is a headline; so is the first sentence you write in a letter, and the first words a salesman says to a customer.

How you begin any proposition can affect the outcome of what you're trying to accomplish. The headline sets a tone that causes the recipient to instinctively react with interest, disinterest, indifference, or even indignation. If your headline bores or antagonizes, the rest of your proposition will be very difficult to get across.

▼

You never get a second chance
to make a first impression.

INSTITUTIONAL ADS VERSUS DIRECT-RESPONSE ADS

There are essentially two types of ads: *institutional* and *direct-response.* Institutional ads are used to reinforce or build a company's image and keep its name before the public. But since these ads don't call for any direct action on the consumer's part, you can't really measure their effectiveness.

Institutional ads can be a bit pretentious. Consumers care much less about how great you are than about how your product can better their lives. Emphasize the benefits of your services or product rather than asking the customer to worship you.

About the only place an institutional ad is worth considering is in a trade directory. Unlike periodicals, which are read then tossed away, trade directories, like *Billboard Buyer's Guide* or the *Midem Directory,* are kept for repeated reference. Thus, your ad stands a chance of being seen several times during the course of a year, enjoying the benefits of repeat advertising at a one-time cost. Just make sure such an ad sends a solid message about your company's benefits.

Repetition is necessary. Some marketing experts reckon people need to see or hear an ad 7 to 12 times before its message is noticed and remembered. But advertising is costly, and you're in competition with the majors, whose budgets are far larger than yours.

Since you can't get much mileage out of one-time print ads, and even less out of one-time broadcast ads, you have to be very careful or shrewd in how and when you advertise.

That's why direct-response ads are best, because they bring immediate, verifiable results. Direct-response ads are used to sell a product, to motivate consumers to go out and buy. Or mail a coupon. Or call an 800 number. Or do *something*, and do it *now!* You can tell within days whether the ad works. Either sales pick up or they don't. You can test various messages, rerun the ones that work, and drop the losers. You will always know to the dollar how effective a direct-response ad has been; you can never quantify the effectiveness of an institutional ad.

DISPLAY ADS

Print ads that are not in the classified section are *display ad*s. Display rates are broken down in various ways, depending upon the publication. Some publications set display rates by *column inch*. Other publications sell space by the *number of lines* used. Still others break pages up into fractions: *full-page, half-page, quarter-page, eighth-page, sixteenth-page.*

Call the publication you want to advertise in and ask the advertising manager to send you a *rate card.* This contains all the information you need for placing an ad: sizes and costs of space available, deadlines for submitting ad copy, issue dates, technical requirements for artwork, payment details (cash with order, deposit required, discounts available, etc.). Then, place the ad by sending the camera-ready copy (sometimes called a *mechanical*) with the *insertion order* to the publication you've targeted.

CLASSIFIED ADS

Classified ads are relatively cheap but can be a waste of money unless carefully crafted and placed where you're sure your audience will see them. And they must be repeated over and over again. Headlines assume an even greater importance with classified ads, because there are no graphics or pictures to grab attention.

Classified ads are sold by the number of lines or words used, so the discipline is to say the most using the fewest possible words. That's not a bad thing, but it can be false economy to slash wording to the point where an ad is so cryptic it's meaningless. Provide enough information using as many hot-button buzz words as necessary to make the ad tantalizing.

Classified ads are opportunities to draw potential customers rather than actually make a sale. Classifieds can be used to spark interest so that people request a catalog, sample, or further information, wherein you can make your spiel with more elaboration.

There is a definite art to writing, placing, and testing classified ads. In fact, all advertising requires expertise, which is why professional assistance is recommended, unless you're prepared to really master the subject.

But, again, don't let the egos of professional consultants rule (and ruin) your marketing efforts. Beware of pros striving to win advertising awards. Keep your message focused to sell your product. Don't fall for cop-outs, such as being told the ad can't be measured by short-term results, that it is "image building." Advertising is salesmanship, pure and simple; it's not a vehicle to show how clever and creative its designer is.

PER INQUIRY ADS (PI)/PER ORDER ADS (PO)

Numerous publications as well as radio and television stations accept ads on a *PI* or *PO* basis. PI means *per inquiry*; PO means *per order.* Instead of paying for your ad upfront, the media outlet collects a set sum for each inquiry or order the ad generates. From your standpoint, it's best to do a PO, because you only pay for definite orders, whereas a PI obliges you to pay for each person who responds, whether or not they actually buy.

Broadcasters and publishers depend on ad revenue for survival, but they frequently have space and time that isn't sold. They fill these gaps with *public service announcements* (*PSAs*) that bring in no revenue. So if you offer them a PO ad, they can run it in place of a PSA.

Say you're selling CDs at $15.98 (plus P&H), and a radio station normally gets $100 for a 60-second spot. The station accepts your PO in return for 25% of the retail price of each CD sold. Say the ad pulls 75 orders. Instead of $100 upfront for the ad, the station gets $300 on the back end. Meanwhile, you've grossed $898.50 ($15.98 x 75 = $1,198.50 - $300) without putting up any money. It's a 60/60 deal for both parties.

Parlay the success of this ad to persuade other stations to run your PO. If 100 stations produce the same results, you gross $89,850 with no upfront advertising costs.

Don't expect stations to run POs during prime time when spots are easier to sell and rates are higher. POs run during off-peak hours when time is available (and, unfortunately, fewer people are tuned in).

REMNANTS

A *remnant* is the term for left-over print advertising space when a publication deadline rolls round. Remnants are similar to POs in the sense that you can take cost-cutting advantage of a publication's unsold space. But you do pay upfront, rather than giving up a percentage of your sales. However, instead of paying the full price for the ad, you can save up to 50% off the normal advertising cost.

And, if you set up your own ad agency (see below), you could knock an additional 15% off the discounted rate. Tell the publication you want their remnant (unsold) space, send your check with the ad copy, and wait. When space becomes available, your ad runs. The only drawback is that you can't dictate which issue you want the ad to run in, nor can you dictate exactly where in the publication you want it to appear.

GANG RUNS

Big printing companies frequently do large, full color print-runs for major clients, and are thus geared up to run smaller orders on their presses at the end of the original job. These *gang runs* can shave 50% to 75% off the normal cost of your brochures, posters, mailing pieces, etc.

Of course, like remnants, you must have patience to take advantage of the savings. You can't give the printer a deadline; your job will run at his convenience. But by planning ahead with a *marketing calendar*, you'll know your print needs far enough in advance to place a gang run order in plenty of time.

TV/RADIO RATE REDUCTIONS

Stated rates are more negotiable than car sticker-prices, and big reductions can be yours simply for asking. You may have a hard time negotiating lower drive-time and prime-time rates, since it's easier for stations to sell such spots. But, stations are anxious to fill unsold spots at other times, and they will indeed deal, rather than run nonpaying PSAs.

AD SIZE/DURATION

As previously mentioned, consistency is vitally important for your ad to be effective. Large ads may look impressive, but they won't work nearly so well as running several smaller ads, which you can do for the same price. The same goes for running more 15- or 30-second radio or TV spots versus fewer 60-second spots.

AD AGENCY DISCOUNTS

When an agency places a magazine ad for a client, it pays the publication 85% of the open rate and charges the client 100% of the rate. The 15% difference is the agency's fee for placing the ad. You can make that 15% discount yours.

Unless you plan to advertise in hundreds of publications and really need an agency to buy and monitor the ads, you probably know exactly which magazines are the best ones to reach your intended market. So place the ads yourself. Set up an additional profit center: an advertising agency. Give it a name different from your company's and print up

separate stationery and *insertion orders.* (See following for a sample insertion order.)

When you place ads, you then pay the discounted rate, saving up to 15% off the normal cost. Thus, an ad rate of $2,000 will actually cost you $1,700. And if you pay up front, many publications will give you a further 2% discount. Then, for ad space retailing at $2,000, you, through your agency, only pay $1,666.

$$.85 \ x \ \$2,000 = \$1700 \ x \ .98 = \$1,666$$

And, if you buy remnant space through your own agency, with a cash discount, the $2,000 ad only costs you $833.

$$\$2000 \ x \ .50 = \$1,000 \ x \ .85 = \$850 \ x \ .98 = \$833$$

This way, you can get two $2,000 ads for the price of one with $334 left over.

Sample insertion order

SAM ADVERTISING AGENCY
1800 Abercrombie Ave.
New York, NY 10019
212 555-5555

To: Music Deals Magazine
125 Fiftieth St.   Order No.: 100
Los Angeles, CA 90013   Date: 6/01/99

Please publish advertising for:
Smith Music Publishing Co.

Space to be ordered within one year from:
06/01/98 thru 05/30/99

Full Page   Once   July 10, 1998 issue
(Space)   (Times)   (Dates of insertion)

Position:
Right-hand page, Publishing Section

Copy:
See Attached

Rate: $1,000.00
Less agency commision on gross: (15%)$ 150.00
Less cash discount on net: (2%) $ 17.00
[xx] Total enclosed with order: $ 833.00

[ ] Please mail invoice
Accepted for publication by:_____
Date:_____

(Please sign and return to Sam Advertising Agency)

POINT-OF-PURCHASE

Point-of-purchase marketing (*POP*) creates impulse sales. POP materials are aimed at people who are ready to buy. They've come into a store with minds made up to buy product similar to yours, so you want your product visually positioned to attract their attention.

You can use special boxes with pop-up displays, racks, bins, posters, banners, streamers, stickers, balloons, pennants, window displays, etc. In-store play of your product is a very effective form of POP. Autograph signings and personal appearances by artists at retail outlets are perfect focal points for POP.

ADD-ON SALES/SPECIAL OFFERS

You can include package inserts with your product providing information about other product, perhaps offering discounts or samplers to those who write or phone. Names and addresses of people who respond go into your contact or customer database so you can regularly send them information about new product.

Record labels introducing new acts, or pushing back-catalog sales, might offer *two-fors* (buy one album, get a second free), discounts on additional purchases, free single with album purchase, or free T-shirts, concert tickets, or other items related to (and further promoting) the company. Prizes or other incentives can be given to dealers or distributors who move certain amounts of product.

CROSS-SELLING

Customers interested in one type of product are natural prospects for similar products. That's why compilation albums of various artists follow a generic theme (*Greatest Disco Hits, Romantic Movie Themes*, etc.). If you're promoting an established artist's new album, you might cross-sell his back catalog, or an "as told to" autobiography, or some other related product at the same time. Retailers can cross-sell an artist's records with concert tickets to his local performances.

SPECIALTY ADVERTISING/GIVEAWAYS

Advertising specialties can draw attention to a specific product or to your company in general. They're akin to institutional ads in that they're image builders and keep the name of your company or product before the public. However, like trade directory ads, they have the benefit of repeat advertising, since they're produced at a one-time cost, and recipients usually keep or use them for some period of time.

Specialty giveaways include items like calendars, desk-sets, pens, pencils, T-shirts, sweatshirts, jackets, caps, jewelry, rulers, paperweights, wall clocks, watches, cigarette lighters, scratch-pads, mugs, cups, playing cards, toys, ashtrays, bags, buttons, stickers, belt buckles, matchbooks, boxes of candy or other foodstuffs, key chains, and so on. Needless to say, your company name, address, phone/fax numbers, and logo are imprinted on each item.

The effectiveness of giveaways as a marketing tool depends on who you give them to and exactly what you choose to give away. Anything shoddy or off-color could do more harm than good. But goodwill can be created with items that are truly useful, interesting, novel, and of perceived value to the recipient.

Usually, specialty giveaways are targeted at business-related customers whose goodwill you need to further your success, such as deejays, program directors, retailers, buyers, booking agents, distributors, licensees, A&R personnel, producers, journalists, reviewers, etc. Specialty advertising should be coordinated with specific events, such as new product releases or holidays. They're particularly useful at trade shows, like MIDEM, SXSW, NAIRD, NARM, NMS, POPKOMM, etc.

Giveaways to consumers must be very selectively targeted in order to be worthwhile. They could be offered as premiums or incentives to buy product. For instance, album buyers could get coupons for sweatshirts or caps emblazoned with your artist's name and likeness, or your company logo.

When you (or one of your songwriters, acts, or product lines) achieve enough brand recognition, you can actually turn specialties into a separate profit center. Coca-Cola, Disney, and Warner Brothers sell all sorts of items imprinted with their names and logos, thus having the best of all worlds: they multiply their marketing reach, as consumers pay for the privilege to walk around with items advertising the companies selling them.

REMINDER ADVERTISING

Billboards/Signs/Banners/Parties/Miscellaneous Ideas

Your imagination can run wild with ideas for *reminder advertising*: skywriting, banners towed by airplanes, rent-a-pickets (people parading with signs touting your product or wearing A-frame sandwich boards), bumper stickers, signs plastered on sides or rear panels of buses and taxi cabs, placards posted in subway and commuter rail stations or inside buses, trains, and subways—even buskers performing where there's a lot of foot traffic. Some of these ideas require permits. Some are a total waste of money unless you're sure the people most likely to see them are really potential customers of your product.

Company sponsored parties, picnics, and barbecues are opportunities to gather by invitation potential customers and people who can help promote your product or your business generally. Not only can you solidify relationships, win friends and customers, you can focus attention on your product with performances by your acts, and by giving invitees a chance to rub shoulders with the "stars."

Publicity/public relations

Public relations (*PR*) is something you engage in anytime you deal with people outside your company. This includes attending conventions, making charitable donations, taking someone to lunch (networking) and, of course, publicity.

Publicity in print, as well as on radio and TV, gives you credibility and authority. It provides stature, believability, and reinforces identity. Best of all, it's free.

You can generate publicity through press releases, interviews, articles, feature stories, and reviews. It is more effective than paid advertising, because people read and watch news, feature stories, and reviews more often than they pay attention to ads.

However, you can't always control publicity. Since you don't pay media outlets to publicize your message, you can't dictate when it runs, how it's presented, or whether it will be accurate.

You can't censure bad publicity or reviews either. You can hire press agents and PR reps to fashion your publicity professionally and give it the widest possible media exposure. But, more often than not, you can generate publicity yourself.

Sometimes, the best tactics can be the least expensive; creativity can cut costs while stretching the impact of what you do. A publicity angle might be so unique or newsworthy that the national media picks up the story and spreads it far and wide.

To get publicity, you need something newsworthy to the particular audience you want to reach. The following ideas constitute newsworthy material.

PUBLICITY ANGLES

- *New offices*. An address change is always worth a mention in trade magazines. But you can develop it into a story warranting wider coverage if there's something special about the new premises, such as architectural features, location, history, or facilities.
- *Personnel changes*. Hiring staff is newsworthy. You can always get a brief trade magazine mention. But, again, you can expand coverage if there's more of a story. Give credentials of new staffers, detail what their roles will be, and say how they'll benefit your organization. Quote the CEO ("Joe's impressive track record in A&R and management brings a new dimension to our creative department"), and the hiree ("I'm very excited to be joining the talented team at this company and working with its quality songwriting roster.").
- *Signings*. Anytime you sign a writer, overseas licens-

ing deal, or major licensing agreement, you have a newsworthy item. Try to find an angle to enlarge upon the story so you can get more than a few lines. Detail the credentials of both parties to the signing and include quotes from the principals that build each other up.

- *Human interest*. Dash off a press release whenever something interesting is done by (or happens to) one of your writers, staffers, or executives (or their close family members). Newsworthy events include: marriages, births, deaths, serious illnesses, accidents, honors, awards, major tours, major TV or movie appearances, unusual hobbies, arrests(!), and oddball things—like having a pet rhino.
- *Opinion pieces*. Keep up with developments in the business. If you feel strongly about some trend or a recent action or statement by someone in the industry, write an *op-ed* piece or a letter to the editor to submit to the trades. Make sure what you have to say is forceful, well-written, and interesting. Don't worry about being provocative. Controversy at least generates publicity.
- *Something unusual about your product*. A rap version of one of Shakespeare's sonnets; a song that laid forgotten in a drawer for years before being found, recorded, and becoming a hit, etc.
- *Anecdotes*. How an artist got his first big break; what was in the mind of the writer when he wrote that big hit, etc. Anecdotal stories can be developed with enough human-interest angle to gain widespread coverage beyond the trades. Wire-services can pick up these stories from local media and scatter them around the country. And they don't necessarily have to be about big stars or hits to resonate.
- *Stage an event*. Conduct a talent search, an annual barbecue, a concert to benefit charity, a seminar, ribbon-cutting ceremony for new offices or studio, an album premier party, etc.
- *Hometown advantage*. Whenever you have a new release, blitz the artist's (and writer's) hometown media with press kits and sample product.
- *Timeliness and topicality*. Songs centered around elections, wars, deaths of famous people, notorious characters, or other big news events can be done as spoofs, elegies, tributes, and commentaries. This could be worthy of national or, at least regional, media attention.
- *Provide information*. Knowledge you take for granted about your business might be fascinating to laymen. You could write freelance articles about particular aspects of the business in which you weave your company and product as part of the story.
- *Sponsorships*. A small scholarship fund, award, trophy, benefit dinner, etc. can help your community and give you great public relations mileage.

- *Anniversaries*. Celebrate your company's anniversaries with press announcements, citing accomplishments since its inception; you can also issue sampler albums, throw parties, etc.

▼

The point is: Look for angles.

PRESS RELEASES

Sometimes newsworthiness is not always obvious, but looked at sideways, upside down, and inside out, you can usually find some hook that will interest editors. You have to tailor press releases to specific media. What's newsworthy to *Billboard* subscribers isn't necessarily interesting to people who read *Newsweek*. Once you've gotten an angle, you'll know the audience to target and whether it's of interest only to trade magazines, local newspapers, or significant enough to interest the general public via national media.

When you issue a press release, make sure you reach the right person, or your item may never see publication. What's the nature of your release? If it's of interest to readers of a metropolitan newspaper, should you send it to the features editor, or to the entertainment editor? If the item is slated for a trade magazine, should you send it to the news editor or the editor who covers your specific type of business or the product's musical genre?

Call the publication, find out the appropriate editor's name, and send your press release, press kit, picture, record, etc., directly to that person. (You don't need to speak to the editor personally at this point.) Send a brief cover letter with the publicity material. Don't try to pressure the editor into running the piece by offering to advertise or threatening not to.

You may follow up with a phone call a few days later and politely inquire if the material was received. Again, apply no pressure; don't ask if the piece will be run. Never ask for a copy of the printed article. The purpose of your polite, unobtrusive call is just to remind the editor that your information is available to fill up that glaring gap on page three in the coming edition. Editors have got to fill space. If your item is in fact newsworthy, they'll welcome and use it.

You can send a press release simultaneously to every publication you feel might run it. If your release is timely (announcing an event to take place on a certain date, for example), you should be aware of the publication's deadlines in order to have the item appear in time to do you the most good.

The release must be precise, concise, and well-written. Don't use superlatives (*best, greatest*, etc.), except when quoting someone who's making the claim. Eliminate all unessential words; keep the text punchy, make the story flow logically, and make it interesting to the readers of the particular publication you're targeting. Edit carefully so there are no typing, spelling, or punctuation errors.

Press releases follow a fairly standard format:
- Use white letter-sized bond.
- Double-space text.
- Margins: one inch on each side of the text, and two inches on the bottom.
- Top left of the page: your name, address, and phone number.
- Top right of the page: (full caps) *FOR IMMEDIATE RELEASE* (or *FOR RELEASE AFTER* [*whatever date*]).
- Center your headline (full caps, underlined). Keep it short, punchy, attention-grabbing, and related to the story that follows.
- Start the article with a dateline (e.g., New York, NY, January 5, 1999).
- The lead paragraph should contain the most essential part of the story.
- Subsequent paragraphs elaborate in less essential detail. Editors make cuts from the bottom of a story up. So get the essentials (who, what, when, where, how) in early, within the first couple of paragraphs.
- One page is best, but if you need additional pages, type "- MORE -" at the bottom center of the page.
- Type "[*headline*] page [*number*]" at the top left hand of each succeeding page.
- At the end of the story, center the text and type: "- END -", or "###."

Sample press release cover letter

SMITH MUSIC PUBLISHING CO.
1800 Abercrombie Ave.
New York, NY 10019
212 555-5555

Ms. Jane Doe
News Editor
Music Deals Magazine
125 Fiftieth Street
Hollywood, CA 90013

June 5, 1999

Dear Ms. Doe:

Enclosed please find information, concerning new licensing agreements for Smith Music Publishing, that we trust will be of interest to your readers.

Please call if you need further details.

Thanks.

Yours sincerely,

Sammy Smith
President
Smith Music Publ'g Co.

Sample press release

SMITH MUSIC PUBLISHING CO.
1800 Abercrombie Ave.
New York, NY 10019
212 555-5555

CONTACT: SAMMY SMITH   FOR IMMEDIATE RELEASE

SMITH PACTS NEW EURO DEALS

New York, 1 June 1999 - Smith Music has concluded new subpublishing agreements with Bulldog Music, Ltd. for the United Kingdom and Republic of Ireland, and with Great Gouda Music BV for the Netherlands, Belgium, and Luxembourg.

Smith Music recently scored three Top 20 hits in the U.S. with "I Love You" (written by John Johnson and recorded by The Crumbs), "You Love Me" (written by Joan Jones and recorded by The Blots), and "Everybody Loves Everybody" (written by Adam Mada and recorded by Levon Novel). The two-year-old company is based in New York.

Smith Music's president, Samuel A. Smith, said, "We talked with several companies in England and Holland before deciding to go with Bulldog and Great Gouda. We wanted to make sure we had the best possible representatives for our catalog in these important territories. I am certain that Nigel Wretch of Bulldog and Frans de Hook of Great Gouda will do outstanding jobs for us."

- MORE -

SMITH PACTS NEW EURO DEALS (Cont'd)   Page 2

Nigel Wretch, Managing Director of Bulldog, noted, "We've been much impressed with Smith Music's success Stateside, and we're tremendously keen to play a part in their continued growth."

Great Gouda's Frans de Hook added, "Sam Smith has a great ear for what today's market wants. We consider it a coup to represent his company, and we're certain of a long, mutually profitable relationship."

Smith concluded the deal with Bulldog during a recent trip to London. Discussions with Great Gouda were initiated at Midem last January, and the agreement was finalized in early May. Both agreements take effect June 1.

- END -

PITCH LETTERS

Instead of providing all the details a press release covers, *pitch letters* are used to motivate editors, station news directors, and talk-show producers to set up interviews or to send reporters to cover whatever it is you're promoting. A pitch letter should make the recipient want to know more and to feel your suggestion for coverage is indeed newsworthy.

Address the pitch letter personally to the editor, program director, news director, or talk-show producer. Get to the point, present the angle of the story. Include any supporting information, such as reviews, clippings, album copies, photos, bios, press kits—anything that builds the case for further coverage. You can also make pitches by telephone and then follow up with a letter and relevant information.

You can often gain more publicity coverage through pitch letters than you can with a press release, but you'll have less control over what is printed or said, since you can't dictate what a reporter writes or an interviewer asks. Still, since the story is exclusively developed by the publication or station, they feel more proprietorship. They are inclined to give your story rather more coverage than if they had been just one of many media outlets regurgitating your press release.

Once you get local coverage, expand it to regional level by sending press releases or pitch letters with locally generated clippings to media in other areas. Then, attack the national media, using regional and local clippings to show the growing interest in your topic. (Don't deluge recipients with too many clippings, just enough to whet appetites and make your point.)

PRESS KITS

Press kits usually include biographies, clippings, news releases, and photos. Many also include sample product and videos. You should have press kits for all your acts, writers, producers, and for your company as well. Slip the contents into glossy folders with your logo imprinted on the cover.

The biography should contain only factual information (not hype), presenting background information that an editor or reporter can use to structure an interview or flesh out a story. Compact the information into two single-spaced pages, and make it an interesting read, not a dry resume.

PHOTOGRAPHS

Pictures are an asset when seeking publicity coverage. Although they won't always be used, you'll get more space when they are, and your item will more likely be noticed and read. If Sammy Smith's news release (above) was accompanied by a photo of himself,

Nigel, and Frans uncorking a celebratory bottle of champagne, people would undoubtedly pause, look, then read the caption to see what it was all about, and Sammy's story about his new subpublishing deals would gain a wider audience.

Photos for press releases should be high contrast, black and white. They must be professional quality, sized 8x10 or 5x7. On the back of each photo, identify the subjects lightly in pencil or affix a typed caption. Use cardboard backing when you mail the photos with your press releases or pitch letters.

NETWORKING

Join trade associations; attend trade shows, seminars, meetings, and conventions; and take people to lunch. Make yourself known, and get to know as many key players in the business as you can. This public relations exercise raises your identity level with the added benefit of keeping you abreast of market and technological changes and what your competitors are doing. It also stimulates ideas for marketing strategies, product development and acquisitions, and widens your circle of useful contacts for future sources of information, talent, strategic alliances, etc.

NEWSLETTERS

Produce newsletters featuring articles about your company, songwriters, artists, and new releases. Mail them to your contact list. If your newsletters are interesting enough and professionally produced, you might also distribute them in batches for retail outlets to rack as freebies alongside regional music-oriented publications and magazines like *Rolling Stone*.

800/900 NUMBERS

Recorded messages at the end of an 800 number can be used with great effect to promote new product and key songwriters, producers, or artists. Callers can hear a tantalizing slice of a new song or record release and a sales pitch. You can also publicize tour information and other current activities of your songwriters, producers, and artists.

Your 800 number can be listed on album covers or inserts, in your company's newsletter, as well as in classified or display ads in fanzines, etc., with invitations to call for special offers or news. You might have an artist record the message for added impact.

Artists who have established a large enough fan base can even set up an additional profit center with a 900 number. Callers actually pay each time they dial the 900 number to hear recorded greetings from the artist and news about upcoming product and tours. The phone company collects the charges, deducts a percentage, and remits the balance to you.

STRATEGIC ALLIANCES

Working with other companies leverages marketing expenditures and gives your message further reach than you can achieve on your own. Potential alliance partners can come from related companies, even competitors in some instances. You can also team with nonmusic companies whose product is targeted at the same market as yours.

Strategic partners should ensure both parties profit equitably and proportionally to their respective contributions, and that both understand the target market and goals of the joint project undertaken. The partners must share ethical standards, because one party's failures or misdeeds can reflect badly on the other's.

Examples of strategic alliances:
- *Cooperative ads (co-ops).* Two or more companies share the costs of an ad or mailing that features their respective product equally. A common example is a newspaper ad by a local record store featuring new album releases from certain labels. Co-ops are also done by major companies in other industries; you might, for instance, see a soft drink company join with a fast-food chain in a media blitz.
- *Customer referrals.* Competitors or companies selling other products to your target market have lists of customers that could be potential customers for your product as well. Many of these companies will rent you their mailing lists. And, as you build your own customer database, you'll find your list a valuable commodity as an extra profit center that you can rent to competitors or companies in other fields. You can also form strategic alliances to swap mailing lists.
- *Distribution.* For indie record labels, a primary goal is to make alliances with regional distributors (or one national distributor) to get product into stores. But, if you're in the embryonic stage, you might not yet have national distribution firmed up. You might, then, distribute your product in your own region, and form alliances with indies based in other regions: You agree to distribute their product in your area, and they handle your product in their territories.
- *Licenses.* Licensing extends the reach of your product to areas you could never effectively cover yourself. Particular examples include licensing print rights to sheet music distributors and overseas rights to subpublishers.
- *Bundling.* This is when two or more companies join their respective products together into one package, in order to enhance the perceived benefits for the customer. Bundling can be effective in many

ways if you're operating an in-house record label. You could work with other labels to offer two-fors, or you could work with nonrelated companies, such as a shirt manufacturer, to give away your product as a premium to customers; or vice versa. Another example of bundling is when two established artists plug into each other's fan base by recording a duet.

Until you have a substantial back-catalog or a range of services that allows you to cross-sell your products at the same marketing cost, it may make very good sense to arrange to sell other companies' products as add-ons to your product line. After all, a direct-mail shot costs the same whether you're offering one album or ten. And if the recipient isn't interested in your product, you might as well profit from selling someone else's. That sale helps pay for your marketing campaign, and it lands you proven prospects for further propositions to convert into paying customers.

For instance, a couple of small, indie publishers might agree to bundle songs and split songplugging targets. If one of the publishers gets the other's song cut, he receives a percentage of the mechanical royalty income for a specified period of time.

- **Sponsors.** Many corporate giants seek the benefits of attaching "Star Power" to their products. Thus, companies like Pepsi-Cola, Nike, and Miller Beer contribute to tours and concerts in return for high profile association with particular artists. The major sponsorships come only when an artist has reached a certain level. But don't overlook smaller companies who might see value in tapping into an emerging artist's growing fan base on a local or regional basis.

CHAPTER 18

Company Management

▼

*Business discipline is
essential for creative success.*

How do some publishers consistently come up with
hit after hit, while others languish in mediocrity or
crash in flames after just one or two hits? What
anoints the blessed? God-given talent? Luck?

Talent and luck certainly help, but they are not
enough. Many talented people never make it; and
luck doesn't last forever. While there is no magic formula, *sustained* success is a result of vision, strong
leadership, and intelligent management. Companies
that consistently roll out hits seem to be led by people with similar characteristics.

1. Management is enthusiastic and obsessive about its
   product. New signings, songs, and releases are primary topics of conversation, not petty office politics.
2. Management keeps its ears to the ground, "listening to customers." They are in tune with contemporary tastes and popular culture, visiting clubs,
   attending concerts, networking with peers, retailers, deejays, and others.
3. Management constantly makes benchmark comparisons with competitors. Every signing, marketing campaign, licensing deal, and management
   decision is measured against what the most successful companies in the industry are doing. The
   standard is to be "better than," not "as good as."
4. Management disciplines are applied to product
   creation. While creativity is encouraged and given
   free rein, the process is not allowed to degenerate
   into time- and money-wasting chaos.
5. Strong leadership is applied to every step of the
   publishing process. The highest standards are demanded from those accountable for acquisition,

product creation, catalog management, marketing,
copyright administration, financial management,
and personnel management. Just one weak link
can cause the chain of success to break.

6. Intelligent leadership knows success is a never-
   ending challenge. You can never relax. The financial and psychological rewards of sustained success
   are tremendous, but they stop coming when you
   step off the treadmill.

The publisher's challenge

Strong management is essential to maximize productivity and efficiency so that music publishers can generate the profits necessary for creative elements to
flourish. The challenge is to reconcile artistically created product with commercial considerations. Management disciplines must be used to channel creative
people towards crafting commercially oriented music.
Likewise, management disciplines must be imposed
on methods used to bring music into the marketplace.

Some of the following management techniques
used by large publishing companies can be tailored
to any size operation to bring a disciplined approach
to a creative environment.

Management by objectives (MBO)

Whether you're striving to manage a demo session or
a world war, it is unlikely you'll succeed unless you
have a clear idea of what you're trying to achieve.
Every action (or lack of action) has a consequence.
The trick is to ensure that every action has an *intended*
consequence, a simply understood and attainable
objective. Leave nothing to chance. This is the essence
of *managing by objectives.*

Management and subordinates should together set goals for employees to meet within a given period of time. Management then meets with employees at regular intervals during that time frame in order to assess progress towards the objectives. At the end of the period they meet again to evaluate how well the tasks were done.

Effective means of managing by objectives include weekly staff meetings and monthly activity reports, as discussed below. Minuted meetings and reports document goals and tabulate progress in writing. End results can thus be measured so that there is no room for misinterpreting what was expected versus what was actually achieved.

MEETINGS

It is important to know the difference between meetings and sessions. Meetings have set agendas to accomplish specific purposes; they're scheduled to start and stop at certain times; they're restrictive in scope, and must be run with discipline. Sessions, on the other hand, are designed for open, creative, and far-ranging debate in order to solve problems, identify opportunities, clear the air, inform, and educate.

Meetings are a pain for some people, but they are as unavoidable as they are essential to good management. They become a pain when improperly conducted, ramble on unfocused, and produce no discernible results. But, when held for a specific purpose, and kept to a rigid format, meetings can be energizing and provide the channels of communication, information, and feedback necessary for a well-run company.

Rules for conducting successful meetings:
- Call meetings only when necessary.
- Line up allies for support and agree on a strategy in advance.
- Limit participation to people whose attendance is absolutely necessary.
- Provide an agenda and any other information or materials needed for attendees to prepare themselves.
- Structure the agenda to address issues by order of importance. If controversial issues are slated, however, schedule less contentious topics first so they can be settled and gotten out of the way.
- Drill participants to arrive promptly and keep to the points at hand.
- Don't allow meetings to turn into "sessions." Focus on the agenda.
- Schedule morning meetings, never immediately after lunch, when people may be somewhat sluggish.
- If meetings run more than two hours, offer refreshments, or schedule a break or a working lunch.

- Set a stop time and enforce it.
- Appoint someone to take minutes. There should be a clear record of all decisions, assignments, and objectives arising from the meeting.

WEEKLY STAFF MEETINGS

When a company has only a handful of people, formal staff meetings may seem pretentious. Everyone works side-by-side every day, so there's not much to discuss that hasn't already been bandied back-and-forth informally. Still, there should be periodic meetings which are minuted. Minutes serve to set objectives in stone so that individuals are accountable for moving the company forward. As the company adds personnel, and its affairs become more complex, weekly staff meetings become a major tool for keeping operations focused.
- In order to reap benefits, staff meetings should be held with scheduled regularity.
- Participants should not be allowed to skip meetings, nor should management allow meetings to be postponed or rescheduled, except in extraordinary circumstances. Hold everyone's feet to the fire to ensure accountability.
- All management personnel should attend weekly staff meetings chaired by their respective department heads. The purpose is to coordinate departmental activities and ensure that the company functions smoothly.

  Weekly management meetings. All department heads should attend a weekly management meeting chaired by the CEO. The management meeting's purpose is to coordinate activities between departments and keep the company on course.

  Weekly professional staff meetings. All professional managers (songpluggers) should attend a weekly professional staff meeting chaired by the creative director. The meeting's purpose is to apply management discipline to creative development, product acquisition, and catalog exploitation.

  Weekly administrative staff meetings. All administrative personnel should attend an administration staff meeting each week, chaired by the business affairs manager. The meeting's purpose is to review progress on licensing, registration, collections, contracts, catalog documentation, and liaison with licensees, rights societies, accounts department, creative department, etc.
- Each participant must come fully prepared to discuss his or her activities of the previous week and to provide a personal agenda for the coming week.
- Keep the length of weekly staff meetings fairly consistent so participants can schedule the rest of their day without conflict.
- Schedule weekly meetings for Mondays, if possible,

so that participants can set objectives for the week ahead and plan activities accordingly.

- Minutes of weekly meetings should be transcribed and circulated to all participants within 24 hours. The minutes serve as a written plan of action for the coming week.

Weekly staff meeting agenda:

1. Review minutes from the previous week's meeting for follow-up.
   - ✔ Have all objectives been reached?
   - ✔ What remains to be done?
   - ✔ Have problems arisen that need solving?
   - ✔ What follow-up actions should be taken, and by whom?
2. Focus on information gathered by the participants since the last meeting regarding topics relevant to the department's function (e.g., chart activity, covers status, ancillary activities [tours, concerts, film, radio, TV productions, etc.], sales figures, international activity, etc.).
3. Discuss status of projects in development, such as artists or writers in the studio, marketing campaigns, release schedules, etc.
4. Review potential acquisitions, including status of negotiations, options, and extensions on prospective and current signings.
5. Target opportunities to pursue. (For instance, review the list of A&R contacts needing songs to record, determine which songs best match casting requirements, and make songplugging assignments.)
6. Listen to new product and make recommendations. A&R staff, for example, might review finished tracks and make decisions whether to approve mixes or test pressings, etc. Marketing staff might review finished product and discuss promotional ideas.
7. Discuss personnel, management, or operational problems.
8. Open the floor for discussion of any other business relevant to the participants' functions not covered earlier.

MONTHLY ACTIVITY REPORTS

At the end of each month, all management staff should prepare reports summarizing their activities of the month just ending and outlining activities and goals for the month ahead. Staff should review their activity reports one-on-one with their immediate supervisor to determine how well goals were met during the previous month and how best to set and achieve goals for the month ahead.

Activity reports serve several management purposes:

- Informs management of progress and flags problems needing executive direction.
- Holds staff accountable for their activities—or lack of activities.
- Motivates staff to set their own goals and prioritize tasks to be accomplished.
- Measures job performance in a fashion not left open to debate so that staff can readily identify areas of weakness and take initiative for corrective action.
- Like minutes of weekly staff meetings, which specify weekly objectives, an activity report provides an action blueprint for the coming month. During the course of the month, objectives enumerated in the report help individuals measure their progress and warns them when performance is slipping.

Education and information

Management should act as *mentors* to employees. Management's role is to advise, guide, educate, and motivate. Treat employees as protégés and give them all the tools necessary to do their jobs effectively.

One of the most important tools is information. Key employees should know the financial ramifications their decisions and actions can have on the company. Equip them to apply intelligent analysis to every idea, project, and acquisition before committing time and money.

- Educate staff on the economics of publishing. For example: exactly how many record sales does it take to earn a professional manager's salary, pay for a demo session, recoup an advance? How many sales are needed to justify a promotional campaign, travel to MIDEM, produce a video?
- Professional managers should know the royalty breakdown of every copyright for which they have promotional responsibility and the effects of splits, cut-ins, and rates on the bottom line.
- Encourage awareness of new technologies for exploitation opportunities, as well as creative thinking about new promotional ideas in existing media.
- Creative staff should review selected new chart entries each week in order to keep abreast of new artists and trends, identify prospective acquisitions, and identify new targets for exploitation.
- Maintain an updated contact database with applicable reference notes for catalog exploitation, media promotion, and licensing opportunities.
- Conduct daily telephone surveys using the contact database to uncover exploitation opportunities.
- Study domestic and international trade magazines for exploitation targets, licensing opportunities, and acquisition sources for new product.

MANAGEMENT INFORMATION SYSTEMS (MIS)

Management and key employees need to be fully informed about everything relating to the company's activities. While monthly activity reports and weekly staff meetings serve to keep management informed of the status of various projects, much of the information is historic; certain problems may fester and compound before management becomes aware of them and can take action.

The purpose of a functioning MIS is to make information available in real time. Thus data is processed as events occur (sales, airplay adds, licenses and contracts issued, manufacturing orders placed, payments made, orders shipped, recording sessions scheduled, etc.). Every department should be linked to a central MIS as well as having its own internal MIS.

Virtually every department has operating functions that management needs to track in real time. Management Information Systems give managers instant access to updated information that is vital for decisions and actions related to virtually all functions of a business, including finance, marketing, sales, R&D, purchasing, shipping, personnel.

While many of these operational details can be entered into a computer database for instant retrieval in report-form as needed, others are less routine and require more than a few keystrokes. Examples include contract proposals and negotiating points exchanged between the company and artists, writers, producers, licensees, or licensors; proposals to and from consultants; and general correspondence covering all the company's concerns, great and small.

As a company grows, the need for an MIS becomes more acute, and the system itself requires more sophistication. Indeed, large companies often appoint a technically-oriented systems manager to oversee the collection and distribution of information. But even small start-ups need some effective MIS to function efficiently.

There are a variety of off-the-shelf MIS software programs, but as you grow, you may need your own programs written to accommodate specific MIS needs. You may consider linking each department's PC to a central mainframe (such a linked network is called *LAN*), so that each manager can access information as needed. But there must also be controls to prevent unauthorized input of data, because incorrect entries can skewer the accuracy of data you must rely on for running the business.

MANUALLY MAINTAINED INFORMATION SYSTEMS

Not every MIS has to be computer-generated. There are several, manually maintained types of records that provide vital information to management and staff alike.

Chron files

To enable senior management to track operational matters in real time, every department should maintain a *chron file* in which copies of each employee's correspondence are chronologically filed. Each department head should read through his or her department's file daily, and scan the day files of other departments at least monthly (if not more often), in order to be thoroughly familiar with all facets of the company's progress, lack of progress, problems, and potential problems.

Reading other people's correspondence in this manner is a valid management technique, not a violation of privacy. No correspondence related to the company should be considered "personal." No one should ever send a letter to someone outside the company that would be embarrassing for colleagues to read. Chron files are to inform management of the status of various activities and to stimulate suggestions, solutions, and ideas.

Licensing register

There should be a centrally kept book, ledger, or log, in which all new record releases are entered as new mechanical license requests come in. Employees should reference the book regularly to be aware of new releases. Professional managers can think through promotional ideas and notify writers involved when their songs are recorded. The register should also include details of newly issued synchronization, transcription, print, and other types of licenses.

Professional managers would be embarrassed to learn about a cover after the writer finds out about it. Professional managers are supposed to be looking after the songs, and, therefore, the first to know.

Who's Looking register

Keep a centrally located *Who's Looking* register, ledger, or blackboard. Whenever an employee learns of an artist looking for songs, enter the artist's name with details of types of songs needed and whom to contact.

The Who's Looking Register should get everyone thinking about what songs in the catalog might be suitable for artists listed; it should spark casting ideas. It might be best to assign one professional manager to each artist listed and funnel all submissions through that person.

TITLE: _____ DATE: _____

WRITER: (1)_____ SHARE: _____%
ADDRESS:_____ S.S. NO: _____
☐ contract sent/date: _____ ASCAP/BMI/SESAC
☐ returned signed/date: _____ ADVANCE: $ _____

WRITER: (2)_____ SHARE: _____%
ADDRESS:_____ S.S. NO: _____
☐ contract sent/date: _____ ASCAP/BMI/SESAC
☐ returned signed/date: _____ ADVANCE: $ _____

WRITER: (3)_____ SHARE: _____%
ADDRESS:_____ S.S. NO: _____
☐ contract sent/date: _____ ASCAP/BMI/SESAC
☐ returned signed/date: _____ ADVANCE: $ _____

CO-PUBLISHER (1) _____ SHARE: _____%
ADDRESS:_____ I.D. NO: _____
☐ contract sent/date: _____ ASCAP/BMI/SESAC
☐ returned signed/date: _____ ADVANCE: $ _____

CO-PUBLISHER (2) _____ SHARE: _____%
ADDRESS:_____ I.D. NO: _____
☐ contract sent/date: _____ ASCAP/BMI/SESAC
☐ returned signed/date: _____ ADVANCE: $ _____

CO-PUBLISHER (3) _____ SHARE: _____%
ADDRESS:_____ I.D. NO: _____
☐ contract sent/date: _____ ASCAP/BMI/SESAC
☐ returned signed/date: _____ ADVANCE: $ _____

☐ ISWC # applied for   date: _____
☐ ISWC #: _____
☐ master file opened   date: _____
☐ accounts dept. notified   date: _____
☐ signed contracts filed   date: _____
☐ lead sheet ordered   date: _____
☐ lead sheet filed   date: _____
☐ demo filed   date: _____
☐ copyright registered   date: _____
☐ copyright certificate filed   date: _____
☐ perf. right clearance sent   date: _____
☐ perf. right cleared   date: _____
☐ notify foreign licensees   date: _____
☐ print licensee notified   date: _____
☐ mechanical license sent   date: _____
☐ cue sheet filed   date: _____
Special Instructions: _____
_____

A *mechanical license worksheet* is also needed if you do your own licensing. It may also serve as a form of transmittal to a mechanical-right licensing agent, such as the Harry Fox Agency, in order to instruct the agent how to issue a license on your behalf.

Title: _____ ISWC # _____

Writer(s): _____

Publisher (1) _____ Share _____ %

Publisher (2) _____ Share _____ %

Publisher (3) _____ Share _____ %

Publisher (4) _____ Share _____ %

Issue a mechanical license as follows:

Record Company: _____

Address: _____

Artist:: _____

Album Title: _____

Release Date: _____ Record No: _____ Rate: _____

Configuration:

[ ] CD   [ ] CD Single   [ ] Cassette   [ ] Cassette Single

[ ] 45   [ ] 33 Single   [ ] 33 LP   [ ] DAT   [ ] _____

ADMINISTRATIVE SYSTEMS

Copyright administration is no less vital than exploitation. Some creative people tend to treat paperwork as an afterthought, or even a nuisance to be avoided. This can lead to mislaid bits of paper, forgotten registrations, and clerical errors and omissions that result in financial loss, or even loss of copyright.

The person responsible for administration is usually called the administrator, copyright manager, or business affairs director. This person must ride herd on creative staff and songwriters to ensure they provide all copyright and contract details in a timely and accurate manner. There must be an MIS system linking the creative department with administration, accounts, and business affairs to assist with the flow of contracts, licenses, royalty breakdowns, and copyright details.

Administration needs complete details of all new works for file opening, database entry, procurement of lead sheets, and to make relevant registrations and notifications to the Library of Congress, licensees, and performing- and mechanical-right societies. Accounts need details of songwriter and co-publisher shares for royalty accounting, and business affairs require deal summaries and royalty information in order to draft contracts and licenses.

A shared MIS between departments should be in place to ensure that all administrative functions are completed for each work, that there are clear channels for follow-through, that all transactions are documented and completed, that contracts are returned signed, and that all registrations and notifications are confirmed, etc.

Copyright administration involves many routine procedures that must be followed for each song, license, and contract. The simplest method of controlling the flow of information and ensuring each administrative step is completed is to devise check lists or worksheets for each new title. The administrative process usually begins with professional managers filling out a worksheet, then passing copies to administration, accounts, and business affairs.

The following sample worksheet serves as a model from which to tailor your own. It also demonstrates the many administrative steps necessary for each copyright.

Management games

Management games are useful for honing management skills and negotiating strategies with mock scenarios or hypothetical business models. A management game is both a training exercise and a method to shape a desired management style.

Participants can tackle a range of issues from problem solving to opportunity assessment, and they can learn from mistakes without the real world costs of making wrong decisions. Management games can also be played by dividing participants into adversarial teams representing two sides of a contract negotiation or conflict resolution. It often helps to have the game presided over by an outside consultant who brings special expertise to the subject and impartial judgment about the outcome.

Catalog and roster reporting

It is essential to communicate regularly with songwriters, co-publishers, managers, and licensors to let them know what's going on with their product. No news, in this business, is not good news.

Creative people need motivation in order to do their job well, and since your product's quality hinges on how well they do their job, you must reassure them that their product doesn't simply disappear into a black hole once it is in your hands.

- Make each professional manager accountable for a specific segment of the songwriter roster or catalog.
- Each month, professional managers must write a memorandum, note, or letter to the owners or creators of the product for which they're accountable, summarizing activity during the previous month regarding airplay, covers, plugging attempts, chart positions, reviews, clippings, etc. Include promotional objectives planned for the month ahead.

These monthly communiqués help maintain good relations with the product creators, and they document activities to show the product has been conscientiously promoted. In addition, these reports help professional managers formulate objectives and keep track of commitments. Just knowing that a report must be written serves to spur action so that there is actually something to report.

EXTERNAL SERVICING

Branch offices, overseas affiliates, print distributors, subpublishers, and other catalog licensees should automatically be serviced with details of new titles, lead sheets, copies of new demos and product releases, press kits, and all related promotional items.

External servicing should be centrally coordinated to ensure there is no duplication of effort. There must be clear channels for follow-through to ensure all transactions are documented and completed.

There should be close and regular communications with international licensees. When your songs are released in your territory, encourage overseas licensees to secure record releases from local record companies in their territories and to coordinate promotional efforts with local record companies. Relevant promotional aids and information should be sent to licensees to facilitate their activities.

Actively encourage international licensees to obtain local recordings of new, unrecorded songs, and to get cover recordings on local acts. Seek information from licensees about local acts needing material for which your writers can specifically "write to order."

Creative management control

The onus is on the professional or creative division to increase annual net turnover. This requires professional staff to possess two fundamental qualifications:
1. The ability to recognize and acquire songs, writers, and catalogs with clear commercial potential.
2. The ability to market songs to the right targets at the right time.

These qualifications are not mutually exclusive; neither is much use without the other. However, the matching of these two abilities results in expertise that benefits the company in the short term (increasing net turnover) and in the long term (increasing catalog net worth/company value).

Most professional managers understand creative psychology, since they tend to come from the ranks of songwriters, musicians, producers, etc. Their challenge is to channel creative forces to produce commercial product and to maintain a creative environment while operating on sound business principles. Thus, senior management must see that creative staff are knowledgeably equipped with the facts of business life and can function within the budgets and systems devised by the company.

CATALOG AND ROSTER MANAGEMENT

- Assign each professional manager responsibility for creative control over specific segments of the songwriter roster or catalog.
- Professional managers must maintain relationships of mutual trust and respect with their respective songwriters.
- Professional managers should help their writers define and achieve career goals.
- Creative personnel should be able to conceptualize projects, guide writers to specific targets, and alert them to new trends that might stimulate ideas.
- Creative control entails working with writers to improve commerciality of their craft. Writers should realize that a "good 'B' side" or "album cut" is merely an excuse for product that doesn't quite make it. Professional managers must work with writers to refine lyrics, storylines, and melodic structure to ensure songs are reworked to 'A' side standards before demo sessions are authorized.
- Creative management includes tracking budgetary and quality control of demo sessions.
- Professional managers should make performance reviews of newly signed writers each month. Assessments of more established writers should be done quarterly. Every songwriter's performance should be reviewed on the following merits:

- ✔ Commerciality of material
- ✔ Frequency of submitted material
- ✔ Demo expenditures vis à vis quantity and quality of songs demoed
- ✔ Financial progress (sales, recoupment, demo/promo costs, etc.)
- ✔ Nature of promotional activity generated and subsequent results
- ✔ Compatibility between professional manager and writer
- ✔ Effectiveness of professional manager and writer relationship
- ✔ Is writer being guided in the right direction?
- ✔ Should writer be reassigned to another professional manager?
- ✔ New marketing tactics for consideration

- Creative managers must ensure all demos are cataloged and filed in the tape vaults. Absent a full-time librarian, one creative staff member should assume the important role of librarian. A librarian's duties include tape duplication, editing, supplies, equipment maintenance, mailing, filing, and cataloging and indexing all demos, lead sheets, printed editions, and recorded releases.

- The creative department must maintain a formal liaison with the administration, accounts, and business affairs departments to ensure copyright and contractual details of all new works are reported. Professional managers must liaise between songwriters and administration/business affairs to assist with inquiries, procure contractual signatures, obtain lyrics for lead sheets, etc.

General personnel management

Affordable computer technology offers administrative efficiency and scope for expansion without the attendant labor and social costs that were required just a few years ago. Savings on administrative costs, therefore, can be put to more productive use in development, acquisitions, and promotion.

Your company should be a streamlined operation with proper tools to accomplish the tasks at hand. A successful publishing operation should be structured as a unified, innovative company, from top to bottom, in its relations between management, owners, and staff.

Under-occupied staff are inevitably demoralized. In turn, this affects the staff that *is* being utilized properly. It is therefore more efficient to hire a lean staff with competitive salaries and/or performance benefits.

Staff turnover is costly in recruiting, training, acclimatization, and morale. Provide performance-based incentives that bond employees to the company. Profit centers might be set up for various departments (creative, administration, etc.) that allow key employees scope to feel that it is their company too, without diluting owners' equity. An innovative approach is needed to allow each employee to progress at his or her own chosen pace within the company.

MAKE SURE PIECES OF THE PUZZLE FIT

There's fallacy in the conventional wisdom that the best performers in a company ultimately deserve promotion to senior management, with fancy titles, perks, and high salaries. In reality, management and operational functions require different attributes. The famed Peter Principle states that people rise to their level of incompetence. Thus, a great producer may be unable to handle administrative chores or work within the management systems required of an A&R director. Likewise, a brilliant promotion man may completely botch the responsibilities of marketing director.

This is not to say promotion men can't make good marketing directors, or songpluggers can't make good publishing execs. In fact, senior executives aren't born; they all start somewhere lower on the ladder. But it does mean careful thought and thorough testing should go into any role changes. Before you "reward" a key-employee with senior management status, make sure you don't lose an effective performer while gaining an incompetent manager. (And never promote a key-employee until you've hired a suitable replacement for his old job.)

Still, top performers expect and deserve recognition. To ensure they remain happily motivated doing what they do best, you must be fair and provide incentives that reward them in proportion to their contributions. If that means a songplugger ultimately earns more than the creative director, or a creative director makes more than the CEO, so be it. The key is to keep what works working. If it seems only senior mangers reap the rewards of a company's success, then key-employees will naturally push for promotion to senior management; and, if they're not promoted or otherwise fairly compensated, they'll cease to perform or jump ship.

Hiring managers and key-employees

ESSENTIAL POSTS TO FILL

There are four categories of employees:
1. directors
2. management
3. key-employees
4. nonkey-employees

Directors are appointed by shareholders or company owners. They have legal responsibilities and are directly accountable to the shareholders. Although senior managers may also hold directorships, there are distinctions between the functions. Directors do not actively manage the company's operations. Instead, they collectively establish company policy, oversee *how* the company is run, and decide whether and when to pay dividends. Actual day-to-day management is the responsibility of senior managers (company officers), who are appointed by the directors.

Senior management is in the hands of company officers: chief executive officer (CEO) or president, chief operating officer (COO) or executive vice president, chief financial officer (CFO) or vice president, and so on. Officers are appointed by and are responsible to the directors. They're entrusted with organizing the company, strategic planning and tactical decisions, and hiring, motivating, guiding, and controlling performance of personnel so that the company meets its objectives.

Key-employees are appointed by and accountable to senior management. Though they don't have the authority to make major decisions, their advice and input may be crucial to decisions made by management. The difference between key-employees and nonkey-employees is that the first have talents and skills that are crucial to management's success and are not easily replaced. Examples include a creative director with a gift for spotting talent, or a songplugger whose flair and contacts are unique.

Nonkey-employees, on the other hand, while essential for operational functions, have less unique talents or skills. Secretaries and bookkeepers, for instance, are examples of nonkey-employees who can readily be found on the open job market, whereas it would take a more discriminatory search to find such key-employees as recording mixers and songpluggers.

QUALIFYING CANDIDATES FOR YOUR TEAM

Before you attempt to attract senior managers and key-employees, write out detailed job descriptions for each post you need to fill and include the qualifications each successful candidate must possess. Go beyond experience to include personal traits when listing required qualifications.

For instance, each senior manager should have energy, flexibility, dedication, perseverance, creativity, organization, dependability, and youthful enthusiasm tempered by mature analytical ability. They should be sober, honest, healthy, decisive, dynamic, literate, articulate, ambitious, self-motivated, and

proactive. They must be able to motivate and manage people, and they must be leaders but must also work well as team players.

Don't hide the above criteria from your candidates. Let them know this is what you expect and that they'll be tested before being asked to join the team. It is difficult for anyone to meet all these qualifications all of the time, but the tests you'll put them through in the interview sessions will eliminate most of those who can't measure up. And if some manage to fool you in the initial interview, they'll tend to reveal their flaws during the more arduous follow-up panel interview, discussed below.

MAJOR PUBLISHING EXECUTIVE JOB DESCRIPTION

Make job descriptions very definitive, including levels of responsibilities and how you expect various positions to interact with each of the others. The job description below is one that might be written to define the qualities and credentials looked for by an entertainment company seeking someone to run its newly-created music publishing division.

Vice President, Music Publishing
Job Description and Qualifications

The successful candidate will report to the CEO. He or she will be responsible for structuring the music publishing division and hiring qualified personnel to fill the following positions, all of whom will report directly to him/her: (1) Creative Director, (2) Copyright Administrator, (3) Assistant Administrator, (4) Songplugger, (5) Secretary/Librarian. He or she will:

- write job descriptions and qualifications criteria for the above positions, set salaries and benefits, set a timeline for filling each post, and personally recruit the personnel;
- monitor and conduct ongoing management evaluations of publishing personnel and be responsible for motivating and managing staff to surpass divisional objectives;
- be 90% responsible for writing the music publishing section of the company's business plan and 90% responsible for presenting that portion of the plan to investors and lending institutions;
- with the finance director, devise pro forma budgets for the division and be accountable for meeting projections within expenditures;
- with the marketing and sales directors, make sales forecasts for the division;
- with the marketing director, make marketing analyses, identify market opportunities, and devise marketing campaigns to promote the music publishing division generally, and writers, copyrights, and individual projects specifically;

- be responsible for building the publishing catalog through acquisitions of existing copyrights, signing songwriters and making co-publishing agreements, and licensing domestic subpublishing rights to foreign catalogs from overseas publishers;
- be authorized to negotiate and sign copyright acquisition deals within preset budgetary limits;
- be responsible for exploiting and promoting the division's copyrights in all sound, visual, and print media, including recordings, airplay, synchronization, jingles, print, etc.;
- be responsible for all copyright registration and licensing;
- with the accounting department, be responsible for all music publishing royalty and advance payments and collections;
- with the A&R department, work to sign the record division's artists and producers to the music publishing division, and find suitable material for the record division's artists to record;
- scout for acts and masters for the record division to acquire;
- with the director of operations, set a timeline and budget for building and operating a demo studio;
- set a timeline and budget for setting up an independent production unit to sign, develop, and produce artists with commercial viability outside the record division's target markets, which he/she will then be responsible for leasing or licensing to other record companies;
- be responsible for negotiating and entering into foreign subpublishing agreements with reputable publishing companies in all major territories within the first year;
- be responsible for negotiating and entering into an exclusive print licensing arrangement with a major sheet music distributor;
- be responsible for generating income equal to 20% of the publishing division's first year's overhead within nine months. He/she will be expected to generate income equal to 50% of the publishing division's second year's overhead by the end of the second year; he/she will be responsible for generating cash equal to the third year's overhead, thus reaching the division's break-even point, by the end of the third year of operations;
- with the directors of the following divisions, be responsible for establishing *management-information systems* to interface with (1) business affairs, (2) finance, (3) A&R, (4) international, (5) marketing, (6) sales, (7) operations, and (8) personnel.

The qualified candidate will be financially literate, experienced in hands-on copyright management, an adept negotiator, a strong manager, good communicator, familiar with business management systems, have a thorough knowledge of record company operations, marketing concepts, and the music geared to the company's target market.

He/she must be familiar with the operational functions of all other departments within the company.

He/she must have CEO qualifications and will serve on the board of directors, since the music publishing division will function as a stand-alone profit center within the overall company.

He/she will interface with all external entities where music publishing is concerned (e.g., performing-right and mechanical licensing societies, trade associations, etc.).

The successful candidate will maintain the respect and goodwill of all other managers and staff within the company, as well as all others in the industry with which the music publishing division interfaces.

This is a high-profile position, so the successful candidate must be able and willing to travel, to favorably represent the company, and to show the flag at important trade and media events.

INTERVIEWING CANDIDATES

Initial interview

Remember, the very life of your company depends upon the caliber of the people you select. Therefore, you have to try and penetrate the "best-behavior" veneer that candidates wear when you interview them, because each person you employ, by virtue of personality, decisions, and performance, has the unwitting power to destroy or build your company.

Before you interview a candidate, you should already know the qualifications you're looking for in the position under consideration. You may have read the candidate's resume and been impressed by paper credentials. Still, the interview is no mere formality. It is the crux by which you decide whether or not it is worth the time and effort the company must invest to bring the candidate on board.

The best time and place to interview a potential senior manager is over breakfast, lunch, or dinner in a nice restaurant. First impressions do count, and you want to see how the candidate responds in a setting that requires a certain amount of decorum. Senior managers must often interact in social settings with top executives of other companies, and with foreign associates, bankers, lawyers, investors, etc. You hardly want your company represented by someone who eats peas with a spoon and sips wine through a straw.

The other advantage to this setting is that it is somewhat less rigid. There is no desk imposed between you, so your subject may be more inclined to open up and reveal more of his or her true personality.

If you haven't yet seen the candidate's resume, don't read it now. You only have so much time to spend during the interview, and you want to utilize it all to get a sense of how the candidate ticks. If you're sufficiently impressed, read the resume later when you can study it without interruption. Then phone the references listed (don't neglect to do that), and you can phone the candidate if you have any follow-up points to discuss as a result of the interview, the resume, or comments from references.

Break the ice by summarizing what your company is all about, its goals, the image you want to project, and the kinds of people you're looking for. Emphasize that you're looking for first-rate people, and explain why. The natural tendency then is for the candidate to convince you that he or she is first rate. This is what you want. If the candidate can't sell you on his or her qualifications for the job, it is unlikely he or she can sell others on the company's product.

You will, of course, be somewhat familiar with the candidate's career history since you've invited him or her for this interview. You therefore don't need to waste time asking the usual questions regarding past experience (it should all be in the resume anyway). Instead, pose a series of hypothetical questions, which don't necessarily have right or wrong answers, but which are designed to give you an idea of how the candidate thinks, reacts, and functions. Although there are no correct answers, as such, the replies will tell you whether the candidate jibes with the type of people your company needs for success.

The responses indicate whether the candidate has the key qualities necessary to forcefully and convincingly articulate his or her thinking. This, in turn, tells you if the candidate has leadership ability, and can organize his or her thoughts. And you will know whether the candidate is creative and flexible, knows his or her stuff, and has a common sense approach to business problems. In short, you should be able to draw out enough information to make a preliminary judgment as to whether the candidate is a solid, firmly rooted person with self-confidence and personal priorities—or if he or she is a flake.

Sample interview questions

Depending upon the type of position you're seeking to fill, here are examples of various hypothetical questions you might ask.

- Our record division wants to impose controlled composition clauses on all its artists. These artists write much of their own material, which is published by your division. What's your position on this vis à vis the record division?
- The manager of a new singer-songwriter demands posters and other POP materials as well as full page ads placed in *Billboard* corresponding with the singer-songwriter's debut album, although the act is totally unknown nationally. How would you respond?
- You gave a "hold" on a song to a relatively unknown artist, but now a really major international act wants to cut the song. What do you do?
- We just signed a songwriter recommended by your assistant. This assistant has great ears, and his previous recommendations proved very successful. But you now learn the songwriter's manager gave him a kickback from the advance we paid. What do you do?
- A valued (but prickly) songwriter wants a budget to cut demos on five new songs he feels very strongly about, but you and your staff unanimously judge four of the songs as decidedly sub par. How do you handle the situation?
- What do you see yourself doing 5/10/20 years from now?
- You must groom a successor for your position. What qualities do you look for?
- Describe the ideal company you'd like to work for.
- What company support and authority do you need to do the job as you see it?
- How much money/compensation do you need during the first year?
- How much would you expect to earn in the third year and how do you justify that amount?
- Have you ever wanted to own your own company? Why (or why not)?
- What motivates you?
- How would you motivate subordinates?

The above examples are intended to spark your imagination so that you can develop a series of penetrating questions relative to your venture. Remember, the idea is to let the candidate bubble and reveal what kind of person he or she is. You're looking for more than a capable functionary. You need an inspirational team player who will really boost your company's performance.

If you decide this person can be an asset, ask him or her to let you know by a specific date if he or she is interested. Then go away, check the references, read the resume, and prepare any follow-up questions you may have in the event he or she accepts. If you don't think the candidate makes the grade, however, have the courage and courtesy to say so, outlining the reasons why in a constructive manner.

Panel interview session

Invite those candidates who make it past the initial interview to a second session with other key managers already on your team. Introduce the candidate to the panel. Restate your company's goals and how the position under offer is designed to further your objectives. Explain the importance of meeting those on the panel. Every senior manager must have a sense of each other's capabilities and personalities, strengths and weaknesses. After the introduction, ask the candidate to make a 5-10 minute summary of his or her experience, qualifications, accomplishments, and goals.

Then, ask the candidate to outline how he or she would structure and operate the department that is managed by the post under consideration. Specifically, you want the candidate's thoughts on the following strategic and tactical aspects of the department for which he or she will be given responsibility:

- priorities, goals, objectives, and milestones for a three-year period
- rough timelines to accomplish the above during the three-year period
- rough budget requirements to accomplish the above for the period
- how the department should interface with other divisions of the company
- the image the department should project

The panel then probes the candidate on his or her responses and plays devil's advocate. Facing a panel and defending positions under pressure reveals a candidate's leadership strengths and ability to perform under stress. It will also reveal which candidates are most committed. Some may melt away after the panel interview, in which case you're better off than if they wash out later and leave you in the lurch. This session is the crunch. You'll find out who's competent and confident and who's not.

▼

Careful selection of personnel is as important as copyright acquisition, since it is the personnel who ultimately determine the degree of success the company will achieve.

Appendix

BOOKS FOR FURTHER READING
(available through Mix Bookshelf)

The Art of Music Licensing
by Al & Bob Kohn
Prentice Hall

This Business of Music
by Sydney Shemel and Wm.
  Krasilovsky
Billboard Books

More About This Business of Music
by Sydney Shemel and Wm.
  Krasilovsky
Billboard Books

Music Business (All you Need
  to Know About)
by Donald Passman
Simon & Schuster

Music Business Handbook
by David Baskerville
Sage Publications

Musician's Legal Guide
by Mark Halloran
Prentice Hall

Music, Money & Success
by Brabec and Brabec
Schirmer

Nimmer on Copyright
by Melville B. Nimmer
Matthew Bender

Lindey on Entertainment, Publishing
& Arts; Agreements & the Law
by Alexander Lindey
Clark Boardman

CONSUMER PUBLICATIONS

BAM
3470 Buskirk
Concord, CA 94523

Circus
6 W. 18th St., Fl. 2
New York, NY 10011

Country Music Magazine
342 Madison Ave.
New York, NY 10173

Down Beat
102 Haven Rd.
Elmhurst, IL 60126

Music City News
50 Music Sq. W., Suite 601
Nashville, TN 37203

Rolling Stone
1290 Ave. of the Americas
New York, NY 10104

Spin
6 W 18 St., Fl. 11
New York, NY 10011

MECHANICAL LICENSING

American Mechanical Rights Assn.
(AMRA)
333 S. Camiani Trail
Venice, FL 34825

Copyright Management, Inc.
(CMI)
1102 17th Ave. S., Suite 401
Nashville, TN 37212
(615) 327-1517

Harry Fox Agency
711 3rd Ave.
New York, NY 10017
(212) 370-5330

Songwriters Guild of America
(SGA)
1500 Harbor Blvd.
Weehawken, NJ 07087
(201) 867-7603

ONLINE DATABASES

Billboard Information Network
(BIN)
1515 Broadway
New York, NY 10036
212 536-5319 or (212) 536-5040
Fax: (212) 536-5351

Billboard Online
Billboard Electronic Publishing
1515 Broadway
New York, NY 10036
(800) 449-1402 or (212) 536-5341
Fax: (212) 536-5310

Broadcast Data Systems (BDS)
Billboard Electronic Publishing
1515 Broadway
New York, NY 10036
(800) 449-1402 or (212) 536-5349
Fax: (212) 536-5312

Cendata (Census Bureau)
Data User Services Division
Bureau of the Census
Washington, DC 20233

Fedworld
National Technical
Information Service
Department of Commerce
Washington, DC 20233
(703) 321-8020

Soundscan
c/o Billboard
1515 Broadway
New York, NY 10036
(212) 536-5319 or (212) 536-5040
Fax: (212) 536-5351

PERFORMING-RIGHT SOCIETIES

American Society of Composers,
Authors & Publishers (ASCAP)
One Lincoln Plaza, Fl. 16
New York, NY 10023
(212) 595-3050

Broadcast Music, Inc. (BMI)
320 W. 57th St.
New York, NY 10019
(212) 586-2000

SESAC, Inc.
55 Music Square E.
Nashville, TN 37203
(800) 826-9996

SELECTED OVERSEAS LICENSING AGENCIES

Australia/New Zealand
Australasian Mechanical Copyright
Owners Assn. (AMCOS)
14th Fl., 56 Berry St.
North Sydney, NSW 2060
(02) 954-3655
Fax: (02) 954-3664
http://www.amcos.com.au

Australian Performing Right Assoc.
(APRA)
1A Eden St., Crows Nest, NSW 2065
(02) 922-6422
http://www.apra.com.au

Canada
Canadian Musical Reproduction
Rights Agency (CMRRA)
56 Wellesley St. West, Suite 320
Toronto, Ont. M5S 2S3
(416) 926-1966
http://www.cmrra.ca

Society of Composers, Authors &
Music Publishers of Canada
(SOCAN)
41 Valleybrook Dr.
Don Mills, Ontario M3B 2S6
(416) 445-8700
http://www.socan.ca

Denmark/Scandinavia
KODA
Maltegardsvej 24
Gentofte, Denmark 2820
http://www.koda.dk

Nordisk Copyright Bureau (NCB)
Frederiksgade 17, P.O. Box 3064
Copenhagen DK 1021
(01) 12.87.00
http://www.sn.no/~tono/ncbdept.html

France
Societe des Auteurs, Compositeurs
& Editeurs (SACEM)
http://www.sacem.org

Germany/Austria
Gesellschaft fr Musikalische
Auffurungs-und-mechanische
(GEMA)
http://www.gema.de

Ireland
Irish Music Rights Organisation
(IMRO)
2 Pembroke Row, off Baggot St.
Dublin 2
(01) 66 14 844
http://www.imro.ie

Japan
Japanese Society for Rights of
Authors, Composers & Publishers
(JASRAC)
http://www.jasrac.or.jp/ejhp

The Netherlands
BUMA/STEMRA
http://www.buma.nl

Spain
Sociedad General de Autores de
Espana (SGAE)
http://sgae.es

United Kingdom
Mechanical-Copyright Protection
Society (MCPS)
Elgar House
41 Streatham High Rd.
London SW16 1ER
(08) 17 69 44 00
http://www.mcps.co.uk

Performing Right Society (PRS)
29/33 Berners St.
London W1P 4AA
(07) 15 80 55 44
http://www.prs.co.uk

TRADE ASSOCIATIONS AND SUPPORT GROUPS

Academy of Country Music
6255 Sunset Blvd. #923
Hollywood, CA 90028
(213) 462-2351

American Federation of Musicians
(AFM)
1501 Broadway, Suite 600
New York, NY 10036
(212) 869-1330

American Federation of Television
& Radio Artists (AFTRA)
260 Madison Ave.
New York, NY 10016
(212) 532-0800

American Society of Composers
Authors & Publishers (ASCAP)
One Lincoln Plaza
New York, NY 10023
(212) 595-3020

Assoc. of Independent Music
Publishers (AIM)
P.O. Box 1561
Burbank, CA 91507
(818) 842-6257

Broadcast Music, Inc. (BMI)
320 W. 57 St.
New York, NY 10019
(212) 586-2000

California Lawyers for the Arts
(CLA)
1641 18th St.
Santa Monica, CA 90404
(310) 998-5590

Canadian Musical Reproduction
Rights Agency (CMRRA)
56 Wellesley St. West, Suite 320
Toronto, Ontario M5S 2S3, Canada
(416) 926-1966

The Clearing House
405 Riverside Dr.
Burbank, CA 91506
(213) 469-3186

Country Music Assoc. (CMA)
1 Music Circle North
Nashville, TN 37203
(615) 244-2840

Electronic Industries Assoc. (EIA)
20001 Pennsylvania Ave, NW
Washington, DC 20006
(202) 457-8700

Gospel Music Assoc.
7 Music Circle North
Nashville, TN 37203
(615) 242-0303

The Harry Fox Agency
711 3rd Ave.
New York, NY 10017
(212) 370-5330

Nashville Songwriters Assoc. Int'l
(NSAI)
15 Music Sq. W.
Nashville, TN 37203
(615) 256-3354

Nat'l Academy of Recording Arts &
Sciences (NARAS)
3402 Pico Blvd.
Santa Monica, CA 90405
(310) 392-3777

Nat'l Academy of Songwriters
(NAS)
6381 Hollywood Blvd., Suite 780
Hollywood, CA 90028
(213) 463-7178

Nat'l Assoc. of Broadcasters (NAB)
1771 "N" St. NW
Washington, DC 20036-2891
(202) 293-3500

Nat'l Assoc. of Independent
Record Distributors &
Manufacturers (NAIRD)
P.O. Box 988
Whitesburg, KY 41858
(606) 633-0946

Nat'l Assoc. of Music Merchants
(NAMM)
5140 Avenida Encinas
Carlsbad, CA 92008-4391
(619) 438-8001

Nat'l Assoc. of Record
Merchandisers (NARM)
11 Eves Dr., Suite 140
Marlton, NJ 08053
(609) 596-2221

Nat'l Music Publishers Assoc.
(NMPA)
711 3rd Ave.
New York, NY 10017
(212) 370-5330

Recording Industry Assoc. of
America (RIAA)
1020 19th St. NW, Suite 200
Washington, DC 20036
(202) 775-0101

SESAC
421 W. 54th St., Fl. 4
New York, NY 10019
(212) 586-3450

Society of Composers, Authors &
Music Publishers of Canada
(SOCAN)
41 Valleybrook Dr.
Don Mills, Ontario M3B 2S6,
Canada
(416) 445-8700

Society of Composers & Lyricists
(SCL)
400 S. Beverly Dr., Suite 214
Beverly Hills, CA 90212
(310) 281-2812

Songwriters Guild of America
(SGA)
1500 Harbor Blvd.
Weehawken, NJ 07087
(201) 867-7603

Video Software Dealers Assoc.
(VSDA)
16530 Ventura Blvd., Suite 400
Encino, CA 91436
(818) 385-1500

TRADE DIRECTORIES AND GUIDES

Album Network Yellow Pages
120 N. Victory Blvd.
Burbank, CA 91502
(818) 955-4000

A&R 411 Directory
SRS Publishing
7510 Sunset Blvd.
Los Angeles, CA 90046
(818) 769-2722

Billboard Directories
1515 Broadway
New York, NY 10036
(212) 764-7300
• *Country Music Sourcebook*
  & Directory
• *Int'l Buyer's Guide*
• *Int'l Directory of Manufacturing*
  & Packaging
• *Int'l Recording Equipment*
  & Studio Guide
• *Int'l Talent & Touring Directory*
• *Record Retailing Directory*

Film & TV Music Supervisors List
SRS Publishing
7510 Sunset Blvd.
Los Angeles, CA 90046
(818) 769-2722

Mix Bookshelf
6400 Hollis St., Suite 12
Emeryville, CA 94608
(510) 653-3307

Music Week Directory
Greater London House
Hampstead Rd.
London NW1 7QZ, England

New on the Charts
70 Laurel Pl.
New Rochelle, NY 10803
(914) 632-3349

Performance Annual Guides
1101 University, Suite 108
Ft. Worth, TX 76107
• *Talent/Personal Mgmt.*
• *Booking Agencies*
• *Promoters/Clubs*
• *Concert Production*
• *Facilities*
• *Transport/Accommodation*
• *Services/Personnel*
• *International*

Phonolog
Music Dept.
10996 Torreyana Rd.
San Diego, CA 92121
(619) 457-5920

Recording Industry Sourcebook
6400 Hollis St., Suite 12
Emeryville, CA 94608
(510) 653-3307

Songplugger Directory of Recording
Artists & Contacts
MIDAS
P.O. Box 16591
Jackson, MS 39236
(601) 957-7027

TRADE PUBLICATIONS

Airplay Monitor
c/o Billboard
1515 Broadway
New York, NY 10036
(212) 764-7300

Album Network
120 N. Victory Blvd.
Burbank, CA 91502
(818) 955-4000

Billboard
1515 Broadway
New York, NY 10036
(212) 764-7300

CMJ New Music Report
11 Middle Neck Rd
Great Neck, NY 11021

Daily Variety
1400 N. Cahuenga Blvd.
Hollywood, CA 90028

Dance Music Report
33-39 22 St.
Long Island City, NY 11106

Entertainment Law Reporter
2118 Wilshire Blvd., Suite 311
Santa Monica, CA 90403
(310) 829-9335

Gavin Report
140 Second St.
San Francisco, CA 94105
(415) 495-1990

Hollywood Reporter
5055 Wilshire Blvd., Suite 600
Los Angeles, CA 90036
(213) 525-2000

International Musician
1501 Broadway, Suite 600
New York, NY 10036
(212) 869-1330

Mix
6400 Hollis St., Suite 12
Emeryville, CA 94608
(510) 653-3307

Music & Media
c/o Billboard Publications
1515 Broadway
New York, NY 10036
(212) 764-7300

Music Trades
80 West St.
Englewood, NJ 07631
(201) 871-1965

Music Week
Greater London House
Hampstead Rd.
London NW1 7QZ, England

Musician
1515 Broadway
New York, NY 10036
(212) 536-5208

New on the Charts
70 Laurel Pl.
New Rochelle, NY 10803
(914) 632-3349

Performance
1101 University, Suite 108
Ft. Worth, TX 76107
(817) 338-9444

Pollstar
4697 W. Jacquelyn Ave.
Fresno, CA 93722
(209) 271-7900

Producer Report
115 S. Topanga Canyon Blvd.,
Suite 114
Topanga, CA 90290
(310) 455-0888

Pro Sound News
460 Park Ave. S., 9th Fl
New York, NY 10016
(212) 378-0400

Radio & Records
10100 Santa Monica Blvd., 5th Fl
Los Angeles, CA 90067-4004
(310) 553-4330

RPM
6 Brentcliffe Rd.
Toronto, Ontario M4G 3Y2,
Canada
(416) 425-0257

Song Link Int'l
23 Belsize Crescent
London NW3 5QY, England
(01) 71 794-2540

Songplugger
Greater London House
Hampstead Rd.
London NW1 7QZ, England

Songtalk
6255 Sunset Blvd., Suite 1023
Hollywood, CA 90028
(213) 463-7178

Songwriter
Limerick City, Ireland

Variety
475 Park Ave S.
New York, NY 10016

TRADE SHOWS AND CONVENTIONS

CMJ Music Marathon
11 Middle Neck Rd., Suite 400
Great Neck, NY 11021
(516) 466-6000

Midem
475 Park Ave. South, 9th Fl
N.Y., NY 10016
(212) 689-4220

New Music Seminar
632 Broadway, 9th Fl.
New York, NY 10012
(212) 473-4343

Popkomm
Rottscheider Str. 6
D-42329 Wuppertal 11, Germany 49
(202) 27 83 10

South by Southwest (SXSW)
P.O. Box 4999
Austin, TX 78765
(512) 467-7979

U.S. GOVERNMENT

U.S. Government Printing Office
Attn: Superintendent of
    Documents
Washington, DC 20233
(202) 783-3238
Fax: (202) 275-0019

United States Copyright Office
Register of Copyrights
Copyright Office
Library of Congress
Washington, DC 20559
(202) 707-3000
Hotline for copyright forms:
    (202) 707-9100

Trademark Register
of the United States
454 Washington Bldg.
Washington, DC 20005

WEB SITES

ASCAP
http://www.ascap.com/ascap.html

Billboard Online
http://www.billboard-online.com

BMI
http://bmi.com/

Cirpa
http://www.cmrra.ca/cirpares/man
date.html

Inmusic & Media
http://www.immedia.com.au/im_/
index2.html

MCPS
http://www.mcps.co.uk/

Mix Bookshelf
http://www.mixbookshelf.com

Music Connection Magazine
http://www.musicconnection.com

Music Interactive
http://www.musicinteractive.com/

Performing Right Society (PRS)
http://www.prs.co.uk/

Popkomm
http://www.musikkomm.de/pop
komm

Producer Report
http://www.mojavemusic.com

SESAC
http://sesac.com/

Songlink International
http://www.webcom.com/genoa
grp/songlink

Songscape
http://www.webcom.com/genoa
grp/sngscape/html

Songwriters Collaboration Network
http://www.websites.earthlink.net/
songmd/

Studiobase (UK)
http://www.deomn.co.uk/studio
base/

Index

1909 Copyright Act, 55
1976 Copyright Act, 52, 55, 56
80/20 Rule, 169
accounting(s), 63, 65, 116
acknowledgment letter(s), 68, 70
acquisition philosophy, 36
acquisition(s), 9, 36
acquisitions made in the normal
  course of business, 108
acquisitions made outside the
  normal course of business, 108
activity reports, 189
ad agency discounts, 180
ad size, 180
ad testing, 131
adaptations, 66
add-on sales, 181
adds, 174
administer, 73
administering performing-
  rights, 87
administration deals, 73
administration fees, 74
administration of co-published
  works, 73
administration of foreign
  rights, 75
administrative fee, 75
administrative publishers, 13
administrative systems, 192
administrator, 73, 75
advance for a catalog of songs, 39
advance to acquire one song, 39
advance(s), 37, 38, 61, 64,
  65, 69, 114, 139
advertising agencies, 128
advertising, 176, 177, 178,
  179, 180, 181
Airplay Monitor, 145
album covers and inserts, 123
all media, 101
All Rights Reserved, 52
all television, 101
alternative quotes, 97
America Online, 84, 140
AMRA (American Mechanical
  Rights Association), 83

Amusement and Music Operators
  Association (AMOA), 90
ancillary benefits of copyright
  ownership, 18
ancillary income, 127
appraisal of copyrights, 47
arrangements, 66
artist development, 156
artist/producer development, 156
artwork, 166
ASCAP (Association of
  Composers, Authors &
  Publishers), 86, 87, 88, 89,
  90, 91, 92, 94, 98, 104, 140,
  143, 161
ASCAP payment system, 88
ASCAP's four funds basis, 89
ASCAP, 141
assignment, 76
at arm's length, 61
at source, 62, 63, 117, 118
audiovisual work(s), 93, 99
audiovisual, 93
audits, 66, 116
back catalog, 146, 160
background music, 141
backward Integration, 171
ballets, 124
banker publishers, 13
benefits of owning a music
  publishing company, 16
Berne Convention
  Implementation Act, 58
Berne Convention, 52, 53
best case/worst case scenarios, 45
best edition, 54
Billboard Buyer's Guide, 178
Billboard Information Network
  (BIN), 144, 145, 174
Billboard International Buyers
  Guide, 110, 162
Billboard magazine, 5, 41, 48, 88,
  144
Billboard online, 144, 174
Billboard, 89, 146
black box, 91
blanket agreements, 121

blanket catalog agreement, 107
blanket licenses, 87
blanket synchronization
  licenses, 160
blended royalty rate, 40
block license, 141
bluebirds, 159
BMI (Broadcast Music, Inc.), 86,
  87, 88, 89, 90, 91, 92, 94, 98,
  104, 140, 143, 161
BMI Broadcast media rates, 88
board games, 123
books, 122
brand extension, 166
brand recognition, 166
Broadcast Data System (BDS), 88,
  90, 144, 145, 174
Broadway musicals, 127
Broadway, 126, 127
Buenos Aires Convention, 52
bumpers, 101
bundle of rights, 59
business cycles, 34
business plans, 31
buy-outs, 82, 99, 101
buying and selling process, 48
cable television, 57, 103
calculating advances, 38
Canadian Mechanical Rights
  Reproduction Agency
  (CMRRA), 84
CAPAC, 90
capitalization, 126
CARP (Copyright Arbitration
  Royalty Panel), 103
Cash Box, 89, 146
cash cow, 169
cash flow management, 20
cash flow(s), 10, 23, 38
cash vs. accrual valuations, 48
catalog agreements, 121
catalog and roster reporting, 193
catalog manager, 146
CD-ROM, 137
changes, 66
changing lyrics, 134
chart activity, 46

chron files, 190
classified ads, 179
clearing houses, 158
close corporations, 30
CMI (Copyright Music, Inc.), 83
co-publishing contract, 75
co-publishing, 72
coin-operated, 58
collaboration, 87
collecting overseas performance
  royalties, 90
collection agreement(s), 107
collection deal(s), 114, 115
College Music Journal (*CMJ*), 89
commercial advertising, 128
commercial lifespan of a song, 4
commercials, 161
commissioned work, 69
commissioning fees for television
  productions, 159
commissioning fees for theatrical
  releases, 159
common law copyright, 53
Common Market, 109
company formation, 27
company management, 187
company name, 20, 48, 165, 166
comparative analysis, 41
compensation, 114, 137, 139
competition, 34
compilation albums, 161
compulsory licenses(ing), 57, 80,
  102, 135, 136, 141
compulsory licensing
  provision(s), 80, 102
compulsory mechanical
  licenses(ing), 80, 134
CompuServe, 84, 140, 141
computer games, 123
concept folios, 119
conflicts, 134
consideration of agreement, 64
consultants, 164, 165, 179
consumer press, 146
consumer products, 142
contact database, 150
contacts, 150

controlled composition, 78, 79
Copyright Act of 1909, 51, 52, 56
Copyright Act of 1976, 51, 54, 90
copyright administration, 192
Copyright Arbitration Royalty
    Panel (CARP), 77
copyright fees, 55
copyright life, 7, 52
copyright notice, 53, 75, 113,
    122, 123
Copyright Office, 52, 54, 81
copyright protection, 7, 51, 52, 55
copyright registration, 53, 54
Copyright Royalty Tribunal
    (CRT), 77, 90
copyright symbol, 53
copyright to arrangements, 139
copyright, 51
copyright-holding companies, 13
copyrighted arrangements
    of PD material, 120
corporations, 29
cost analysis, 176
costs of product, 9
CPM formula, 176
CPM media analysis, 176
creative control, 66
creative management control, 193
creative manager, 146
credibility, 167, 173, 174
credits, 88
cross-collateralization, 47, 62
cross-selling, 181
crossing over, 175
cue sheet(s), 88, 98, 104
currency exchange rates, 109
cut-in(s), 79, 97
cyberspace, 84, 91, 104, 140, 141
DART, 142, 143
default(s), 66, 117
defining your message, 166
delphi method, 41
demo costs, 148
demo studios, 148
demo(s), 67, 147, 149
Democratic Pool, 41
demographic sources of
    copyright income, 3
departmental functions, 14, 15
deposit, 54
derivative rights to demos, 148
derivative works, 56, 69
desk drawer publishers, 13
different kinds of publishers, 12
digital audio recorders
    and tape, 142
direct-response ads, 178
directories, 146
directors, 195
display ads, 179
distribution channels, 170
distribution levels, 171
divisibility of rights, 59
divisibility, 60
division of ownership, 73
Doctrine of Unfair
    Competition, 52
dog, 169
dolls, 142
dramatic performance rights, 125
dramatic performance, 124, 125
dramatic rights, 124
dramatic work, 124

dramatico-musical works, 124
dramatists' guild, 126
dramatizations, 66, 112, 124
due diligence, 49
duration of copyright
    assignment, 69
duration of license term, 134
duration of performance, 134
duration of services, 68
duration, 61, 95, 113, 180
earnings history, 114
edits, 66
electrical transcription
    license(s), 131, 141
electrical transcription, 141
electronic bulletin boards, 84, 91
employee for hire, 52, 61, 69
employees for hire, 57, 94, 158
equipment and furnishings, 23
equipment, 23
escalating royalty, 79
european union (EU), 109
evergreens, 159
exclusions, 60
exclusive catalog agreements, 108
exclusive songwriter
    agreements, 82
exclusive songwriter contract, 59
exclusivity, 96, 130, 134
executive judgment, 41
executive summary, 31
exploitation, 144
expression vs. ideas, 51
extent of usage, 134
external servicing, 193
fair use, 57
fake books, 120
fiduciary responsibility, 18
filing fee, 54
Film & TV Music Supervisor's
    List, 158
film producer's budget, 95
Film Producers, Studios, Agents
    & Casting Directors Guide, 158
financial aspects
    of acquisitions, 37
financial evaluation of
    copyrights, 47
financial projections, 32
financials, 49
first sale, 51
first use, 58, 60, 80, 81
fixation, 139
fixed, 7, 52, 53
fixing fee, 138, 139
flat fee, 82
flow of rights, 7
forecasting a multiproduct
    line, 42
forecasting sales, 40
forecasting the sales blend, 43
foreign acquisitions, 110
foreign administration, 74
foreign licensing, 106
foreign taxes, 109
foreign theatrical
    distribution, 102
Form CA, 55
Form PA, 55
Form SR, 55
Form TX, 55
Form VA, 55
forward integration, 171

four Ps, 168
Harry Fox (Agency), 83, 84,
    140, 141, 143
free television, 100
full-service publisher, 13, 14
furnishings, 23
games, 123
gang runs, 180
Gavin Report, 89, 146
general partnerships, 28
generic catalog marketing, 160
giveaways, 181
grand rights, 112, 124,
    125, 126, 127
greeting cards, 121, 122, 123
Group Discussion, 41
headlines, 178
hiring, 194
historical-based forecasting, 41
history of music publishing, 6
hit song, 10
holding companies, 30
holds, 96, 146, 147
Hollywood Reporter, 146, 158
home taping, 142
home video rights, 101
home video, 82
impact on future income, 134
importance of the copyright, 134
importance of the song, 95
in-flight programming, 142
incentive assignments, 72
incidental music, 124
incorporation, 30, 31
incremental advances, 46
independent promotion, 160
indie publishers, 15
individual song contract, 59
information superhighway, 91,
    104, 140
information, 189
infringement, 55, 57,
    125, 135, 142
initial interview, 196
insertion order, 179
institutional ads, 178
Insurance 23
intangible assets, 8
integration, 171
interactive compact disk
    (CD-I), 137
interactive media, 137
international copyright
    protection, 52
international copyright, 52
international scope
    of the market, 4
International Television
    & Video Almanac, 158
Internet, 84, 91, 104, 140
interview, 197, 198
interviewing candidates, 196
investment, 9
investors, 31, 32
ISBN number (International
    Standard Book Number), 91
ISRC [International Standard
    Recording Code], 91
ISWC (International Standard
    Work Code), 53, 91
jingle production companies, 128
jingles, 128, 161

JLO (Juke Box Licensing
    Office), 58
job descriptions, 195
joint copyright registration, 74
joint ventures, 28
joint-administration
    agreements, 75
joint-administration, 73, 74
Jukebox License Office (JLO), 90
jukeboxes, 57, 90
jurisdiction, 67, 76, 118
jury of experts, 41
karaoke synchronization
    licenses, 138
karaoke, 138
key-employees, 195
key-man insurance, 24
lead sheet, 54
leads, 167
legal empowerment, 118
legal entity, 27
legal, 24
legalities, 49, 70
length of performance, 95
Librarian of Congress, 77
librarian, 194
Library of Congress, 54, 55, 56,
    57, 74, 81
libretto, 124
licensed territory, 117
licenses and regulations, 24
licensing foreign catalogs, 110
licensing period, 130
licensing principles, 133
licensing register, 190
life of copyright, 61, 101
limitations on administrator's
    control, 73
limited partnerships, 28
limiting retention rights, 113
literary content, 124, 126
litigation, 76
live performances, 161
living stage performance, 127
living stage, 124
local cover(s), 114, 115, 118
local covers only, 116
location, 21
logo, 165, 166
lone rangers, 13
lyric changes, 96, 129
lyric reprint licenses, 121
macromarketing, 164
management by objectives
    (MBO), 187
management games, 192
management information
    systems (MIS), 105, 190, 192
management team, 25
managing promotion
    personnel, 174
market genre segments, 4
market research, 144
market surveys, 41
market targeting, 144
market, 150
marketing consistency, 163
marketing mix, 168
marketing plans, 164
marketing tools, 173
marketing, 163
matching folios, 120
mechanical income, 9, 77

mechanical license, 77, 81
mechanical licenses for
    cyberspace, 104
mechanical reproduction, 77
mechanical rights for
    videograms, 99
mechanical rights
    in cyberspace, 84
mechanical royalties
    on local covers, 116
mechanical royalty(ies), 77
mechanical-right licensing
    societies, 83
mechanical-right licensing, 77
medley, 134
meetings, 188
method books, 119
micromarketing, 164
Midem Directory, 178
MIDEM, 110, 162, 181
MIDI files, 136
MIDI rights license(s), 136, 137
MIDI sequence market, 136
MIDI sequence program, 136
MIDI sequence, 136, 137
MIDI software, 136
MIDI, 136
milestone achievements, 45, 63,
    70, 114, 117
milestone performance
    obligations, 66
million-selling record, 11, 12
minimum/maximum advance
    formula, 46
mixed folios, 120
monopoly of rights, 57
most favored nation, 135
most favored nations
    clause, 95, 139
movie soundtracks, 94
movies and television shows
    based on existing songs, 103
movies, 93, 157, 159
multimedia, 137
multiple, 47
music boxes, 142
music clearance companies, 158
music licensing in
    cyberspace, 140
music publishing career, 16
music supervisors, 158
musical instrument
    digital interface, 136
musicals, 124
Muzak, 141
NAIRD, 181
NARM, 181
National Music Publishers
    Association (NMPA), 83
National Public Radio (NPR), 57
nature of agreement, 67, 76
nature of product, 134
nature of rights, 112
nature of usage, 133
nature of use, 94
negotiated licenses, 58
negotiated mechanical
    licenses, 81
negotiating, 115
negotiating advances, 37
negotiating synchronization
    fees, 94
negotiating, 60, 79, 101,
    114, 126, 130, 134, 135

negotiations, 70
networking, 182, 185
new media, 133, 136
New on the Charts, 146
newsletters, 185
Nielsen Report, 90
Nintendo, 139
NMS, 162, 181
nonreturnable, 62
noncommercial broadcasts, 102
noncommercial transmissions, 57
nondramatic performances, 125
nondramatic, 124
nonkey-employees, 195
nonmusical plays, 124
nonreturnable, 37
nonroutine license, 74
nontheatrical synchronization
    licenses, 98
notice of copyright, 53
notice(s) of intention, 81
notifications, 104
nsertion order, 180
number of other works, 134
number of uses, 96
off-air test, 131
off-Broadway theater, 127
off-Broadway, 126
office facilities, 22
one-man corporations, 29
online databases, 144
online mechanical licenses, 140
online performing-right
    licenses, 140
online synchronization
    license, 141
operas, 124
operettas, 124
option fees, 96
option price, 103
option(s), 45, 63, 68, 96,
    101, 103, 134
orchestral arrangements, 161
overseas mechanical-right
    licensing societies, 84
overseas mechanical-right
    societies, 84
overseas performing-right
    societies, 90, 91
package deals, 96, 160
packaging, 152, 166
panel interview session, 198
paper adds, 174
parody, 134
partial use, 102
partnerships, 28, 29
pay-per-play, 90
pay-per-view, 100
paying indie promo men, 174
PBS licenses, 103
PBS, 103
PD, 55, 120, 137
per inquiry ads (PI), 179
per order ads (PO), 179
per unit royalty, 99
performance clause(s), 63, 66,
    70, 76
performance fee, 97, 98
performance income, 10, 65
performance obligations, 114
performance rights for
    videograms, 99
performance rights, 139

performance royalties
    on local covers, 115
performance royalties, 87, 88,
    115, 160
performance uses, 86
performing-right licensing, 85
performing-right societies, 56,
    86, 125
performing-right society
    membership requirements, 90
performing-rights for
    synchronized usages, 97
periodicals, 122
permanent retention, 112
permissions, 133
persistence, 175
personal service contracts, 68
personality folios, 120
personnel management, 194
personnel, 26
photographs, 184
piano copy(ies), 64, 119
piped music, 141
pipeline income, 113
pitch letters, 184
pitching, 146
place, 168, 170
playlists, 174
plays with music, 124
point-of-purchase, 181
poor man's copyright, 55
POP materials, 181
POPKOMM, 110, 162, 181
positioning, 178
post chart payments, 90
power of attorney, 67
PPD (published price
    to dealers), 78
premium giveaway(s), 80, 82
press kits, 184
press release format, 183
press release(s), 183
price, 168, 172
pricing policies, 172
print advertisements, 122
print advertising, 131
print rights, 119
printed editions, 64
printed music formats, 119
problem child, 169
PROCAN, 90
product development, 5
product life cycle, 168
product management, 169
product, 8, 36, 148, 168
professional copies, 65
professional manager, 146
program budget, 102
prohibitions, 137
projecting your message, 165
promo spots, 101
promo video clips, 161
promoting copyrights
    overseas, 162
promotion man, 173
promotion, 152, 168, 172
promotional video clips, 100
promotional videos, 82
pros and cons of exclusive
    catalog deals, 108
prospectus, 48
PSAs, 131
Public Broadcasting System
    (PBS), 57, 102

public domain, 53, 55, 56, 120
public relations (PR), 182
public service announcements
    (PSAs), 131, 179
publication date, 56
publicity angles, 182
publicity, 182
publicly owned corporations, 30
published and unpublished
    works, 52
"published" vs. "unpublished"
    works, 52
pull strategy, 173
purchasing copyrights, 47
purpose of advertising, 178
push strategy, 173
R.O.W. ("Rest of World"), 106
Radio and Records, 89, 146
radio commercials, 131
radio programming, 174
radio, 142, 160
raising capital, 25, 28
rate card, 179
rate discounts, 79
rates, 79
reciprocal agreements, 84
recognized works, 89
record clubs, 80
record production royalties, 155
record production, 154, 155
record promotion, 173, 174
record releases, 46
recorded music libraries, 142, 161
recording-right license fee, 98
recoup, 37, 40, 62
recouping expenses, 46
recoupment of expenses, 62, 67
recurring use(s), 96, 102
red tape, 25
reduced fees for TV licenses, 102
reduced fees, 100
reduced royalty rates, 60
regional (or local) test, 131
regional testing, 175
Register of Copyrights, 54, 55
registrations, 75
rejections of copyright claims, 55
release commitments, 113
release money, 89
reminder advertising, 181
remnants, 179
renewal option(s), 130, 138
renewal period, 56
renewal reminders, 105
renewal rights, 52
renewals, 101
reprint fees, 122
reprint license(s), 122
reserves, 82, 120
restrictions, 134
retail selling price (RSP), 78
retention period, 69, 113
retention rights, 113
return on investment, 19
return privileges, 120
revue, 124, 127
RIAA, 145
right of assignment, 67, 117
right of retention, 69
right to audit, 75
right to change lyrics, 101
right to copy, 51
right to publicize name
    and likeness, 67

Music Publishing: The Real Road to Music Business Success

rights licensed by music publishers, 7
risks of integration, 171
road shows, 126
rollover advance(s), 99, 101, 136, 139
R.O.W., 111
royalties, 62, 64, 65, 115, 120, 139
royalty statements, 63
royalty-bearing songs, 120
royalty-bearing, 137
RSP (retail selling price), 78
"S" corporations, 30
sales management, 167
sales process, 152, 167
sales, 166
samples, 113
sampling, 135
score, 159
secondary stations, 174
secondary transmission, 57
Sega, 139
sell-off period, 121
senior management, 195
Serial Copyright Management System (SCMS), 143
serious music publishers, 14
SESAC (Society of European Stage Authors & Composers), 86, 89, 90, 92
SESAC'S royalty system, 89
SESAC, 98, 104, 161
sheet music retail prices, 120
sheet music, 119
short-term licenses, 100, 102
single-song contract, 64
single-song agreements, 121
small rights, 124, 125, 126, 127
Society of Composers, Authors, & Music Publishers of Canada (SOCAN), 90
sole proprietorship, 27, 28
song delivery, 45
SongLink Int'l, 146
songplugger(s), 119, 146
songplugging techniques, 148
songplugging, 146
songs written before January 1, 1978, 52
songwriter contracts, 59
Songwriters Guild, 83
Soundscan, 41, 144, 145, 174
soundtrack album guarantee, 95
sources of copyright income, 9
special distributions, 89
special offers, 181
special product packagers, 80
special products, 80
special use permits, 133
specialization, 20
specialty advertising, 181
split copyright(s), 72, 73
split publishing, 72
splits, 79, 97
staff meetings, 188
standards, 159
star power, 95
star, 169
start-up costs, 21
start-up money, 18
statements, 116
statutory mechanical royalty, 77
statutory rate, 77, 78, 80
statutory royalty rate(s), 84, 104

strategic alliances, 185
structuring advances, 45
subpublisher, 107
subpublishing agreements, 111
subpublishing, 107
subscription television, 101
substantial similarity, 57
SXSW, 162, 181
synchronization fees, 102
synchronization license, 93, 97
synchronization licenses for commercial advertising, 104
synchronization right licensing, 93
synchronization rights in cyberspace, 104
synchronization, 93
syndicated radio programs, 142
tangible assets, 8
target market, 144
tax-exemption certificates, 109
television synchronization licenses, 100
television, 157, 161
temporary assignment, 112
termination of publishers' rights, 56
termination, 56, 113, 117, 118, 121
territory, 61, 111, 130, 134
testing, 175
theatrical distribution, 102
theatrical exhibitions, 94, 98
theatrical synchronization fees, 94
theatrical synchronization licenses, 93
theme commissioning, 158, 159
third-party legal actions, 67
timing of advance payments, 62
timing of ASCAP and BMI royalty distributions, 89
timing of royalty statements, 65
timing, 152
tip sheets, 167
title of the program, 101
titles, 52
toys, 142
tracking submissions, 154
trade associations, 145
trade magazines, 146
trade shows, 176
transcription fee, 131, 142
transcription licenses, 142
translations, 66, 112, 122
Treaty of Rome, 109
trend analysis, 42, 43
TV Data, 90
TV Guide, 90
TV/radio rate reductions, 180
type of performance, 133
unauthorized copy, 57
underscore, 159
undivided interest, 60
uniqueness of the work, 134
Universal Copyright Convention (UCC), 52
unpublished work(s), 52, 54
valuing the catalog, 47, 48
Variety, 146, 158
vertical integration, 171
video arcades, 140
video games, 139
video production, 157
videocassettes, 82

videogram synchronization license(s), 98, 99
videogram, 99
visual presentation, 33
warrant of exclusivity, 64
Web sites, 141
weighted, 88
what it takes to be a publisher, 18
Who's Looking register, 190
work(s) for hire, 52, 57, 61, 69, 94
working capital, 9
working relationships with subpublishers, 111
worksheet(s), 191, 192
WorksNet, 91
World Wide Web, 84, 91, 104, 140
worldwide music publishing revenues, 10
worldwide publishing revenues, 106
worldwide synchronization licenses, 112
writer collaborations, 72
writer's obligations, 70
writer's right to audit, 66

A Music Bookstore At Your Fingertips...
FREE!

Since 1982, *Mix Bookshelf* has been the world's leading resource for information on recording technology and the music industry. Tens of thousands of musicians and audio professionals rely on the *Mix Bookshelf* catalog for the best selection of how-to books, career guides, reference manuals, textbooks, instructional videos, instructional and business software, and sample CDs available anywhere. **If there's *anything* you need to learn about the recording, technology, business, or composition of music, *Mix Bookshelf* has the information.**

We offer:

• The most comprehensive listing of resources for music industry professionals and hobbyists

• Convenient and cost-efficient "one-stop shopping" for retailers and school bookstores

• Discounts and review copies for educators and established music business and recording programs

For a free *Mix Bookshelf* catalog call (800) 233-9604

or write to
Mix Bookshelf; c/o Whitehurst & Clark, Inc.; 100 Newfield Ave.; Edison, NJ 08837-3817
(908) 417-9575; Fax (908) 225-1562

or check us out on the Web! You can browse our catalog and order Bookshelf items at **http://www.mixbookshelf.com**

You'll find information on hundreds of topics including:

Career Development
Studio Business
Music Business Software
Resource Guides
Music Publishing
The Internet
Music Business
Studio Recording
Engineering
Studio Design and Construction
Home Recording
Live Sound
Lighting
Handbooks
Dictionaries
Construction Projects
Maintenance
Digital Audio
Audio for Video and Film
MIDI Guides
MIDI Software Manuals
Multimedia
Synthesis
Computer Music
Instrument-Specific Guides
Samples
Sound Effects
CD-ROMs
Music Theory
Songwriting
Arranging
Lyrics
Composing Alternatives
Instructional Software
Performance
Vocal Training
Keyboards
Guitar
Bass
Rhythm Section
Drums
Saxophone
Accessories

MIX
BOOKSHELF
INFORMATION RESOURCES FOR MUSIC PROFESSIONALS